MUSIC RESEARCH AND INFORMATION GUIDES

MUSIC RESEARCH
AND INFORMATION GUIDES
VOL. 17

MUSIC AND WAR

GARLAND REFERENCE LIB
OF THE HUMANITIES
(VOL. 1581)

MUSIC AND WAR

*A Research
and Information Guide*

Ben Arnold

Michael Saffle
consulting editor

GARLAND PUBLISHING, INC.
New York & London / 1993

Library of Congress Cataloging-in-Publication Data

Arnold, Ben, 1955–
    Music and war : a research and information guide / Ben
Arnold.
        p.   cm. — (Garland reference library of the humani-
ties ; vol. 1581) (Music research and information guides ;
vol. 17)
    Includes bibliographical references and indexes.
    ISBN 0–8153–0826–4 (alk. paper)
    1. Music and war—Bibliography. I. Title. II. Series.
III. Series: Music research and information guides ; vol. 17.
ML128.W2A75   1993
016.7815'99—dc20   93–24938
                                                         CIP
                                                          MN

Printed on acid-free, 250-year-life paper
Manufactured in the United States of America

for Christopher, Anthony,
Mary Adrianne, and Norman

CONTENTS

ILLUSTRATIONS
(following page 362)

TO READERS OF THIS RESEARCH GUIDE

War-related compositions are presented in the annotated listings and supplements at the end of each chapter. Each composition included in these listings and supplements is identified and cross-referenced by number. (Occasionally, cross-referenced works are identified by a "•" sign.) These reference numbers are used, as well, to identify works when they are first discussed in the chapters. The annotated listings are arranged alphabetically first by nationality and then by composer; the supplements are arranged alphabetically by composer only. Each entry uses the following symbols for clarification:

Date of composition (in brackets): i.e., [1900]
Date of first performance: "1st:"
Publishing information: "#"
Recording information: "*"

In the event of multiple compositions by one composer, each follows successively in alphabetical order without restating the composer's name. If the reader does not know the nationality of a composer, the index in the back will provide the identification numbers of all annotations dealing with a particular composer.

PREFACE

The idea for this book arose from a desire to examine music and its relationship to some programmatic, literary, or descriptive topic. I selected the idea of music and war because of its social importance, its long tradition, and its richness of significant compositions, particularly in this century. The study of music and war provided the opportunity to look at music's ability to represent, depict, suggest, or symbolize through various means war and the intended death and destruction it creates. At the same time, the idea of music and war offered the possibility of viewing composers and their places in society. How do composers go about exploring ways and idioms to treat war and its horrors in music? What, if any, are the conventions that became standard in these compositions? Is there a consistent musical way to fire a cannon shot, depict the suffering of those wounded, or suggest the feeling of loss for loved ones killed in war? How do these depictions and representations change through the ages?

The music discussed in this book deals specifically with art compositions related to war and to one of its possible extremes, the end of the world through nuclear means. The emphasis is on Western art music, chiefly compositions written in the European tradition and primarily by composers living in the West (although some Japanese and Chinese works are included). Art compositions from the former Soviet-bloc countries are often relegated in this study to the supplements because of their large numbers, uneven quality, and lack of availability. Patriotic and military works per se (e.g., the numerous marches, quicksteps, sonatas, symphonies, and concerti, many of which were dedicated to famous generals and leaders) are omitted, unless they deal with a particular battle, or some unusual or pressing reason exists for including them. Some propaganda works (e.g., Earl Robinson's *Battle Hymn*) are included, however, if there is actual war-depicting music within them. Film and television music is omitted, too, unless it received independent publication and performance (e.g., Sergey Prokofiev's *Alexander Nevsky*). The two hundred peace works that have been written in this century are omitted largely because "music and peace" is a topic in itself. Compositions based on the idea of the end of the world brought about through nuclear war are included, but works based on other apocalyptic possibilities are not. Upon occasion, war songs of a popular or traditional character are discussed to illustrate parallels between them and art music composed on similar themes, especially during the Vietnam era. These popular and folk works, however, are omitted entirely from the listings at the ends of the chapters, since numerous studies examine these thousands of war songs from various wars.

Opera poses a problem because so many are set during war time. I have mentioned only the better-known operas that include specific battle scenes, unless the opera is specifically about war (e.g., Luigi Nono's *Intolleranza*). Battle-like scenes from operas by Giuseppe Verdi, Richard Wagner, or Peter Ilyich Tchaikovsky are included because they help illustrate how composers attempt to create artistic battle situations. I have omitted "battle scenes" between human beings and animals (e.g., in Wolfgang Amadeus Mozart's *Magic Flute* or Wagner's *Siegfried*).

This book, therefore, is intended to be selective rather than comprehensive. I have not attempted to catalog or even mention every popular, folk, or art composition related to war. Instead, I have tried to show how composers through the ages have written war-related music. The compositions I have selected to discuss are not always of high musical value; some have been chosen for their innovative ways of depicting war sounds or for purpose of historical documentation. I have avoided highly technical analyses of each work; instead, I have tried to place works in their historical contexts and to examine unusual or significant techniques or characterizations only of selected compositions.

In order to study the development of war-related art music, I examined more than 1300 compositions from the Middle Ages to 1991. I concentrated primarily on art music of the twentieth century, since this music is, I feel, the most worthy of attention. In a project of this magnitude, it is inescapable that important war-related works have eluded me, and I apologize in advance for these omissions.

In selecting individual works, attention was given to composers' own words and any dedications they had given their works. Some compositions have been included because other writers have suggested that these works are war-related, even if the composers in question did not indicate clearly that their works were about war.

My book consists primarily of an introduction and two major sections. The introduction presents an overview of the music and examines some of the significant ideas about the subject of war-related music and its role in society. Part I is organized chronologically, corresponding to the standard historical divisions in music:

Medieval/Renaissance, Baroque, Classic, and Romantic. The only diversion from this scheme is the "Annotated Listing of American Civil War Music," placed at the end of Chapter IV, even though it contains music written since 1900 dealing with the American Civil War. Over sixty composers wrote pieces about the civil war, and it is the only historic war prior to this century that continues to inspire large numbers of contemporary (chiefly American) composers.

At the turn of the twentieth century, war music changed radically as perceptions of war altered. Consequently, Part II examines these changes and the substantial war compositions of this century. It is organized according to the major wars: World War I, World War II (with particular attention to the Holocaust and the effects of the atomic bomb on Hiroshima and Nagasaki), and the Vietnam conflict. War-related works not written specifically about these wars are grouped together in four general listings and supplements covering the following years: 1900-1913; 1919-1938; 1946-1964; and 1965-1990. Works dealing with the Russian Revolution, the Spanish Civil War, and the Korean War are mentioned only in passing and are not grouped together in separate listings.

Chapters I through VIII are followed by: a) annotated listings of works (each numbered consecutively) dealing with the themes of each chapter; and b) supplements of less important works. The annotated listings include each composer's name, dates, and nationality, as well as specific information about each composition: title, genre or instrumentation, dates of composition and of first performance, score and recording information, author(s) of text(s), Library of Congress (LC) call number (when available), and a brief description of the work. Only one or two scores or recordings are cited, even though many may exist. The purpose of the information provided is to let the reader know that the music has been published and/or recorded. These listings are not, however, to be considered as recommendations. Furthermore, many of these recordings may be out of print and difficult to find. The New York Public Library (NYPL) owns numerous items that I could not locate at the Library of Congress, and NYPL catalog numbers are given frequently in lieu of LC numbers. If I have been unable to find a call number for a particular score, I have cited instead a source of information about this composition. The supplements follow the same format as the main listings, but supplement information is less complete and all items follow one after the other without separations.

Titles are italicized except for generic titles like concerto or symphony, unless such works also have a descriptive title (e.g., *Schlacht-Sinfonie*) and except for titles of songs and poems, which are put in quotation marks. Spellings are given in their original form, even if this creates some discrepancies. For example, "battaglia" (or its French version "bataille") appears as "bataglia," "batalla," "batala," "batalia," "bathala," "battaille," "battalia," "battala," and "battaia." The spellings of Soviet-bloc names generally follow those used in Allan Ho and Dmitry Feofanov's *Biographical Dictionary of Russian/Soviet Composers* (Westport, Conn.: Greenwood, 1989). Exceptions are made for familiar spellings like Tchaikovsky (not "Chaikovsky") and Prokofiev (not "Prokof'yev").

Many composers are identified as "Soviet," even though the Soviet Union has broken up, because their works were composed during its existence. In order to use the indexes at the back of this book, readers are not required to know by nationality the Soviet composers cited below; instead, the nationality of each composer is given in post-Soviet form after his or her dates (e.g., "Shostakovich, Dmitry (1906-1975). Russia").

It is my intention that composers and performers alike will seek out the music described below in order to study it, to learn from it, and, most important, to perform it. I hope the ideas raised here and the compilation of this body of material will stimulate interest in the musical ramifications of war. The atrocities of our time have forever changed both music and the ways composers view war and the role it plays in our civilization. On the surface, music may seem to have little to do with war; certainly they are uneasy bedfellows. But these two disparate facets of life have been intertwined throughout their histories, joining forces to delight, enrage, and/or horrify, just as wars by themselves have done at one time or another throughout the ages.

I wish to thank the Emory University Research Committee and the Summer Developmental Awards of Emory University for their generous support in providing release time for writing and for travel funds to conduct research at several libraries: The Library of Congress; the New York Public Library and the American Music Center; the Free Library of Philadelphia; the British Library; and the libraries of the University of Kentucky, the University of Georgia, the University of North Carolina at Chapel Hill, and Emory University. I greatly appreciate the attention and assistance staff members have provided me at these libraries. I would also like to give special thanks to Marie Hansen and the staff at the Interlibrary Loan Department of Emory University.

Numerous composers of war-related music have provided me with scores, recordings, and bibliographical information. For such help I would like to thank Joseph Baber, Leonardo Balada, Irwin Bazelon, Harold Blumenfeld, Alan Bush, Joseph Byrd, Ján Cikker, Phil Corner, Jean Coulthard, George Crumb, Norman Dello Joio, Kenneth Garburo, Roger Hannay, Lou Harrison, Arthur Hills, Kent Holliday, Zoran Hristić, Karel Husa, Warner Hutchison, Gunnar Johansen, Jerome Kitzke, Alcides

Lanza, Andrzej Panufnik, Barbara Pentland, Ned Rorem, Arnold Rosner, Marcel Rubin, R. Murray Schafer, Francis Schwartz, Elie Siegmeister, Ben Steinberg, and Richard Wernick. The following publishers and music centers have also been helpful in providing me with much hard-to-find information: E.B. Marks, Doblinger, Donemus Amsterdam, Editions Salabert, Theodore Presser, Peer Southern, G. Schirmer, the Australian Music Centre, the Canadian Music Centre, the Information Centre of the Czech Music Fund, Instituto de Cultura Puertorriqueña, the Israeli Centre, and the Swedish Music Information Center.

Countless people have told me about war-related compositions of which I was unaware, and although I am unable to recall everyone who has assisted me in this quest over the past decade, I would like to acknowledge the following for their special interest in this topic: Jamee Ard, Sarah Brown, Lance Brunner, Jonathan Glixon, Richard Golden, Mark King, Leonard Lehrman, Rey M. Longyear, Dick Ringler, and Whit Whittington.

I am also grateful for numerous friends, colleagues, and students who have contributed significantly to this study: Allan Ho and David Cox for their time and input during the numerous discussions we have had on the topic and for their support over the years; Stephen Crist for his reading and suggestions in an earlier paper dealing with the Holocaust; Dmitry Feofanov for his kind assistance in translating passages in Russian; Kenneth DeLong for his expertise and experience in finding sources in Czechoslovakia; Whit Whittington and Mark King for their many hours of searching for names, dates, scores, and other bibliographic information; and Michael Rintamaa and Jonathan DeLoach for their careful proofreading and assistance with the index.

I owe special gratitude to my editor Michael Saffle who graciously and patiently answered question after question and guided me through the writing of this book. With his encouragement and guidance, this book has moved from fantasy to reality. Finally, I want to thank Marie Ellen Larcada and the staff at Garland for their encouragement and experience in seeing this project to its completion.

Ben Arnold
Atlanta, Ga.
8 March 1993

ACKNOWLEDGMENTS

Portions of Chapter 7 ("The Aftermath of World War II") appeared in a different version in *Holocaust and Genocide Studies*, © 1992, Pergamon Press. Used with permission.

Chapter 8 ("The American-Vietnam Conflict") is based on an earlier article that appeared in *The Musical Quarterly*, © 1991, Oxford University Press, Inc. Used with permission.

AN INTRODUCTION
TO WAR-RELATED MUSIC

The history of war-related music has been a rich and multifarious one. From the time of the ancient Greeks, the theme of war has often been presented in music. The heroic battle ode began to dominate war-related music in the compositions of Heinrich Isaac and Clément Janequin in the late fifteenth and early sixteenth centuries. While war laments or peace compositions were occasionally written, the battaglias and other compositions attempting to depict battles in music became the most popular and influential type of war-related work.

Before this century many of the greatest composers wrote various types of battle compositions. Heading the list are Janequin, William Byrd, Andrea Gabrieli, Girolamo Frescobaldi, Claudio Monteverdi, Jean-Baptiste Lully, George Frideric Handel, Ludwig van Beethoven, Carl Maria von Weber, Franz Liszt, Hector Berlioz, Richard Wagner, Giuseppi Verdi, Bedřich Smetana, Peter Ilyich Tchaikovsky, and Nicolai Rimsky-Korsakov. Even Wolfgang Amadeus Mozart wrote a small contredanz in celebration of a military victory.

Many of these compositions were as innovative as they were popular. Heinrich Biber, Monteverdi, Jean François Dandrieu, and Johann Klöffler contributed novel programmatic techniques in their music, including polyrhythms, polytonality, tremolos, pizzicati, and clusters; Peter von Winter's *Schlacht-Sinfonie* was one of the earliest choral symphonies, and Beethoven composed his *Wellington's Victory* for the new and unusual instrument, the Panharmonikon. After the French Revolution, war music was decisive in the development of the oratorio and programmatic symphony. With few exceptions, however, the quality of these works was generally poor, especially in the seventeenth, eighteenth, and nineteenth centuries. Although composers established a vast body of war-related compositions prior to this century, only a few of these compositions are known today, and fewer still continue to be performed.

Since 1900 composers have produced over a thousand compositions that treat the subjects of war and its possible consequence, the end of the world through nuclear means. These works have continued the victory celebrations of earlier ones (particularly during the first half of the century), greatly intensified the lament tradition (and in essence re-created it during and immediately after World War I), and evolved into a new genre attempting to show the horror of war in a serious and tragic manner. Scholars have investigated these twentieth-century compositions as a genre only briefly, even though major composers of this century have written a significant number of works. Leonard Bernstein, Benjamin Britten, Aaron Copland, Paul Hindemith, Darius Milhaud, Luigi Nono, Andrzej Panufnik, Sergei Prokofiev, Arnold Schoenberg, William Schuman, Dmitry Shostakovich, Richard Strauss, Igor Stravinsky, and hosts of prominent living composers have contributed to this genre.

The violence and destruction of past wars and fears over future conflicts have elicited some of the most powerful artistic statements of the twentieth century. As scientists and businesses continue to improve weapons and warfare in this century to the point where they threaten our entire civilization with destruction, the outcry against war through various artistic media has become more intense and pervasive. These artistic statements cut across linguistic and geographical boundaries and are prevalent in all the arts.

Whether in lament for those who died in war or in outrage at the horrors of war, composers, like other artists, have turned to their art to express their feelings about war and the suffering and destruction it brings. Many composers believe they have an important role in society and that their music can serve as a vehicle for elevating social awareness. In writing about his *Threnody,* R. Murray Schafer proclaimed that "music is used here as the swiftest means of transporting the audience to the emotion-point where they realize the stupidity of war, of all war, of all apologies of war."[1] In the preface to his *Apotheosis of The Earth,* Karel Husa wrote, "The composer hopes that the destruction of this beautiful earth can be stopped, so that the tragedy of destruction—musically projected here in the second movement . . . can exist only as fantasy, never to become reality."[2]

These examples reveal how composers take an active role in society using the force of music to heighten social awareness. Many twentieth-century composers no longer produce purely abstract works without social significance. Robert P. Morgan goes so far as to assert that "the musical work [of the twentieth century] seems to be in the process of being transformed from an object intended primarily for aesthetic appreciation to a kind of document, a position statement concerning contemporary existence."[3]

Much of the war music since 1945 is essentially protest music or music with a message. During World War II a large number of compositions were patriotic works intended to unify the people in their struggle against the enemy, and some works, mostly written at the war's conclusion, even applauded victory. After the war, however, the largest number of war-related compositions were horrific representations of war, dirges, or requiems for those who died and suffered in war. Several composers lost family members and friends in the world wars, Korea, or Vietnam, and express their anguish and despair in their music. Through their music and texts, many composers graphically illustrate the terrors and horrors that war has inflicted on society in the past, and that war might once again unleash upon us if we do not heed the calls for peace.

With the rise of Fascism, Communism, two world wars, Korea, Vietnam, and the omnipresent threat of nuclear war and the extinction of the human race, composers in this century rarely praise war or the "heroics" of war as they often did in previous centuries. Now they depict its horrors and preach its futility. Theodore Adorno, in his *Philosophy of Modern Music,* wrote that "art is able to aid enlightenment only by relating the clarity of the world consciously to its own darkness."[4] Perhaps through their vivid music composers in this century can "enlighten" people and make them better aware of the need for peace and the dangers and darkness any war might inflict on society. This is certainly not the only function of art, but it is an essential one. Without Hitler and the two world wars, or without the cold war and Vietnam, composers would not have had reasons to write *The Last Ten Minutes, A Survivor From Warsaw,* or *Threnody to the Victims of Hiroshima.* These compositions are, to be sure, outgrowths of the society in which they were created.

NOTES

1. R. Murray Schafer, "Threnody: A Religious Piece For Our Time," *American Organist* 4 (May 1970), p. 33.

2. Karel Husa, "Preface" to *Apotheosis of This Earth* (New York: Associated Music, 1970).

3. Robert P. Morgan, "On the Analysis of Recent Music," *Critical Inquiry* 4 (Autumn 1977), p. 51.

4. Theodore W. Adorno, *Philosophy of Modern Music*, trans. Anne G. Mitchell (New York: Seabury, 1973), p. 15.

ABBREVIATIONS

The following abbreviations are used chiefly for citations in the annotated listings and supplements:

AMC   The American Music Center, 30th W. 26 Street, New York

BAKER   Slonimsky, Nicolas, ed. *Baker's Biographical Dictionary of Musicians*, 8th ed. New York: Schirmer, 1990.

BROWN   Brown, Howard Mayer. *Instrumental Music Printed Before 1600*. Cambridge: Harvard University Press, 1965.

CZECH   Information Center of the Czech Music Fund, 11800 Prague 1, Besední 3, Czechoslovakia

GLÄSEL   Gläsel, Rudolf. *Zur Geschichte der Battaglia*. Leipzig: Ph.D. dissertation, 1931.

HO   Ho, Allan, and Dmitry Feofanov. *Biographical Dictionary of Russian/Soviet Composers*. Westport, Conn.: Greenwood, 1989.

LC   The Library of Congress

MGG   Blume, Friedrich, ed. *Die Musik in Geschichte und Gegenwart*. Kassel & Basel: Bärenreiter, 1949-1967.

NEW GROVE	Sadie, Stanley, ed. *The New Grove Dictionary of Music and Musicians*. London: Macmillan, 1980.
NYPL	New York Public Library
RISM	*Répertoire International des Sources Musicales.* Kassel: Bärenreiter, 1971.
SLONIMSKY	Slonimsky, Nicolas. *Music Since 1900.* 4th ed. New York: Charles Scribner's Sons, 1971.
[ ]	Date of composition (in brackets), e.g., [1945]
1st:	Date of first performance
#	Publishing information
*	Recording information

Music and War

I. WAR MUSIC BEFORE 1600

THE ANCIENT WORLD

Over three millennia ago Hammurabi proclaimed, "I made an end of war." The boast of this great Babylonian king has been disproven thousands upon thousands of times, as armies have fought one against the other in all parts of the world. Long before Hammurabi flourished, man had been fighting man, man had been killing man. Still today, with all the technical advancements and supposed cultural sophistication, no end to war is in sight. For at least five thousand years, representations or depictions of war with its victories and defeats found their way into art, literature, and music.

As early as 3500 B.C.E. a Neolithic rock painting found in the Tassili Plateau of the Sahara depicted archers in combat.[1] In Mesopotamia a monument depicted "on one side of a stone the victorious troops of Eannatum of Lagash marching over the prostrate bodies of the army of Umma, while vultures and lions devour the corpses."[2] The Egyptian Pharaohs had sculptures and paintings of battle made in their honor, such as the thirteenth-century B.C.E. stone relief carved on the Great Temple of Abu Simbel, showing Rameses II slaying his enemy. In ancient Greece numerous vase paintings, architectural friezes, and sculptures depicted Greek warriors and scenes of battle. The famous Painted Colonnade in the Athenian Agora contained paintings of the fall of Troy and the Battle of Marathon. Often, Greek artists depicted their gods in battle, as in the frieze of the Siphnian Treasury which represented a battle between the gods and the giants.

The earliest literature is also occupied with war. In a portion of the *Epic of Gilgamesh* dating from around 2000 B.C.E., Gilgamesh and Enkidu victoriously defended Uruk against Elam. A few hundred years later, an Egyptian victory hymn was written in honor of Thutmose III. Homer's great epic of the Trojan War, *The Iliad*, found its form some time around 800 B.C.E.[3] *Exodus* and *Samuel* provided Biblical accounts of battle, and *Joshua* presented one of the earliest descriptions of musical instruments in battle. During the sixth-century B.C.E. fall of Jericho, Joshua and his followers, with their seven trumpets of rams' horns and their seven days of shouting, forced the walls of Jericho to crumble and "utterly destroyed all that was in the city."[4]

The Greeks first represented the idea of war in theater and music. Music played a significant role in the Greek dramas of Aeschylus, Sophocles, Euripedes, and others, although only a few musical fragments are now extant. In addition to drama, the Greek poets composed and sang short odes depicting the valor of Greek warriors. One of the most famous poet-singers, Simonides, composed ballads which eulogized those who died in battle. It is likely that these performers sang their songs of praise and victory in a specific musical mode, since the Greeks formulated a system in which each mode was considered to possess a specific character or emotion. The philosophers, as well, speculated on the power of these musical modes and their effects on the citizens of the Greek city-states. In his *Republic* Plato wrote that the Mixolydian and Lydian modes were "suitable for dirges," and that Ionian and Lydian were considered "languid" and unsuitable for soldiers. He accepted only the Dorian and Phrygian modes, believing that Dorian represented bravery and "any dangerous undertaking," while Phrygian represented peace.[5] Plato, therefore, not only believed in the significant social effect of the modes on the citizens, but also specifically distinguished between the musical modes of conflict and peace.

Aristotle also made distinctions among the modes and separated them into three categories: the ethical, the practical, and the passionate.[6] He made no specific distinction between war and peace as Plato did, but further reinforced the tradition of assigning certain emotional characteristics to the modes—a practice that continued until the establishment of major and minor tonalities in the Baroque period.

The ancient Greeks also thought music could fulfill a practical function on the battlefield itself. During the battle of Mantinea in 418 B.C.E., Thucydides reported that the "Spartans came on slowly and to the music of many flute-players in their ranks. This custom . . . is designed to make them keep in step and move forward steadily without breaking their ranks, as large armies often do when they are just about to join battle."[7] Paul Henry Lang reinforced this idea and added that "before the battle the aulete played a 'prelude' which was supposed to put the soldiers in the proper mood for fighting, while the so-called Castor-song gave the signal for the attack."[8] No detailed musical description of the "prelude" exists, but the fact that a certain work of music could place the soldiers in the mood for battle further emphasizes the early role that music played in the military life of Greece. Therefore, we could consider this prelude as one of the first war-related compositions of which we have a record.

The Romans continued the tradition of representing war in art and literature. Horace wrote numerous poems about battles and war, and Virgil devoted the last four books of his *Aeneid* to the description of the war between the Trojans and Italians. Virgil also provided a poignant statement about war at the end of the first book of his *Georgics*. Frequently the Romans used paintings and sculptures to celebrate victories over their enemies.[9]

Although music played an active role in ancient Rome, no musical compositions are extant. The Roman army used a variety of trumpets in its military bands, and it is possible that these bands performed specific music to prepare the Roman soldiers for battle, as the early Greeks had done. Drums, which are prominent in military bands of later civilizations, had no place in either Greek or Roman military music. Rather, "women in the cults of Dionysos and Cybele . . . almost exclusively played" Greek and Roman drums.[10]

THE MEDIEVAL PERIOD: 400-1450

There is little evidence that musicians continued to perform war-related music during the early Middle Ages. Literature and paintings on the subject of war appeared only sporadically during these centuries, and they exhibited little change in attitude toward the idea of war. With few exceptions, these arts captured the triumphant side of war, the glorious victory. War was a noble pursuit, filled with the challenge of hand-to-hand combat. In 1229 the people felt cheated of a glorious military victory when Frederick II took Jerusalem, Nazareth, and Bethlehem through negotiations instead of battle.[11] Men looked forward to fighting in order to demonstrate their bravery and strength; war was not something that they feared.

Although documentation of war-related music during the Middle Ages is scarce, music was likely prominent in military operations. In his *History of the British Army*, J.W. Fortescue suggested that one of the functional roles of Saracen musicians during a battle in the time of the Crusades was "to gather the minstrels around the standards and bid them blow and beat strenuously and unceasingly during the action. The silence of the band was taken as a proof that a battalion had been broken and that the colours were in danger."[12] Unfortunately, we have no idea of what type of music they played or whether it was simply noise that served a military purpose. Pattee Evenson claimed this music seriously affected the Crusaders and "the confusion which it created in their ranks was so profound as to lead subsequently to the adoption and expansion of military music in the forces of the Crusaders themselves."[13]

The earliest examples of war-related music in the Medieval period for which manuscripts are available, however, were not compositions used for battle. Several of the early songs from the Crusades were laments for the death of a leader or for the destruction of a city. The monophonic conductus *Sede Syon, in pulvere* (no. 3), dating from approximately 1195, bewails the destruction of Jerusalem, which Saladin sacked in 1187. *Fortz chaussa es* laments the death of one of the most famous leaders of the Crusades, the English king Richard Coeur de Lion. The music to these songs, however, appears to be no different from other Medieval songs dating from the same time. The text alone makes these pieces "war" songs; the music serves only as a vehicle of expression. Medieval composers did not attempt to portray realistic battle scenes in musical terms as composers of future generations did.

Guillaume Dufay's motets of the mid-fifteenth century are in a similar vein. *C'est bien raison de devoir essaucier* (no. 4) celebrates the restoration of peace in Florence, Venice, and Milan in 1433, and *Supremum est mortalibus bonum* (no. 6) was written for the Peace Treaty of Viterbo in the same year. Neither has musical material that in any way depicts or symbolizes war. Dufay also later composed a marvelous lament on the fall of Constantinople: *Lamentatio sanctae matris ecclesiae constantinopolitanae: O très piteux de tout espoir fontaine* (no. 5).

THE RENAISSANCE PERIOD: 1450-1600

The Renaissance witnessed changes in many facets of war and the arts, partially because of the influence of the ancient Greeks and Romans. Unlike the armies of the Greeks and Romans, however, the Renaissance armies employed drummers in their military bands. In *Instructions sur le faict de la guerre* (1549), Forquevaux wrote that each infantry legion should contain two drummers,[14] and according to J.T. Arbeau in his *Orchésographie*, drums played a significant role in the battle, serving as a "signal and warning to the soldiers to strike camp, to advance, & to withdraw; and to give them heart, boldness and courage to attack the enemy on sight; and to defend themselves manfully and vigorously."[15]

The earliest extant battle composition by a known composer is Isaac's *Alla battaglia* (c. 1485-1487) (no. 18). Although it has been a popular instrumental work since its modern publication in 1908, recent research indicates that it originally contained a text.[16] Timothy McGee persuasively argues that a version including text was probably performed in Florence in 1485 during a grand ceremony connected with the installation of the new captain-general of the Florentine army.[17] That the work was at first known to modern scholars as an instrumental piece is not that unusual, because it was common for instrumental transcriptions to be made of such works. Janequin's texted *La guerre* also appears without words in several manuscripts from the Renaissance period.

The music of Isaac's three-part *Alla battaglia* is in F-Ionian and opens with a distinct rhythmic motive that is used more often than any other in battle compositions throughout the next four centuries (Example 1).

Example 1: Rhythmic motive from Isaac, *Alla battaglia*:

Isaac's battaglia also contains repeated-note patterns, open fifths, and a sectionalized form, elements that are common in many later battle compositions.

It was not until the sixteenth century, however, that war-related musical compositions flourished. In his *Zur Geschichte der Battaglia* (1931), Rudolf Gläsel catalogued nearly eighty compositions written between 1500 and 1600 that are related to battle.[18] The one work chiefly responsible for the increasing interest in battle music during the sixteenth century was Clément Janequin's *La guerre* (no. 22). Howard Brown wrote that this work "became one of the best-known pieces of the entire century, copied by many other composers and arranged for keyboard or lute solo and for all varieties of instrumental ensemble."[19] Most likely composed to commemorate the victory of Francis I at the Battle of Marignano in 1515, *La guerre* was an innovative work which established many characteristics of war-related music that are still employed in compositions in the twentieth century.

Published in 1528, *La guerre* appeared in several published editions during the sixteenth century. It is divided into two distinct, through-composed sections, each tonally closed and clearly in F-Ionian, the same mode as Isaac's *Alla battaglia*. The relatively static harmony consists primarily of major tonic and dominant triads. The harmonic interval of a perfect fifth is used extensively, and the melody, possibly imitating trumpet calls, often outlines the major triad. The pandemonium of the battle itself is created not through dissonance, but through a lively tempo, fast repeated notes, short scalar patterns, consistent use of imitation and onomatopoetic devices, and a conspicuous rhythmic motive of four sixteenth notes followed by two eighths (Example 2). *La guerre* contains virtually no dissonance.

Example 2: Rhythmic motive from Janequin, *La guerre*:

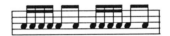

The text of *La guerre* represents the nobleness of warfare, the grandeur of victory. It tells of a battle between courageous warriors engaged in honorable man-to-man combat. "Gallant nobles, be valiant! Strike to kill! Tarirarirayne. Trique tac patac. Give blow on blow. Beat back the foe! Courage! . . . Victory to the noble King Francis!" With this engaging text and these various musical characteristics, Janequin created a pleasant and enjoyable composition—one completely devoid of the tribulations, sufferings, and horrors of war.

Janequin's *La guerre* was so successful that he composed further battle chansons, *La bataille de Metz* (no. 21) and *La guerre de Renty* (no. 24), made another version of *La guerre* called *La guerre: Escoutés tous gentils* in 1555 (no. 23), and incorporated his original chanson into his *Messa la battaille* (no. 25) Francisco Guerrero and Tomás Luis de Victoria continued this parody tradition and based their masses *Missa de la batalla escoutez* (no. 50) and *Missa pro Victoria* (1600) (no. 135) on *La guerre* as well. Both Andrea Gabrieli and Annibale Padovano closely modeled their eight-voice battaglias for wind instruments on Janequin's chanson, using the same organization, mode, rhythmic motives, scales, meter changes, and repeated notes that Janequin employed in 1528. Many little-known composers, such as Melchiore de Barberiis, Guilio Barbetta, Francesco Canova de Milano, and Marc'Antonio Pifaro, also based instrumental works on or made transcriptions of *La guerre*.

Following Janequin's lead, several other composers turned to vocal works descriptive of battle. In addition to his battaglia for wind instruments, Andrea Gabrieli wrote another Battaglia for eight voices (no. 39) modeled on *La guerre*, but independent in style. Like Janequin, Gabrieli used onomatopoetic devices, repeated notes and rhythmic patterns; he divided the work into two sections and concluded it victoriously. Near the end of the sixteenth century, Andriano Banchieri wrote a similar eight-voice *La battaglia* in G major (no. 33), and Guillaume Costeley and Mateo Flecha composed extended four-voice works in the same tradition. In England William Byrd wrote a different type of work, an actual song of lament for the dead entitled *In Fields Abroad* (no. 16).

With the rise of instrumental music during the Renaissance, composers moved beyond transcriptions of vocal battle chansons and began writing independent instrumental battle works in the late sixteenth century, particularly for lute and keyboard. The lute pieces were generally on a smaller scale and written by lesser-known composers such as Ludovico Agostini, Guilio Cesare Barbetta, Grégoire Brayssing, Francesco Canova de Milano, and Giocomo Gorzanis. Several of these lute pieces, and as well some keyboard works, were brief dances (e.g., *Pavane de la guerre* or *Gaillarde sur la bataille*) which had little to do with battle or war other than the titles the composers gave them. In 1591, however, William Byrd expanded upon some of Janequin's ideas and wrote one of the best-known battle compositions for keyboard. Instead of the two sections of Janequin's *La guerre*, Byrd illustrates the program by dividing *The Battle* (no. 15) into ten separate pieces, each depicting a certain phase of the battle. The battle starts with the "Soldiers' Summons," followed by a series of marches and instrumental fanfares, and proceeds to the battle itself, the retreat, and the burying of the dead. Although the battle remains in C-Ionian throughout, Byrd uses different rhythmic patterns and keyboard figurations to depict the events represented in the titles. "The Battle Joined" illustrates the use of repeated chords to depict a battle. The first line contains only tonic and dominant chords that are repeated steadily, foreshadowing Monteverdi's use of *stile concitato* in his eighth book of madrigals. The texture is thicker than in any of the other pieces employing three notes in each hand. The work ends with "The Burying of the Dead," which consists almost completely of half notes. This section represents the inactivity of the dead as opposed to the repeated eighth notes that represented the fighting in the battle scene. It remains clearly in C-Ionian and does not employ any of the dissonance or chromaticism that are associated with later laments.

By the end of the Renaissance, numerous war-related traditions had begun. Although none of the music from this time represented the horrors of war or contained much use of dissonance, songs and chansons told of battles and glorious victories, occasionally lamenting lost rulers or important leaders. The parody battle masses had begun with Janequin and Francisco Guerrero, and instrumental transcriptions of chansons led to battle pieces written for lute, keyboard, and larger instrumental ensembles, including intimate little dance pieces such as Sebastian Vredeman's *Branle de bataille* (no. 72) and Adrian Le Roy's *Pavane de la guerre* (no. 68). These innovations and remarkable compositions laid a solid foundation of war-related music upon which the Baroque composers would build.

ANNOTATED LISTING OF MEDIEVAL WAR MUSIC:
1100-1450

Anonymous

1. *Bogurodzica (Mother of God)* [before 1410].
   [Cited in Gustave Reese, *Music in the Renaissance*, 2nd ed.
   (New York: W.W. Norton, 1959), p. 742]
   A battle hymn that legend has being sung at Tannenberg
   (1410).

2. *Deo gracias, Anglia (Agincourt Carol)*. Medieval carol [c. 1415].
   #*Music Britannica IV*, ed. John Stevens (London: Stainer & Bell,
   1952), p. 6. Reprinted in *The Chester Book of Madrigals
   (Warfare)*, ed. Anthony G. Petti (London: Chester Music, 1986),
   vol. 7, pp. 2-3.
   M1578.W37 1986
   In two voices (occasionally three) and five verses, this carol
   narrates the battle at Agincourt in 1415.

3. *Sede Syon, in pulvere*. Monophonic conductus [c. 1195].
   [No LC number available]
   A lament for Jerusalem after Saladin captured it in 1187.

France

Dufay, Guillaume (c. 1400-1474)

4. *C'est bien raison de devoir essaucier*. Ballad [26 April 1433].
   #*Guillaume Dufay, Opera Omnia*, ed. Heinrich Besseler (Rome:
   American Institute of Musicology in Rome, 1964), vol. 6, pp. 31-
   32.
   M3.D9 v. 6
   In fifty-four measures, with three voices and three parts in F-
   Ionian, only the top voice contains text.

5. *Lamentatio sanctae matris ecclesiae constantinopolitanae: O très
   piteux de tout espoir fontaine*: Latin song, probably for woman's
   voice [1454]. 1st: 17 February 1454. #*Guillaume Dufay, Opera
   Omnia*, vol. 6, pp. 19-21.
   M3.D9 v. 6

An eighty-four measure lament written in F-Lydian/Ionian. The top two voices and bass are in 3/4 and the tenor is in 2 x 3/4.

6. *Supremum est mortalibus bonum/ Supremum.* Isorhythmic motet [18 April 1433]. *#Guillaume Dufay, Opera Omnia*, vol. 1, pp. 23-27.
    M3.D9 v. 1 pt. 2
    Deals with the Peace Treaty of Viterbo. Contains 127 measures, with two voices and one instrumental part.

Grimace (fl. 1350-1375)

7. *Alarme, alarme.* Voices [late 14th c.]. *#French Secular Music of the Late Fourteenth Century*, ed. Willi Apel, p. 122. *Vanguard SRV-298SD.
    M2.A535F7
    The text is more about love than war, but it is an early piece combining the theme of love and war, a pairing which continues throughout the Baroque.

ANNOTATED LISTING OF RENAISSANCE WAR MUSIC:
1450-1600

Anonymous

8. *Alla bataglia.* 3 voices [c. 1470]. Found in *Chansonnier Pixérécourt.*
    [Cited in NEW GROVE, vol. 2, p. 290]
    In three parts and uses repeated chords.

9. *Bataglia Francese di Clemens Janecquin* [sic] *Prima parte.* Keyboard [1577]. *#Musica de diversi autori* (Venice: Angelo Gardano, 1577), no. 1.
    [Cited in BROWN, p. 289]
    A keyboard work based on Janequin's *La guerre.*

10.   *Branle de bataille* (no. 118); *Battaille*; *Victoire*; *La gailliarde de la bataille* (no. 152). Cittern [1582]. *#Hortulus cithare vulgaris continens optimes* (Paris: Pierre Phalèse & Jean Bellère, 1582). [Cited in BROWN, pp. 312-13]
       Phalèse and Bellère published a number of battle pieces without supplying composers' names in various editions during the latter half of the sixteenth century. See BROWN for a more complete listing.

11.   *A Historical Song*: "*A Song of the Captivity and Sad Constraint of the Land of Hungary.*" Four-voice song [c. 1558]. *#Zamosc Song Book*, printed in *Music of the Polish Renaissance*, ed. Jozef M. Chomiński and Zofia Lissa (Warsaw: Polskie Wydawnictwo Muzyczne, 1955), pp. 188-92.
       M2.M9813
       In four voices with five verses, this thirty-nine measure song is in C-harmonic minor and in the form ABBAA.

12.   *A Historical Song*: "*A New Song of the Victory at Byczyna.*" Song [c. 1588]. *#Music of the Polish Renaissance*, pp. 193-96.
       M2.M9813
       A strophic song in nineteen measures and five verses telling of the victory at Byczyna.

13.   *Duma.* Song [c. 1589]. *#Music of the Polish Renaissance*, pp. 197-201.
       M2.M9813
       Modeled on Janequin, this text is particularly gory for its time. The song of fifty-eight measures is in C-Ionian, 4/4, and almost completely diatonic with strong syncopations in the beginning. Before the text was discovered, *Duma* was thought to have been an instrumental work (as was the case with Isaac's *Alla battaglia* [no. 18]).

14.   *La guerre.* Lute [c. 1529]. #Sammlung Attaingnant 1529. Reprinted in *Laute und Lautenmusik bis zur mitte des 16. Jahrhunderts,* ed. Oswald Körte (Leipzig: Breitkopf & Härtel, 1901), p. 153.
       ML1010.K85
       In F-Lydian, a one-page work with repeated notes and rhythms with six repeated sections.

England

Byrd, William (1543-1623)

15. *The Battle.* Keyboard [1591]. #*My Ladye Nevells Booke.* Reprinted
     (New York: Dover, 1969). *London CS 7221 (brass version)
     M2.B95M9 1969
     Contains ten independent movements (all in C-Ionian),
     moving from "The Soldier's Summons" through various marches,
     "The Battle Joined," "Retreat," and "The Burying of the Dead." See
     Olivier Neighbour, *The Consort: Keyboard Music of William Byrd*
     (London: Faber & Faber, 1978), pp. 172-74.

16. *In Fields Abroad.* Consort Song. #*The Byrd Edition*, "Madrigals,
     Songs, and Canons" (London: Stainer & Bell, 1976), vol. 16, pp.
     106-09.
     M3.B992 v. 16
     In four verses and AAB form, this song laments the dead lying
     on foreign fields.

17. *Look and Bow Down.* Consort Song [1588]. #*The Byrd Edition*,
     vol. 16, pp. 178-79. Text by Queen Elizabeth I.
     M3.B992 v. 16
     Written on the defeat of the Spanish Armada; in G minor.

Flemish

Isaac, Heinrich (c. 1450-1517)

18. *Alla battaglia.* Four voices [c. 1485-1487]. #*Denkmäler der
     Tonkunst in Österreich* (Graz: Akademische Druck-u.
     Verlagsanstalt, 1959), vol. 32, pp. 221-24. *MCA 25953.
     M2.D36 Bd. 32
     Contains 213 measures and is in three sections, each of which
     opens imitatively. This is the earliest extant battle piece composed
     originally with text. See note 16 on page 25.

France

Costeley, Guillaume (1531-1606)

19. *La prise de Calais (Hardis françoys).* Four-voice chanson [after
     1558]. #*Les maîtres musiciens de la renaissance française* (Paris:

Alphonse Leduc, 1894-1908), vol. 19, pp. 12-22. Reprinted in *The Chester Book of Madrigals (Warfare)*, ed. Anthony G. Petti (London: Chester Music, 1986), vol. 7, pp. 21-28.

M2.M23 or M1578.W37 1986

A 228-measure suite in F-Ionian with some imitation, particularly in the trio for three imitative voices. Does not contain nonsense syllables or many repeated notes, but makes use of repeated patterns at times. Retells the French taking Calais in 1558.

20. *La prise du Havre (Approche toy, jeune roy)*. Four-voice chanson. *#Les maîtres musiciens de la renaissance française*, vol. 19, pp. 50-66.

M2.M23

Similar in style and writing of *La prise de Calais*, with few programmatic effects.

Janequin, Clément (c. 1475-1558)

21. *La bataille de Metz (Or sus branslés)*. Chanson [1555]. *#Clément Janequin Chansons Polyphoniques* (Monaco: Éditions de L'oiseau-lyre, 1965), vol. 6, pp. 78-116.

M3.1.J3M5 v. 6

In five polyphonic voices and two major sections, this chanson uses nonsense syllables and repeated notes in the tradition of *La guerre*.

22. *La guerre*. Chanson [c. 1528]. *#Clément Janequin Chansons Polyphoniques*, vol. 1, pp. 23-53. *Vanguard SRV-298SD.

M3.1.J3M5 v. 1

The most famous song about war in the Renaissance was composed most likely to commemorate Francis I's victory at the Battle of Marignano in 1515. *La guerre* also appeared in purely instrumental arrangements. See, for example, the two lute arrangements in *The Lute Music of Francesco Canova de Milano (1497-1543)* (Cambridge: Harvard University Press, 1970), pp. 299-326.

See also items 13, 23, 25, 29-30, 34, 37-38, 42-44, 50, 52, 106, and 135. For Janequin's reworking of this work, see A. Tillman Merritt, "Janequin: Reworkings of Some Early Chansons," *Aspects of Medieval and Renaissance Music: A Birthday Offering to Gustave Reese*, ed. Jan LaRue (New York: W.W. Norton, 1978), pp. 603-13.

23. *La guerre: Escoutés tous gentils.* Chanson [1555]. *#Clément Janequin Chansons Polyphoniques,* vol. 6, pp. 41-77.
    M3.1.J3M5 v. 6
    Another version of his 1528 *La guerre,* the spellings of text are different and the text itself is different at the end of part I. The first part of this version is twenty-four measures longer than the original chanson. The second part uses more repeated pitches in the faster notes than in the earlier version, and although the first thirty-nine measures of part II are similar in both, the text and music following this point are much different.

24. *La guerre de Renty (Branlez vos piques).* Chanson [1559]. *#Clément Janequin Chansons Polyphoniques,* vol. 6, pp. 167-76.
    M3.1.J3M5 v. 6
    A four-voice polyphonic chanson of only eighty-seven measures and without the nonsense syllables and battle-like figures found in *La guerre.*

25. *Messe la battaille.* Four-voice mass [1555]. #Paris: Salabert, 1947.
    M2011.J3B3
    An A-major setting of the ordinary in four voices based upon melodies from *La guerre.*

France and Catalina

Brudieu, Joan (c. 1520-1591)

26. *Oid, oid.* Four-voice madrigal [1585]. *#Sección de música publicaciones* (Barcelona: Biblioteca de Catalunya, 1963), vol. 1, pp. 22-27.
    M2.B28 v. 1
    In the tradition of Janequin with onomatopoetic devices. Written to celebrate the Victory at Lepanto on 7 October 1571. See André Mangeot's "The Madrigals of Joan Brudieu," *The Score* 7 (1952), pp. 25-31.

Germany

Löffelholtz, Christoph (1572-1619)

27. *Die kleine Schlacht.* Organ [1585]. *Musical Heritage Society 1790. #Berlin State Library.
    [No LC number available]

A three-minute work using the opening rhythm of *La guerre* frequently. Contains repeated static chords over which run faster-note passages. Some imitation and contrasting sections before closing with a fanfare.

Neusidler, Hans (c. 1508-1563)

28. *Hie volget die Frantzösisch Schlacht die heist Signori.* Lute [1544]. *#Ein new künstlich Lautten Buch* in *Denkmäler der Tonkunst in Österreich* (Vienna: Österreichischer Bundesverlag), vol. 37, pp. 46-55.
     M2.D36
     In three parts, this highly diatonic, D-Ionian work uses numerous repeated notes and rhythms throughout in a three-voice texture and with changing meters. Another brief battaglia (forty-seven measures) follows on pp. 56-58 in G-Ionian with more scale passages and sustained notes: *Sula battaglia.*

Paix, Jakob (1556-after 1623)

29. *La bataille. Escoutez.* Keyboard [1583]. *#Orgel Tablaturbuch* (1583), no. 38.
     [RISM P640]
     In four-voice texture, based on Janequin's *La guerre.*

Waissel, Matthäus (c. 1540 - d. 1602)

30. *La battaglia.* Lute [1573]. *#Tabulatura* (1573), ed. Dániel Benko (Budapest: Editio Musica, 1980), vol. 1, pp. 26-27.
     M140.W34T3 v. 1
     Based on *La guerre* but highly ornamented and transposed to D-Ionian as well as abridged.

Werrekoren, Hermann Mathias (16th c.)

31. *La battaglia taliana.* Four-voice chorus [1544]. #Brussels: Tirnbass, 1931 and Peer: Musica Alamire, 1987. First published as *Die Schlacht vor Pavia.*
     JMB 91-57 (NYPL call number)
     Composed in honor of Francesco Sforza and possibly written about the Battle of Pavia (1525) or the Battle of Marignan. It contains battle cries, onomatopoeias, and various languages.

Italy

Agostini, Ludovico (1534-1590)

32. *All'arm 'all'arme.* Five-voice canzona [1574]. #*Monumenti di musica italiana*, Serie II: Polifonia (Kassel: Bärenreiter & Brescia: L'Organo, 1963), vol. 1, pp. 25-28.
     M2.M48442. v. 1
     A forty-measure, strophic canzona setting "all'arm" to repeated pitches in a homophonic texture.

Banchieri, Adriano (1568-1634)

33. *La battaglia.* Eight voices (or eight instruments) [1596]. #*Canzoni all francese a quattro voci per sonare. . . in fine una battaglia a otto* . . . (Venice: Ricciardo Amadino, 1596). Reprinted (Macomb, Ill.: R. Dean Publishing, 1974). *Argo ZRG 932 (brass version).
     M1531.B268C32
     Using nonsense syllables, repeated notes, and dotted rhythms like Janequin's *La guerre*, this delightful work in G-Ionian emphasizes sixteenth notes in successive imitation.

Barbetta, Guilio Cesare (c. 1540-after 1630)

34. *Pass' e mezzo, Sopra la battaglia.* Lute [1569]. #*Il primo libro dell' intavolatura de liuto* (Venice: Girolamo Scotto, 1569), no. 18; also in *Lautenspieler des 16. Jahrhunderts*, ed. Oscar Chilesotti (Leipzig: Breitkopf & Härtel, 1929), pp. 72-75.
     M2.C61
     In D-Ionian, an ornamental version of Janequin's *La guerre* dedicated to "Al molto magnifico et prudentissimo Signor, il Signor Melchioro Adiebes, dignissimo Consigliero dell Illustre nation Alemana."

Cimello, Tomaso (c. 1500-after 1579)

35. *Venimo tre soldati.* Chanson. #*Canzone villanesche al modo napolitano a tre voci: libro primo* (Venice: A. Bardane, 1545).
     [OCLC 18515607 - at University of California, Riverside]
     "A spiritual battle-piece in the tradition of the programme chanson characterized by the repetition of three note motifs" (NEW GROVE, vol. 4, pp. 403-04).

Festa, Contanzo (c. 1490-1545)

36. *Deus venerut gentes.* Five-voice motet. #Manuscript at the
     Bibliotoca Vallicelliana in Rome, no. 45; *Italia sacra musica*, ed.
     K. Jeppesen (1962), vol. 1.
     [No LC number available]
     Edward Lowinsky argues that this was a war-related work. See
     "A Newly Discovered Sixteenth-Century Motet Manuscript at the
     Bibliotoca Vallicelliana in Rome," *Journal of the American
     Musicological Society* 3 (1950), pp. 173-232. Alexander Main
     suggests it was "probably intended as a protest against the invasion
     of Rome, 1527" (NEW GROVE, vol. 6, p. 501).

Francesco da Milano (1497-1543)

37. *La bataglia.* Lute [1536]. *#Intavolatura de viola o vero lauto*, 1536
     in *Opere complete per liuto* (Milan: Edizioni Suvini Zerboni,
     1971), vol. 2, pp. 127-77.
     M140.F8C5 v. 2
     Two different and complete transcriptions of Janequin's *La
     guerre.*

Gabrieli, Andrea (c. 1510-1586)

38. *Aria della battaglia.* Eight-part instrumental. *#Instituzioni e
     Monumenti dell'arte musicale italiana* (Milan: Ricordi, 1931-
     1939), vol. 1, p. 93. *London LDR 71081 (brass transcription).
     M2.I87 v. 1
     Closely modeled on Janequin's *La guerre*, this work is in F-
     Ionian and uses numerous repeated notes and chords.

39. *Battaglia.* Eight texted voices. *#Instituzioni e Monumenti dell'arte
     musicale italiana* (Milan: Ricordi, 1931-1939), vol. 1, p. 203.
     *Erato ECD 88168.
     M2.I87 v. 1
     Influenced by Janequin in technique but uses different musical
     materials, all in C- or G-Ionian. Contains nonsense syllables and
     ends with a victory celebration.

Lupacchino, Bernardino (d. c. 1555)

40.   *Sopra la battaglia.* Two recorders [before 1555]. *#Tre Composizioni per 2 flauti dolci* (Padova: G. Zanibon, 1974), pp. 9-11.
       M289.L96D9
       In F-Ionian, this work looks back in some ways to Janequin but is much simpler and rhythmically somewhat static.

Negri, Cesare de (c. 1535-after 1604)

41.   *La battaglia.* Lute [1580]. *#Danze Del Secolo XVI,* transcribed by Oscar Chilesotti (Bologna: Forni editore, 1969), pp. 64-65.
       M140.N48N4 Th. 2
       An unusual battle piece with repeats every three or four measures; includes highly rhythmic figurations and ornamental thirty-second notes. It begins in A-Ionian but ends in B-Ionian.

Padovano, Annibale (1527-1575)

42.   *Battaglia per strumenti da fiato.* Eight voices [1590]. *#Instituzioni e Monumenti dell'arte musicale italiana* (Milan: Ricordi, 1931-1939), vol. 1, p. 177. *Archiv Produktion 2533 468.
       M2.I87 v. 1
       Once performed by an ensemble of forty, this work was modeled closely on Janequin's *La guerre,* using several of the same motives, harmonies, and rhythms in its two parts.

Pifaro, Marc'Antonio [del] (c. 1500-?)

43.   *La bataglia. Chiarenzana.* Lute [before 1546]. *#Intavolatura de lauto di Marcantonio del Pifaro* (Venice: 1546). Reprinted (Geneva: Minkoff Reprint, 1981), no. 9.
       M140.P53I67
       Based in part on Janequin's *La guerre.* In lute notation.

Susato, Tylman (c. 1500-c. 1561)

44.   *Pavane: La batille.* Instrumental ensemble *a* 4 [1551]. *#Dances from Danserye* (London & New York: Schott, 1983), pp. 13-14. *Erato ECD 88168.
       JMF 86-880 (NYPL call number)

Consists of thirty-two measures in four repeated sections of C-Ionian, largely homophonic. The last section uses repeated sixteenth notes. Based on Janequin's *La guerre*. Susato also published a beautiful copy of *La guerre* in 1545. See NEW GROVE, vol. 18, p. 378 for a reproduction of the first page of the score.

Valentini, Giovanni (1582-1649)

45. *Iubilate Deo.* Motet [c. 1621]. #*Messa, Magnificat et Iubilate Deo a sette chori concertati con le trombe* (Vienna: M. Formica, 1621).
[No LC number available]
      In his article "The Hapsburg Court of Ferdinand II and the *Messa, Magnificat et Iubilate Deo a sette chori concertati con le trombe* (1621) of Giovanni Valentini," Steven Saunders suggests this motet was written "for the celebrations in Vienna of the imperial troops' victory over the Bohemian forces at White Mountain, the first major battle of the Thirty Years War," *Journal of the American Musicological Society* 44 (1991), p. 378.

Verdelot, Philippe (between 1470 and 1480-before 1552)

46. *Italia mia bench'el parlar'.* Madrigal [1538]. #*Dei madrigali di Verdelotto et de altri eccellentissimi autori a cincque voci, libro secondo* (Venice: O. Scotto, 1538), no. 13. Reprinted in *The Chester Book of Madrigals* (London: Chester Music, 1987), vol. 8. *Columbia M36664. Text by Petrarch.
      M1578.W37 v. 8
      In his article "The 'Sack of Rome' Set to Music," *Renaissance Quarterly* 23 (1970), pp. 412-21, Don Harrán writes that this was a war lament mentioning "divine intervention to heal the wounds inflicted by the enemy" (p. 420).

47. *Trista Amarilli mia.* Madrigal [1530]. #*Madrigali de diversi musici libro primo de la serena* (Rome: Valerio da Bressa, 1530), fol. 3.
      [Cited in Harrán. See item 46.]
      Harrán suggests this work also treated the sack of Rome allegorically. He writes that it is "the only piece in the sacro-secular repertory of its time to refer, more or less explicitly, to the invasion of Rome and its aftermath" (p. 419).

Spain

Encina [Enzina], Juan del (1468-1529)

48. *Una sañósa Porfía.* Madrigal [after 1492]. #*The Chester Book of
     Madrigals, (Warfare),* vol. 7, pp. 44-45. *Erato ECD 88168.
     M1578.W37 1986
     A lament dealing with the retaking of Granada from the Moors
     in 1492 and an early example of folía.

Flecha, Mateo (ii) (1530-1604)

49. *Guerre* from *Las Ensaladas.* Four voices [1595]. #*Sección de
     música publicaciones* (Barcelona: Biblioteca de Catalunya, 1963),
     vol. 16, pp. 47-61.
     M2.B28 vol.16
     An extended (267-measure) work similar to Janequin's *La
     guerre* in spirit and technique. Uses numerous nonsense syllables
     ("fa la la," "tope tope tope," and "duf duf duf") in F-Ionian.

Guerrero, Francisco (1527-1599)

50. *Missa de la batalla escoutez.* Five voices. #London: Mapa Mundi,
     1978.
     M2011.G95B4
     A parody mass incorporating themes of Janequin's *La guerre.*

SUPPLEMENT OF RENAISSANCE WAR MUSIC:
1450-1600

51. Abondante, Giulo (fl. 1546-1587). Italy. *Pass'e mezo de la
     bataglia.* Lute [1586]. #*Il quinto libro de tabolatura da liuto*
     (Venice: Angelo Gardano, 1587). Reprinted (Geneva: Minkoff
     Reprint, 1982), no. 25, pp. 165-69. M140.A26. In two parts and
     in lute notation.
52. Barberiis, Melchiore de (fl. 1545-1550). Italy. *Pass'e mezo della
     battaia, Saltarello dell Pass'e mezo della battaia.* Lute [1549].
     #*Intabolatura di lauto libro nona, intitulato il Bembo* (Venice,

1549), no. 18. [Cited in BROWN, p. 113]. Based on Janequin's *La guerre.*

53. Biffi, Gioseffo (fl. 1596-1606). Italy. *A battaglia.* Six voices [1596]. *#Il primo libro delle canzonette à sei voci per cantar & sonare, insieme con alcun latine, una todesca, & una battaglia* (Nuremberg: Paul Kauffmann, 1596). [RISM B2632].

54. Bonagionta, Giulio (d. after 1582). Italy. *All' arme,* nos. 1 and 3. Three voices [1565]. [Cited in GLÄSEL, p. 93].

55. Brayssing, Grégoire (fl. 1547-1560). Germany. *Pavane de la guerre avec sa gailliarde.* Guitar [1553]. *#Troisième livre de tabulature de guiterre.*

56. _____. *La guerre, faicte a plaisir.* Guitar [1553]. *#Quart livre de tabulature de guiterre* (Paris: Adrian Le Roy & Robert Ballard, 1553), no. 25. [RISM B4295].

57. Cimello, Tomaso (c. 1500-after 1579). Italy. *Battaglia villanesca* [1545]. [Cited in GLÄSEL, p. 92].

58. Corfini [Corsini], Jacopo (c. 1540-1591). Italy. *All' arme.* Five voices [1568]. *#Il secondo libro di madrigali* (Venice, 1568). [Cited in GLÄSEL, p. 93].

59. Crisci, Oratio (fl. 1581-1589). Italy. *Pria che la tromba spaventosa.* Madrigal [1588]. [Cited in GLÄSEL, p. 93].

60. Des Bordes (16th c.). France. *La guerre marine* [1555]. #Le Roy & Ballard's 11th Book. [Cited in MGG, vol. 1, p. 1407]. Uses onomatopoeia.

61. Estrées [Estrée], Jean d' (d. 1576). France. *Premier bransle de la guerre.* Instrumental ensemble *a* 4 [1559]. *#Second livre de danseries* (Paris, 1559), no. 46. [RISM E884].

62. _____. *Pavane de la guerre.* Instrumental ensemble *a* 4 [1559]. *#Tiers livre de danseries* (Paris, 1559), no. 10. [RISM E884].

63. Gervaise, Claude (fl. 1540-1560). France. *Pavanne de la guerre, Gaillarde [de la guerre]* (no. 4); *Gaillard [du ton de la guerre]* (no. 5); *Gaillard [du ton de la guerre]* (no. 6). Instrumental ensemble *a* 4 [1557]. *#Troisieme livre de danceries* (Paris, 1557). M4.C36 no. 66.

64. Gorlier, Simon (fl. 1550-1584). France. *La premiere partie de la bataille de Janequin à trois.* Solo four-course guitar [1551]. *#Le troysieme livre conetnant plusieurs duos et trios, avec la bataille de Janequin à trois, nouvellement mis entabulature de guiterne* (Paris, 1551), no. 15.

65. Gorzanis, Giacomo (c. 1520-between 1575 and 1579). Italy. *Pass e mezo della bataglia, Padoana dell bataglia, Saltarello della bataglia.* Lute [1564]. *#Il terzo libro de intabolatura di liuto* (Venice:

Antonio Gardano, 1564). Reprinted (Geneva: Minkoff Reprint, 1981), no. 11. M140.G5.

66. Kargel, Sixt (c. 1540 after 1594). Germany. *Passomezo bataglia.* Solo cittern [1570]. *#Renovata cythara* (Strassburg, 1578), no. 58. M128.K27.

67. Las Infantas, Fernando de (1534-c. 1610). Spain. *Cantemus Domino.* Deals with the Victory of Lepanto.

68. Le Roy, Adrian (c. 1520-1598). France. *Pavane de la guerre.* Guitar [1552]. *#Tiers livre de tabulature de guiterre* (Paris, 1552), no. 10. *Erato STU 71334. [Cited in BROWN, p. 136].

69. _____. *Galliard de la guerre.* Guitar [1552]. *Tiers livre de tabulature de guiterre* (Paris, 1552), no. 10. *Erato STU 71334. [RISM L2045].

70. Tasso, Gioan Marie (16th c.). Italy. *Sopra la battaglia. a 2* [1565]. *#Il primo libro a note negre a due voci* (1565), no. 35. [Cited in BROWN, p. 220].

71. Viaera, Fredericus (fl. 1563-1564). The Netherlands. *Passemezo bataglia.* Cittern [1564]. *#Nova et elegantissma in cythara ludenda carmina quae videlicet in sola cythara ...* (1564), no. 10. [Cited in BROWN, p. 215].

72. Vredeman, Sebastian (c. 1542-late 16th or early 17th c.). The Netherlands. *Le petit bataille* (no. 48); *Branle de bataille* (no. 87). Cittern [1568]. *#Nova longeque elegantissima cithara ludenda carmina cum Gallica tum etiam Germanica* (1568). [RISM V2566].

73. _____. *Gailliarde de battaille.* Cittern [1569]. *#Carminum quae cythara pulsantur liber secundus* (1569), no. 83. [RISM 2567].

74. Waissel, Matthäus (c. 1540-d. 1602). Germany. *Pavana sur la battaglia, Gaillierda sur la battaglia.* Lute [1591]. *#Tabulatura* (1591), no. 128. [RISM W76].

NOTES

1. *Man Through His Art: War and Peace*, ed. Anil de Silva, Otto von Simson, and Roger Hinks (Greenwich, Conn.: New York Graphic Society, 1964), vol. 1, p. 44.
2. Chester G. Starr, *A History of the Ancient World*, 3rd ed. (Oxford: Oxford University Press, 1983), p. 44.
3. Considerable controversy surrounds the dates of Homer and the *Iliad*. See Starr, p. 203.
4. Joshua 6:21.
5. Plato, *The Republic*, 2nd ed., rev., trans. Desmond Lee (Middlesex: Penguin, 1974), p. 159.
6. Warren Anderson, "Aristotle," *The New Grove Dictionary of Music and Musicians*, ed. Stanley Sadie (London: MacMillan, 1980), vol. 1, p. 589. Hereafter "NEW GROVE."
7. Thucydides, *History of the Peloponnesian War* (London: Penguin, 1954), p. 392.
8. Paul Henry Lang, *Music in Western Civilization* (New York: W.W. Norton, 1941), p. 16.
9. See Mortimer Wheeler, *Roman Art and Architecture* (New York: Oxford University Press, 1964), p. 174.
10. Curt Sachs, *The History of Musical Instruments* (New York: W.W. Norton, 1940), p. 149.
11. Steven Runciman, *A History of the Crusades* (Cambridge: Cambridge University Press, 1954), vol. 3, pp. 187-188.
12. Henry George Farmer, *Military Music* (New York: Chanticleer, 1950), p. 12.
13. Pattee E. Evenson, *A History of Brass Instruments, Their Usage, Music, and Performance Practices in Ensembles During the Baroque Era* (Ph.D. dissertation: University of Southern California, 1960), p. 300.
14. Raymond de Beccarie de Pavie, sire de Fourquevaux, '*Instructions sur le faict de la guerre.*' Cited by Malcolm Vale, *War and Chivalry* (Athens, Ga: University of Georgia Press, 1981), p. 152.
15. Jean Thoinot *dit* Arbeau, *Orchesographie*. Quoted in Vale, p. 153.
16. Timothy J. McGee, "'Alla Battaglia': Music and Ceremony in Fifteenth-Century Florence," *Journal of the American Musicological Society* 36 (1983), pp. 287-302.
17. McGee, pp. 290-91.
18. Rudolf Gläsel, *Zur Geschichte der Battaglia* (Ph.D. dissertation: Leipzig, 1931), pp. 91-105. This work contains a more complete listing

of early battle works and provides manuscript information. Hereafter "GLÄSEL."

19. Howard M. Brown, *Music in the Renaissance* (Englewood Cliffs, N.J.: Prentice-Hall, 1976), p. 215.

II. WAR MUSIC OF THE BAROQUE PERIOD: 1600-1750

During the one hundred and fifty years between 1600 and 1750, political and religious wars raged throughout Europe. The entire region participated in the Thirty Years War (1618-1648), the English Civil War (1642-1647), the Dutch Wars, various Turkish wars and sieges, the Great Northern War (1700-1721), or the Wars of the Spanish (1701-1714) and Austrian (1740-1748) Successions. Throughout the suffering and bloodshed, war retained, for the most part, its glorious side in literature, painting, and music.

The Baroque period also saw the rise of realistic art, including the earliest anti-war art. D.J.R. Bruckner calls Jacques Callot's book of anti-war sketches the "grandfather of all modern art against war."[1] Callot's *Miseries and Disasters of War* contains twenty-four plates of anti-war art created in the years 1633 to 1635. Peter Paul Rubens followed in 1637 with *The Horrors of War* commissioned by the Medici family. Not all Baroque art, however, was against war. Diego Rodríguez de Silva y Velásquez's *Surrender of Breda* (1634-1635) is a majestic portrait of Spanish victory. Furthermore, war had never been more glorious in the minds of European kings. Louis XIV had a "War Drawing Room" built in his Versailles palace with decor that celebrated the French military victories leading to the Treaty of Nijmegen.

Composers did not write anti-war compositions during this era but continued and expanded upon the traditions of the Renaissance. During the early seventeenth century, several composers, Giovanni Anerio, Joan Cereols, Francesco Foggia, and Tomás Luis de Victoria, continued the tradition of writing battle masses. This tradition, however, did not continue into the eighteenth century. Vocal interest is renewed and intensified in the madrigals of Claudio Monteverdi and carried over into the operatic tradition with Monteverdi, Jean-Baptiste Lully, Henry Purcell, and George Frideric Handel.

The Baroque age witnessed a major development not only in the genre of war music, but also in music history, with Monteverdi's invention of the *stile concitato*. This technique, consisting of rapid repeated notes, appeared first in his war composition *Il combattimento di Tancredi e Clorinda* (1624) (no. 121), based on a poem of Torquato Tasso. Monteverdi chose this poem because he wanted "the opportunity of describing in music contrary passions, namely warfare and entreaty and death."[2] He further described this style and its inception in the preface to his eighth book of madrigals, the *Madrigali guerrieri ed amorosi* (1638). He wrote of his "rediscovery" of an agitated, warlike style which he developed while studying the philosophies of Plato and Boethius, and how this style best resembled the passions to suggest war in a musical setting.[3] This agitated style appears in several of Monteverdi's greatest compositions. Although he did not write battle music per se, he attempted to portray musically the intensity and anxiousness of war. By developing the *stile concitato* and by using it to express the text, Monteverdi was among the first composers to treat seriously the subject of war in music.

As did the composers who preceded him, Monteverdi sets his war music in an Ionian or major tonality. In *Il combattimento* he uses G minor from measures 73 to 132; as soon as the war section begins at measure 133, however, he changes to G major. Fast repeated notes play an even greater role in Monteverdi than in earlier composers as illustrated by his use of extended passages in *Il combattimento*. In measures 159 to 174 and 299 to 315, Monteverdi uses repeated sixteenth notes in each of these measures (Example 3).

Example 3: Monteverdi, *Il combattimento di Tancredi e Clorinda*:

In *Altri canti d'amor* (no. 120) Monteverdi uses fast scale passages as Janequin did in *La guerre*, but Monteverdi stresses the conflict by presenting them in contrary motion. He also uses duple meters and repeated rhythmic patterns, and occasionally constructs his melodies from triads (mm. 120-22 and 135-37). Monteverdi's war madrigals are sectional, but sectionalization is completely dependent upon text. *Altri canti d'amor* contains four distinct sections, and only in the second of these dealing with Mars and "fatal crashes and fearless battles" does Monteverdi write warlike music.

Monteverdi also composed a brief instrumental "Sinfonia de guerra" for his opera *Il ritorno d' Ulisse in patria* (1641) (no. 123). This section in G major consists of only twenty-two measures, which are repeated, and uses the stock devices of his military vocal compositions: major tonality, fast scale passages, triadic melodies, and repeated pedal points. This sinfonia is also important because it is one of the earliest instrumental battle scenes that appears in a Baroque opera.

A more elaborate operatic battle scene appears in Act II of Lully's *Alceste* (1674) (no. 105). In scene iii, the besieging soldiers sing a marching song and plan their attack. The actual battle takes place in scene iv: with the cries, "A l'assault, a l'assault" of the besiegers and those of "Aux armes, aux armes" of the besieged, a full-fledged battle rages until the city falls after a gallant fight. Although the tempo is lively throughout, Lully greatly varies the rhythmic interest. Characteristics of French Baroque music, such as frequent shifts in meter from triple to duple and various dotted rhythmic patterns, are present. The tonality remains major throughout, often C major. Trumpets and drums establish much of the heroic nature of the music and, as in the earlier war-related compositions, dissonance plays no role.

The battle scene in Purcell's *King Arthur* ("Come if You Dare") (no. 99) is also in C major, featuring the trumpets and using the chorus only for the victory celebration at the end. Similar battle scenes appear in several of Handel's operas and oratorios. Short war pieces representing battle appear in *Belshazzar, Guilio Cesare, Riccardo Primo*, and *Saul* (nos. 88, 90, 94, 96). Other than employing rapid sixteenth-note passages, fast tempos, and timpani and brass, these works have few of the characteristics of earlier battle music and create no effects that bring to mind a battle. Handel also composed victory hymns and martial music for *Joshua* (no. 91) and *An Occasional Oratorio* (no. 93) and helped establish a tradition for large-scale choral and orchestral works to be performed in celebration of victory. In July of 1713 he wrote his *Utrecht Te Deum* and *Utrecht Jubilate* (no. 97) in celebration of the Peace of Utrecht, which ended the War of the Spanish Succession. Thirty years later, in 1743, he composed his *Dettingen Anthem ("The King Shall Rejoice")* and *Dettingen Te Deum* (no. 89) in order to celebrate the victory of King George II against the French in the War of the Austrian Succession. All of these compositions are in the key of D major and are clearly works of jubilation.

Like the battle pieces of Janequin and Byrd, Handel's Te Deums were extremely popular. Paul Henry Lang wrote that the *Utrecht Te Deum* "became a 'repertory' item at St. Paul's Cathedral for decades until displaced by the *Dettingen Te Deum*. . . . This music and this manner the English public felt to be the very embodiment of their feeling and beliefs."[4] Handel's Te Deums were important in establishing the spectacular role music played in military celebrations. His influence is apparent in Carl Heinrich Graun's 1756 *Te Deum* celebrating Frederick's victory at the Battle of Prague and the Te Deums and anthems of François-Joseph Gossec, Étienne Nicolas Méhul, Charles-Simon Catel, and others composed during the French Revolution.

Like the vocal and operatic war music of the Baroque, instrumental music underwent several changes. The keyboard battle pieces quickly replaced the lute compositions that vanished soon after the turn of the seventeenth century. The organ battle pieces in Portugal during the seventeenth century by Pedro de Araujo, Antonio Martin y Coll, Diego da Conçeicão, and Frey Joseph Torrelhas were all sectionalized and used similar techniques found in the early keyboard works of Girolamo Frescobaldi, John Bull, Juan Cabanilles, Johann Krieger, Bernardo Storace, José Ximénez, and Johann Kaspar Kerll. These compositions included a plethora of repeated notes, considerable imitation, fanfares, drone basses, and fast scale passages, with no unusual dissonance or irregular rhythmic constructions. Most of these works were in major keys and duple meter, and generally sectionalized, but they did not contain descriptive headings and only a few programmatic effects. Except for Johann Kuhnau's *Biblical Sonata No. 1* (no. 110), which narrated the fight between David and Goliath with descriptive passages over the music indicating what is happening, war composers largely abandoned the suite-like keyboard work typified by Byrd's *The Battle*.

The newest programmatic effect for the keyboard to be developed in the Baroque appeared in 1724 with Jean François Dandrieu's transcription of his symphonic composition *Les caractères de la guerre* (no. 104) for the harpsichord. In the preface to this version, Dandrieu described one of the earliest uses of tone clusters for the keyboard, almost two hundred years before Henry Cowell supposedly invented the technique.[5] Dandrieu called these passages "cannon shots" and instructed the performer to "strike the lowest notes on the keyboard with the entire length of the flat of the hand."[6] Like other works up to this time, *Les caractères de la guerre* consists of several movements with descriptive subtitles. The work is in D major throughout and relies on rapid, repeated notes and rhythmic patterns. In the orchestral version, Dandrieu provided a new feature in the extensive use of drum rolls in addition to the usual rapid scales, fanfares, and repeated rhythmic patterns. From beginning to end, the composition expresses only the heroic nature of battle.

Less than two decades later Graun managed to fit the idea of battle music into sonata form in his *La battaglia del re di Prussia* (1740) (no. 107), using considerable amounts of Alberti bass in the process. The first theme consists of a fanfare built on F-major triads and with a common rhythmic motive. The second theme provides a "boom" of gun fire with its three-octave leaps in the right hand "smashing" a single bass note. Repeated notes do not figure as greatly in this work, but Graun uses fast scales, repeated rhythmic patterns, and sequences. Harmonically, he dwells on the basic I, IV, and V chords; other than an occasional diminished chord, no dissonance is present. Although this composition retains many of the stock characteristics of battle music, its importance to the battle literature lies in its use of sonata form.

The instrumental battle for ensembles continued with Samuel Scheidt's *Galliard battaglia* (no. 112) in 1621, and then made major leaps in technique and innovations with Heinrich Biber's *Battalia* (no. 81) in 1673, a year before Lully's *Alceste*. Biber dedicated his work not to the war god Mars but ironically to Bacchus, the god of wine and "promoter of civilization . . . and lover of peace."[7] On the surface Biber's *Battalia* appears to be similar to the earlier suite-like battle pieces. It is a suite of six movements with such titles as "Der Mars," "Die Schlacht," and "Lamento der Verwundten Musquetirer." All of them have a D-major tonality, except for the lament which begins in B minor. Fast tempos with repeated notes and rhythmic patterns abound. What distinguishes Biber's battle composition from the earlier ones, however, is his imaginative use of special instrumental effects.

At certain points in the first movement, Biber requests the string performers to strike their instruments with the wood of the bows, one of the earliest uses of *col legno* (though not the first). In the second movement Biber uses eight different melodies at the same time and entitles this section "Die liederliche Gesellschaft von allerley Humor." Nonetheless, the dissonance that polytonality creates here does not generate harsh or grating sounds; it simply portrays an entertaining, somewhat jarring, good-natured ribaldry of soldiers in their camp. The fundamental meter is 4/4, but the first violin enters with triplets, creating a 12/8 meter in its part. Because of this simultaneous use of 4/4 and 12/8, relatively complex rhythms are established, such as three against four and two against three. When the seventh voice enters on the first beat in measure 34, the different notes sounding at that time are D, E, F, F#, G, and A. All are either a quarter note or dotted quarter in length and create daring dissonances for this era (Example 4).

Example 4: Biber, *Battalia* ("Die liederliche Gesellschaft"):

Biber instructs the double basses in "Der Mars" to place a sheet of paper under the A string to give the effect of a snare drum. From measures 52 to 62 the double bass plays only one note in various rhythmic patterns while the violin plays repeated thirty-second note patterns above it (Example 5).

Example 5: Biber, *Battalia* ("Der Mars"):

In the battle movement he uses tremolos and dotted rhythms and instructs the performers to jerk the string forcefully. After all the adventurous musical effects of the first five movements, Biber chooses to conclude his battle work with an Adagio lament for the wounded instead of the customary victory celebration. Although it ends in D major, it is the only movement that begins in a minor key.

Biber's *Battalia* provides an example of how composers look for novel effects or techniques to express a musical program. Had he not attempted to express musically the passion of war, Monteverdi may not have invented *stile concitato*. Had he not tried to capture the confusion of battle, Janequin may not have conceived fast repeated notes and onomatopoetic sounds. Moreover, because of the programmatic nature of his *Battalia*, Biber used polytonality, *col legno*, "percussive" string basses, and "cannon-sounding" pizzicati over two hundred years before the experimental composers of the twentieth century.

Anonymous

75. *Batalla de 5. Tono*. Organ. *#Organa hispanica* (Heidelberg:
Süddeutscher Musikverlag, 1971), vol. 1, pp. 2-4.
M6.O678 Heft 1
Sixty-eight measures long, it begins with slow chords and
changes dramatically at m. 45 with fast sixteenth-note scale
passages, closing with energetic imitations in C major.

76. *Batalla famossa*. Organ. *#Organa hispanica*, vol. 1, pp. 11-18.
*Gallo CD-440.
M6.O678 Heft 1
A 188-measure, C-major work opening with a chordal fanfare,
evolving soon into sixteenth-note scalar patterns that dominate
throughout, often in parallel thirds or tenths.

77. *Batalha de 6. Tom*. Organ. *#Organa hispanica*, vol. 1, pp. 19-25.
M6.O678 Heft 1
A 185-measure, F-major work that is much thicker in texture
and requires more virtuosity than the other five battle works in this
edition. It contains dotted rhythmic passages in imitation, extended
triplet and brilliant sixteenth-note passages, and numerous repeated
notes and continuous eighth-note chordal passages. One of the
most descriptive early organ battle works.

78. *Battaglia* in the Chigi Manuscript of the Vatican Library. *#Corpus
of Early Keyboard Music—Seventeenth-Century Keyboard Music,*
"Toccatas, Dances and Miscellaneous Forms" (American Institute
of Musicology, 1968), vol. 2, pp. 59-62.
M2.C8 no. 32 v. 2
A C-major, diatonic work which opens with triadic triplets
leading to repeated chords in a dotted quarter—eighth—quarter
rhythm. These eighty-two measures are in binary form and include
numerous repeated notes, trills, and triplets.

79. *Kdož jsú boží bojouníci* (*"Ye Who are Warriors of God"*). Taborite
     battle song. #Gustav Reese, *Music in the Renaissance* (New York:
     W.W. Norton, 1954), p. 734.
       ML172.R42
       In three sections and three stanzas in 6/8; used in numerous
     twentieth-century war-related compositions, particularly by Czech
     composers.

80. *Rebels' Song* from "A Record of the Deeds Described Hereafter."
     #*Zamosc Song Book*, printed in *Music of the Polish Renaissance*,
     ed. Jozef M. Chomiński and Zofia Lissa (Warsaw: Polskie
     Wydawnictwo Muzyczne, 1955).
       M2.M9813
       A defiant song: even though they are small, they will
     overcome a larger enemy.

Bohemia

Biber, Heinrich Ignaz Franz von (1644-1704)

81. *Battalia*. Strings and basso continuo [1673]. #Vienna: Doblinger,
     1971. *Nonesuch 71146 and Telefunken 9579-B.
       M1103.B55B4
       One of the most extreme war pieces of its time, incorporating
     polyrhythms, unusual dissonances, prepared instruments, pizzicati,
     and *col legno* to depict the sounds of war. See pages 31 to 32 for
     additional information.

Burgundia

Besard, Jean Baptiste (1567-1625)

82. *Battaille de Pavie*. Lute [1603]. #*Lautenspieler des 16.
     Jahrhunderts*, ed. Oscar Chilesotti (Leipzig: Breitkopf & Härtel,
     1929), p. 210.
       M2.C61
       A diatonic, D-major lute work with repeated dotted rhythms
     and notes, ending with a flourish of thirty-second notes.

England

Bull, John (c. 1562-1628)

83.   *A Battle and No Battle.* "Phrygian Music for two players."
      Keyboard with ground "to be played to the battle." #*Musica
      Britannica, John Bull, Keyboard Music: II*, transcribed and ed.
      Thurston Dart (London: Stainer & Bell, 1963), vol. 19, pp. 111-
      17.
         M2.M638 v. 19
         Built on a bass ground, this 144-measure work in F-
      Mixolydian was possibly influenced by Byrd's famous battle work.
      It is sectionalized using repeated pitches, scales, static harmonies,
      meter changes, and virtually no dissonance. The ending is unusual
      with its "The knell, first slow, then quick ten times" followed by
      "Bells of Osney, very quick twenty times," and then "The
      conclusion, after the battle, and knell." See Walker Cunningham,
      The Keyboard Music of John Bull. Studies in Musicology, no. 71
      (Ann Arbor, Mich.: UMI Research Press, 1984), pp. 181-82.

84.   *Battle Pavan.* Keyboard. #*Musica Britannica,* vol. 19, p. 118.
         M2.M638 v. 19
         Possibly by Richardson, this pavane contains twenty-eight
      measures in F major frequently using sixteenth- and thirty-second-
      note scale passages. See also item 85 below.

85.   *Battle Galliard.* Keyboard. #*Musica Britannica,* vol. 19, p. 119.
         M2.M638 v. 19
         Consists of twenty-eight measures in F major. See also item
      84 above.

86.   *Coranto Battle.* Keyboard. #*Musica Britannica,* vol. 19, p. 109.
      *Musical Heritage Society 1790.
         M2.M638 v. 19
         A twenty-nine measure, C-major work in binary form that
      uses numerous repetitive rhythms.

Dowland, John (1563-1626)

87.   *Round Battle Galliard.* Lute [1616]. #*Collected Lute Music of John
      Dowland,* transcribed and ed. Diana Poultan and Basi Carr (London:
      Faber Music, 1974), vol. 1, p. 131.
         M110.R4E85 v. 1

A twenty-three measure, diatonic work in G major; it is in triple meter with some syncopations and in three distinct, repeated sections.

Handel, George Frideric [Händel, Georg Friedrich] (1685-1759) [German-born]

88. *Belshazzar.* Oratorio [1745]. 1st: 27 March 1745. #*The Works of George Frideric Handel* printed for the German Handel Society. Reprinted (Ridgewood, N.J.: Gregg, 1965), vol. 19. *Vox SVBX 5209.
   M3.H27 v. 19 or M2003.H14B42
   Includes a "Martial Symphony" in D major during which Belshazzar is killed (pp. 219-21). The highly diatonic orchestral passage emphasizes the brass and is full of repeated notes and martial rhythms.

89. *Dettingen Anthem ("The King Shall Rejoice").* Anthem for chorus, soloists, and orchestra [17 July 1743–3 August 1743]. 1st: 22 November 1743. #*The Works of George Frideric Handel*, vol. 25. *DG ARC-410647-2 AH.
   M2023.H13C744
   Written to celebrate the British victory at Dettingen on 27 June 1743, this martial, D-major work opens with trumpets and timpani and develops into an enormous praise to God for achieving their victory.
   Handel also wrote the *Te Deum "Dettingen."* Anthem [27 November 1743]. #Philadelphia: Geo. F. Blake, 18--. *DG ARC-410647-2 AH. M2023.H13D45.

90. *Guilio Caesare.* Opera [1723]. 1st: 20 February 1724. #*The Works of George Frideric Handel*, vol. 68. *RCA 6182-2-RG.
   M1503.H135J75
   Near the beginning of Act III (p. 96) is a battle symphony in D major fought between the soldiers of Cleopatra and those of Ptolomey. Scored for oboe, violin, viola, and basses, it uses repeated notes and continuous sixteenth-note activity in a highly diatonic tonality.

91. *Joshua.* Oratorio [1747]. 1st: London, 9 March 1748. #*The Works of George Frideric Handel*, vol. 17. *University of Missouri S-1004.
   M2003.H14J6

Near the beginning of Act II (pp. 97-101), the walls of Jericho fall amidst the burning flames (ascending sixteenth notes, continuous rhythmic activity, and considerable chromaticism). Toward the end of the act, Handel writes a lament in E minor for the defeated Israelites and a "Warlike Symphony" (pp. 142-45); he notates only one measure, indicating the rhythm to be played (incidentally the same opening rhythm as Janequin's *La guerre*). According to the preface of the score, Handel intended to borrow war-like music from his earlier works, most likely the battle music from his opera *Ricardo Primo*. See item number 94 below.

92. *Music for the Royal Fireworks.* Orchestra with twelve trumpets and horns [1749]. 1st: London (Green Park), 27 April 1749. #Leipzig: Breitkopf & Härtel, 19--. *Oiseau 400059-2 and Philips 411122-2PH.

    M2023.H2314B9

    One of Handel's most famous works, written to celebrate the Peace of Aix-la-Chapelle in 1748. This suite consists of several movements, including "La Paix" and "Réjouissance."

93. *Occasional Oratorio.* Oratorio [1746]. 1st: 14 February 1746. #Leipzig: Breitkopf & Härtel, 1935.

    M2003.H14F3

    Includes a G-major battle scene and an aria, "When warlike ensigns wave on high." In his *Handel's Dramatic Oratorios and Masques* (London: Oxford University Press, 1959), Winton Dean writes that this oratorio "was not a celebration, as is often supposed, but a declaration of faith and a blast of encouragement to the loyalists. Like the pageants in honor of the Services produced at the Albert Hall during the 1939-45 war, it was a piece of propaganda" (p. 460).

94. *Riccardo Primo.* Opera [1727]. 1st: London, 11 November 1727. #*The Works of George Frideric Handel*, vol. 74.

    M3.H27. V. 74

    An extended da capo movement in C major illustrates the excitement of war with fast sixteenth notes, martial rhythms, and cries of "guerra, guerra" (pp. 83-87).

95. *Rinaldo.* Opera. 1st: 24 February 1711. #*The Works of George Frideric Handel.* *RCA ARL1-0084.

    M3.H138 v. 58B

    The opera opens with "The City of Jerusalem besieg'd."

96.   *Saul.* Oratorio. 1st: 16 January 1739. #Leipzig: Breitkopf & Härtel, 1909. *Teldec 8.35687 ZA.
       M2003.H14S45
       Opens with a tremendous C-major victory celebrating the triumph over Goliath and the Philistines.

97.   *Utrecht Te Deum* and *Jubilate "Utrecht."* Chorus and orchestra [1713]. 1st: London, 7 July 1713. #*The Works of George Frideric Handel,* vol. 31. *Teldec 8.42955 ZK and Oiseau 414413-2 OH.
       M3. H27 v. 31
       Two D-major victory celebrations written in honor of the Peace of Utrecht. See Stoddard Lincoln's "Handel's Music for Queen Anne," *Musical Quarterly* 45 (1959), pp. 191-207.

Jenkins, John (1592-1678)

98.   *Newark Siege Fantasia.* Consort of viols [after 1646]. #n.p.: Viola da Gamba Society, 196-. *London CS 7221 (brass transcription by Peter Reeve).
       M990.J45N5
       A five-minute, sectionalized work, with repeated rhythms and notes; deals with the Siege of Newark during the English Civil War (1642-1646).

Purcell, Henry (1659-1695)

99.   *King Arthur,* Act I, scene ii ("Come If You Dare"). Semi-opera [1692]. #London: (Purcell Society) Novello & Ewer, 1878-1965, vol. 26. *Erato ECD 88056.
       M3.P93 v. 26
       An instrumental battle scene in C major, using repeated notes in the trumpets and concluding with a choral victory celebration.

100.   *Ode for St. Cecilia's Day,* No. 11 ("The Fife and all the Harmony of War"). Alto and orchestra [1692]. #London: (Purcell Society) Novello & Ewer, 1878-1965, vol. 8. *Vanguard SRV 286 SD.
       M3.P93 v. 8
       A thirteen-part ode which takes turns praising various instruments. In no. 11 Purcell plays on the association of the fife with war by writing fanfares with trumpets and timpani.

France

Chambonnières, Jacques Champion (1601 or 1602-1672)

101. *Allemande la Dunquerque.* Keyboard [1670]. *#Les pièces de clavessin . . . livre premier* (Paris, 1670), no. 7. Reprinted (Courlay: Edition J.M. Fuzeau, 1989).
   M24.C427P51 1989
   Written for the commemoration of the capture of Dunkirk in 1646.

102. *Les baricades.* Keyboard [c. 1670]. *#Les pièces de clavessin . . . livre premier* (Paris, 1670), no. 16. Reprinted (Courlay: Edition J.M. Fuzeau, 1989).
   M24.C427P51 1989
   Written about an uprising that began in Fronde in 1648.

Couperin, François (le grand) (1668-1773)

103. *La steinquerque.* Trio sonata [c. 1692]. *#François Couperin œuvres complètes* (Paris: Éditions de l'Oiseau-lyre, 1932-1933), vol. 10. *Denon 33C37-7811 and Vox SVBX 5142. It has also been arranged for wind octet: #Paris: G. Billaudot, 1972.
   M3.C85B7 v. 10
   In B-flat major, the first movement "Gayement" is given the subtitle "Bruits de guerre." The music is imitative with repeated rhythms and notes in nearly every measure. The other movements are "Air," "Gravement," "Legerement," "Mouvement de fanfares," "Lentement," "Gravement," and "Gayement."

Dandrieu, Jean François (1682-1738)

104. *Les caractères de la guerre.* Orchestra [1718]. Keyboard arrangement [1724]. #Paris: Ballard, 1718; Reprinted (Courlay: J.M. Fuzeau, 1989).
   [RISM D892]
   The harpsichord arrangement of this suite-like work in D major is important for its use of clusters; also includes descriptive titles. See pages 30 and 31 for additional information.

Lully, Jean-Baptiste (1632-1687) [Italian-born]

105. *Alceste.* Opera [1674]. #*Jean-Baptiste Lully œuvres complètes*
      (Paris: La revue musicale, 1932), vol. 2. *Columbia M3 34580.
            M3.L9525 v. 2
            In Act II, scenes iii-iv, Lully illustrates the besieging soldiers
      planning their attack and fighting until they conquer the city. See
      page 29 for additional information.

Germany

Fabricius, Petrus (1587-1651)

106. *La battaglia.* Lute [1605]. #Wilhelm Tappert, *Sang und Klang aus
      alter Zeit* (Berlin 1906), pp. 61-62.
            *XML-500 (NYPL call number)
            An abridged variant of *La guerre* in G major filled in with
      more eighth notes. In two parts with imitation in the second.

Graun, Carl Heinrich (1704-1759)

107. *La battaglia del re di Prussia.* Piano [1740]. #London, Harrison,
      1798?
            OCLC 23760597
            Simple harmonies and a basic sonata form encase this battle
      piece crowned with the right hand crossing over the left to ring out
      an occasional single, low bass note simulating a gun shot or
      cannon blast. Deals with the Austrian Succession in 1740. For
      additional versions of and commentary on the score, see Albert
      Mayer-Reinach, "Carl Heinrich Graun, La battaglia del Re di
      Prussia," *Internationale Musik-Gesellschaft* 4 (1903), pp. 478-84;
      and J.W. Enmschedé, "Zur Battaglia del Re di Prussia,"
      Internationale Musik-Gesellschaft 4 (1903), pp. 677-85.

Kerll, Johann Kaspar (1627-1693)

108. *Battaglia.* Organ. #*Denkmäler der Tonkunst in Bayern*, pp. 47-50
      and *Antologia di musica antica e moderna per pianofort* (Milan,
      1931), vol. 7, pp. 99-105. *Disques Pierre Verany PV. 786094.
            M2.D4 2. jahrg., bd. 3
            A seven-minute work in C major, with dotted rhythms,
      extended trills, and repeated notes. Highly diatonic and in three
      main parts, with programmatic depictions of marching soldiers in

the second part and of a triumphant, light-hearted victory celebration in the third.

Krieger, Johann (1651-1735)

109. *Schlacht.* Keyboard. *Musical Heritage Society 1790.
[No LC number available]
A three-minute work in binary form in duple meter, with static, repeated chords broken up with faster trill-like patterns.

Kuhnau, Johann (1660-1722)

110. *Biblical Sonata No. 1 ("The Fight Between David and Goliath").* Keyboard [1700]. #New York: Broude, 1953, pp. 4-12. *Archive Production ARC 3095.
M23.K97B63 1976
Depicts the battle between David and Goliath and the killing of Goliath. The music contains narration above each section and then paints the scene in music. A flurry of thirty-second and sixty-fourth notes appear in a rapid scale pattern to illustrate David's throw toward Goliath. Goliath's fall is represented with a descending F-minor scale, and sixteenth-note scales in C major represent the flight of the Philistines.

Praetorius, Michael (1571-1621)

111. *Courante de la guerre, Courante de bataglia,* and *Galliarde de la guerre* in *Terpsichore* [1612]. #*Gesamtausgabe der musikalischen Werken von Michael Praetorius* (Wolfenbüttel: G. Kallmeyer, 1928-1960), vol. 15, pp. 47-48 and p. 173. *Hyperion CDA 66200 and Angel CDM 69024.
M3.P82 v. 15
The Courantes are binary dances in D major of 22 and 35 measures (respectively). The Galliarde of forty measures is in F major with three repeated sections. None of the dances has programmatic indications other than the title.

Scheidt, Samuel (1587-1654)

112. *Galliard battaglia.* Five unspecified instruments [1621]. #*Samuel Scheidts Werke* (Ugrino: Abteilung, 1928), vol. 2/3, pp. 27-29. Version arranged by the Canadian Brass: #Toronto: G. Thompson, 1982. *Disques Corelia CC681299.

M3.S28 v. 2/3

A three-part composition in G major in which each section is repeated. Uses static harmonies, repeated-note accompaniment, echo effects, and florid melodies.

Holland

Eyck, Jacob van (c. 1589-1657)

113. *Battalia* from *Der Fluyten Lust-hof.* Recorder [1646]. #Amsterdam: Muziekuitgeverij Ixijzet, 1957), pp. 49-50.
      M110.R4E85 1970
      A monophonic work in four sections with descriptive headings, including "Batali" and "Alarm."

Italy

Anerio, Giovanni F. (1567-1630)

114. *Missa della battaglia.* Mixed voices and organ [1608]. #*Musica divina* (Regensburg: Friedrich Pustet, 1955), vol. 11.
      M2011.A53B3
      A complete setting of the Ordinary in F major. The music has some imitation and paired voices, but much of it is homophonic. The text setting in the Gloria and the Credo is particularly declamatory.

Banchieri, Adriano (1568-1634)

115. *La battaglia* from *L'organo suonarino*, op. 25. Keyboard [1611]. #*Antologia di musica antica e moderna per pianofort* (Milano, 1931), vol. 3, pp. 87-88. *Musical Heritage Society 1790.
      *MYD+ (NYPL call number)
      A three-minute, F-major work in ten sections with varying tempos, followed by a suite-like "Canzone Italiana" and "Dialogo."

Castaldi, Bellerofonte (c. 1580-1649)

116. *Capriccio di battaglia a due stromenti.* Lute [1625]. #*Capricci a due stromenti cioe tiorba e tiorbino* (Geneva: Minkoff Reprint, 1981), pp. 4-10.
      M142.T4C37

An extensive lute score with numerous repeated notes and rhythms.

Falconieri, Andrea (1586-1656)

117.   *Teiple à tre*: *Battala de Barabaso Yerno de Satanas.* Two violins, bass, and basso continuo [1650]. #*Componimenti diversi* (Milan: L'Arte musicale in Italia, 1968), vol. 7, pp. 128-142.
       M2.T67 vol. 7
       In C major and full of repeated notes and rhythms. The second section in 3/2 consists of half notes in parallel thirds, followed by a section of fast, imitative sixteenth notes. It is highly sectionalized but does not include descriptive headings.

Frescobaldi, Girolamo (1583-1643)

118.   *Capriccio sopra la battaglia.* Keyboard [1637]. #*Gesamtausgabe nach dem Urtext,* ed. Pierre Pidoux: *Das Erste Buch der Toccaten, Partiten usw. 1637* (Kassel: Bärenreiter, n.d.), vol. 3, p. 89. *Disques Pierre Verany PV. 786094. (Also transcribed by Gorden Binkerd. See item number 1214.)
       M24.F872T61
       Begins and ends in G major and goes through the keys of D, A, E, C, and F. Every few measures have an immediate repeat and include triadic, fanfare-like outlines, triplet patterns, and repeated rhythms.

Garli, Donino (17th c.)

119.   *Battaglia des Donino Garli da Parma.* Ein Schlachtgemälde for lute [1620]. #*Lautenbuche des Kasimir Stanislaus Rudomina Dusiacki* (Paduoa, 1626) in Wilhelm Tappert, *Sang und Klang aus alter Zeit* (Berlin 1906), pp. 69-71.
       *MYD (NYPL call number)
       In F major with an F pedal throughout its 106 measures. Completely diatonic, including numerous repeated notes, dotted rhythms, changes in meter, and consecutive alternating thirds or fifths.

Monteverdi, Claudio (1567-1643)

120.   *Altri canti d'amor.* Madrigal from Book 8: *Madrigali guerrieri et amorosi* [1638]. #Paris: Heugel, 1973. *Philips 6500 197.

M1531.M85M313

In four sections, the second uses fast, repeated sixteenth notes to illustrate the men at war. See pages 28 to 29 for additional information.

121. *Il combattimento di Tancredi e Clorinda.* Madrigal [1624]. #Milan: Società anonima notari, 1921. *DG ARC-415296-2 GH and Teldec 8.43054 ZK. Text from Tasso's *La Gerusalemme liberata.*
M2.C6328 vol. 19

Important for Monteverdi's use of *stile concitato* and for the quality it brought to the tradition of war-related music. See page 28 for additional information.

122. *Hor che' l ciel e la terra.* Madrigal from Book 8 *Madrigali guerrieri et amorosi* [1638]. #Milan & New York: Ricordi, 1958. *Musikproduktion Dabringhaus und Grimm L-3081.
M1530.M

A good example alternating between the faster, *forte* sections of war and the slower, softer sections of peace, both in a major key.

123. *Il ritorno di Ulisse in patria* ("*Sinfonie di guerra*"). Opera [1641]. #Mainz & New York: Schott, 1988 or *Tutte le opere di Claudio Monteverdi*, pp. 167-169. *Telefunken SKB-T-23/1-4.
M1506.M65R63 1988

This section at the end of Act II is only twenty measures that repeat. See page 29 for additional information.

Storace, Bernardo (fl. late 17th c.)

124. *Ballo della battaglia* [before 1664]. #*Bernardo Storace: Selva di varie compositioni d' intavolature per cimbalo ed organo, Corpus of Early Keyboard Music*, vol. 7, pp. 121-24. *Desto DC 7191
M2.C8 no. 7

A fifty-one measure work in D major and G major; in rounded binary form using frequent repetitions of patterns; remains in 4/4 throughout.

Portugal

Araujo, Pedro de (? -1684)

125. *Batalha de 6. Tom.* Keyboard. #*Organa hispanica* (Heidelberg: Süddeutscher Musikverlag, 1971), vol. 1, pp. 26-32.
M6.O678 Heft 1
A 203-measure, F-major work. Contains alternating passages of slow imitative and chordal writing, with faster passages of eighth-note fanfares, brilliant sixteenth-note scales, and dotted rhythms.

Conçeicão, Diego da (fl. 1695)

126. *Batalha de 5° Tom.* Organ [before 1695]. *Delos D.CD 3077 and Musical Heritage Society 1790.
A six-minute, sectionalized work more rhythmically complex (with unusual syncopations) than the early battaglias, but still contains numerous repeated notes and chords along with parallel third passages and florid notes over drone basses.

Martin y Coll, Fray Antonio (17th c.)

127. *Batalla de 5. Tono.* Organ. #*Organa hispanica* (Heidelberg: Süddeutscher Musikverlag, 1971), vol. 1, pp. 5-6.
M6.O678 Heft 1
A fifty-five-measure work in three repeated sections, the first two of which are largely chordal and the last full of fanfare-like eighth-note passages all built around C or G major.

Spain

Bruna, Pablo (1611-1679)

128. *Batalla de 6 tone.* Organ. #*Cinque composizioni inedite* (Milan: Editioni Suvini Zerboni, 1979), pp. 26-35.
M7.B889S8
A 234-measure, F-major work in two parts (4/4 and 6/4). Both parts are imitative and have parallel thirds in the right hand.

Cabanilles, Juan (1644-1712)

129. *Tiento XXI de batalla partido de mano derecha 6*. Organ. #*Musici Organici: Johannis Cabanilles (1644-1712) Opera Omnia* (Barcelona: Biblioteca de Cataluña, 1927), vol. 4, pp. 130-40.
     M2.B28 vol. 4
     A 156-measure, F-major work which opens with a three-voice fugue in 4/4. The second part shifts to 12/8 and contains numerous scale passages and, near the end, arpeggios. Uses considerable chromaticism and ends with a sixteenth-note flourish.

130. *Tiento XXV de batalla 8*. Organ. #*Musici Organici: Johannis Cabanilles (1644-1712) Opera Omnia*, vol. 4, pp. 170-81.
     M2.B28 vol. 4
     A 195-measures work in G major. The first part is a four-voice fugue in 4/4 with frequent broken chords and expressive suspensions. The second part beginning at measure 116 switches to 3/4 and ends with an extensive sixteenth- and thirty-second-note flourish of five measures on a D-major chord.
     Cabanilles composed four other battle works for organ, all published in *Musici Organici: Johannis Cabanilles (1644-1712) Opera Omnia*, vol. 4: *Tiento lleno de batalla, 8 tono* (pp. 11-15); *Tiento par de batalla 8 tone* (pp. 125-26); *Tiento par de batalla 5 tone* (pp. 148-53); and *Tiento par de batalla mano drecha, 6 tone* (pp. 300-03).

Cererols, Joan (1618-1680)

131. *Missa de batalla*. Twelve-voice mass for three choruses and basso continuo. #*Joan Cererols Obres Completes* (Montserrat: Monestic de Monteserrat, 1982), pp. 53-122. *Deutsche Harmonia Mundi 77057-2-RG.
     M2.M33 vol. 2
     A complete, F-major setting of the ordinary in a highly imitative style with fanfare-like melodies based on the Portuguese organ battle works.

Corrêa de Arauxo' Francisco (c. 1576 or 1577-1654)

132. *Batalha*. Organ [c. 1626]. #*Libro de Tientos y Discursos de Musica Practica y Teorica de Organo*, 1626. Reprinted (Geneva: Minkoff Reprint, 1981), pp. 60-62. *Gallo CD-440.

M7.C67L5 1981
A three-page work that deals with the Battle of Morales.

Nebra, José de (1702-1768)

133. *Batalla de clarines.* Keyboard. #*Obras ineditas para tecla* (Madrid: Socieded Española de Musicología, 1984), pp. 39-42.
JMG 92-372 (NYPL call number)
In sixteen measures, with arpeggios, repeated notes, and trills in D major followed by a thirty-measure minuet.

Torrelhas, Frey Joseph (fl. c. 1700)

134. *Batalha de 6. Tom.* Organ. #*Organa hispanica* (Heidelberg: Süddeutscher Musikverlag, 1971), vol. 1, pp. 7-10.
M6.O678 Heft 1
A 142-measure, F-major work with a canonic opening and in two basic parts. The meter shifts to 3/2 at m. 58, and the closing twenty measures consist of dotted rhythms and repeated notes over long sustained chords.

Victoria, Tomás Luis de (1548-1611)

135. *Missa pro victoria.* Mass [1600]. #*Opera Omnia* (Wiesbaden: Breitkopf & Härtel, 1909). Reprinted (Ridgewood, N. J.: Gregg, 1966), vol. 6, pp. 26-38. *Discourses ABM 20.
M3.V645 v. 6
Partially based on Janequin's *La guerre*, it is written for double chorus and organ in F major.

Ximénez [Jimenez], José [Joseph] (1601-1672)

136. *Batalla de Sexto Tono No. 1.* Keyboard. #*Joseph Jimenez Collected Organ Compositions, Corpus of Early Keyboard Music* ed. Willi Apel (American Institute of Musicology, 1975), vol. 31, pp. 33-40. *Musical Heritage Society 1790.
M2.C8 no. 31
A 230-measure, F-major work which includes repeated notes, scales, and rhythms. Imitation and parallel thirds also appear in this sectionalized work.

137. *Batalla de Sexto Tono No. 2.* Keyboard. #*Joseph Jimenez Collected Organ Compositions,* vol. 31, pp. 40-45.

M2.C8 no. 31

Very similar to item number 136 above, but includes more imitative writing and repeated notes in its 155 measures in F major.

Tuscany

Poglietti, Alessandro (?-1683)

138. *Suite: sopra la ribellione di Ungheria.* Keyboard suite [1671]. *#Denkmäler der Tonkunst in Österreich* (Vienna: Österreichischer Bundesverlag, 1959), vol. 27, pp. 32-36. *Hyperion A66096.

   M2.D36 v. 27

   A thirteen-minute programmatic suite in E minor dealing with the uprising against the Hapsburgs in 1671 led by three noblemen who were captured and beheaded. The suite contains: Toccatina; Allemande ("La prissonie"); Courente ("La procès"); Sarabande ("La sentence"); Gigue ("La lige"); "La décapitation, avec discretion"; Passacaglia; and "Les kloches" ("Requiem aternam dona eis domine"). The decapitation is a four-voice fugue with a dotted rhythmic subject with a downward skip of a diminished seventh providing a descriptive, programmatic touch.

139. *Toccata fatta sopra l'Assedio.* Keyboard [1676]. #Harpsichord Music (University Park: Pennsylvania State University Press, 1966). *Hyperion A66096.

   M22.P8N5

   A five-minute, three-part (fast-slow-fast) work beginning with imitative fanfares and brilliant scale patterns written after Duke of Lorraine's siege of Philippsburg in 1676.

SUPPLEMENT OF WAR MUSIC IN THE BAROQUE:
1600-1750

140. Altenburg, Michael (1584-1640). Germany. *Die engelische Schlacht* [1617]. [Cited in GLÄSEL, p. 97].
141. Dedekind, Henning (1562-1626). Germany. *Dodekas musicarum deliciarum. Soldatenleben.* Voices [1628]. [Cited in GLÄSEL, p. 97].
142. Demantius, Christoph (1567-1643). Germany. *Tympanum militaire.* Six voices [1600]. Enlarged and revised in 1615. (Collection of martial songs dealing with the recapture of the Raab fortress from the Turks.) [RISM D1531 and D1540].
143. Heredia, Pedro (de) (d. 1648). Italy. *Batalla.* Organ. [Cited in Gustave Reese, *Music in the Renaissance,* 2nd ed. (New York, 1959), p. 629].
144. Jelich, Vincentius (1596-?1636). Austria. *Parnassia militia concertuum unius* [1622]. #Zagreb: Isdavacki zavod Jugoslavenske akademije, 1957. M2.J47.
145. Mancinus, Thomas (1550-c. 1611). Germany. *The Battle of Sievershausen* [1608]. #Helmstedt: Jacob Lucius, 1608. [RISM M320].
146. Melii, Pietro Pauolo (fl. 1612-1620). Italy. *Corrente sopra una batalia della guerriera.* Lute [1616]. #*Intavolatura di liuto libro quarto* (Florence: Studio Per Edizioni Scelte, 1979), vol. 19, pp. 27-28. M2.A72 v. 19 pt. 3.
147. Uccellini, Marco (c. 1603-1680). Italy. *La gran battaglia.* Symphony from *"Sinfonie Boscareccie."* Strings and continuo [1669]. #Anversa: Presso i heredi Pietro Phalesio, 1669. M412.2.U33 op. 8 1669.

NOTES

1. D.J.R. Bruckner, Seymour Chwast, and Steven Heller, *Art Against War* (New York: Abbeville, 1984), p. 23.

2. Claudio Monteverdi, *Madrigali guerrieri ed amorosi*, Foreword in *Source Readings in Music History*, ed. Oliver Strunk (New York: W.W. Norton, 1950), p. 414.

3. Monteverdi, pp. 413-14.

4. Paul Henry Lang, *George Frideric Handel* (New York: W.W. Norton, 1966), p. 223.

5. Both *The New Grove Dictionary* [article unsigned] and Christoph von Blumroder in Eggebrecht's *Handwörterbuch der musikalischen Terminologie* (Wiesbaden: F. Steiner, c. 1972-) credit Henry Cowell with inventing the technique of tone clusters in their articles "Cluster." Clusters, however, appeared much earlier in numerous programmatic compositions by Jean François Dandrieu, Domenico Scarlatti, Daniel Steibelt, Bernard Viguerie, Charles Alkan, and Thomas Bethune.

6. Arthur Loesser, *Men, Women & Pianos: A Social History* (New York: Simon & Schuster, 1954), p. 170.

7. Thomas Bullfinch, *The Age of Fable or Beauties of Mythology* (New York: New American Library, 1962), p. 38.

III. WAR MUSIC OF THE CLASSIC AND EARLY ROMANTIC PERIOD: 1750-1827

During the last half of the eighteenth century and the first quarter of the nineteenth—the age of the American and French Revolutions and of Napoleon and Wellington—the western world underwent a remarkable transformation, as revolutions and wars shattered governments and traditions on two western continents. Reflecting this situation was the popularity and frequency of battle music and victory pieces, as some examples of military music appeared in almost every kind of composition during this time. Franz Joseph Haydn and François-Joseph Gossec composed military symphonies, Franz Schubert penned military marches, and Mozart and Beethoven, influenced by the military concertos of the French violin school, composed military-like piano concertos.[1]

A new development also took place during this period that significantly transformed the character of war music: for the first time composers incorporated national airs or popular military tunes into larger forms of traditionally "serious" music. Tunes such as "La marseillaise," "Ah ça ira," "Marlborough," "Yankee Doodle," and "Hail Columbia" found their way into overtures, suites, sonatas, symphonies, oratorios, cantatas, and operas. The recently formed French government even required "La marseillaise" to be performed before the beginning of every opera given in France after the Revolution.[2]

One unfortunate outcome of this practice, however, was to lower dramatically the quality of patriotic compositions as a whole. Composers became more socially and politically engaged and often pandered to the public taste at the expense of artistic value. Few patriotic compositions that Gossec, Etienne Nicolas Méhul, Jean François Le Sueur, or other composers of the French Revolution wrote are performed today. Instrumental battle music particularly suffered in quality during this era, and some critics consider it one of the lowest possible forms of musical composition. While writing about battle music of this period, Frederick Niecks claimed that "not a single work of the kind ever created has high artistic value, not even Beethoven's battle [piece], and extremely few have as much as a modicum of value."[3] It is at this point that numerous battle works, in a sense, lost their status as "art music" and entered the realm of what Carl Dahlhaus calls "trivial music": mass-produced lowbrow music.[4]

Artistically valuable or not, these works were immensely popular with the newly formed middle class who flocked to the public concerts and who tried them out on their pianos at home. Battle music had been popular in the time of Janequin and Byrd, but it became the public craze in post-revolutionary Europe and America. The piano, with its sudden popularity and availability, soon became the chief instrument for which composers wrote battle music. Composers and publishers quickly profited from the public's insatiable demand for piano battles, by offering works such as Beethoven's *Wellington's Victory* in solo, four-hand, and two-piano arrangements.[5] In his *Men, Women & Pianos*, Arthur Loesser has colorfully described this phenomenon of battle music for the keyboard:

> It is certainly true that toward the end of the eighteenth century pianistic battle pieces came into great general favor and were dished up in large quantity, if not variety, by publishers, composers, virtuosos, and of course young ladies—the ultimate retailers. These compositions were, indeed, extraordinarily conventional in conception; they all show a remarkable family resemblance, not always short of actual plagiarism: all are rigorously provided with approach marches, bugle calls, cannon shots, cavalry charges, fog of battle, cries of the wounded, national anthems, and victory balls. . . . The names of the battles, however—and therefore the titles—did vary considerably, on the sound commercial principle that you can always sell the same hokum over again under a different label.[6]

One outcome of this popularity of battle pieces led to manufacturers actually adding percussive pedals to a number of pianos in the early nineteenth century so that composers and performers could add even more realistic sounds to their "battle re-enactments."[7]

James Hewitt, František Koczwara, Johann Wanhal, Bernard Vignerie, Daniel Steibelt, Jan Dussek (or Dusík), Ferdinand Kauer, and Benjamin Carr wrote numerous battle pieces during the eighteenth and early nineteenth centuries. Koczwara is remembered today solely because of the overwhelming popularity of his *Battle of Prague* (1788) (no. 172) for piano and optional violin and cello. For over sixty years this particular keyboard work was the most famous battle piece, frequently transcribed and arranged for a wide assortment of instruments. Casual reference to the work appears in nineteenth-century literature in the works of Henry David Thoreau, William Thackeray, and (upon three occasions) Mark Twain.[8] In *A Tramp Abroad* Twain gives a clever account of a woman playing the work in Switzerland:

> [She] turned on all the horrors of the 'Battle of Prague,' that venerable shivaree, and waded chin deep in the blood of the slain. She made a fair and honorable average of two false notes in every five, but her soul was in arms and she never stopped to correct. The audience stood it with pretty fair grit for a while; but when the cannonade waxed hotter and fiercer and the discord average rose to four in five, the procession began to move. A few stragglers held their ground ten minutes longer, but when the girl began to bring the true inwardness out of the 'cries of the wounded' they struck their colors and retired in a kind of panic.[9]

The American James Hewitt greatly profited from the popularity of battle music by composing works dealing with the American Revolution. In 1792 he wrote the *Battle of Trenton* (no. 156) for piano and the *Battle Overture* for orchestra, and he completed his military sonata *The 4th of July* (no. 157) nearly two decades later. Dedicated to George Washington, the *Battle of Trenton* contains a detailed program centered around his wartime adventures. The lengthy program is typical of its time:

> Introduction. The Army in Motion. Acclamation of the Americans. Drums Beat to Arms. Washington's March. The American Army Crossing the Delaware. Ardor of the Americans at Landing. Trumpets Sound the Charge. Attack. Cannons. Bombs. Defeat of the Hessians. Flight of the Hessians. The Hessians Begging Quarter. Grief of the Americans for the Loss of Their Comrades Killed in the Engagement. Drums and Fifes. Quick Step for the Band. Trumpets for Victory. General Rejoicing.[10]

Predominantly in the key of D major, *The Battle of Trenton* contains the stock battle devices of triadic outlines, fast repeated notes, dotted rhythms, triplets, and popular songs. Hewitt ventures into the minor mode in the laments "Grief of the Americans for the Loss of Their Comrades Killed in the Engagement" and "The Hessians Begging Quarter." The Hessians surrender in the key of G major, and toward the end, the American popular tunes "Yankee Doodle" and "Roslin Castle" appear.

Kauer's *La conquete d' Oczakow* (1788) (no. 168) consists of twelve "representations" of the Russian conquest of the Turkish fortress in Oczakau the same year. Kauer depicts the Russian assault in ascending sequences, and the "bloody battle" between the Turks and Russians takes place in scenes viii-ix with continuous sixteenth-note sequential and repetitive patterns for thirty-four consecutive measures. No dynamic markings are supplied anywhere in the score, but the titles presented over each representation adequately provide the performer with all the necessary information needed to play the work according to the composer's wishes. Kauer's battle work concludes with the joy of the victors in D major.

Carr's battle composition *Siege of Tripoli* (c. 1801) (no. 154) was more innovative than many of the other battle pieces from this time. Although it follows the same procedures as many other battle pieces with a descriptive title above each section, the *Siege of Tripoli* features virtuoso piano writing that distinguishes it from the other compositions. Carr employs four-octave scales, thirty-second-note-diminished-seventh arpeggios, and an ascending two-octave glissando for the right hand in sixths to represent "a gallant defence [that] nobly blows up the Vessel rather than be taken Captives to Tripoli." After a cascading diminished chord, which represents a "Tower of a Mosque destroyed," Carr writes a full measure of rest with the notice, "Chief Battery silenced." Soon after the lament of the Americans, represented by a Largo in D minor, the work concludes with a rondo version of "Yankee Doodle" in A major.

Composers continued turning out battle works after Napoleon's defeat in 1815, when all became relatively quiet in central Europe and America. Five years after Waterloo, Johann Nepomuk Hummel composed his most popular work and one of the best known compositions of his generation: *Six Waltzes Followed by a Great Battle*, Op. 91 (no. 197). Hummel, an astute businessman, made seven arrangements of this work for various instrumental combinations and piano four-hands. This rather trite composition quotes "Marlborough" and contains repeated-note fanfares and drum rolls combined in an agreeable waltz rhythm. The public, however, eagerly purchased this type of music.

Orchestral battle compositions continued to develop during this period, in length if not in substance. Johann Klöffler, Franz Neubauer, Ignazio Raimondi, Paul Wranitzky, Peter von Winter, and Beethoven himself contributed large-scale battle symphonies. In 1777 Klöffler composed one of the most unusual battle symphonies, foreshadowing the Ivesian idea of having two orchestras "battle" one another within a single composition. Between 1777 and 1787 his *Bataille für zwei Orchester* (no. 198) received performances in twenty major cities, including Amsterdam,

London, Copenhagen, Moscow, and Vienna. The program consisted of twenty-eight separate numbers depicting the various stages of the battle.[11] Except for the use of the minor mode illustrating the complaints and groaning of the wounded, the entire work is in D major. The size of the combined orchestras varied in the cities where it was performed, but the number of performers was usually around fifty or sixty. A master publicist who aroused the curiosity of the public, Klöffler performed to larger than usual audiences. A reviewer of the London concert on 26 May 1783 noted: "The audience expressed as much pleasure as it is capable of producing, to the highest degree of delight and satisfaction, and turned toward their homes uncommonly stirred by the evening's entertainment."[12]

Franz Neubauer's *La bataille* (1794) (no. 173) is also an extensive programmatic symphony lasting approximately twenty-five minutes. It contains seven movements, beginning with the morning of the battle and followed by the preparations for battle, the conflict itself, and the obligatory victory celebration at the end. The third movement, entitled "Harangue aux guerriers," adds considerable humor to this grandiose work by featuring a lengthy bassoon solo. The battle movement contains some sudden dynamic outbursts and considerable use of drone basses and imitation, in addition to the expected rapid scales, repeated notes, and major tonality.

Paul Wranitzky's *Grande sinfonie caractèristique pour la paix avec la République française* (1797) (no. 176) is important for its incorporation of the idea of peace into battle music. After the battle Wranitzky sets "The Peace Negotiations" in a lilting 6/8 meter and labels the movement Andante grazioso. This work also had the unusual distinction of being banned because the government considered its title provocative.[13]

Beethoven's Symphony No. 3 ("Eroica") (no. 194), composed in 1803, is not a battle work, but a war-related one that was originally entitled "Bonaparte" and that shares characteristics of the French Revolutionary funeral march. Maynard Solomon and Claude V. Palisca have examined this relationship carefully,[14] while George Grove wrote that upon hearing of Napoleon's death "[Beethoven] said, 'I have already composed the proper music for that catastrophe,' meaning the Funeral March . . . if indeed he did not mean the whole symphony."[15] It seems plausible that the revolutionary nature of the symphony both in length and content would not have been this extreme had the symphony not intended to be a tribute to Napoleon.

Considering Beethoven's great symphonies, piano sonatas, and string quartets, it is indeed ironic that during his lifetime *Wellington's Victory* (no. 195) was his best-known work.[16] The idea for the composition was apparently not Beethoven's, but that of Johann Mälzel, the inventor of a mechanical organ called the "Panharmonikon." Beethoven originally wrote the battle piece for the Panharmonikon, and with Mälzel's encouragement, he later orchestrated it. *Wellington's Victory* found great favor with the public, but often not with critics and other contemporary composers. Another composer of war-related music, Carl Maria von Weber, was "unable to give his opinion of this work, since the appalling din of cannon, rattles etc. made it impossible for him to hear the actual music properly," upon hearing *Wellington's Victory* the first time.[17] A number of writers have criticized *Wellington's Victory*, but Paul Mies in *The New Oxford History of Music* argued that this criticism is not totally warranted because "Beethoven himself took it very seriously, as is shown by his comprehensive instructions for performance; it had great success; and it contains its full share of Beethoven's individual traits."[18]

Beethoven divides the composition into two major parts, the battle and the victory symphony. The battle section opens with parallel introductions of the two opposing forces. First the British march to a drum cadence and trumpet fanfares before the full orchestra enters with the march "Rule Britania" in the "heroic" key of E-flat major. Then the French enter similarly with drums and trumpets, leading to the full orchestra which plays the French march "Marlborough" in the key of C major. The trumpets from each side again play solo fanfares announcing the beginning of the battle. Throughout the ensuing battle scene, Beethoven symbolically retains the E-flat trumpet for the British side and the C trumpet for the French.

The battle proper starts *ff* in B major (Allegro) and in a duple meter. Cannons from each side are soon heard and are used repeatedly throughout the battle scene. In the score the French and British cannons are distinguished from one another by special symbols, and each side is also represented by its own trumpet and rattle. The battle quickly moves away from B major, through C minor, to C major. The tempo changes to Meno allegro and the meter to 3/8. The French trumpet exchanges blows with the British trumpet, both employing the same rhythm, while the rattles from each side are heard. With the change of key to A-flat major and the beginning of the "Sturm March," the British begin to dominate the fighting. The French rattle and trumpet are no longer heard, and Beethoven indicates in the score that the English drums have broken through to the French side. The French cannons still fire occasionally, but not as frequently as the British cannons. The battle moves harmonically by step from A-flat, to A, B-flat, and B before skipping to the British key of E-flat, as the tempo increases to Sempre più allegro and finally Presto. The French cannons are no longer heard, and the sounds of the British cannons continue unopposed for the last seventy-seven measures of the battle sequence. Before the movement ends, however, a wonderful symbolic moment occurs in the Andante section. The music returns to the 6/8 meter which Beethoven had previously used only for the introduction of the French army. In this slow tempo, he writes a variation on the French "Marlborough" in F-sharp minor, clearly serving as a dirge for the defeated French troops (Example 6).

Example 6: Beethoven, *Wellington's Victory*:

The victory symphony that comprises the second part is musically superior to the opening battle movement largely because it contains no cannons, rattles, or trumpet fanfares. The victory movement is in D major, except when "God Save the King" is briefly stated in the third-related key of B-flat. Beethoven limits the use of this tune, however, and most of the movement contains original material. In the coda, he treats the British tune to fragmentation and diminution as he drives to a rousing conclusion.

Beethoven's victory piece had competition in 1813, however, because in that same year Peter von Winter's *Schlacht-Sinfonie* (no. 209) appeared. At the time a reviewer for the *Allgemeine musikalische Zeitung* considered Winter's symphony more significant than Beethoven's:

> Herr van Beethoven's composition appears to us, nevertheless, only an occasional work, on which he had applied little industry. Without special preparation, he began immediately with the cannons and now depicted the material of a battle. However, our Winter, whose composition was mentioned in an earlier report, opens with much forethought, the concern for which the listener is rewarded and which appeals more to his spirit.[19]

The *Schlacht-Sinfonie* was one of the earliest choral symphonies, predating the completion of Beethoven's Ninth by over a decade. Even though it is called a symphony, the work is in one continuous movement. Winter composed the work in commemoration of the German victory over Napoleon in October 1813 and dedicated it to the Bavarian King Maximilian Joseph. The first performance was a grandiose affair consisting of five orchestras and a mixed choir. The *Allgemeine musikalische Zeitung* reported its success:

> Loud cries of joy rose from all sides of the hall, accompanied along with the fiery music which continued streaming forth in triumphant song, and did not subside, till after the sound [of the music] had long become silent. It was a moment where all present were filled with enthusiasm and cheerful presentiment. . . . [To Winter], this evening was a beautiful reward for so much, which he had intelligently begun, and always skillfully achieved during his long artistic life. With just pride may he look back at what he has achieved for his name will forever remain high in the annals of musical art.[20]

After a tonally unstable orchestral introduction of twenty-nine measures, the four-part chorus enters heroically in C major and in march rhythm. This first section uses the martial dotted rhythms, fast scales, and repeated note patterns. The chorus sings through five strophes of similar patriotic verse, all set syllabically, for over one hundred measures at a dynamic level of *forte* or louder. Beginning at the Allegro giusto in measure 138, the next three hundred measures are solely instrumental. The chorus enters again in measure 548, and the work ends with a triumphal final chorus in C major. Because of his tremendous success with the *Schlacht-Sinfonie*, Winter followed it with a peace cantata *Germania* (1815). In his introduction to a modern edition of the score, Donald Henderson suggested these two works were paired together as a program of war and peace.[21]

While instrumental battle music flourished during the period from 1750 to 1827, several types of war-related vocal compositions were also quite prominent. During the American Revolution, the principal American composer William Billings served the Revolution by composing anthems and songs (nos. 150-153). These compositions in no way tried to imitate the furor of battle or the spirit of glorious victory. Instead, the composer expressed his distaste for war and his desire for peace. The music itself was not programmatic but merely served as a peace. The music itself was not programmatic but merely served as a vehicle to express the text—a function similar to that of the Medieval conductus centuries ago and of many popular songs in this century. The descriptive texts are set in a relatively simple four-part harmony with no sounds of battle, no dissonance, no fast repeated notes. Unlike the music of the later French Revolution, Billings's compositions needed no trumpets, drums, military bands, or choruses of thousands.

On the other hand, the French Revolutionary composers established a tradition of revolutionary hymns, cantatas, and oratorios. Earlier composers like Handel and Graun had written choral victory works, but Gossec, Méhul, Catel, Cherubini, and hosts of others composed works of these kinds with relentless revolutionary fervor. According to David Charlton, at least 1,374 revolutionary hymns were composed or arranged from the beginning of the French Revolution to 1803.[22] In *The Spirit of Revolution in 1789*, Cornwell Rogers indicated that composers had written over 3,000 politically related songs in France between 1789 and 1800.[23]

Moreover, the musical celebrations after the French Revolution were such grand events that theaters could not accommodate them. Many were held in the open air so that the masses could attend. The Robespierre Fête de l'Etre Supreme on 8 June 1794 consisted of 2,400 vocal and instrumental performers along with 130 pieces of artillery.[24] Winton Dean notes that these massive oratorios and celebrations enormously influenced later French musicians: "The grand operas of Spontini and the whole aesthetic of Berlioz would be unthinkable without them."[25]

This revolutionary music is almost never performed today; it was music for the moment, music to keep the revolutionary fires burning. We should nonetheless not so quickly dismiss it, because its importance

> lies not so much in its intrinsic value, as in the role it plays in a great social movement. Organized music, which had for so long served lords spiritual or temporal, now made articulate the will of the people. . . . Thus in these festal and ceremonial odes and hymns the musical function of the chorus is transcended by its symbolic representation of the brotherhood of man entering, full of hope, upon a new epoch and uplifted in the first, undimmed glow of idealism.[26]

Masses and other traditionally religious genres did not escape the influence of the revolutionary age. Haydn entitled one of his own masses *Missa in tempore belli* (1796) (no. 166)—a work that was directly influenced by the threat of Napoleon's coming to Vienna. The solemn,

Agnus Dei illustrate the influence of the impending war upon the composer. On the words "Dona nobis pacem" in the Agnus Dei, Haydn has the choir enter on high Gs while the brass and winds are playing loud fanfares. In writing about this passage, H.C.R. Landon speculates that "Haydn seems almost to have changed the words from 'Give us peace' to 'We demand peace.'"[27] This mass also illustrates how the events of war have led composers to make innovations in works other than the programmatic battle compositions. Landon further claims that the first performance of Haydn's mass "will have left the audience shaken in a way that possibly no religious music had done since the days of Bach and Handel."[28] Napoleon's rise no doubt had considerable influence on Haydn's compositions during the last decade of the eighteenth century. In addition to his *Missa in tempore belli*, Haydn composed the *Lord Nelson Mass* and *Lines from the Battle of the Nile* (nos. 166, 165), as well as two symphonies the "Military" and the "Drum Roll."

Beethoven, too, turned to choral music to celebrate the events of war and Napoleon's defeat. In addition to *Wellington's Victory*, Beethoven wrote in 1814 a grandiose cantata *Der glorreiche Augenblick*, Op. 136 (no. 191), and several smaller works including *Germania* (190), *Ihr weisen Gründer glücklicher Staaten*, and *Es ist vollbracht* (189).[29] These works were all patriotic compositions in honor of the Congress of Vienna or in response to the surrender of Paris. Although Beethoven rode a crest of unprecedented popularity with these war-related works, critics have been harsh in their judgements of them. Maynard Solomon suggested that these choral works were "filled with bombastic rhetoric and 'patriotic' excesses . . . [and] mark the nadir of Beethoven's artistic career. In them his heroic style is revived, but as parody and farce."[30] Nonetheless, they show how Beethoven was swept up with the events taking place around him. He seemed eager to compose them and clearly enjoyed the success that they brought. While we may be critical of them out of context today, during their time they must have been heroic works of the first order.

The only other great composer to write a major vocal composition about Napoleon's defeat was Carl Maria von Weber. Weber planned his *Kampf und Sieg* (1815) (no. 206) immediately after Napoleon's defeat at Waterloo and took considerable pains to avoid the trap of writing a musically inferior victory cantata. Nonetheless, although it was enthusiastically received at its first performance on 22 December 1815, the composition received harsh criticism from the press. In an article sent to various musical journals, Weber defended his work by describing in detail how his composition was written, and why it was justifiably superior to the other victory cantatas written during the time.

Weber describes the opening of the work, which begins in D minor, as "abrupt–stormy–lamenting–vehemently accented."[31] The battle itself also begins in D minor and is one of the earliest compositions to use the minor mode specifically to depict part of a battle; however, the battle scene soon leaves the minor mode to continue raging in D major, E-flat major, and stepping up to E major. After various solos and trios, the work concludes majestically with the full chorus and orchestra in D major.

Although orchestral battle music of this era is better known today than most war-related vocal music, composers were most active in the vocal genres. As has been shown, cantatas, oratorios, anthems, hymns, and the sacred mass were chosen to lament or celebrate the wars and revolutions which dominated the era. War compositions of this era more frequently contained laments or expressions of grief than in previous generations, even if such serious aspects remained a small part of the literature. No musical compositions achieved the power of Goya's *Third of May* (1808) or his visual catalog of the *Disasters of War* (1810-1821). Goya's vision, however, was a personal statement, not representative of the age in which he lived. The idea that war was grand and heroic continued to persist through a period of war and revolution, through a period of killing, decapitation, hanging, and torture. Weber may have partially depicted a battle scene in the more somber key of D minor, but *Kampf und Sieg* ends with a triumphant victory celebration in the key of D major. War remained a heroic adventure, at least as represented in the world of music.

Anonymous

148. *Bataille geshilet.* Piano or organ. Nymegen den 20 July 1792.
#[n.p. 179-?].
*MYD (NYPL call number)
An eleven-page work in which the "Attaque" contains
continuous repeated-note triplets in both hands building up to a
cadence on the dominant and immediately turning into sixteenth-
note descending and then ascending scales. A handwritten
manuscript beginning with a D-minor introduction and ending in D
major.

149. *The Battle of Copenhagen: A Grand Characteristic Sonata.* Piano.
#Dublin: Goulding, [n.d.].
M23. B3
A seventeen-page battle piece with over twenty descriptive
sections. This work uses related keys of C major, C minor, and E-
flat major, but oddly places the "Cries of the Wounded" in C
major, adding considerable chromaticism and minor seconds.

America

Billings, William (1746-1800)

150. *Chester* from *New-England Psalm-Singer.* Chorus [1770]. #*The
Complete Works of William Billings* (Boston: The American
Musicological Society and The Colonial Society of Massachusetts,
1977), vol. 2, pp. 72-73.
M1584.B or M2116.B59S4 1781 Case
A strophic, sixteen-measure patriotic song illustrating how the
youthful Americans can defeat their older enemies. Billings's most
popular patriotic song.

151. *Lamentation over Boston* from the *Singing Master's Assistant.*
Anthem for chorus. #New York: Mercury Music, 1949 or *The
Complete Works of William Billings*, vol. 2, pp. 136-47. Based
on Psalm 137.

M1584.B
Written while Boston was occupied by the British; it is possible that Samuel Adams assisted in writing this anthem.

152. *Retrospect* from *Singing Master's Assistant*. Anthem for chorus [1778]. #Boston: Draper and Folsom, 1778 or *The Complete Works of William Billings*, vol. 2, pp. 231-43.
M1584.B or M2116.B59 S4 1781 Case
A protest against war calling for the citizens to "Beat your swords into plowshares and your spears into pruning hooks, and learn war no more" (Isaiah 2:4).

153. *Victory* from *The Continental Harmony*. Chorus [c. 1794]. #Boston: Andrews and Thomas, 1794 or *The Complete Works of William Billings*, vol. 4, pp. 254-55.
M2.B53C7 or M2116.B59C5 1794a
A twenty-five measure work in B-flat major thanking God for the American victory.

Carr, Benjamin (1768-1831)

154. *The Siege of Tripolli: An Historical Naval Sonata*. Piano [c. 1801]. #Philadelphia: G. Blake, 181- or *Anthology of Early American Keyboard Music 1787-1830*, Part I, ed. J. Bunker Clark in *Recent Researches in American Music* (Madison: A-R Editions, 1977), vol. 1, pp. 77-91.
M1.A1C
More innovative than many of the battle pieces of its time. See page 54 for additional information.

Etienne, Denis-Germain (1781-1859)

155. *Battle of New Orleans*. Piano [1816]. #Boston: G. Graupner, 181-?
M1.A1E
A nineteen-page work beginning with the following instructions: "C: Sign of the Drum Pedal for the Cannon" and "Ø: Sign of the Drum Pedal with the little bells." It begins with "The Night Calm" in C minor, moving to C major for the "Distant March of the Enemy" (*pp*). The battle is quite frenetic with sixteenth-note arpeggios, tremolos, and chromaticism. "Terrible Carnage" is in C major with an occasional diminished chord thrown in. "Hail Columbia" and "Yankee Doodle" end the work. Dedicated to the "American Nation."

Hewitt, James (1770-1827)

156. *Battle of Trenton.* Piano [1792]. #*Recent Researches in American Music* (Madison: A-R Editions, 1980), vol. 7, pp. 88. Complete score also reprinted in John Waldorf Wagner's *James Hewitt: His Life and Works* (Indiana University: dissertation, 1969), pp. 522-36. E. Power Biggs made an arrangement for organ: #Bryn Mawr: Merion Music, 1974.
     M1.A1H Case
     Depicts Washington's attack on and victory over the Hessians on Christmas Eve. Highly sectionalized, with descriptive titles, and includes popular tunes such as "Yankee Doodle" and "Twinkle, Twinkle Little Star." See page 53 for additional information.

157. *The 4th of July—A Grand Military Sonata.* Piano [1801-1811]. #Miami, Florida: Belwin, 1989. *Desto/CMS 6445-6447.
     M1.A1H Case
     A highly sectionalized work with titles beginning with "Day break. Cannon . . . General Beat" and ending with "Hail Columbia" and a victory celebration.

158. *The Grand March and Tammany Quick Step.* Piano [1808].
     M1.A1H case
     "Composed for the solemn funeral procession to accompany the interment of the remains of 11,500 American Seamen, soldiers, and citizens who died while on British War ships during the Revolutionary War."
     Hewitt also composed the now lost *Overture in 9 Movements, Expressive of a Battle.* Orchestra [1792].

Masi, Francesco (19th c.)

159. *The Battles of Lake Champlain and Plattsburg.* Grand piano sonata [1815]. #Boston: The Composer, 1815?
     **M.445.128 (Boston Public Library call number)
     A fourteen-page work "respectfully dedicated to the American heroes who achieved the glorious victories." See J. Bunker Clark, *The Dawning of American Keyboard Music* (New York & Westport, Conn.: Greenwood, 1988), pp. 244-46.

Ricksecker, Peter (fl. 1811)

160. *The Battle of New Orleans*. Piano [1816]. #Philadelphia: G.
Willig, 1816.
M1.A1R
A ten-page, highly sectionalized battle piece in D major with
an unusual number of subtitles. It begins Grave with the heading
"The Americans await with calmness the approach of the Enemy
who are seen advancing from a distance." A sign with "cannon"
written above it presumably indicated a cluster as in earlier battle
works. "A tremendous fire" is represented by sixteenth-note
arpeggiated chords for over fourteen measures. The work concludes
with marches dedicated to three generals.

Trisobio, Filippo (fl. 1796)

161. *The Clock of Lombardy, or the Surrender of Milan to General
Buonaparte*. Piano [1796-1798]. #Philadelphia: Trisobio, c. 1796.
OCLC 25263304 (At the University of Pennsylvania)
A fifteen-page work in various major keys that is an
entertainment more than a battle piece. It contains marches, dotted
rhythms, and descriptive headings, e.g., "Entry of General
Buonaparte into the Milanese Territory," "The troops under arms,"
or "The Soldiery with the Country Girls in the Dance Peculiar to
the Country." When Napoleon communicates with his officers, the
music is a "Recitativo ad Libitum." The battle itself is in B-flat
major with repeated sixteenth-note B-flats in the bass throughout
the section. The work as a whole is more light-hearted than other
battle works of the time.

Austria

Diabelli, Antonio (1781-1858)

162. *Der 18te October, oder das große militarische Prater-Fest in Wien
anno 1814*. Piano [1814]. #Vienna: S.A. Steiner, 1814. Text by
Kanne.
Mus. Res. MYD (NYPL call number)
This beautifully published score in seventeen pages could in
reality serve as a melodrama because the text, an actual poem, is
used extensively. The music remains sectionalized and features
chordal textures, Alberti bass, syncopation, and staccato passages.

Haslinger, Tobias (1787-1842)

163. *Deutschlands Triumph oder der Einzug der verbündten Mächte zu Paris, Europas Siegesfeier grosse musikalische Darstellung für die turk. Musik.* Piano [c. 1826]. #Vienna: Auf Kosten des Herausgebers, c. 1826.
     M25.H Case
     A twenty-page, sectionalized battle piece closing with "Dank der Völker, für die Palme des Friedens"; requires considerable virtuosity.

164. *Die Schlacht bey Paris gekrönt durch die Emnahme der Hauptstadt Frankreichs. Eine grosse Musikalische Schlacht-Darstellung für das Pianoforte.* Piano [c. 1814]. #Vienna: T. Haslinger, c. 1814.
     *MYD+ Mus. Res. (NYPL call number)
     A virtuosic, twenty-one page work which modulates through several keys to retell the Battle of Paris from 25 to 31 March 1814. Uses chromatic descending scales to represent fires, tremolos and fast ascending scales for the attack, and fast repeated notes and arpeggios in a highly energetic tempo to represent the cavalry. The lament for the wounded moves to G minor (Andante lamentoso).

Haydn, Franz Joseph (1732-1809)

165. *Lines from the Battle of the Nile.* Aria for soprano and piano. #Berlin: Adler, 1931. #Vienna: Doblinger, 1981. *Adda 81069. Text by Cornelia Knight.
     M3.3.H19N3 Case
     A highly sectionalized work moving from its stern C-minor opening with text of grief, going through C major with renewed hope, and concluding in B-flat major praising the great Lord Nelson and his victory at Aboukir Bay. Haydn uses much text-painting when appropriate.

166. *Missa in tempore belli.* Chorus and orchestra [1796]. #Kassel: Bärenreiter, 1967. *Philips 412734-2 PH and Angel CDC-47425.
     M2013.H4 no. 9 M5
     Influenced by Napoleon's march on Vienna. See page 60 for additional information.
     Another of Haydn's masses was influenced by Napoleon's march: *Mass in D minor* (*"Lord Nelson Mass"*). Chorus and orchestra [1798]. #Kassel: Bärenreiter, 1967. *Philips 416358-2 PH and DG ARC-423097-2 AH. M2013.H4.HXXII, 11 1963.

Hoffmeister, Franz Anton (1754-1812)

167. Symphony ("La festa della pace 1791"). Orchestra [c. 1792]. #*The Symphony 1720-1840*, Barry S. Brook, ed.-in-chief (New York: Garland, 1984), Series B, vol. 5, pp. 1-71.
      M1001.H72 Op. 9 no. 1 1984
      Written soon after the peace Leopold III concluded with the Ottoman Turks, this work includes four movements (Allegro; poco Adagio; Menuetto: Allegretto; and Allegro molto, Tuchesco). The "Turkish" finale includes extensive percussion (triangle, bells, etc.) and an active piccolo part.

Kauer, Ferdinand (1751-1831)

168. *La conquete d'Oczakow: Sonata Militaire.* Piano [1788]. #in Bland, John, compiler. *"Erschröckliche und ergötzliche Geschichten"* RBM 3064.
      M20.B642 Case
      Deals with the war between the Russians and the Turks at Oczakau in 1788. To indicate "the powder magazine is blown up" the pianist is called upon to play a sixty-fourth-note passage in consecutive sixths in the right hand. "The cries of the wounded, the women and children" is highly chromatic and made up of diminished sevenths. See page 54 for additional information.
      Kauer composed numerous other battle pieces: *Darstellung der Geschichte des Wiener Aufgeboths, nach der Angabe Ihro K.K. Majestat Maria Theresia.* Orchestra [1802-1803]; *Nelsons Grosse Schlacht.* Wind ensemble or piano trio [c. 1798]. Dedicated to Duke of Sussex; *La siège de Belgrad.* [Cited in MGG, vol. 1, p. 1409]; *Tone-Painting of the Destruction of the Bandit City of Algiers and the Burning of its Fleet.* [Cited in R.M. Longyear, "Ferdinand Kauer's Percussion Enterprises," *The Gatlin Society Journal* (May 1974), p. 2]; and *Wellington's and Blucher's Famous Battle Near Waterloo* [after 1815].

Mozart, Wolfgang Amadeus (1756-1791)

169. *Contretanz* ("La bataille"), K. 535. Orchestra [1788]. #Leipzig: Breitkopf & Härtel, 19-- or *Wolfgang Amadeus Mozart "Orchesterwerke"* (Kassel: Bärenreiter, 1988), vol. 13, pp. 44-47.
      M3. M92 v. 13 Pt. 1 Sec. 2
      A highly diatonic C-major work in five sections ending with a "Marcia turca" full of dotted rhythms. Geoffrey Winters made an

arrangement for recorders, percussion, and piano with optional violins and cello.

170. *Contretanz* ("Der Sieg vom Helden Koburg"), K. 587. Orchestra [1789]. 1st: December 1789. *#Wolfgang Amadeus Mozart "Orchesterwerke,"* vol. 13, pp. 148-52. *Nonesuch H71146. M3. M92 v. 13 Pt. 1 Sec. 2

   An eighty-measure work in C major written to celebrate Coburg's victory over the Turks at the Battle of Martinestie in 1789. Nonetheless, it remains typical Mozart with no programmatic references other than dotted rhythmic patterns.

Bohemia

Dussek [or Dusík], Jan Ladislav (1760-1812)

171. *Die Leiden der Königin Marie Antoinette (The Sufferings of the Queen Marie Antoinette)*, Op. 23. Harpsichord [1793]. #Paris: Silbcr, No. 1451. *Musikszcnc Schwciz EL 17002.
   [RISM D4373]

   An intensely programmatic suite dealing more with revolution than with war, but certainly an outgrowth of fighting and persecution. The suite contains ten movements dealing with Marie Antoinette's imprisonment, her trial, and decapitation—the most famous part of the score using a descending glissando to depict the event.

   Dussek also composed *The Naval Combat: Total Defeat of the Dutch Fleet by Admiral Duncan, October 15, 1797.* Sonata for piano, violin, cello, grand tambour, and lute [1797]. #Offenbach: Johann André, No. 2494.—St. [RISM D4094]; and *Elegie harmonique* in F-sharp minor, Op. 61. Piano sonata [1806-1807]. #Leipzig and New York: Peters, 1949. M23.D97 Op. 61 Case or M2.M637 vol. 53. Dedicated to Prince Louis Ferdinand who fell at the Battle of Saalfeld.

Koczwara, František (1730-1791)

172. *The Battle of Prague.* Piano, violin, and cello [c. 1788]. #England?: s.n., 180-? *New World NW 299.
   M1.A1K

   The British Library alone has over thirty different printings and arrangements of this work. The music begins with a slow march in F major, followed by a "Word of Command" and "First

Signal." The "Cannon" is sounded by an octave of bass Cs. The bugle horns and trumpet call sound, this time with cannons depicted by a triplet four-note figure. The attack consists of a continuous Alberti bass, with single-note cannon shots in the bass. The right hand includes rapid sixteenth-note scales, trills, and tremolos. The "Cries of the Wounded" is in F minor and precedes "God Save the King." An Allegro finale concludes the work. See pages 52 to 53 for additional information.

Neubauer, Franz (1760-1795)

173. *La bataille*, Op. 11. Orchestra [1794]. *Nonesuch H71146.
       [No LC number available]
       A seven-part description of the Battle of Martinesti against the Turks; includes many trumpet fanfares, drum rolls, repeated notes, and fast scale passages. See page 55 for additional information.

Wanhal, Johann (1739-1813)

174. *Le combat naval de Trafalger et la mort de Nelson.* Piano. #Vienna: J. Elder, 18--.
       M25.W
       A thirteen-page, C-major battle with subtitles in German and French. A funeral march for Nelson is in C minor. The battle itself contains low octaves or single notes with "bom" placed under them, rapid sixteenth-notes treble tremolos, and arpeggios.

175. *Die Schlacht bei Würzburg.* Piano [1796]. #Vienna: Jos. Elder, 1796?
       M25.W Case
       An eleven-page battle in C major with descriptive subheadings. Wanhal uses low and high single notes for the "Heftige Kanonade." The attack section uses bass notes for cannon shots and sixteenth-note treble arpeggios for the confusion of battle in combination with some minor keys and diminished seventh chords. It ends with "Danksagung an unsere Helden die Retter Deutschlands."
       Wanhal also composed *The Threatening or the Liberation of Vienna.*

Wranitzky, Paul (1756-1808)

176. *Grande sinfonie caractéristique pour la paix avec la République française*, Op. 31. Orchestra [1797]. #Augsbourg: Gombart, 1797? *A. Charlin CL 44.
M1001.A2W94 Op. 31P
The first movement is entitled "The Revolution" and contains a couple of marches. The second is a lament on the death of Louis XVI and a funeral march. The third begins with two marches before the C-major battle breaks out. The last movement begins with "The Peace negotiations" in G major and ends with "Rejoicing on the Conclusion of Peace." See page 55 for additional information.

France

Balbastre, Claude-Bénigne (1727-1799)

177. *Marche des Marseillois* [sic] *et l'air Ça ira*. Organ or piano [1792]. *#Pièces de clavecin d'orgue et de forte piano* (Paris: Heugel, 1973), pp. 88-93. *Disques Pierre Verany PV.785032-33 and Musikszene Schweiz EL 17002.
M22.B223C8
Consists of a theme and two variations on "La marseillaise." During the second variation, Balbastre includes "Combat" (dotted rhythms), "Fuites des ennemis" (sixteenth-note ascending scales), and "Canon" (unmetered whole notes in a descending scale). The work concludes with "Ah ça ira."

Berlioz, Hector (1803-1869)

178. *Scène héroïque (La révolution grecque)*. Chorus and orchestra [1825]. (Second version written in 1833.) 1st: 26 May 1828. *Hector Berlioz New Edition of the Complete Works* (Kassel: Bärenreiter, 1991), vol. 12, pt. 1. Text by Farrand.
M3.B47 v. 12 pt. 1
Influenced by the Greek struggle against Turkey. The four movements are "Récitatif et Air (un chef grec)," "Chœur des guerriers," "Prière (chœur de femmes)," and "Final (chœur général)." The last chorus is taken from his *Le cri de guerre du Brisgaw*.

Devienne, François (1759-1803)

179. *The Battle of Gemappe.* Piano or harpsichord with violin and cello
      accompaniment [1796]. #London: Longman & Broderip, 17--.
         M314.D Case
         After the opening fanfares, "La marseillaise" appears. The
      work is sectionalized with subheadings, and the music is simple
      and diatonic. "Cries and Lamentations of the Wounded" is in D
      minor and the piece ends with "The Carmagnole" and "Ah ça ira."

Darcier, Joseph (1820-?)

180. *La bataillon de la Moselle.* Souvenir historique for voice and
      piano. #Paris: L. Viellot, 18--. Text by C. Gille.
         *MO (French) box (NYPL call number)
         A strophic song in three parts (D minor, A major, and D
      minor). Its five verses retell the battle while the music remains
      highly diatonic.

Fuchs, Georg-Friedrich (1752-1821) [German born]

181. *The Battle of Jena.* Piano with violin accompaniment [1807-1809].
      #Philadelphia: G. Willig, 1807-1809. An arrangement also exists
      for two flutes.
         M1.A1F
         An eleven-page work in F major that is more imaginative than
      most of the other battle works of this period. The music is more
      syncopated and the concluding section is particularly novel
      rhythmically. After the "Retreat of the Prussians" and the "Groans
      of the Wounded," Fuch quotes "Marlborough." The work ends with
      a victory march as the "French enter Berlin," concluding with a
      tonic-chord tremolo in both hands *ff.*
         Fuchs also composed *Cinquième harmonie, ou bataille de
      Gemmappes et prise de la ville de Mons.* Four clarinets, two
      horns, two bassoons, trumpet, and drum. #Paris: Henri Naderman,
      aux adresses ordinaires.—St. [RISM F2044].

Gossec, François-Joseph (1734-1829)

182. *Le triomphe de la République ou La camp de grand Pré.*
      Divertissement lyrique in one act [1794]. #Paris: Chez Cochet,
      [n.d.]. Text by M.J. Chénier; ballet by Cardel.
         Mus. Res. *MSI (NYPL call number)

A victory celebration. Uses "canon" blasts in the overture which also contains considerable dotted rhythms and arpeggios.

Gossec's other war-related works include *Trois chant du 14 Juillet sous la Révolution.* *MFp.v. 10, no. 10 (NYPL call number); *La chant des triomphes de la France* [1794]. *EMI CDC 7494732PM518; and *Te Deum.* Chorus. *Adda AD 185. See NEW GROVE for a more complete listing of Gossec's revolutionary works, vol. 7, pp. 560-63.

Jadin, Louis Emmanuel (1768-1853)

183. *Le grande bataille d'Austerlitz.* Piano. Also arranged for other instruments [c. 1806].
     M25.J Case
     A thirteen-page battle piece sectionalized with fanfares, descriptive French subtitles and special effects, rapid bass trills, and fast sixteenth-note Alberti basses.

Le Mière de Corvey, Jean Frédéric Auguste (1770-1832)

184. *La bataille de Jena.* Piano [c. 1806]. #Vienna: Jean Cappi, c. 1806.
     M35.L
     A seventeen-page battle piece with German subtitles. The sections are small and pass through numerous keys. The "Wehklagen der Verwundeten" is set in C minor.

Méhul, Etienne-Nicolas (1763-1817)

185. *Les chant des victoires: hymne de guerre.* Song [c. 1794]. #Paris: Magasín de musique, c. 1794. Text by M.J. Chénier.
     M1731.M Case
     A two-page strophic song in B-flat major with four verses and refrain with texts including "Gloire au Peuple Français" and "Vive la république, et périssent les Rois."

186. *Le chant du départ: hymne de guerre.* Song [c. 1794]. #Paris: Magasin de musique, 1794. Text by M.J. Chénier.
     M1731.M Case
     A two-page C-major song: diatonic, heroic, and loud.

187. *Chant national du 14 juillet 1800.* Three choruses and orchestras [1800]. #Paris: Gravé par Made. Leroy, c. 1800. *EMI

7494702PM518 and Musifrance WE 810-ZK. Text by Louis de Fontanes.

M1737.M49

An ambitious twenty-minute work praising the victorious revolution and the peace now brought about (temporarily). The third orchestra and chorus contains only harps, horn, and women's voices.

Méhul composed many other revolutionary works after the French Revolution. See NEW GROVE for a more complete listing, vol. 12, pp. 62-67. See *EMI CDC 7494732, *EMI CDC 794702, and *Musikszene Schweiz EL 17002 for more recorded compositions pertaining to the French Revolution.

Viguerie, Bernard (c. 1761-1819)

188. *Battle of Maringo: A Military and Historical Piece.* Piano with violin and cello accompaniment [1802]. #Boston: Gottlieb Graupner, 1802?

M1.A1V or M312.V68 Case

A thirteen-page, C-major battle important for its use of a symbol to indicate a three-octave cluster to be played with both hands in the bass. Viguerie calls this the "coup de canon." The work is highly sectionalized with subheadings every two or three staves on the average. It ends with three extended airs in different styles.

Viguerie also composed the *Battle of Prague.* Piano with violin and cello accompaniment. #Paris: Auteur, No. 33.—St. [RISM V1507].

Germany

Beethoven, Ludwig van (1770-1827)

189. *Es is vollbracht,* WoO 97. Chorus and orchestra [1814]. #*Beethoven Complete Edition* (New York: Kalmus, [n.d.]), vol. 27. Text by F. Treitschke.

M3.B4 1967 v. 27

A D-major, heroic work praising God for the Kaiser who gave them the victory over Napoleon.

190. *Germania,* WoO 94. Bass, chorus, and orchestra [1814]. #*Beethoven Complete Edition,* vol. 27, no. 207d.

M3.B4 1967 v. 27

A brief, B-flat major strophic song ending *fff* on the words "Germania." Composed in celebration of the capitulation of Paris on 31 March 1814. (See Solomon, *Beethoven*, p. 222.)

191. *Der glorreiche Augenblick (The Glorious Moment)*, Op. 136. Cantata [1814]. #*Beethoven Complete Edition*, vol. 28.
        M3.B4 1967 v. 28
        An elaborate cantata in six sections beginning in A major and ending in C major with an enormous amount of repeated notes and continuous dotted rhythms. Beethoven wrote this work and a chorus *Ihr weisen Gründer glücklicher Staaten*, WoO 95, as "a tribute to the Congress of Vienna." (See Solomon, *Beethoven*, p. 222.)

192. *Kriegslied der Oesterreicher*, WoO 122. Voices and piano [1796]. #*Beethoven Complete Edition*, vol. 26. Text by Friedelberg.
        M3.B4 1967 v. 26
        A two-page strophic song in C major that is completely diatonic with triadic melodies and dotted rhythms setting an anti-Napoleon text.

193. *Ruins of Athens*, Op. 113. Cantata [1811-1812]. #New York: Kalmus, [n.d.]. *EMI CDC 7 499272-2.
        M1512.B47R84
        An eight-part work beginning in G major and ending in A major, written for the opening of the imperial theater in Pesth. Contains a "Marcia alla turca" with numerous militaristic effects.

194. Symphony No. 3 ("Eroica"). Orchestra [1803]. 1st: #London: Eulenberg, 1936. *RCA RCD1-7197 or Angel CDC-47410.
        M1001.B4 Op. 55 1935
        Originally dedicated to Napoleon Bonaparte, the symphony began a new era for Beethoven in its expansion of sonata form. Not a battle piece like his *Wellington's Victory*, but the slow movement is a funeral march in the French Revolutionary tradition of Gossec. See Maynard Solomon's article "Beethoven and Bonaparte," *The Music Review* 29 (1968), pp. 96-105.

195. *Wellington's Victory*, Op. 91. Orchestra (Originally written for panharmonicon) [1813]. #*Beethoven Werke* "Ouverturen und Wellingtons Sieg" ed. Hans-Werner Küthen (Munich: G. Henle, 1974), vol. 2, pt. 1, pp. 133-219. *DG 419624-2 GH and Telarc CD-80079.

M3.B44 v. 2 pt. 1

The most important war composition of the early nineteenth century and Beethoven's most popular composition. See pages 55 to 57 for additional information.

Graun, Carl Heinrich (1704-1759)

196. *Te Deum Laudamus Commemorating Frederick's Victory at the Battle of Prague 1756.* Soloists, Chorus, and orchestra [1757]. #London: Novello & Ewer, 189-?

M2020.G75T32 Case or M2023.G77T4

In eleven sections in D major and in the Handelian tradition of the *Dettingen Te Deum.*

Hummel, Johann Nepomuk (1778-1837)

197. *Six Waltzes followed by a Great Battle*, Op. 91. Orchestra [1820].

M211.H92 Op. 91 Case

Using drum rolls and fanfares, and quoting "Marlborough," Hummel presents a clever and rather typical battle work. See page 54 for additional information.

Klöffler, Johann Friedrich (1725-1790)

198. *Bataille.* Symphony for two orchestras representing opposing forces [1777]. 1st: Amsterdam, 28 October 1777.

[No LC number available]

Extraordinarily popular between 1777 and 1787 and performed throughout Europe during these years. The D-major composition was written for fifty to sixty instruments and was based on a plan to illustrate numerous positions of battle. For more information, see pages 54 to 55.

Simrock, N. (Nikolaus? 1751-1832)

199. *Battle of Dunkirk.* Piano. #Baltimore: C. Hupfeld, [n.d.].

JPG 78-15 (NYPL call number)

A ten-page score with special mention of playing cannons by striking the palms of both hands on the keys. It opens and closes with fanfares and marches and the sounds of cannons in D major and minor.

Steibelt, Daniel (1765-1823)

200. *Défaite des Espagnole par l'armée française.* Sonata militaire for piano [c. 1797]. #Paris: Boyer, 1797.
    M23.S82D4 Case
    An eighteen-page sonata with a slow introduction in E-flat major ("Le calme de la nuit") leading ("pas de charge") to an extended Allegro. The music is dominated by repetitive dotted rhythms, tremolos, rapid scales, and Alberti basses. The Allegro is a continuous movement of nearly sixteen pages and is not sectionalized with subheadings like the usual battle works.

201. *Die Schlacht bei Leipzig.* Piano [c. 1814]. #V. Simmrock.
    M25.S Case
    A sectionalized battle piece with great uses of repetition in D major. The work includes various marches and fanfares in its seven pages.

202. *Die Zerstörung von Moskwa (The Destruction of Moscow)*, Op. 101. Piano [1814]. #Leipzig: C. F. Peters, 18--.
    M1.S35 Vol. 56 Case or M25.S Case
    A twenty-page, sixteen-section, virtuosic battle with numerous descriptive passages and headings dealing with Napoleon's entering Moscow. Quotes "Marlborough" and "God Save the King" and uses numerous tremolos and rapid scales to represent the "Anfang der Feuersbrunst" or the "Explosion des Kremlin." It concludes with a "Freude der Sieger: Russischer Tanz" in G major with seven variations and a coda.
    Steibelt composed numerous other war-related works: *Admiral Duncan's Victory* [1797]; *Brittania, an allegorical overture in commemoration of the signal naval victory obtained by Admiral Duncan over the Dutch Fleet the 11th of October 1797.* Piano. #London: Longman & Broderip. [Closed shelf M1739.S818 University of Rochester and RISM S5447] and a slightly different title: *Brittania. An overture for the piano forte in commemoration of His Britannic Majesty's solemn procession to the Cathedral of St. Paul's to return the Almighty thanks for the splendid victories obtained by his navy over the fleets of France, Spain and Holland.* Piano. #London: Longman & Broderip. [RISM S5448]; *Le combat naval*, Op. 41. Piano, violin, cello, and tambour [c. 1800]. #Paris: Imbault, 1800. M25.S; *La bataille de Gemappe et Neerwinden.* [Cited in Niecks, *Programme Music in the Last Four Centuries.* (New York: Haskell House, 1969), p. 19]; *La fête de Mars.*

Intermezzo [1806]. 1st: 4 March 1806. Celebrated Napoleon's victory at Austerlitz; and *La journée d'Ulm*. Piano [c. 1815]. #Philadelphia: G. Willig, c. 1815. *Oryx 1811. M1.A1S.

Riotte, Philipp Jakob (1776-1856)

203. *The Battle of Leipsig* [sic] *or Liberation of Germany*. Piano [c. 1814]. #Philadelphia: Bacon, 1814 or Vienna: Thadé Weigl, 1816; Reprinted (Wilhelmshaven: Heinrichshofen, 1963).
      M1.A1R
      A massive nineteen-page battle piece, highly sectionalized with numerous descriptive headings (some of considerable length) and key changes. The piano writing is highly virtuosic for its time, using tremolos, Alberti basses, thick repeated chords, and hand crossings.

Vogler, Abt (George J.) (1749-1814)

204. *Variations sur l'air de Marlborough*. Piano and orchestra [1791]. #Mainz: Schott, 1951. *Musikszene Schweiz EL 18002.
      M1010.V885V38
      Contains eleven variations and a capriccio on the famous French tune, but without particular battle characteristics. Over twenty minutes long.

205. *Das Wiederkehren des verwundeten baierischen Kriegers*. Ode for four vocal parts. #Munich: Falterischen Musikhandlung, 17--.
      M1584.V Case
      A C-major work with a contrasting C-minor section. In general a praise for the brave warrior.
      Vogler also composed *Der Fall der Mauren von Jericho* and *Seeschlacht*. [Cited in MGG, vol. 1, p. 1409].

Weber, Carl Maria von (1786-1826)

206. *Kampf und Sieg: Kantate zur Feier der Vernichtung des Feindes in Juny 1815 bei Bell-Alliance und Waterloo*, Op. 44. Cantata [1815]. #Berlin: Schlesingerschen Buchund Musikhandlung, 1815. *Urania UR 7126. Text by Johann Gottfried Wohlbrück.
      M1533.W373K3
      Weber's response to Napoleon's defeat at Waterloo. The work has thirteen sections, the last of which is to praise God. It includes a war choir in sections five and six and an instrumental

arrangement of "God Save the King." Weber took this work seriously and was upset when it was criticized, prompting him to write in defense of the work. See pages 60 to 61 for additional information.

Weber, Gottfried (1779-1839)

207. *Requiem den manen der sieger bei Leipzig und La Belle—Alliance geweiht.* Male chorus and orchestra. #Offenbach: M. André, 182-? M2010.W38 Op. 24
A setting of the five-movement ordinary of the mass with a brief, four-part chorale interspersed between each of the mass movements.

208. *Te Deum, Deutschlands siegreichen Heeren gewidmet,* Op. 18 in D minor. Chorus and Orchestra [1814]. #1815.
*MRDI NYPL
A large-scale Te Deum written to celebrate the defeat of Napoleon.

Winter, Peter von (1754-1825)

209. *Schlacht-Sinfonie.* Choral symphony [1813]. #*Peter von Winter,* ed. Donald McCorkle, Thor Johnson, and Donald G. Henderson in *The Symphony 1720-1840,* Series C, vol. 11 (New York: Garland, 1982).
M1530.W78S3P2
Dedicated to the Bavarian King Maximilian Joseph, a large-scale work in continuous movements written after the Germans defeated Napoleon in October 1813. See pages 57 to 58 for additional information.
Winter composed a companion work, *Germania.* Peace cantata [1815]. [Cited in MGG, vol. 14, pp. 714-20].

Great Britain

Dale, Joseph (1750-1821)

210. *The Siege of Valenciennes,* Op. 9. Piano or harpsichord with violin accompaniment [c. 1793]. #London: G. Dale, [n.d.].
Mus. Res. *MYK (NYPL call number)
A ten-page piece sectionalized with descriptive headings, including a B-flat major version of the "Lamentation of the

French." After a Rondo militaire, it closes with a four-part chorus singing "God Save the King" in B-flat major.

Dale's other battle works include *Admiral Duncan's Victory Over the Grand Dutch Fleet the 11th of October 1797*, Op. 13. Piano or harpsichord [c. 1797]. #London: Author. [RISM D757] and *Nelson and the Navy. A Sonata for Piano . . . in Commemoration of the Glorious 1st August, 1798* [c. 1798]. #London: Author. [RISM D763].

Gildon, John (19th c.)

211. *The Glorious Victory of Salamanca, on the Ever Memorable 22d of July 1812*. Piano with accompaniments for violin and cello [1812-1814]. #London: Goulding, D'Almaine, & Potter, c. 1813.
       M1.A1G
       *MYD Box (NYPL call number)
       "Composed and most gratefully inscribed to the most noble General the Marquis Wellington and his brave and gallant warriors." A fourteen-page work in B-flat major with bugle calls and quick steps. "The enemy commences the attack at Castrejon" uses broken octaves, sixteenth-note scales, and later cannon shots (low bass notes and chords). After "God Save the King" in E-flat major, "The Glorious News Arrives in England" begins with ascending thirty-second note scales celebrating the festivities.

Hook, James (1746-1827)

212. *The Battle of Salamanca: A Grand Martial Sonata*. Piano. #London: G. Walker, [n.d.].
       M23.A2H79
       In five sections, four of which are marches and one of which is "The Battle," full of cannon shots (low notes) and fast Alberti-bass patterns.

King, Matthew Peter (1773-1823)

213. *The Battle off Trafalgar: A Sonata for the piano forte descriptive of that glorious event and signal victory achieved by the revered Lord Viscount Nelson*. Piano. #London: Preston, [n.d.].
       M786.41.K53b
       In fourteen extended sections with descriptive titles, this work opens in C major with simple blocked and broken chords. It remains in major throughout and concludes with a stirring D-major

"Rule Brittannia." Some section titles include "The Fleet of Lord Nelson cruizing off Cadiz," "The Battle," "Lord Nelson Shot," "Sinking the Spanish Ship," and "Shouts of Victory."

214. *The Siege of Valenciennes.* Piano or harpsichord with violin accompaniment [c. 1794]. #London: Longman & Broderip, 1794? An arrangement for military band also exists: #London: Longman & Broderip [RISM K601].
    M221.K Case
    An eight-page piece in E-flat major. In the extended "Siege," low octaves are called "Bombs," descending sixteenth-note scales represent the "Fall of buildings," tremolos represent the "Horses advancing," and trills are used to show the "Town on fire." Concludes with a military rondo.

Mazzinghi, Joseph (1765-1844)

215. *Admiral Lord Nelson's Victory* or *The Battle of the Nile*, Op. 36. Piano sonata [1798]. #Philadelphia: G. Willig, 180-- or London: Goulding, Phipps, & D'Allmaine, 1799.
    M1.A1M
    "In commemoration of the glorious 1st of August 1798." An atypical battle piece because it has no descriptive headings. After a slow C-minor introduction, Mazzinghi writes four extended movements in different tempos and keys. The music relies heavily on broken-chord accompaniments and simple melodies.

Ogilvy, C. (19th c.)

216. *The Battle of Waterloo.* Piano and final chorus [c. 1818]. #Philadelphia: G. Willig, c. 1820.
    M1.A1O Case
    Composed and dedicated to the Duke of Wellington and arranged for the piano by G. Anderson. A simplistic, five-page piece in sections with descriptive headings. The Battle is an Allegro con spirito in G major with blocked chord accompaniment and arpeggios in the right hand. Includes a "Lamention [sic] for the slain" in G major and concludes with a four-part chorus singing "Britons strike home, revenge your Country's Wrongs" in C major.
    Later Anderson printed the work without crediting Ogilvy at all. See #Boston: Oliver Ditson, 186-? and *The American Collection of Vocal and Instrumental War Music* (New York &

Chicago: National Music, 1898), pp. 37-40. M25.A or M1.A13B Case.

Panormo, Ferdinand Charles (19th c.)

217. *Moscow or Buonaparte's Retreat*. Piano [c. 1814]. #London: G. Walker, c. 1814.
   *MYD Special Collections (NYPL call number)
   A seven-page work which opens with an air in A minor, followed by a dotted rhythmic "Alarm of the Russians." The battle rages with thirty-second note arpeggios in contrary motion. The "Crash of the Cremlin [sic]" is represented by two *fff* A-minor chords and concludes with "The Russians drive the French," remaining throughout in A minor.

Reeve, William (1757-1815)

218. *Battle Piece* from *Oscar and Malvina*. Piano. #London: Longman & Broderip, 17--, pp. 24-26.
   M1526.R Case
   The battle remains in D major (and almost exclusively diatonic) throughout its "Single Combat," "Skirmish of Foot Soldiers," "General Attack," "Groans of the Wounded," and "Retreat." The attack sections use fast, sixteenth-note repeated patterns and scales to create the battle-like effect.

Rimbault, Stephen Francis (1773-1837)

219. *The Battle of Navarino*. Piano [c. 1827]. #London: W. Hodsoll, [18--].
   M25.R
   Dedicated to the Admirals of the combined squadrons. A typical D-major battle piece, sectionalized, diatonic, with titles such as "Boat sails from the Dartmouth," "General attack," and "The pilot killed." Includes "Turkish" music and "Rule Britannia."

220. *The Hero of the Nile or Nelson Victorious*. A Song on that glorious event [c. 1798]. #London: T. Preston, 1798.
   M1741.R Case
   A four-stanza, strophic song in G major, almost completely diatonic throughout its two pages.

Weldon, Peter (19th c.)

221. *The Battle of Baylen, and the Surrender of General Dupont's Army to the Patriotic Spanish Army under the Command of Generals Castanos & Redding.* Piano with accompaniment for violin and bass [1808?]. #London: Goulding, Phipps, & D'Almaine, 1810?
    M1.A1W
    A typical sectionalized battle piece with descriptive titles in organization; the music is somewhat different, however, with more sixteenth-note scales passages and broken octaves. The score itself is most attractive, with an exquisite title page and a pictorial scene interspersed into the score showing people praying for the wounded after the trumpets of victory have sounded. See illustration no. 1.
    Weldon also composed *The Siege of Gerona.* Piano with violin and bass accompaniment [1810-1812]. See J. Bunker Clark, *The Dawning of American Keyboard Music* (New York & Westport, Conn.: Greenwood, 1988), pp. 242-43.

Italy

Pacini, Giovanni (1796-1867)

222. *Batille de St. Chaumont.* Piano and final chorus [c. 1815]. #Hamburg: J.A. Bohme, 1815-1820.
    JMG 74-598 (NYPL call number)
    A twenty-page, C-major work full of tremolos and subtitles. The "Battaille générale" moves to F minor with rolled chords, sixteenth-note arpeggios, scales, and tremolos. Before the final celebratory dances, the chorus sings the "Cantique des Parisiens" and the "Chant français national."

Raimondi, Ignazio (c. 1737-1813)

223. *The Battle.* Symphony adapted for piano with violin and cello accompaniments [1785]. #London: Printed by author, 1791.
    *MX (NYPL call number)
    A fifteen-page, eight-movement work. The sixth movement is a battaglia in D major with tremolo figures, Alberti bass, trills, scales patterns, alternating dynamics, and alternating syncopated chords; followed by a D-minor lament before ending with a D-major victory movement.

Salieri, Antonio (1750-1825)

224. *Der tyroler Landsturm.* Cantata. 1st: 23 May 1799.
      [No LC number available]
      Contains quotations from "La marseillaise" and Haydn's
      "Kaiser Hymn" and is in the patriotic French Revolution tradition.
      See Maynard Solomon, *Beethoven* (New York: Schirmer, 1977),
      p. 193.

Russia

Degtyaryov, Stepan A. (1788-1813)

225. *Minin and Pozharsky or The Liberation of Moscow.* Oratorio
      [1811]. #Moscow: Muzyka, 1986.
      M2007.D
      Called "the first Russian oratorio on a patriotic subject" (HO,
      p. 111). See C. Hughes, *The Origin of the First Russian Patriotic
      Oratorio: S.A. Degtiarev's "Minin i Pozharskii" (1811)* (Ph.D.
      dissertation: University of North Carolina, 1984).
      Degtyaryov also began *The Triumph of Russia or the Rout of
      Napoleon.* Incomplete oratorio [1812]. Cited in HO, p. 111.

SUPPLEMENT OF CLASSIC AND EARLY ROMANTIC WAR
MUSIC: 1750-1827

226. Abel, Frederick (1794-1820). America. *General Jackson's Triumph.*
      Piano duet [c. 1818].
227. Beauvarlet-Charpentier, Jacques Marie (1766-1834) France. *Bataille
      d'Austerlitz.* Piano and violin [c. 1806]. [RISM B1504].
228. _____. *Victoire de l'armée d'Italie, ou bataille de Montenotte.*
      Organ. #Paris: Auteur, chez les marchands de musique.-St.
      *Disques Pierre Verany PV.785032-33. [RISM B1506].
229. Berkenhead, John L. (fl. 1796). Great Britain. *Abolition of the
      Bastille.* Harpsichord.

230. Blewitt, Jonathan (1782-1853). Great Britain. *The Battle of Waterloo*. Piano sonata [1816-1818].
231. _____. *The Battle and Victory of Salamanca*. Piano sonata [1812].
232. Catel, Charles-Simon (1773-1830). France. *Hymne à la victorie sur la bataille de Fleurus*. Vocal [1794]. See NEW GROVE for a more complete listing of revolutionary works, vol. 4, pp. 7-8.
233. Cherubini, Luigi (1760-1842). Italy. *Lodoiska*. Opera. 1st: Paris, 1791. #"Early Romantic Opera," vol. 33 (New York: Garland, 1978). *Nuova 2236-7. Libretto by Claude François Fillette-Loraux. M1500.E270 1978 v. 33.
234. Clementi, Muzio (1752-1832). Italy. *La consolation*. Dedicated to the memory of Prince Louis Ferdinand, who fell at Saalfeld in 1806.
235. Corri, Natale (1765-1822). Great Britain?. *The Siege & Surrender of Valenciennes*. Piano or harpsichord, with violin accompaniment. #Edinburgh: Corri. M221.C Case.
236. Delaval, Mme. (18th c.). France. *Les adieux de l'infortune Louis XVI à son peuple*. Cantata [1794].
237. Donizetti, Gaetano (1797-1848). Italy. *Il capitan battaglia* in E-flat major. Piano duet [1819]. #Roma: Boccaccini and Spada, 1983. M202.D66C3 1983.
238. Dourlen, Victor-Charle-Paul (1780-1864). France. *Bataille de Jena*. Piano [1807].
239. _____. *Bataille de Marengo, sonate militaire*. Piano [1801]. M1.A1 M98 Case.
240. Farina, Edoardo (19th c.). Italy? *Sonata per orchestra detta "La battaglia."* Orchestra. #Milan: Casa musicale Sonzogne, 1964. *MTO (NYPL call number). A nine-minute work in three movements. Opens with fanfares, moves to double-dotted rhythms before turning into a march with three-note bass clusters.
241. Janiewicz, Feliks (1762-1848). Poland. *The Battle of Deine* [c. 1805]. Formerly called *The Birthday of Freedom*.
242. Kambra, Karl (19th c.). Germany. *The Battle of Trafalgar*. Piano sonata [c. 1808]. Case Newberry Library, Chicago SA 21.
243. _____. *The Siege of Valenciennes*. Piano [c. 1793]. #New York: G. Gilfert. [RISM K61].
244. Laroque, Philip (19th c.). America. *Battle of the Memorable 8th of January 1815*. Piano [1815]. "Most respectfully dedicated by him to the fair sex of America." M1.A1L.
245. Le Sueur, Jean François (1760-1837). France. *Scène patriotique*. Chorus [1794]. M380.14 (Boston Public Library). See NEW GROVE for other compositions that Le Sueur wrote dealing with the French Revolution, vol. 10, pp. 694-97.

246. Lyon, James (1735-1794). America. *The Military Glory of Great Britain*. "An entertainment given by the late candidates for Bachelor's Degree at the close of the anniversary commencement held in Nassau-Hall, New Jersey, September 29th, 1762" [1762]. #Philadelphia: William Bradford, 1762. Music attributed to James Lyon and the text to Rev. Samuel Davies. AC901 .H3 vol. 22, no. 4.

247. Messemaeckers, Hendrik (19th c.). France? *Bataille de Belle Alliance*. Piano. M25.M. An elaborate twenty-three page battle composition with all the usual subtitles (given in French). Deals with Wellington leading his troops at the Battle of Waterloo and uses minor keys to show the suffering of the wounded. Includes "Rule Britannia."

248. Munro, John (19th c.). The Netherlands? *The Battle of Vittoria: A Characteristic Sonata*. Piano [c. 1815]. #Amsterdam: H.C. Steup, 181-. M23.M72.B3 Case. A thirteen-page, highly sectionalized battle piece with the usual descriptive titles.

249. Richmond, T.R. (19th c.). England. *Huzza! Brother Britons, Rejoice, Sing, and Dance. Admiral Nelson's Glorious Victory Over the French, August 1st, 1798*. #London: G. Goulding, [1798?]. G.425 pp (18) (British Library).

250. Simrock, Heinrich (b. 1760?). Germany. *The Battle of Wagram*. Piano [1810].

251. Smith, John Stafford (1750-1836). Great Britain. *The Battle of the Wabash*. A patriotic song [c. 1812]. #Philadelphia: G.E. Blake, 1812? Text by Joseph Hutton, set to "Anacreon in Heaven" (or "The Star Spangled Banner"). M1630.3.S76B2 1812? Case. Celebrates the Battle of Tippecanoe.

252. Spohr, Louis (1784-1859). Germany. *Das befreite Deutschland*. Cantata [1814]. #Cassel?, 181-?. Text by C. Pilcher. M243.29 (Boston Public Library call number).

253. Spontini, Gaspare (1774-1851). Italy. *Ferdinand Cortez*. Opera [1809]. #"Early Romantic Opera," vol. 43 (New York: Garland, 1980). M1500.S76F22 1969 Case.

254. Voight, Augustus. *The Battle of Trafalgar*. Voice and piano [180-]. #London: Purday & Button, 180-. Text by E. Button. OCLC 17708533. "A grand lyrical tribute to the memory of the immortal Nelson."

255. Wölfl, Joseph (1773-1812). Austria. *Combat naval*. Piano. [Cited in MGG, vol. 1, p. 1409].

256. Würfel, Vaclav Wilhelm (1790-1832). Bohemia. *Belle—Alliance*. Piano. [Cited in MGG, vol. 1, p. 1409].

NOTES

1. In particular, Mozart's Piano Concerto, K. 467 and Beethoven's Piano Concerto No. 5 ("Emperor")—two peaks in the history of the military concertos. See Boris Schwarz, "Beethoven and the French Violin School," *Musical Quarterly* (1958), pp. 431-47.

2. David Charlton, "Revolutionary Hymn," NEW GROVE, vol. 15, p. 777.

3. Frederick Niecks, *Programme Music in the Last Four Centuries* (New York: Haskell House, 1969), p. 104.

4. Carl Dahlhaus, *Nineteenth Century Music*, trans. J. Bradford Robinson (Berkeley and Los Angeles: University of California Press, 1989), pp. 311-20.

5. As was customary for Beethoven's symphonic works, arrangements were made for piano trio and string quartet as well.

6. Arthur Loesser, *Men, Women & Pianos: A Social History* (New York: Simon & Schuster, 1954), pp. 167-68.

7. Rosamond Harding, *The Piano-Forte: Its History Traced to the Great Exhibition of 1851*, 2nd ed. (Cambridge: Cambridge University Press, 1978), p. 118.

8. Henry Bollman, "Query on 'Prague,'" *Saturday Review* 44 (29 April 1961), pp. 54-55.

9. Cited in Bollman, "Query on 'Prague,'" p. 55.

10. Headings taken from score in *Recent Researches in American Music* 7 (Madison: A-R Editions, 1980), pp. 88ff.

11. Some performance programs only listed twenty-one major sections with smaller sections grouped together.

12. Ursula Goetze, *Johann Friedrich Klöffler* (Dissertation: Westfalischen Wilhelms-Universität zu Munster, 1965), p. 116. ["Die Versammlung äusserte so viel Vergnügen, als der höchste Grad der Wonne und Zufriedenheit zu verursachen fähig ist, und kehrte ungemein geruhrt von dieser Abendunterhaltung nach Hause."]

13. Milan Poštolka, "Paul Wranitzky," NEW GROVE, vol. 20, p. 539.

14. Maynard Solomon, "Beethoven and Bonaparte," *Music Review* 29 (1968), pp. 96-105; Claude V. Palisca, "French Revolutionary Models for Beethoven's *Eroica* Funeral March," *Music and Context: Essays for John M. Ward*, ed. Anne Dhu Shapiro (Cambridge, Mass.: Department of Music, Harvard University, 1985), pp. 198-209.

15. George Grove, *Beethoven and His Nine Symphonies*, 3rd. ed. (London: Novello & Ewer, 1898), reprint (New York: Dover, 1962), p. 54.

16. Charles Rosen, *The Classical Style: Haydn, Mozart, Beethoven* (New York: W.W. Norton, 1972), p. 401.

17. John Warrack, ed., *Carl Maria von Weber: Writings on Music*, trans. Martin Cooper (Cambridge: Cambridge University Press, 1981), p. 174.

18. Paul Mies, "Beethoven's Orchestral Works," in *The New Oxford History Of Music*, vol. 8 (London: Oxford University Press, 1982), p. 149.

19. *Allgemeine musikalische Zeitung* (April 1814), p. 291. ["Hrn. v. Beetho.s Composition scheint uns dessen ungeachtet nur eine gelegentliche Arbeit, auf welche er wenig Fleiss verwended hat. Ohne sonderliche Vorbereitung fängt er sogleich mit der Kanonade an, und schildert nun das Materielle einer Schlacht, indess unser Winter, in der im vorigen Berichte erwahnten Composition, mit vielem Vorbedacht die Sache einleitet, den Zuhörer für sich gewinnt, und mehr dessen Geist anspricht."]

20. *Allgemeine musikalische Zeitung* (January 1814), p. 76. ["Lautes Freudengeschrey erhob sich von allen Seiten des Saales, begleitete lange die feurige Musik, die immer im Triumphgesange fortströmte, und verlohr sich erst, nachdem die Töne schon lange geschwiegen hatten. Es war ein Augenblick, der alle Anwesende mit Begeisterung und froher Ahnung erfüllte. . . . Ihm ist dieser Abend ein schöner Lohn für so Vieles, dass er während eines langen Künstlerlebens verständig begonnen, und immer geschickt vollbracht hat. Mit gerechtem Stolze darf er auf das, was er geleistet, zurücksehen: denn immer wird sein Name in den Annalen der Tonkunst aufgezeichnet bleiben."]

21. *The Symphony 1720-1840: Peter von Winter*, ed. Donald McCorkle, Thor Johnson, and Donald G. Henderson, Series C, vol. 11 (New York: Garland, 1982), p. xxviii.

22. Charlton, vol. 15, p. 777.

23. Cornwell B. Rogers, *The Spirit of Revolution in 1789* (Princeton: Princeton University Press, 1949), pp. 5-6.

24. Winton Dean, "French Opera," in *The New Oxford History of Music*, vol. 8 (London: Oxford University Press, 1982), p. 28.

25. Dean, p. 28.

26. Anthony Lewis, "Choral Music," in *The New Oxford History of Music*, vol. 8 (London: Oxford University Press, 1982), p. 657.

27. H.C. Robbins Landon, *Haydn: The Years of 'The Creation' 1796-1800* (Bloomington: Indiana University Press, 1977), p. 174.

28. Robbins Landon, p. 175.

29. See Maynard Solomon, *Beethoven* (New York: G. Schirmer, 1977), pp. 222-26.

30. Solomon, *Beethoven*, p. 222.

31. Warrack, p. 161.

IV. WAR MUSIC OF THE ROMANTIC PERIOD: 1828-1900

War-related music remained a steady enterprise for many composers during the nineteenth century, a century that includes the Opium Wars (1839-1842, 1856-1858), the Mexican War (1846-1848), the European revolutions of 1848, the Crimean War (1853-1856), the American Civil War (1861-1865), the Franco-Prussian War (1870-1871), the Spanish-American War (1898), and several other smaller wars and revolutions. Largely because of the type and length of wars fought in Europe between 1848 and 1900, however, composers wrote fewer war-related compositions that dealt with contemporary wars. Often these wars were of short duration or were colonial wars; in both circumstances, the public was not involved sufficiently to sustain the fervent patriotic feelings for an extended time that might later be expressed in art. Consequently, the war-related music changed significantly on the continent.

European composers turned from contemporary wars to historical subjects for their musical descriptions of battle. Franz Liszt's *Hunnenschlacht* (1857) depicted the battle in the Catalaunian Fields between the Huns and the Christians in 451. In 1846 Edouard Gregoir wrote a historical symphony about the Crusades. Bedřich Smetana composed several symphonic poems dealing with the Hussite wars in the fifteenth century. Numerous battle scenes appeared in war-related operas dealing with earlier eras: Wagner's *Rienzi* (1840) is set in fourteenth-century Rome; Verdi's *I Lombardi* (1843) takes place in 1096-1097, *Alzira* (1845) in the sixteenth century, *Jérusalem* (1847), a revision of *I Lombardi*, between 1095-1099, and *La battaglia de Legnano* in 1176; and Tchaikovsky's *Mazeppa* (1883) takes place during the seventeenth century. Tchaikovsky and Berlioz composed symphonic works in honor of past battles and revolutions that took place earlier in the nineteenth century.

Significant changes in battle music, however, occurred in this century. Liszt elevated the battle genre in his novel "battle" work *Hunnenschlacht* (no. 306). In this symphonic poem, Liszt depicts a battle that is more psychological than realistic. The work, based upon a fresco by Wilhelm von Kaulbach, presents survivors of the great battle who envision it continuing between the souls of the slain in the heavens. Liszt had heard Kaulbach discuss the symbolism of the fresco in which Attila the Hun and the Christian Theodoric represented two principles, "barbarism and civilization, the past and the future of humanity."[1]

After listening to Kaulbach and carefully studying the painting, Liszt decided to represent musically the story depicted in the fresco using two distinct motives to symbolize the Huns and the Christians. He described how he envisioned the work (referring to himself as "the musician"):

> The musician thought that he heard in the midst of a sanguinary fight the cries of the combatants, the clash of arms, the wails of the wounded, the imprecations of the conquered, the groans of the dying, mingling in a terrible chorus, while at the same time as if coming from a distance he recognized the accents of a prayer, the sacred hymn, mounting to heaven from the depths of the cloister, whose silence it alone breaks. The more deafening the tumult of the battle became, the more this hymn increased in force and power. The two motives, gradually approaching each other, finish by uniting; pressing upon each other they contend in a hand-to-hand combat, like two giants, till the one which is identified with divine truth, universal charity, the progress of humanity, and the hope of the world, is victorious and sheds over all things a radiant, transfiguring, and eternal light.[2]

Liszt requires no roaring cannons, national airs, or slashing swords. Rather he creates the aura of battle without resorting to these stock devices that have been used for centuries. In the first part, depicting the battle itself, Liszt uses a tempetuoso tempo and syncopated rhythms, predominantly in the minor tonalities of C and F-sharp. The composition opens with dark, foreboding colors and grows into a frenzied battle. At measure 77, the theme of the barbarous Huns is introduced in the low strings and bassoons. At measure 98, "Crux fidelis," the chorale which Liszt uses to represent the Christians, follows softly in the trumpets. The theme of the Huns prevails throughout the battle scene. At the Maestoso assai, the theme of the Huns roars triple *forte* in the brass instruments, followed immediately by "Crux fidelis" performed softly on the organ (Example 7).

Example 7: Liszt, *Hunnenschlacht*:

This exchange takes place two more times before a new E-flat major theme modeled on "Crux fidelis" enters at measure 312 in the strings and winds. By measure 352 Liszt has arrived at the key of C major, and it is clear the Christians will be victorious even though both themes continue to be used. "Crux fidelis" again asserts itself and runs unopposed for the last twenty bars of the symphonic poem.

Liszt also composed the symphonic poem *Héroïde funèbre* (no. 304), a grand funeral march representing the heroes lost in battle. Part of this work was based on Liszt's earlier five movement *Revolutionary Symphony*, which was sketched in 1830 but never completed. Later, during the European uprisings of 1848, Liszt again turned to this symphony, but only completed *Héroïde funèbre*, the first movement of the projected five. Liszt's most important work to come out of the 1848 and 1849 revolutions was his *Funérailles* (no. 303). This work, among his best compositions, is a powerful lament and a heroic tribute expressed with powerful tolling bells and triumphal energy, far different from war-related piano compositions during the time of Napoleon.

Liszt's friend and contemporary Hector Berlioz also contributed significantly to the genre of war-related music. In addition to his youthful cantata for chorus and orchestra *La révolution grecque* (1825-1826) and his war song for chorus and piano *Chant guerrier* (1829), he arranged "La marseillaise" for double chorus and full orchestra in 1830. The French government commissioned his major war-related composition *Grande symphonie funèbre et triomphale* (1840) (no. 288) to commemorate the tenth anniversary of the 1830 revolution. In his memoirs, Berlioz explained his conception of the work.

> I thought that the simplest plan would be best for such a work,
> and that a large body of wind instruments would alone be

suitable for a symphony which was at least on the first
occasion to be heard in the open air. I wished in the first place
to recall the famous Three Days' Conflict amid the mournful
accents of a solemn march accompanying the procession; to
follow this by a sort of funeral oration, or farewell address to
the illustrious dead . . . and finally to sing a hymn of praise
as an apotheosis.[3]

In addition to these specific war-related works, Berlioz also included
scenes of battle, victory, and lament in his opera *Les Troyens* (no. 289).
The opera opens triumphantly in C major with the Trojans celebrating
the departure of the Greeks who seem to have finally abandoned their
siege. Later in the first act, while Aeneas sleeps, the music portrays the
sounds of distant fighting with moaning woodwinds and strings and
occasional trumpet blasts as the Greeks conquer and burn the city of Troy.
Les Troyens also includes two laments over the fall of Troy: Cassandra's
impassioned prophecy in the first act, and the orchestral prelude which
begins the second part (*Les Troyens à Carthage*). To represent the defeat
of the Trojans, Berlioz transforms his famous Trojan march into B-flat
minor, which he calls "le mode triste." (The key of B-flat minor plays a
prominent role in twentieth-century compositions dealing with the theme
of the tragedies of war, particularly in lament compositions.) When
Berlioz brings back the Trojan march in the fourth and concluding act as
Aeneas is leaving Carthage, he again presents the march in B-flat major,
"le mode triomphal."
    Battle music, victory scenes, and laments for the dead continued to
appear in operas during the nineteenth century. Acts IV and V of
Meyerbeer's *Les Huguenots* (no. 291) include the massacre of the
Huguenots. The short massacre scene includes biting, propelling rhythms
in the brass accompanied by sounds of gunfire and a female chorus
singing the protestant hymn "Ein' feste Burg."
    The two great opera composers and political revolutionaries,
Giuseppe Verdi and Richard Wagner, each contributed significant battle
scenes. Although Wagner only composed one extended battle scene in
Rienzi (no. 300), his first operatic success, Verdi composed numerous
political operas that included patriotic choruses and scenes of battle. Their
political involvement in contemporary events, however, differed greatly.
Verdi confined himself to being engaged through his music. Wagner, on
the other hand, actively participated in political and revolutionary events.
    The battle music in the various sections of Wagner's *Rienzi* (1840)
is in major keys. The war dance in the ballet scene from Act II, which
begins in F major, employs a duple meter with a tempo marking of
Allegro vivace. Rapid scales, dotted rhythms, and the repeated pattern in

trumpet fanfares are all frequently used. Although the war dance appears in 6/8 meter and with various repeated triplet patterns, it remains in a major key (usually D, C, or F). In the action of the opera, the battle hymn Rienzi sings, "Sancto Spiritus," is in B major (Allegro maestoso e energico). It, too, employs a duple meter and trumpet fanfares. Wagner treats the actual battle in the opera offstage, as did Spohr in his use of an offstage invasion march in *The Fall of Babylon* (no. 297). Strands of "Sancto Spiritus" harmonized under a diminished chord and trumpet fanfares periodically interrupt the solemn prayer that is being sung on stage. The victory scene following the battle is in the key of E-flat major.

Verdi wrote numerous operatic battle pieces, chiefly in his earlier "revolutionary era" operas; however, as Julian Budden pointed out, "battles do not show Verdi at his best."[4] Battle music and victory hymns appear in *Lombardi, Giovanna d'Arco, Macbeth, Jérusalem, Il corsaro, La battaglia di Legnano,* and *La forza del destino.*

One of Verdi's earliest and largest battle scenes (lasting nearly 200 measures) is fought between the crusading Lombards and the Musulmans in Act IV of *I Lombardi* (no. 313). At the Allegro vivace (rehearsal no. 17) full orchestra and chorus enter with repeated F-minor chords to the text "Guerra. Guerra. S'impugni la spada." At rehearsal no. 18 Verdi modulates to the relative major, the key for the principal portion of the battle scene. Repeated notes, dotted rhythms, static harmonies, and triadic outlines are used in a fast, duple meter. Budden suggests that Verdi modeled his battle scene on Beethoven's *Wellington's Victory* "with the two opposing forces represented not by anthems but by two melodies which we have already heard them sing. . . . To make the distinction even clearer the Christians have the orchestra while the enemy have to make do with the banda."[5] Near the end of the battle scene, over C pedals, the interval of a minor second played by the banda appears in the melody signifying the defeat of the Musulmans. At this point in the score, Verdi has written "lamentevole," and the music remains at a soft dynamic level for the remainder of the scene. The victory hymn, which concludes the opera, is a C-major Adagio in duple meter ending *fortissimo* with the sopranos singing high Cs. When Verdi later revised the opera as *Jérusalem* (no. 312), he included the same battle interlude as in the original *I Lombardi*. He did, however, omit the two melodies that appeared in the original and did not use the banda to represent the enemy.

Verdi's most unusual battle scene is found in the second version of *Macbeth* (no. 314). It begins *pianississimo* with rapid sixteenth notes over a syncopated E-diminished chord. Soon it leads into triadic patterns in G major with the traditional battle rhythm of an eighth followed by two sixteenths and two eighths. Trumpet fanfares announce the battle proper, and imitative orchestral writing follows to depict the chaos of the battle. Although it begins in C major, it remains highly chromatic and shifts through various key centers. This battle music, near the closing moments of the opera, leads directly into a grand victory hymn replete with double-dotted rhythms, a fast tempo, and a *fortissimo* ending in A major.

The most effective battle music Verdi wrote appears in *La forza del destino* (no. 310). Unlike the previous Verdi examples, which appeared near the end of their operas, the battaglia in *La forza* appears about midway through the opera. Dialogue and action are continuous throughout the concise scene, and the orchestra plays only forty measures without some dialogue interrupting the instrumental battle. Beginning with the customary fanfares in the brass instruments, the music soon leads to a driving rhythmic figure. Harmonically this section is more ambiguous than earlier battle pieces, wavering between F minor and A-flat major. The battle is quickly over, the dynamic level drops to *piano*, and the fast, repeated sixteenth notes cease. Alvaro is carried in unconscious and the battle music is no longer heard.

Both Tchaikovsky's *Mazeppa* (no. 317) and Rimsky-Korsakov's *Legend of the Invisible City of Kitezh* (no. 434) include extended instrumental battle pieces. Like those of Wagner and Verdi, the Russian operatic battle pieces contain fast tempos, repeated notes and rhythms, and a *fortissimo* dynamic level. Rimsky-Korsakov and Tchaikovsky, however, both begin with triple meter and slip into minor keys more frequently than Wagner or Verdi. Rimsky-Korsakov's scene remains throughout in 3/4, although Tchaikovsky's changes into 4/4 beginning with the Allegro giusto, marziale. Tchaikovsky also uses a band to play "against" his orchestra in the same manner as Verdi in *I Lombardi*. Rimsky-Korsakov uses two different themes to illustrate the opposing forces. Both of these works are exciting, brilliantly orchestrated battle pieces.

To Tchaikovsky goes the distinction of writing the most famous, and possibly the most notorious, battle pieces ever composed: the *1812 Overture* (1882) (no. 316). The American public has wholeheartedly endorsed this work for festive celebrations, particularly on the Fourth of July. Nonetheless, the composition has received extraordinarily harsh criticism. Ralph Wood proclaimed that "*1812* must be one of the most dreary and repulsive works in the whole of music."[6] Tchaikovsky himself wrote that his overture would be "very noisy. I wrote it without much warmth of enthusiasm; therefore it has no great artistic value."[7]

Several Czech composers also created war-related compositions. The subject of Šárka, a legendary maiden who leads a mass slaughter of the male population because her lover was unfaithful to her, appeared in Zdeněk Fibich's opera *Šárka* (1896-1897) (no. 284) and Smetana's symphonic poem of the same name (no. 286). In his ambitious cycle of symphonic poems *Má vlast*, Smetana also wrote battle scenes in *Vysehrad*, *Tábor*, and *Blaník*. The Hussite warrior song "Ye who are God's warriors," which Karel Husa later used in his *Music for Prague 1968* in 1968, forms the main theme of *Tábor* (no. 287) and also appears in *Blaník* (no. 285).

In the United States, however, war-related music was quite different. The art tradition was not as firmly established as in Europe, and consequently composers looked back to the earlier forms of war-related music and produced music of limited significance. Furthermore, during the middle of the century, Americans fought in two major wars, the Mexican War and the American Civil War. Both of these wars involved the public to an unprecedented degree, and composers turned out numerous keyboard battle compositions as well as popular war songs in response.

During the Mexican War, keyboard battle pieces were kept alive with works depicting specific battles from the war. Charles Grobe wrote compositions entitled *The Battle of Buena Vista* (no. 271) and *The Battle of Palo Alto and Resaca de La Palma* (no. 272), and Francis Buck the elaborately titled *Fall of Vera Cruz and the Surrender of the City and Castle of St. Juan de Ulúa to the American forces under Major Gen'l Scott 29 March 1847* (no. 264). John Schell, William Cumming, and W. Striby also contributed battle pieces about the Mexican War, but all of these pieces were remarkably similar to the previous battle pieces in their use of descriptive headings, tremolos, dotted figures, and arrangements of popular songs.

THE AMERICAN CIVIL WAR

During the Civil War similar battle pieces proliferated as well. Susan Strother, Hermann Schreiner, Laura Hatch, and James Beckel wrote typical battle works. Charles Grobe composed a series of war works known as *Pictures of the War* (see no. 274), and Thomas Bethune, the black pianist better known as "Blind Tom," contributed his popular *Battle of Manassas* (1866) to the Civil War keyboard repertoire. *Battle of Manassas* (no. 261) makes extensive use of tone clusters in the bass to simulate the cannon fire, while "Yankee Doodle" and "The Star Spangled Banner" are heard above the roar of the artillery. Bethune also requires the performer to whistle in one section in order to depict the whistle of a train carrying supplies and soldiers. In actual performance the work becomes a humorous parody of war. From this piece one could imagine that war was a glorious, delightful event. Nothing could be further from the seriousness and tragedy of the American Civil War than this light-hearted crowd pleaser.

Louis Moreau Gottschalk used similar means to appeal to the patriotism of his audience and to achieve tremendous popularity, but at a step above the typical battle music of the time. During the Civil War, he often performed his famous battle composition, *L'Union* (no. 270), to great acclaim. In Philadelphia, he wrote, "I have played *The Union*. Unheard-of enthusiasm. Circumstances gave it a real interest, which has been the pretext for a noisy and patriotic demonstration by the audience. Recalls, encores, hurrahs, etc!"[8] In *L'Union* Gottschalk uses rapid, interlocking octaves on the lower bass notes to create the "roar" of cannon fire, not just a "boom" created by taking the flat of a hand to blast out a tone cluster (Example 8). Before combining "Yankee Doodle" and "Hail Columbia," he writes a section featuring a rapid five-note scale which supposedly imitates a five stroke drum roll.

Example 8: Gottschalk, *L'Union*:

Gottschalk was quite flexible in "nationalizing" his compositions. In Spain he was nearly responsible for creating riots by his performance of *El sitio de Zaragoza* (*The Siege of Saragossa*), which included famous patriotic tunes of the Spanish. He called the work a symphony for ten pianos. It was replete with popular Spanish tunes, drum rolls, and cannon fire—a typical battle piece with considerably larger forces. Returning to America, he replaced the Spanish national airs with patriotic American tunes and labeled the work a *Grand National Symphony for Ten Pianos*: *Bunker Hill*.

After the Civil War, a former Union Army bandmaster, Patrick Gilmore, staged a couple of supercolossal musical events. In the city square of New Orleans, he led a concert that included "5,000 voices, 500 bandsmen and a trumpet and drum military corps. 'Hail Columbia' was sung, accompanied by a battery of cannon firing on each beat of the drums and [by] the ringing of church bells in the vicinity."[9] In Boston in 1869, he organized the National Peace Jubilee which required a thousand-member orchestra and a chorus of ten thousand. Three years later, in 1872, he expanded the concept from the "National" Peace Jubilee to the "World's" Peace Jubilee and accordingly enlarged his musical forces to include a two-thousand-member orchestra and a chorus of twenty thousand.

The Civil War changed the way Americans looked at war. What started as just another war concluded as the greatest bloodbath in American history. The photographs of Matthew Brady and the poems of Walt Whitman, who served as a nurse during the war, captured the horrors of "battle's reality." In addition to Whitman, the Civil War produced two other poets and writers of "war" literature, Herman Melville and Stephen Crane; however, with the exception of Gottschalk's piano music and the songs of Henry Clay Work, little important war-related music came from the war. Composers in the twentieth century often set Whitman's anti-war poetry to music, but few did so in the nineteenth century. Nevertheless, the battle compositions of Gottschalk and Bethune were some of the last representatives of an exhausted genre of music. Only a small number of composers continued writing battle pieces in the last three decades of the nineteenth century, and the few who did were Americans writing about the Spanish-American War. George Schleiffarth's *Battle of Manila* (1898) (no. 277) and J.L. Baker's *The Battle of Manila* (c. 1902) (no. 411), with their quotes of "Yankee Doodle" yet again, were the last piano battle suites to be written for a contemporary battle.

The music of the Spanish-American War still largely reflected the traditional nineteenth-century war compositions. R. Kelso Carter wrote a victory hymn entitled *The Battle of Manila* (no. 265), and Walter Damrosch, the great German-born conductor, wrote an inspired *Manila Te Deum* (no. 266), praising God for Admiral Dewey's great victory at Manila. Nonetheless, change was in the air and was anticipated by the tearful popular songs of the war such as "Just Break the News to Mother" and "Good-bye, Dolly Gray."

ANNOTATED LISTING OF ROMANTIC WAR MUSIC:
1828-1900

America (United States)

Anderson, G. (19th c.)

257. *Battle of Waterloo*. Piano and chorus. Composed and dedicated to
the Duke of Wellington. See item 216.

Barker, James Nelson (1784-1858)

258. *The Battle of New Orleans*. "Sung on the 8th of January at the
Democratic Festival." Voice and piano [c. 1829]. #Philadelphia:
G.E. Blake, 1829.
   M1.A13C no. 11
   A twenty-measure, C-major strophic song in nine verses, full
of dotted rhythms. One part of the stanza reads: "They fly, see they
fly—O the triumph is glorious/ Our Orleans is rescued—our
Jackson victorious."

Beckel, James Cox (1811-?)

259. *The Battle of Gettysburg*. Piano [c. 1863]. #Boston: Oliver
Ditson, 1891.
   M786.4.B394b 1891
   A typical C-major battle piece, highly sectionalized with texts
describing each section. Some examples include "Attack on the
First and Eleventh Corps, and fall of Gen'l Reynolds," "Gen'l
Reynolds's killed," "Tremendous firing of the Rebel's, answered by
the Union forces," "Grand combined attack of the whole Army
under Gen'l Meade," and "The Rebel's Retreat, flying to all
quarters." Numerous fanfares, scales, and dotted rhythmic patterns
are used, as are the tunes "Yankee Doodle" and "The Star Spangled
Banner."
   Beckel also composed similar works: *Battles of Chattanooga,
Lookout Mountain, and Mission Ridge. November 23rd, 24th, and
25th 1863*. Piano [c. 1863]. #Philadelphia: M.D. Swisher, 1886.
M25.B; and *Major Gen. Geo. E. Pickett's Charge at the Battle of*

Gettysburg, July 3, '63. Piano [c. 1888]. #Philadelphia: James C. Beckel, 1888. M25.B.

260.   *Dead on the Battlefield.* Chorus and piano [c. 1862]. #New York: S.T. Gordon, 1862. Text by M.L. Hoffard.
         M1640.B
         A three-page, B-flat major, heroic lament (Andantino impassionate) in three verses, with the chorus singing of the "bravest of the brave."

Bethune, Thomas [Blind Tom] (1849-1908)

261.   *Battle of Manassas.* Piano [1866]. #Chicago: Root & Cady, 1866. M20.C58B
         A typical battle piece with titles every few measures, drum rolls, cannon-shot clusters (with the flats of both hands), sounds of trains (pianist must "choo choo" and whistle) and "Dixie," "The Star Spangled Banner," "Yankee Doodle," and "La marseillais." Went through numerous editions after its 1866 publication.

Browne, Augusta (? -1858)

262.   *The Warlike Dead in Mexico.* Voice and piano [1848]. #New York: C. Holt, Jr., 1848. Text by Mrs. Balmanno.
         Am. 2-V (NYPL call number)
         A three-part lament (Largo) moving from G minor to B-flat major; written for those killed in action.

Brown, Francis H.Q. (1818-1891)

263.   *The Battle: Descriptive Fantasie* [c. 1862]. #Boston: B. Oliver Ditson, 1862.
         [OCLC 18195010]
         A thirteen-page battle piece in five sections entitled "The Tented Field," "Night Before Battle," "The Soldier's Dream," "Morning: The March," and "The Attack and Battle."

Buck, Francis (19th c.)

264.   *Fall of Vera Cruz and Surrender of the City and Castle of St. Juan D'Ulúa to the American Forces under Major Gen'l Scott 29 March 1847.* Piano [1847]. #Baltimore: Frederick D. Benteen, 1847.
         Drexel 5535 (NYPL call number)

"A descriptive piece composed and respectfully dedicated to the Officers and Men of the U.S. Army and Navy engaged in that Glorious Achievement." In D major, a highly descriptive work with Alberti basses and tremolos, including a funeral march, a storm, cries of the wounded, and concluding with the American army taking possession of the castle.

Carter, R. Kelso (1849-1928)

265. *The Battle of Manila.* Voice and piano [1898]. #Baltimore: R. Kelso Carter, 1898.
     M1644.C
     Dedicated to Admiral Dewey and his men, this is nothing more than a one-page hymn in A-flat major glorifying war and victory.

Damrosch, Walter (1862-1950) [German-born]

266. *Manila Te Deum.* Solo quartet, chorus, and orchestra [1898]. #Cincinnati: J. Church, 1898.
     M2023.D166
     "Composed in honor of the victory won by the American navy under Admiral Dewey at Manila Bay, May 1st 1898." Dedicated "to the sailors and soldiers of the United Sates of America," this is a large-scale work in five movements praising God after the victory won at Manila.

Gottschalk, Louis (1829-1869)

267. *Bataille,* Op. 64 (*Etude de concert*). Piano [c. 1869]. #*The Piano Works of Louis Moreau Gottschalk,* ed. Vera Brodsky Lawrence (New York: Arno Press & the New York Times, 1949), vol. 1, pp. 145-58.
     M22.G687L4
     In two sections (Andante and Allegro marziale), this E-flat major work uses repeated notes and rhythms, heavy chordal textures, and builds to a *fff* "con tutta la forza" extravaganza.

268. *Chant du guerre,* Op. 78. Piano [1857]. #*The Piano Works of Louis Moreau Gottschalk,* vol. 1, pp. 249-62.
     M22.G687L4
     Opens *fff* with octaves in each hand and requires brilliant chromatic octaves, dangerous left-hand leaps, and considerable

endurance as Gottschalk conjures up the energy and recklessness of war.

269. *Chant du soldat: grande caprice de concert*, Op. 23. Piano [1857].
    #*The Piano Works of Louis Moreau Gottschalk*, vol. 2, pp. 1-20.
    M22.G687L4
    In addition to the lyrical, tender "con amore" sections, Gottschalk pulls out the stops in the "Marziale" sections with dotted rhythms, octave tremolos, and brilliant octaves.

270. *L'Union*, Op. 48. Piano [1862]. *Smithsonian Collection ND-033 and Angel S36077, 36090. #*The Piano Works of Louis Moreau Gottschalk*, vol. 5, pp. 265-82. Samuel Adler also made an arrangement for piano and orchestra: #New York: Schirmer, 1972.
    M22.G687L4
    The most virtuosic of Gottschalk's battle compositions, it includes a brilliant cadenza and a dramatic version of "The Star Spangled Banner" in F-sharp major. See page 96 for additional information.
    Gottschalk also wrote *La bataille de Carabova* [1859], a triumphal march for José Antonio Paez, *El sitio de Zaragoza* (*The Siege of Saragossa*) for ten pianos [1851], and *Grand National Symphony: Bunker Hill*, a revision of *El sitio de Zaragoza* [1853-1854].

Grobe, Charles (1817-1880)

271. *The Battle of Buena Vista*, Op. 101. Piano [1847]. #Baltimore: G. Willig Jr., 1847.
    M1.A13G Case
    "Composed and most respectfully inscribed to Genl. Z. Taylor, the hero who never lost a battle." A thirteen-page battle composition with tremolos in the F-major battle scene. Words are used throughout and are highly descriptive, e.g., "Gen. Taylor apprized [sic] of the Mexican approach, breaks up his camp at Agua Nueva and takes post in a strong position at Buena Vista." After a C-minor "Burial of the Dead," Grobe closes with a grandiose and pompous finale.

272. *The Battle of Palo Alto and Resaca de la Palma*, Op. 72. Piano [1846]. #Baltimore: F.D. Benteen, 1846.
    Am 2-I (NYPL call number)

Dedicated "as a tribute of respect to the officers and men of the U.S. Army." A seven-page work in C major recounting the battle, blow by blow, giving times of day and cannon shots fired (five-note descending figures thumping on a long, low great C). Night-time scene changes to A-flat major, and the Victory March concludes in G major with "Yankee Doodle." The title page is a beautiful lithograph of the battle by J.H. Bufford.

273. *Battle of Shiloh or Pittsburgh Landing.* Voice and piano [1862]. #Boston: Oliver Ditson, 1862.
      M1642.G76
      A brief, three-page piece moving from D major to C major in a highly diatonic style with subheadings running throughout.

274. *The Fall of Sebastopol: Descriptive Fantasia.* Piano. #Boston: Oliver Ditson, 1855.
      AM 2-I (NYPL call number)
      A nine-page composition depicting the battle which took place on 5 September 1855. Includes rocket fire with crescendoing, ascending major-minor seventh chord arpeggios and bombardments with alternating sixteenth notes. After a G-minor Marche funèbre with tremolos, it concludes with a B-flat major version of "God Save the Queen" and an E-flat major march.
      Grobe wrote several other battle pieces: *The Battle of New Orleans.* Piano. #Lee & Walker, 1862. AM 2-I (NYPL call number); *The Battle of Port Royal* or *The Bombardment of Forts Walker and Beuregard*, Op. 1385. Piano [c. 1861]. #Boston: Oliver Ditson, 1861. M20.C59G. "Dedicated to Commodore S. F. Dupon and his brave associates"; *The Battle of Prague* of Koczwara's. Revamped, remodeled, and renovated by Grobe. Piano [1860]. #Boston: Russell & Tolman, 1860. M25.K. See no. 172 above; *Battles of Sebastopol.* Piano. #New York: W.H. Hall & Son. AM 2-I (NYPL call number); *The Bombardment and Surrender of Fort Pulaski, April 10 and 11, 1862*, Op. 1406. *Pictures of the War No. 5.* Piano [c. 1862]. #Boston: Oliver Ditson, 1862. M20.C59G; and *The Capture of Island No. 10, April 8th, 1862*, Op. 1401. *Pictures of the War No. 4.* Piano [c. 1862]. #Boston: Oliver Ditson, 1862. M20.C59G.

MacDowell, Edward (1860-1908)

275. *War Song*, Op. 6. Male chorus [1898]. #New York: Arthur P. Schmidt, 1898.

*MP (U.S.) NYPL

A borderline war work in that it is chiefly a march. The continuous quarter-note pulse and the repeated text of "tramp onward on" make it a powerful representation of the inevitability of war.

276. Suite No. 2 ("Indian"), Op. 48. Orchestra [1891-1895]. #Leipzig: Breitkopf & Härtel, 1897. *Turnabout TV-S 34535.
    M3.3.M14 Op. 48
    The third and fourth movements are war-related: "In War-Time" and "Dirge." The music for "In War-Time" is imitative, energetic, and attractive, using long trills and cymbal crashes. The "Dirge" based on an Indian lament often sung by the Kowa is a pleasant work with its sustained repeated notes in the winds and expressive melodies in the strings.

Schleiffarth, George (19th c.)

277. *Battle of Manila: A Descriptive Fantasie.* Piano [1898]. #Chicago: Frank K. Root, 1898.
    M1644.S
    A typical battle piece, with "Yankee Doodle" and "The Star Spangled Banner." It also uses descriptive subheadings and closes with "A Grand March of Victory" in F major.

Schreiner, Hermann L. (1832-1891)

278. *The Soldier's Grave.* Voice and piano [1863]. #Macon, Ga.: John C. Schreiner, 186-. Text by D. Ottolengui.
    M1642.S
    A simple, strophic song in E-flat major about a soldier dying with a smile on his face because he was told of his army's victory. "Tis the grave of a hero."

279. *When Upon the Field of Glory. An Answer to When this Cruel War is Over.* Song for voice and piano [1861]. #Macon & Savannah: J.C. Schreiner, 1861. Text by John H. Hewitt.
    M1642.S
    An A-flat major strophic song about a soldier gladly dying for the cause because "in Heaven we'll meet again."

Striby, W. (19th c.)

280. *The Battle of Buena Vista.* Piano [c. 1848]. #Louisville: H.J.
      Peters.
         M1.A12I v. 19
         A twelve-page battle, highly sectionalized with descriptive
      titles. Contains drum rolls, bugle calls, cannon shots, a Mexican
      quickstep, and numerous marches. The battle itself rages through
      tremolos and broken octaves, and the work ends with "Hail
      Columbia" in C major.

Strother, Susan A. (19th c.)

281. *The Battlefield: A Fantasie on the Battle of Bull Run.* Piano [c.
      1866]. #Washington, D.C.: John F. Ellis, 1866.
         M25.S
         A conventional battle piece with nearly twenty separate
      sections with subtitles ranging from the opening "Reveille"
      through "The Attack," "Sharp Shooter," to the "Route and Flight
      of the Enemy."

Austria

Payer, Hieronymus (1787-1845)

282. *Bataille de Navarien: Fantaisie brillante,* Op. 132. Piano [c. 1828].
      #Hamburg: A. Cranz, 1828.
         *MYD (NYPL call number)
         A fifteen-page, sectionalized, descriptive work full of blocked
      chords, Alberti basses, double-dotted rhythms, tremolos, and
      "Egyptian cannons" (low bass notes over tremolos). Closes with
      English and Russian songs. Subtitles given in French and German.

Belgium

Gregoir, Édouard (1822-1890)

283. *Les croisades: Prise de Jerusalem par Godefroid de Bouillon anno
      1099,* Op. 20. Historical symphony [1846]. #Imp. & Lith. de T.
      and D. Hemelsoet, Gand, 1847.
         M1001.G822
         In four parts: "Le voeu des croisés: Introduction et Prière"; "Le
      départ des croisés: Marche militaire"; "Invocation: solo de

violoncello"; and "Combat: Fanfare, cavalerie, cris des blessés, le retour, March." The "Cries of the Wounded" moves to C minor and incorporates muted strings. The last section is in C major with trumpet calls and chromatic scales before ending with an F-major Marche militaire.

Bohemia

Fibich, Zdeněk (1850-1900)

284. *Šárka*, Op. 51. Opera [1896-1897]. 1st: 28 December 1897. #Prague: Národní hudební vydavatelství, Orbis, 1950. *Supraphon CO-1746/48.
M1503.F443S35
The tales of the Amazonian warrior Šárka, with limp battle scenes in the third act.

Smetana, Bedřich (1824-1884)

285. *Blaník*. Symphonic poem [1879]. #Budapest: Editio Musica, 1990.*Orfeo C-115842 and Philips 420607-2 PH2.
M1002.S638M32
A victory hymn dealing with Blaník Mountain, the place the Hussites took refuge. It consists of five marches and various interludes, often quoting the Hussite chorale "Kdož jst Boži bojovníci" ("Ye who are God's warriors").

286. *Šárka*. Symphonic poem [1875]. #London: Eulenberg, 1976. *Orfeo C-115842 and Philips 420607-2 PH2.
M1002.S638 M35
Through extreme syncopation, agitated tempos, and passionate, chromatic dissonance, Smetana depicts the woman warrior Šárka as she leads a group of women who slaughter the sleeping men.

287. *Tábor*. Symphonic poem [1878]. #London: Eulenberg, 1976. *Orfeo C-115842 and Philips 420607-2 PH2.
M1002.S638M36 1976
Based on the Hussite chorale "Kdož jst Boži bojovníci," this work derives its name from a town where the Hussites stayed.

France

Berlioz, Hector (1803-1869)

288. *Grande symphonie funèbre et triomphale.* Military band, strings,
      and chorus [1840]. 1st: 7 August 1840. *#Hector Berlioz New
      Edition of the Complete Works* (Kassel: Bärenreiter, 1967), vol.
      19. *Philips 416283-2 PH2.
            M3.B52 v. 19
            Commissioned to be performed on 28 July 1840. In three
            movements: "Marche funèbre," "Hymn d'adieu" (later "Oraison
            funèbre"), and "Apothéose."

289. *Les Troyens.* Opera [1856-1858, revised 1859-1860]. 1st: 4
      November 1863. *#Hector Berlioz New Edition of the Complete
      Works*, vol. 2. *Philips 416432-2 PH4. Libretto after Virgil.
            M3.B52 vol. 2 M1500
            Includes the offstage burning of Troy in the first act, two
            laments over its destruction, and a massive choral victory
            celebration which begins the opera.

Litolff, Henry Charles (1818-1891)

290. Piano Concerto No. 3 ("National Hollandais"), Op. 45, in E-flat
      major (4th movement). #New York: Music Treasure, 1973.
            M1011.L79 Op. 45
            In the last movement, Litolff incorporates a Dutch theme from
            a political hymn ("Wien Neerlands bloed") that arose during the
            1830 revolution.

Meyerbeer, Giacomo (1791-1864) [German-born]

291. *Les Huguenots,* Acts IV and V. Opera [1836]. #London: Boosey &
      Hawkes, [n.d.]. *London LON 1437.
            M1503.M623H74
            This five-act opera depicts the massacre in the last two acts.

Germany

Becker, Reinhold (c. 1842-1924)

292. *Vor der Schlacht,* Op. 50. Baritone, male chorus, and orchestra [c.
      1888]. #Leipzig: C.F.W. Siegel, 1888. Text by Theodor Körner.

*MP+ (Germany) (NYPL call number)
An exuberant work moving from F minor to F major with heavy use of brass and dotted rhythms.

Brahms, Johannes (1833-1897)

293. *Triumphlied,* Op. 55. Eight-part chorus, baritone, and orchestra [1870-1871]. 1st: Karlsruhe, 5 June 1872. #New York; Kalmus, [n.d.]. *DG 41937-2 GH3.
       M1530.B81T6
       Written to celebrate the German victory over the French in Franco-Prussian War of 1871. In three sections in D, G, and D major, it remains a praise to God for the victory, with contrapuntal "Hallelujahs" following one after another.

Bruch, Max (1838-1920)

294. *Kriegsgesang* from *Neue Männerchöre,* Op. 68, No. 3. Four-part chorus and orchestra. #Berlin: N. Simrock, 1896. Text from Goethe's *Des Epimendies Erwachen.*
       JMG 86-907 (NYPL call number)
       Moving from D minor to D major, a diatonic and heroic portrayal of glorious victory, using triplets throughout the majority of the work.

Rheinberger, Joseph (1839-1901)

295. *Wallenstein,* Op. 10. Symphonic poem [1867]. #Leipzig: C.F.W. Siegel, 187-.
       M1002.R47
       In four parts: "Vorspiel" (Grand and heroic, going from D minor to D major); "Thekla"; "Wallensteins Lager" (in 2/4, Allegretto, full of repeated rhythms with trio); and "Wallensteins Tod" (in D minor with low strings, timpani rolls, moving to a frenetic Allegro vivace in D major with continuous eighth-notes for extended periods. After a heroic outburst it concludes with a brief coda in D minor).

Schumann, Robert (1810-1856)

296. *Schlachtgesang,* Op. 62, No. 3, from *Drei Gesänge.* Male chorus [1847]. #Complete edition, Ser. 11, no. 2 (Leipzig: Breitkopf & Härtel), pp. 17-20.

M3.S3925 Ser. 10-12
A three-page song in C major including dotted rhythms, a nice balance between homophonic and polyphonic writing, and ending with shouts of "Hurrah."
Schumann also wrote smaller war-related works: *Die beiden Grenadiere*, Op. 49, No. 1 (in *Romanzen und Balladen*. Song. #New York: Schirmer, 1910. *Telefunken 6.42620 and Tactus OY TA 7905. M1621.S); and *Krieglied*, Op. 68, No. 3 (from *Album für die Jugend*. Piano [1848]. M3.S3925 Ser. 7 v. 5, p. 64).

Spohr, Louis (1784-1859)

297. *Fall of Babylon* (no. 24). Oratorio [1839-1840]. #London: Novello, [18--].
M2003.S76F3
This section of the oratorio "Shout aloud!" is a march and chorus of Persian soldiers proclaiming the conflict is ended and Babylon has fallen. The work is full of dotted rhythms and martial figurations, with the chorus singing throughout.

Strauss, Richard (1864-1949)

298. *Ein Heldenleben*. Symphonic poem [1897-1898]. #New York: International Music, 1955. *RCA RCD1-5408 and London 414292-2 LH.
M1002.S91 Op. 40 1955
Contains "The Hero's deeds of war" and "The Hero's works of peace." The battle scene is extraordinary for its imaginative dissonance in a work from 1898.

299. *Kampf und Sieg* from *Lebende Bilder (Living Tableaux)*. Orchestra [1892, revised 1931]. 1st: 8 October 1892. #Magdeburg: Heinrichshofen, 1930. *Records International 7003-1.
M1002.S91K2
Strauss composed four numbers for this collective presentation (along with works by Liszt, Lassen, and Bronsart). Strauss's contribution is a depiction of the Battle of Luetzen of 1632, full of dotted and repetitive rhythms and grandiose gestures, ending in C major.

Wagner, Richard (1813-1883)

300. *Rienzi*, Act III, scene iii. Opera [1840]. 1st: 20 October 1842.
    #(Leipzig: Breitkopf & Härtel, 1914), pp. 371-91. *Angel SELX
    3818.
        M1503.W14 R26 1982
        Amidst the singing of the war hymn "Sancto Spiritus,"
    Wagner notates clashings of swords with a special mark in the
    score (p. 381) while the fighting takes place off-stage in B-flat
    major.

Great Britain

Cumming, William Hayman (1831-1915)

301. *Santa Anna's Retreat from Cerro Cordo*. #W.C. Peters & Sons,
    1847.
        M25.C
        A simple, three-page piece with left-hand notes of only an A
    or G. It begins animato and "gradually increase[s] the movement to
    'Double Quick' Time." It also starts *pp* and crescendos to *ff*. At
    two points along the way, the composer writes in the score: "Santa
    Anna loses his wooden leg" and "Santa Anna loses his Mexican
    hat."

Hungary

Liszt, Franz (1811-1886)

302. *Alexander Petöfi* from *Historische ungarische Bildnisse* (*Historical
    Hungarian Portraits*) and an expansion of the earlier *Petöfi
    Szellémenek—Dem Andenken Petöfis*. #Budapest: Edition Musica,
    1980.
        M3.L772 Ser. I v. 10
        Petöfi, a Hungarian poet who incited people to rebel for
    liberty, was killed in the 1849 revolution. Liszt wrote this
    poignant elegy in his memory; contains numerous recitatives,
    stark harmonies, and lugubrious ostinatos in its eighty-nine
    measures.

303. *Funérailles*. Piano [1849]. #Budapest: Edition Musica, 19--?.
    *RCA 5935-2-RC and Philips 411055-2 PH.
        M3.L772 Ser. I v. 9

Deals with the Hungarian revolution of October 1849. An impassioned, heroic funeral march with its famous middle octave section reminiscent of that in Chopin's A-flat Polonaise.

304. *Héroïde funèbre*. Symphonic poem no. 8 [1848-1850, revised 1854]. 1st: 10 November 1857. #London: Eulenburg, 1976. *Hungaroton HCD-12677/81.

     M1002.L77H47

     Liszt creates a brooding atmosphere with low brass and bells. Parts of this work were taken from Liszt's unfinished *Revolutionary Symphony* started in 1830. Liszt planned to include "La marseillaise" and other revolutionary tunes in this symphony. Lina Ramann suggests that Beethoven's *Wellington's Victory* was the model for Liszt's youthful symphony. For a discussion of this symphony, see Alan Walker, *Franz Liszt: The Virtuoso Years 1811-1847* (New York: Knopf, 1983), p. 144 and Paul Merrick, *Revolution and Religion in the Music of Liszt* (Cambridge: Cambridge University Press, 1987), pp. 3-4. See page 91 above for additional information.

305. *Hungaria 1848*. Cantata for soprano, tenor, baritone, male chorus, and orchestra [1848]. 1st: 21 May 1912. #Budapest, 1961. *Hungaroton HDC 12748. Text by Franz von Schober.

     [No LC number available]

     An eleven-minute cantata in three main sections written during the 1848 Hungarian Revolt. The text refers back to the deeds of Attila the Hun and deals with the Hungarian's courageous struggle for freedom in 1848.

306. *Hunnenschlacht*. Symphonic poem no. 11 [1856-1857]. Based on Wilhelm von Kaulbach's painting. 1st: 29 December 1857. #London: Eulenburg, 1976. *Hungaroton HCD-12677/81.

     M1002.L77H85

     Certainly programmatic, but far better than the usual battle compositions of the time. See pages 89 to 91 above for additional information.

307. *Lyon*. Piano [1834-1835]. #Budapest: Editio Musica, 1976.

     M25.L5 A39 no. 1 1976

     More of a revolutionary work than a war work. This Allegro eroico work deals with an uprising in April 1834 in which a number of the working class were killed. Liszt prefaced the score with "Vivre an travaillant ou mourir en combatant" ("To live working or to die fighting.") Uses dotted rhythms, extremely loud dynamics, tremolos, repeated notes, and thematic transformation to create its battle-like mood.

Italy

Busoni, Ferreuccio (1866-1924)

308. Zweite Orchestersuite ("Geharnischte Suite"), Op. 34a. Orchestra [1895, revised 1902]. #Leipzig: Breitkopf & Härtel, 1905.
     M1003.B97 Op. 34A
     In four movements: "Vorspiel," "Kriegstanz," "Gräbdenkmal," and "Ansturm." The battle dance in B-flat major (Allegro risolutio) is in cut time, with chromaticism, numerous repeated notes, and considerable use of brass and percussion. The funeral march is followed by the "Assault"—another fiery Allegro impetuoso martial movement in D minor.

Verdi, Giuseppe (1813-1901)

309. *La battaglia di Legnano.* Opera [1849]. 1st: 27 January 1849. #New York: Kalmus, 1980? *Replica ARPL 22500. Libretto by Salvatore Cammarano.
     M1503.V484B4
     Includes a victory hymn in G major with bells ringing that leads into a *Te Deum.*

310. *La forza del destino*, Act III ("Scene e battaglia"). Opera [1862]. 1st: 10 November 1862. #(New York: Kalmus, 1968), pp. 189-95. *London 421598-2 LM3 and Angel CDCC047581. Libretto by Francesco Maria Piave.
     M1503.V484F72 1944
     Verdi uses numerous repeated notes and energetic rhythms moving from F minor to A-flat major to depict a brief battle scene in which Alvaro is wounded.

311. *Giovanna d'Arco*, Act III. Opera [1845]. 1st: 15 February 1845. #New York: Kalmus, 197-. *Foyer FO 1040. Libretto by Temistocle Solera.
     M1503.V484G5 1850
     The battle takes place offstage as Giovanna hears the sounds before joining the battle and receiving her death blow.

312. *Jérusalem.* Opera [1847]. 1st: 22 November 1847. A revision of *I Lombardi.* #Mainz: B. Schott, 19--. *Melodram MEL 27004. Libretto by Alphonse Royer and Gustave Vaëz.

    M1503.V484L52

    Verdi retained the battle scene from *I Lombardi* in this revision. See item 313 below.

313. *I Lombardi alla prima Crociata,* Act IV ("Scena, Inno di Guerra e Battaglia"). Opera [1843]. 1st: 2 November 1843. #(Milan: G. Ricordi, 1873), pp. 305-24. *Hungaroton HCD-12498/500. Libretto by Temistocle Solera.

    M1503.V484L4

    Verdi's longest operatic battle scene with the chorus and soloists shouting "Guerra! Guerra!" in F minor. A battle breaks out in essence between the main orchestra and the banda, alternating back and forth.

314. *Macbeth,* Act IV ("Scene e battaglia"). Opera [1847]. 1st: 14 March 1847. #New York: Kalmus, 197 , pp. 280-90. *London 417525-2 LH2 and RCA 4516-2-RG. Libretto by Francesco Maria Piave.

    M1503.V484M2

    Near the end of the work, this chromatic battle scene full of repeated-note trumpet calls and cries of soldiers is followed by a C-major victory hymn.

Norway

Neupert, Edmund (1842-1888)

315. *Vor der Schlacht.* Tone poem, orchestrated by Johan S. Svendsen [c. 1896]. #Copenhagen & Leipzig: Wilhelm Hansen, 1896.

    M1060.N48V5

    A brief, sectionalized C-minor work with some highly jagged sections with dotted rhythms and staccato passages, but nothing particularly explicit about war except for the title.

Russia

Tchaikovsky, Peter Ilyich [Chaikovsky, Pyotr Il'ich] (1840-1893)

316. *1812 Overture,* Op. 49. Orchestra [1882]. #New York: Kalmus, 1900? *DG 400035-2 Gh and CBS MLK-39433.

M1004.C434M3

Perhaps the most popular of all war-related music still in the current repertory; full of brass, drums, and cymbal crashes. Quotes the Russian Hymn "God Preserve Thy People" and the French "La marseillaise." The ending, with its cannon shots, bells ringing, and the Russian national anthem, clearly symbolizes the Russians' defeat of Napoleon and his troops.

317. *Mazeppa* ("Le bataille de Poltawa"). Orchestral scene from opera [1883]. 1st: 15 February 1884. #Moscow: P. Iurgenson, 1899. *Cetra L043.

M1503.T878M35

Begins Act III and is full of repeated notes and rhythms and fast scales; uses a banda against the orchestra to create the two warring factions.

318. *Slavonic March*, Op. 31. Orchestra [1876]. 1st: 17 November 1876. #London: Eulenburg, 1900? *Philips 6880 039.

M1046.T3 Op. 31

Composed for a benefit concert for soldiers wounded during the Serbo-Turkish War and quotes the Russian national anthem and a Serbian folk song.

Switzerland

Barblan, Otto (1860-1943)

319. *Calvenfeier 1499-1899*, Op. 8. Oratorio for chorus and orchestra [1899]. #Chur: Stehli & Keel, 1899. Text by M. Bühler and G. Luck.

M1513.B242C3

Deals with the Rhaetian Republic from 1471 to the unification of Switzerland in 1803. The third and fourth scenes ("Kriegselend an der Grenze" and "Die Schlacht an der Calven") contain laments, marches, and prayers before the battle. The "Totenklage" and victory march are in D major.

SUPPLEMENT OF ROMANTIC WAR MUSIC:
1828-1900

320. Adelburg, August, Ritter von (1830-1873). Of Croatian and Italian descent. *War and Peace*. Oratorio. [Cited in BAKER, p. 10].

321. _____. *Wallenstein*. Opera after Schiller. (Overture [1867]). [Cited in BAKER, p. 10].

322. Berwald, Franz (1796-1868). Sweden. *Slaget vid Leipzig (The Battle of Leipzig)*. Orchestra [1828]. [Cited in NEW GROVE, vol. 2, p. 654].

323. _____. *Gustaf Adolph the Great's Victory and Death at Lützen*. Chorus, winds, and organ [1845]. Text by G. Ingelman. [Cited in NEW GROVE, vol. 2, p. 654].

324. _____. *Charles XII's Victory at Narva*. Four tenors, wind, and organ [1845]. [Cited in NEW GROVE, vol. 2, p. 654].

325. Blockley, John (1800-1882). America. *The Charge of the Light Brigade*. #London: Cramer, Beale, & Wood. Text by Alfred, Lord Tennyson.

326. Boott, Francis (1813-1904). America. *Battle of the Baltic*. Voice and piano [c. 1857]. #Boston: Oliver Ditson, 1857. Text by Campbell. AM 2-V (NYPL call number). An F-major, four-verse song telling the story of the Battle of the Baltic.

327. Delaney, Alfred (19th c.). America. *Dirge sung at the Consecration of the Soldiers' Cemetery at Gettysburg (Nov. 19th, 1863)*. Four voices [1863]. #Philadelphia: Lee & Walker, 1863. Text by James G. Percival. M1640.D. In A minor, this strophic song proclaims in each verse how great it is to die for one's country and the glory that lasts forever.

328. _____. *Gettysburg* from *Songs of the Loyal No. 5*. Voice and piano [1863]. #Philadelphia: B. Lee & Walker, 1863. "Respectfully dedicated to General Meade by Robert Morris. Music adapted by Alfred Delaney."

329. Foster, Stephen C. (1826-1864). America. *Santa Anna's Retreat from Buena Vista*. Piano. #Louisville: W.C. Peters, 1848. Am. 1-I (NYPL call number). A quickstep that is not programmatic other than the title.

330. Goldmark, Karl (1830-1915). Austria-Hungary. *Penthesilea Overture*, Op. 31. Orchestra [1879]. #Mainz: B. Schott, 18--. *Records International 7007-1. M1004.G621 Op. 13 S3. Deals with the Trojan War.

331. Hatch, Laura Hastings (19th c.). America. *Battle of the Wilderness.*
      A descriptive piece composed for the pianoforte [187-]. #Boston:
      Ditson, 187-. No. 4 in **M.446.157 (Boston Public Library call
      number).

332. Indy, Vincent d' (1851-1931). France. *Wallenstein.* Orchestra (also
      arranged for piano solo and piano four-hands) [1873-1881].
      #Miami: Kalmus, 1984. *EMI C06914043. M1002.I42W3.

333. Jennerson (19th c.). America. *Battle of the Baltic.* Voice and piano
      [c. 1847]. #Boston: G.P. Reed, 1847. Text by Campbell. AM 2-V
      (NYPL call number). An E-flat major introduction is followed by a
      four-verse strophic song telling again of Nelson's glorious victory
      with continuous dotted rhythms.

334. Koechlin, Charles (1867-1950). France. *La guerre* (from Op. 14).
      Song [1896-1899]. Text by Banville. [Cited in NEW GROVE,
      vol. 10, p. 147].

335. Lefébure-Wély, Louis-James-Alfred (1817-1869). France. *Après la
      victoire.* Cantata [1863]. [Cited in BAKER, p. 147].

336. Lignoski, B.R. (19th c.) America. *Battle of Palo Alto.* Piano.
      #Baltimore: Willig, 1851. M1.A12I v. 44.

337. Lindpainter, Peter (1791-1856). Germany. *War Jubilee Overture*
      [before 1844].

338. Marx, Adolph Bernhard (1795-1866). Germany. *Schlacht von
      Warschau* [1831]. [Cited in MGG, vol. 1, p. 1410].

339. Massenet, Jules (1842-1912). France. *La Navarraise.* Opera [1894].
      1st: 20 June 1894. #Paris: Heugel, 1894. *Columbia M33506.
      M1503.M415N3. Deals with the nineteenth-century Spanish civil
      war.

340. Mercadante, Saverio (1795-1870). Italy. *Inno guerriero dedicato a
      Garibaldi.* Chorus and orchestra [1861]. #Naples, 1861. [Cited in
      NEW GROVE, vol. 12, p. 175].

341. Mihalovich, Ödön Péter József de (1842-1929). Hungary. *Csatádal
      (Battle Song).* Male voices and orchestra [1871]. #Pest, 1873.
      [Cited in NEW GROVE, vol. 12, p. 286]. Text by Sándor Petőfi.

342. de Mol, William (1846-1874). Belgium. Symphonie ("La guerre").
      Orchestra.

343. Parry, Joseph (1841-1903). Wales. *Blodwen.* Opera [1878]. #Niles:
      Melrose Music, 1912. *Sain 1138R. M1503.P25 1912. Deals
      with Henry IV's campaign.

344. Schell, John. (19th c.). America. *Battle of Resaca de la Palma.*
      Piano [c. 1846]. M1.A122 v. 1.

345. _____. *Bonaparte's Retreat from Moscow.* Piano. #Charleston: J.
      Siegling, 1831-58?. AM 1-I (NYPL call number). A one-page,
      diatonic, G-major battle piece including the use of Alberti bass.

346. Schreiner, Hermann L. (1832-1891). America. *Battle of Manassas* [1861].
347. Shol'tz, Fyodor Yefimovich (1787-1830). Russia [German born]. *Navarinsk Battle*. Fantasy for six pianos [1828]. [Cited in HO, p. 472].
348. Siboni, Erik (1828-1892). The Netherlands. *Slaget ved Murten (Battle of Murton)*. Cantata for solos, male chorus, and orchestra. He also composed *Stormen paa Kjøbenhavn (The Assault of Copenhagen)*. [Cited in NEW GROVE, vol. 17, p. 290].
349. Somervell, Arthur (1863-1937). English. *The Charge of the Light Brigade*. Chorus [1896]. Text by Alfred, Lord Tennyson. [Cited in NEW GROVE, vol. 17, p. 475]. Deals with the Crimean War.
350. Stanford, Charles (1852-1924). Great Britain. *The Battle of the Baltic*, Op. 41. Chorus and orchestra [1891]. #London: Novello, 1891. Text by Thomas Campbell. M1533.S785B3. A heroic E-flat major work, full of pride in war and glory.
351. Zoellner, Heinrich (1854-1941). Germany. *Battle of the Huns*, Op. 12. Soprano, baritone, male chorus, and piano. #Boston: Prüfer, 188-. No. 6 in **M.392.32 (Boston Public Library call number).

ANNOTATED LISTING OF AMERICAN CIVIL WAR MUSIC:
1900-1990

America (United States)

Adams, John (b. 1947)

352. *The Wound Healer.* Baritone and chamber orchestra [1989].
    *Elektra Nonesuch 7559-79218-2. Text by Walt Whitman.
    [No LC number available]
    A nineteen-minute evocation of caring for the wounded
    soldiers, displayed by sensitive writing for the strings, spacious
    harmonies, and a warm lyricism.

Baber, Joseph (b. 1937)

353. *Shiloh and other Songs from Herman Melville's "Battle Pieces."*
    Tenor, horn, and piano. [1991]. 1st: New York, 15 December
    1991. Text by Herman Melville.
    [No LC number available]
    A setting of three poems: "The Portent," "Misgivings," and
    "Shiloh." The music is tonal and highly syncopated, moving from
    the ominous rumors of war (Adagio) to the battle itself (Allegro).
    The tenor represents the "anguished" person in war while the horn
    and piano reflect the "environment of land and battle."

Baron, Maurice (1889-1964)

354. *Ode to Democracy.* Baritone, chorus, and orchestra (or piano).
    #New York: B.M. Baron, 1947. Text by Abraham Lincoln.
    M1533.B263O
    A ten-minute heroic and patriotic setting of Lincoln's
    Gettysburg Address. The baritone sings the entire speech broken up
    with choral interjections that repeat the last phrase of text the
    baritone sang.

Becker, John Joseph (1886-1961)

•   Symphony No. 6 ("Out of Bondage"). See item number 603.

Binkerd, Gordon (b. 1916)

355. *Requiem for Soldiers Lost in Ocean Transports.* SATB Chorus [1984]. #New York: Boosey & Hawkes, 1984. Text by Herman Melville.
     M2011.B56R4 1984
     A nine-minute tonal and polytonal work, largely homophonic but with some imitative polyphony. Does not contain an explicit program or involved text painting.

Bloch, Ernest (1880-1959) [Swiss born]

356. *America.* Chorus and orchestra [1926]. 1st: New York, 20 December 1928. #Boston: C.C. Birchard, 1928. *Vanguard SRV-346SD.
     M1001.B656A5
     Written to show Bloch's appreciation for his adopted country and the admiration he felt for the vision of Lincoln and Whitman. The second movement ("1861-1865 Hours of Joy—Hours of Sorrow") incorporates Civil War songs ("Dixie," "Tramp, Tramp, Tramp," and the "Battle Cry of Freedom") into the polyphonic texture of the movement. The movement ends with the sorrow of the war and the death of Lincoln.

Bottorf, Deane (20th c.)

357. *The Words from Gettysburg.* Mixed voices, brass choir, and timpani. #[n.p.], 1961. Text by Abraham Lincoln.
     M1531.B76W7
     A simplistic setting with the chorus singing virtually unaccompanied, the brass providing only an introduction, interludes, and an intensified conclusion.

Carfagno, Simon A. (b. 1906)

358. *Gettysburg, 1863.* Cantata for soloists, chorus, and orchestra [1961]. #Simon A. Carfagno, 1961.
     M1530.C24G5
     Beginning Largo e Maestoso with trumpets and trombones blaring out repeated notes in C major, this work retains its heroic nature amidst changing meters and polyphonic choral writing.

Carter, John C. (20th c.)

359. *War is Kind.* SATB chorus, baritone, and piano [1976]. #Macomb, Illinois: R. Dean, 1976. Text by Stephen Crane.
M1557.C
Includes a continuous quintal ostinato in the piano over which the chorus sings in a homophonic texture and occasionally speaks. The choral part is predominantly stepwise in simple rhythmic patterns.

Cecconi-Bates, Augusta (b. 1933)

360. *War is Kind.* Soloists and band [1981]. 1st: 5 April 1981. #Holograph at the AMC. Text by Stephen Crane with additional text inserted by the composer.
AMC M1528.C3877W2
A twenty-minute work with a military overture followed by a cantata "After the Battle." The battle section is full of the glory of war, but the cantata itself turns into a funeral dirge.

Copland, Aaron (1900-1990)

• *A Lincoln Portrait.* See item number 607.

Creston, Paul (1906-1985)

361. *Reconciliation* from *Leaves of Grass.* Chorus [1982]. #New York: G. Schirmer, 1982. Text by Walt Whitman.
M1552.C
A slow and simple section, with a women's voice (preferably a contralto) speaking while the chorus sings "Ah." The brief movement is chromatic but contains numerous traditional tertian chords.
Creston also prefaced the twenty-two-measure second movement of his *Three Poems from Walt Whitman*, Op. 4, for cello and piano, with the opening lines from "Reconciliation." #San Diego: Music Graphic Press, 1979.

Curtis-Smith, Curtis O(tto) B(ismark) (b. 1941)

362. *A Civil War Song Cycle.* Voice and piano [1987]. Texts by Walt Whitman and Herman Melville.
AMC M1621.4.C981C5

This setting of several poems begins with the hanging of John Brown and ends with the dead lying in the fields of Shiloh. The music is an imaginative, varied setting using frequent quintal harmonies and stark dissonances in sensitive ways. Contains "The Portent," "The March to Virginia," "Vigil Strange," "The Housetop," "A Night Place," "By the Bivouac's Fitful Flame," "Beat! Beat! Drums!," and "Shiloh."

Dello Joio, Norman (b. 1913)

363. *Songs of Walt Whitman.* Chorus and orchestra or piano [1966]. #New York: Edward B. Marks, 1966. Text by Walt Whitman.
       AMC M1533.D358S6
       Includes settings of "I Sit and Look out upon the World," "The Dalliance of Eagles," "Tears," and "Take our Hand."

Diamond, David (b. 1915)

364. *This Sacred Ground.* Baritone, children's chorus, chorus, and orchestra [1962]. 1st: 17 November 1963. #New York: Southern Music, 1963. Text is Lincoln's *Gettysburg Address.*
       M1533.D5.S32
       In a section dealing with "Now we are engaged in a great civil war," Diamond uses full percussion (including bass drum, slap stick, tenor drum, cymbals, and gong) in accented, syncopated patterns played *ff.* The children's chorus is not used in this section.

Foss, Lukas (b. 1922)

365. *American Cantata.* Double chorus, tenor, and orchestra [1976, revised 1977]. 1st: 24 July 1976. #New York: Boosey & Hawkes, 1981. Texts selected by Arieh Sachs and the composer.
       JNG 83-56 (NYPL call number)
       Foss cites a letter from a dying Civil War soldier in this cantata celebrating the American Bicentennial; makes a strong statement about the tragedy of war.

Gibb, Robert Wilson (1893-1964)

366. *Gettysburg Address.* Male chorus [c. 1957]. #J. Fischer & Brothers, 1957. Text by Abraham Lincoln.
       ML96.G43 Case

A pompous setting beginning in D-flat major and ending in F major; nearly diatonic throughout.

Gillis, Don (1912-1978)

367. *Abe Lincoln, Gettysburg 1863*. Narrator and band [1953]. #New York: Mills, 1953. Text by Abraham Lincoln.
      M1625.G55A2
      A four-minute setting of the *Gettysburg Address* marked "Slowly—with deep emotion and feeling." The work is soft throughout and underscores the seriousness of Lincoln's message and the events surrounding the speech.

Goldmark, Rubin (1872-1936)

368. Requiem. Orchestra [1919]. 1st: New York, 30 January 1919. #New York and Boston: G. Schirmer, 1921.
      M1045.G63R3
      Moves from E-flat minor to E-flat major, a large-scale composition whose structure and contents were suggested by Lincoln's *Gettysburg Address*. The "civil war" section of the speech appears to be the Feroce section played *fff* with brass leading the way in fast repeated, fanfare-like passages. This section is followed by a softer and calmer section where the composer writes the text "Dona eis requiem" in the first violin part. Goldmark also writes in the last line of the address "and the government . . . " *fff* in an elaborate E-flat major coda.

Hadley, Henry (1871-1937)

369. *Gettysburg Address*. Soloist and chorus [c. 1941]. #Boston: C.C. Birchard, 1941. Text by Abraham Lincoln.
      M1557.H
      A brief G-major setting with the soloist declaiming the text, while the chorus hums and then sings in four parts the last few words of text the soloist sang. The text dominates; the music in most every case is only perfunctory.

Hanna, James R. (b. 1922)

370. *War*. A cycle of five songs for voice and piano [1954, revised 1955 and 1958]. #Hattiesburg, Miss.: Tritone, 1961. Text by Walt Whitman.

M1621.4.H35 W3

The songs include "Too Long America," "An Army Corps on the March," "Look Down Fair Moon," "The Bravest Soldier," and "Turn O Libertad." The most striking of these is "Look Down Fair Moon" with its descending motion and chromaticism and its bitonality on "faces, ghastly, swollen, purple."

Hanson, Howard (1896-1981)

371. *Drum Taps.* Baritone, chorus, and orchestra [1935]. #New York: J. Fischer, 1935. *Mercury MG 50073. Text by Walt Whitman.
   M1533.H25S6

   A setting of three songs: "Beat! Beat! Drums!," "By the Bivouac's Fitful Flame," and "To Thee, Old Cause." The first song opens with drum ostinatos, brass fanfares, and quintal winds and continues with some cluster effects and dotted rhythms. The second song is weakened by much "Ah-ing" and humming in the chorus; the third returns to the heroic nature of the first movement closing with a C-major march.

Harris, Roy (1898-1979)

• Symphony No. 6 ("Gettysburg"). See item number 617.

372. Symphony No. 10 ("Abraham Lincoln"). Chorus, brass, percussion, and two pianos [c. 1965]. 1st: 14 April 1965.
   [No LC number available]

   In five movements, the last two dealing directly with war and peace: "Civil War—Brother against Brother" and "Praise and Thanksgiving for Peace." Cited in Dan Stehman, *Roy Harris: An American Musical Pioneer* (Boston: G.K. Hall, 1984), pp. 124-31.

Hennagin, Michael (b. 1936)

373. *The Unknown.* Chorus (SSA), piano, flute, and percussion [c. 1968]. #New York: Walton Music, 1968. Text by Walt Whitman.
   *MP (U.S.) NYPL call number

   Using whispering and spoken texts as well as "free chanting," this angry work is about the men killed in war. Much of the music is sharply punctuated with primitive rhythms and some loud clusters.

Hindemith, Paul (1895-1963) [German born]

374. *Schlagt! Schlagt! Trommeln!*, Op. 14, from *Drei Hymnen*.
      Baritone and piano [1919]. #Mainz: B. Schott's Söhne, 1983. Text
      by Walt Whitman, trans. Johannes Schlaf.
           M1621.H55H9 1983
           With the marking "Nicht sehr schnell; gewichtig." Above an
      active piano part, the voice belts out syllables in a declamatory
      style, concluding *fff* over a powerful, repeated ostinato on B-flats.

375. *When Lilacs Last Bloom'd: A Requiem for Those We Love*.
      Soloists, chorus, and orchestra [1946]. 1st: New York City, 14
      May 1946. #New York: Associated Music, 1948. *Telarc CD-
      80132 and DG 2543825. Text by Walt Whitman.
           M2013.H645W52 1948a
           Along with Britten's *War Requiem*, Hindemith's work
      remains one of the most significant choral compositions influenced
      by war in this century. In eleven numbered parts, this intense
      setting of Whitman captures the elegiac atmosphere of the
      suffering of war directly, poignantly, and simply. Dedicated to the
      memory of President Roosevelt and to the American soldiers killed
      during World War II. See Alec Robertson, *Requiem: Music of
      Mourning and Consolation* (New York: Praeger, 1968), pp. 252-
      59.

Hutchison, Warner (b. 1930)

376. *Mass: For Abraham Lincoln*. Amplified and prepared piano,
      singing, speech, tape, and dramatic action for two or three
      performers [1974]. #Holograph at the AMC. Words of Lincoln
      narrated on tape.
           AMC M204.H98785M4
           An eight-movement, fifty-three minute composition about the
      life and times of Abraham Lincoln beginning with a prologue
      ("The Assassination"), proceeding with "Freedom Versus Slavery,"
      "Portents of Change," "The Conflict," "Aftermath of War,"
      "Restoration," "Liberty and Law," and concluding with "The
      Burial." The work employs imaginative graphic notation (the fifth
      movement is in the shape of a cross and the sixth in the shape of a
      triangle within a circle), strumming and hitting inside the piano,
      and tremendous clusters and dissonances.

Kay, Ulysses (b. 1917)

377. *War is Kind* from the *Stephen Crane Set.* Mixed chorus and
thirteen instruments [1967]. #New York: Duchess Music, 1972.
Text by Stephen Crane.
M1533.K23S852
The last of four songs in this sixteen-minute work. An ironic
song with much unison writing, Kay makes "War is Kind" more
ironic by ending with an incomplete phrase, "war is" followed only
by "war" repeated several times.

Lockwood, Normand (b. 1906)

378. *Dirge for Two Veterans.* Chorus [1936]. #New York: M. Witmark
& Sons, 1937. Text by Walt Whitman.
*MP (U.S.) NYPL call number
A three-minute setting of Whitman's poem in several
tonalities, using occasional cross-rhythms, bitonality, and
numerous repeated note melodies.

Loeffler, Charles Martin (1861-1935)

379. *Beat! Beat! Drums!* Male chorus in unison, six piccolos, three
saxophones, brass, drums, and two pianos [1932]. 1st: Cleveland,
17 November 1932. #Boston: B.C.C. Birchard, 1932. Text by
Walt Whitman.
M1609.L
A conventional, diatonic, heroic march. Opens with a brisk F-
minor march replete with drum-roll figurations and fanfares. F
major and F minor then alternate until the work ends with sixteen-
measures of F major all played *f* or *ff*.

McDonald, Harl (1899-1955)

• *Dirge for Two Veterans.* See item number 627.

Melnik, Henry (20th c.)

380. *Abraham Lincoln's Gettysburg Address.* Narrator and wind
ensemble [c. 1944]. #New York: D. Gornston, 1944.
M1625.M44A2
Moving from B-flat, E-flat, and F to A-flat major, this
patriotic work intends to provide a backdrop for the narrated texts.

The composer provides two endings: 1) a brief ending used during a larger program; and 2) one that leads into a setting of "The Star Spangled Banner."

Moss, Lawrence (b. 1927)

381. *Drumtaps.* Three songs for baritone and piano [1986]. #Lawrence Moss, 1986. Text by Walt Whitman.
       AMC M1621.M913D7
       A setting of "First O Songs for a Prelude," "By the Bivouac's Fitful Flame," and "To the Leven'd Soil They Trod." The music includes parallel fourths and fifths, chromaticism, quintal writing, changing meters, and playing on the inside strings of the piano, particularly "slapping low strings with the palm of the hand."

Nelhybel, Vaclav (b. 1919) [Czech born]

382. *Epitaph for a Soldier.* Soloists and chorus [1964]. #New York: Colombo, 1966. Text by Walt Whitman.
       M1587.N
       Commissioned by and dedicated to the Concert Choir of the Lebanon Valley College, a twelve-minute setting of Whitman's "Come up from the Fields Father" and "The Bravest Soldier." The alto solo sings the words of the mother learning of her son's injury as the chorus comments upon the tragedy. The music throughout is tonal but somewhat dissonant, and the work concludes with the chorus singing a B-minor lament in 4/4.

Pasatieri, Thomas (b. 1945)

383. *Dirge for Two Veterans.* Voice and piano [1973]. #New York: Belwin Mills, 1977. Text by Walt Whitman.
       M1620.P29.B4
       In four sections, this haunting work is highly chromatic and virtuosic, including some changing meters and irregular divisions. The text setting contains some slightly melismatic passages.

Persichetti, Vincent (1915-1987)

384. *A Lincoln Address*, Op. 124. Narrator and orchestra (also arranged for band, Op. 124a) [1973]. #Bryn Mawr: Elkan-Vogel, 1973. 1st: St. Louis, 25 January 1973. *University of Wisconsin-Milwaukee USR 8401. Text from Lincoln's second inaugural address.

M1625.P47L5

A twelve-minute composition originally composed to celebrate President Nixon's second inaugural ceremony, but withdrawn because of its references to war and the threat of potentially embarrassing the President during the Vietnam conflict. The work begins and ends with a slow section, and the narration is broken up frequently with extended musical interludes. In the tradition of Copland's *Lincoln Portrait.*

Raphling, Sam (1910-1988)

385. *Beat! Beat! Drums!* Voice and piano [c. 1968]. #New York: General Music, 1968. Text by Walt Whitman.

   M1621.R36B4

   A highly chromatic, energetic and non-tonal setting of Whitman's text. The vocal line is often doubled by the piano.

Rorem, Ned (b. 1923)

386. *Swords and Plowshares.* Four solo voices and orchestra [1989-1990]. 1st: Boston, 14 November 1991. Texts by Arthur Rimbaud, Lord Byron, W.H. Auden, W.B. Yeats, Archibald MacLeish, Edwin A. Robinson, Emily Dickinson, Walt Whitman, Denise Levertov, and from the Psalms.

   [No LC number available]

   In two parts, each containing seven songs. The first part sets texts of war and the second, texts of peace. The first and last songs are set for vocal quartet, the others equally divided among the soprano, alto, tenor, and bass including solos, duets, and trios.

387. *Tears* from *Whitman Cantata.* Male chorus, twelve brass, and timpani [1983]. 1st: September 1983. #New York: Boosey & Hawkes, 1983.

   M1540.R67W5 1983

   The sixth of seven Whitman settings—this is for unison tenors, in 4/4 throughout, slow, chordal, and full of expressive two-note slurs.

Schuman, William (1910-1992)

•   *A Free Song.* See item number 635.

Sessions, Roger (1896-1985)

388. *When Lilacs in the Dooryard Bloom'd.* Cantata [1964-1970]. 1st:
     23 May 1971. #Bryn Mawr: Theodore Presser, 1974. *New World
     Records NW 296-2. Text by Walt Whitman.
         M1533.S5W5 1974
         A serial composition which resorts to cannon shots during the
     scene that evokes the fighting during the American Civil War (m.
     507 to the end).

Soule, Edmund F. (b. 1915)

389. *War.* Song cycle. Voice and piano [1975]. #Eugene, Or.: Soule,
     1975. Texts by Walt Whitman, Stephen Crane, and A.E.
     Housman.
         M1621.4.S65W3
         A setting of war text, including Housman's "On the Idle Hill
     of Summer," Crane's "War is Kind," and Whitman's "In Midnight
     Sleep." The first and last songs center around B-flat minor,
     although they are highly chromatic at times and occasionally have
     small patches of polytonality. Soule's style is freely dissonant in
     these songs and calls for some use of clusters, whispered text, and
     frequently changing and irregular meters.

Tamul, Jack (b. 1948)

390. *Lament for Gettysburg.* Soprano, voices, and tape. *Spectrum SR-
     134.
         [No LC number available]
         A slow, quiet work built upon a ground bass with voices
     singing or humming only syllables and no complete words. In its
     eight minutes, it uses some indeterminacy, clusters, and sensitive
     glissandi in the voices.

Thall, Peter Morgan (20th c.)

391. *The Gettysburg Address.* Voice and piano written in collaboration
     with Beatrice Hatton Fisk [1956]. #Peter Morgan Thall, 1956.
         M1659.L7T
         A simple, diatonic, syllabic F-major setting of Lincoln's
     speech in a popular style; *Taps* accompanies "and the government
     of the people by the people, for the people shall not perish from
     the earth."

Uber, David (b. 1921)

392. *Gettysburg: Suite for Brass Instruments*. Brass octet for horn, three trumpets and trombones, and tuba [c. 1953]. #New York: Edition musicus, 1953.
M857.U2G4
A brief, simplistic, highly sectionalized, tonal composition with subtitles similar to those found in the nineteenth-century battaglias: "On the Battlefield," "Seminary Hill," "Soldier's Dream," "At the Peace Light," and "Farewell: Gray Cannon, Lonely Plains."

Waters, James (b. 1930)

393. *War is Kind*. Soprano and piano [19--]. Text by Stephen Crane.
AMC M1621.W329W2
A slow lament, with a virtuosic piano part and a disjunct and chromatic vocal part. The intensity of syncopated clusters and thirty-second notes leads to a climax "and a field where a thousand corpses lie" stated recitative-like over a sustained open fifth.

Weinberg, Jacob (1879-1956)

394. *The Gettysburg Address*. Symphonic ode for baritone, chorus, and orchestra (available in three versions: large orchestra, small orchestra, and two pianos) [1936]. 1st: New York, 1936. #New York: Witmark & Sons, 1936. Text by Abraham Lincoln.
M1531.W42G4
A fifteen-minute, pompous, and monumental setting of Lincoln's *Gettysburg Address* including quotations from "The Star Spangled Banner" and choral humming. Ends triumphantly in B-flat major.
Weinberg also wrote two other briefer settings of the address for four-part a cappella chorus (#New York: Transcontinental Music, 1954) and chorus and piano (#New York: Jewish Music Alliance, 1943).

Weinberger, Jaromir (1896-1967) [Czech born]

• *A Lincoln Symphony*. See item number 639.

Woollen, Russell (b. 1923)

395. *Lines of Stephen Crane.* Medium voice, flute, oboe, percussion string quartet, and piano [1981]. #Unpublished.
    ML29e.W84 no. 1 Case
    A cycle consisting of eleven songs, the seventh of which is a setting of "War is Kind." The music is somewhat dissonant and angular with its double-dotted rhythms.

Wright, Rayburn (20th c.)

396. *The War for the Union.* Symphonic suite for orchestra and male chorus [c. 1963]. #Unpublished: Eastman School of Music, 1963.
    M1538.W9W4
    This massive 200-page score is in four movements: "The Fever to War," "The Military Camp Life," "The Homesick Soldier," and "The Realities of War." The last movement includes numerous folk tunes and places for optional narration. The purely instrumental last movement ends with the "Battle Hymn of the Republic" in Lyndel Mitchell's arrangement.

Zaninelli, Luigi (b. 1932)

397. *The Battle of Vicksburg.* A theater piece for soprano, narrator, and piano [c. 1982]. #Toronto: E.C. Kirby, 1982. *Spectrum SR-122.
    M1626.Z
    An introduction and eight songs, each introduced by a narrator giving an account of the Battle of Vicksburg. Much of the piano writing is sparse and delicate, and the twenty-five minute cycle ends with "The question": "Why, Lord? Must we give up all that we hold dear?" Performed on recording without narration.

Germany

Hartmann, Karl Amadeus (1905-1963)

398. *First Symphony: Versuch eines Requiems.* Soprano and orchestra [1937]. 1st: 22 June 1957. #Mainz: B. Schott's Söhne, 1957.
    *Wergo WER 60086. Text by Walt Whitman.
    M1613.H34S9
    A thirty-five minute work consisting of five sections: "Introduktion: Elend" (dominated by vocal recitatives); "Frühling" (a scherzo-like movement); "Thema mit vier Variationen" (purely

instrumental); "Tränen" (a slow, highly chromatic movement with frequent dotted rhythmic patterns); and "Epilog: Bitte" (opens with a vocal recitative and percussion).

Weill, Kurt (1900-1950)

• *Walt Whitman Cycle* See item number 673.

Great Britain

Rands, Bernard (b. 1934)

399. *Look Down Fair Moon* from *Canti lunatici*. Soprano and instruments [1980]. #London: Universal Editions, 1983. *CRI CD 591. Text by Walt Whitman.
M1613.R178C3 1983
Based on a collection of texts dealing with the moon, Rands chose to set one of Whitman's Civil War texts. The graphic poem viewed from the moon looking down on the dead and wounded provided Rands with the most dramatic, albeit brief, moment in his twenty-eight minute cycle.
Rands also composed another war-related work: *Madrigali* (after Monteverdi, arranged by Berio), based on part of Monteverdi's eighth book of madrigals (London: Universal, 1980).

Vaughan Williams, Ralph (1872-1958)

400. *Dona nobis pacem*. Chorus and orchestra [1936]. 1st: Huddersfield, 2 October 1936. #London: Oxford University Press, 1936. *Angel S36972. Text by Walt Whitman and from the Bible.
M2023.U38D62
In five movements, alternating between war, lament, and peace. Whitman's angry "Beat! Beat! Drums!" (a particularly savage setting with harsh dissonances) follows the first movement Agnus Dei. The third movement, a setting of Whitman's "Reconciliation" for baritone and chorus, ends with a soprano singing softly "Dona nobis pacem." The fourth movement is Vaughan Williams's earlier setting of "Dirge for Two Veterans," and the last ends again with the soprano singing "Dona nobis pacem." Lasts forty minutes. See page 139 for additional information.

SUPPLEMENT OF AMERICAN CIVIL WAR MUSIC: 1900-1990

401. Gaul, Harvey Bartlett (1881-1945). America. *Lincoln's Second Inaugural*. Anthem for mixed voices. #New York: H.W. Gray, 1946. M1554.G Rare Bk. Coll.

402. George, Earl (b. 1924). America. *War is Kind*. Male chorus, percussion, trumpet, and piano [1966]. [Cited in BAKER, p. 611].

403. Hansen, John Charles (b. 1957). America. *The Gettysburg Address*. Voice and piano [1987]. 1st: Utah, 28 June 1987. AMC M1621.H249G3. A simple, diatonic song moving from C minor to E-flat major. Not in the least programmatic.

404. _____. *Craneology*. Voice, clarinet, and piano [1974]. #[United States: s.n.], 1974. Text by Stephen Crane, including "War is Kind." M1621.3.H26 C72.

405. Hinderlie, Sanford. (20th c.). America. *War is Kind*. Three choruses and orchestra [1983]. #Microform at University of North Texas at Denton. Text by Stephen Crane. A fifteen-minute work serving as his master's thesis.

406. North, Alex (b. 1910). America. *War is Beautiful* [1936]. [Cited in BAKER, p. 1318].

407. Rogers, Bernard (1893-1968). America. *Dirge for Two Veterans*. #Bryn Mawr: Theodore Presser, 1969. Text by Walt Whitman. M1554.R.

408. Rorem, Ned (b. 1923). America. *Pilgrim Strangers*. Six male voices [1984]. #New York: Boosey & Hawkes, 1984. Text by Walt Whitman. M1590.R.

409. Russo, William J. (b. 1928). America. *The Civil War*. Rock cantata [1968]. [Cited in BAKER, p. 1564].

410. Wallach, Joelle (b. 1946). America. *Whitman Visions: Look Down Fair Moon*. Chorus [1976]. #New York: American Composers Alliance, 1976. Text by Walt Whitman. AMC M1582.W195W6. A five-page setting of this powerful Whitman poem.

NOTES

1. Eugene d'Albert, Otto Taubmann, Aloys Obrist, eds., *Franz Liszts Musikalische Werke* (Leipzig: Breitkopf & Härtel, n.d.), vol. 1, part 6, p. 1.

2. d'Albert, Taubmann, Obrist, p. 1.

3. Ernest Newman, ed., *Memoirs of Hector Berlioz,* trans. Rachel and Eleanor Holmes (New York: Tudor, 1935), p. 232.

4. Julian Budden, *The Operas of Verdi: From Oberto to Rigoletto* (New York & Washington: Praeger, 1973), p. 309.

5. Budden, p. 133.

6. Ralph W. Wood, "Miscellaneous Orchestral Works," in *The Music of Tchaikovsky,* ed. Gerald Abraham (New York: W.W. Norton, 1946), p. 95.

7. Modest Tchaikovsky, ed., *Life and Letters of Peter Ilych Tchaikovsky,* trans. Rosa Newmarch (New York: Haskell House, 1970), vol. 2, p. 390.

8. Louis Moreau Gottschalk, *Notes of a Pianist,* ed. Jeanne Behrend (New York: Knopf, 1964), p. 66.

9. Harold Gleason and Warren Becker, *Early American Music: Music in America from 1620 to 1920,* 2nd ed., *Music Literature Outline Series* (Bloomington: Frangipani, 1981), vol. 3, p. 145.

V. THE EARLY TWENTIETH CENTURY: WORLD WAR I AND ITS AFTERMATH: 1900-1939

BEFORE WORLD WAR I

Numerous wars, uprisings, and revolutions in the last years of the nineteenth century and the first thirteen years of the twentieth served as a prelude to World War I. They include: the Boer War, the Spanish-American War, the Boxer Rebellion, the Russo-Japanese War, the 1905 Russian Revolution, the Turkish-Italian War, the Balkan Wars, and revolutions in Portugal, Mexico, and Central China. The war-related music of these years is as diverse as the numerous wars and revolutions that were fought. War music still had no "cause" and would not until at least World War I and, especially, World War II. During these years Arthur Farewell and Carlos Troyer occupied themselves with insignificant "Indian War Dances" (nos. 412, 413, 415). Gustav Holst wrote a battle march with a text translated from Sanskrit, and Hubert Parry and Charles Stanford continued to write about the historic Napoleonic wars in their *War and Peace* (no. 425) and *Ode to Wellington* (no. 427) respectively. Béla Bartók revived the idea of Kossuth and the 1848 Hungarian revolution in his early symphonic poem *Kossuth* (no. 430). Only a couple of months before World War I broke out, Holst wrote his most ferocious war-related work, *Mars, the Bringer of War* from *The Planets* (no. 474).

Even before World War I, however, the idea of the lament grew more frequent in these war compositions, as seen in Charles Wood's *Dirge for Two Veterans* (1901) (no. 429), Grechaninov's *To the Memory of the Fallen For Freedom* (1905) (no. 432), Charles Loeffler's *For One Who Fell in Battle* (1911) (no. 414), and Lili Boulanger's *Pour les funérailles d'un soldat* (1912) (no. 417). Near the beginning of the war, both Ralph Vaughan Williams and Gustav Holst set Walt Whitman's *Dirge for Two Veterans* (nos. 400, 473). These works are only a prelude to the hundreds

of laments that follow war after war to the present day and indicate the
popularity of Whitman's war poetry, which continues to form the basis
of many twentieth-century war compositions.

WORLD WAR I

The wars and revolutions that opened the century, however, had not
prepared the world for what followed in 1914. World War I began with a
renewed spirit of optimism. Young men eagerly volunteered for duty,
many feeling they would miss out on the most important event of their
age if they failed to participate. By 1916, after the Battle of the Somme,
the optimism had collapsed. The expected short war had grown into an
unprecedented bloodbath. The world, its societies and arts, would never be
the same.

The concert life naturally changed, particularly in the allied countries
where German music had been so widespread. In Great Britain, all German
music was at first banned outright. Although not forbidden in most other
countries, German music was greatly curtailed in nearly all. Musicians
performed more music by native composers in France, England, and
America than before the war.[1] In Paris, musicians gave a concert in 1915
devoted entirely to French composers killed during the war, and on 13
May 1915, Georges Enesco presented a concert to raise funds for the Red
Cross in Paris.[2] *The Musical Times* reported that during the war nearly
250 concerts had taken place in hospitals around Great Britain, and, as
well, numerous concerts were given to help raise money for widows and
children left helpless by the war.[3]

Even though composers wrote numerous compositions during the
war, World War I produced only a few significant war compositions.
Many of the major composers of the period evidently agreed with Richard
Strauss, who suggested that composers, particularly those of lesser fame,
took advantage of the war by writing war-related music in order to get
their music performed.[4] Major composers joining Strauss in not writing
war compositions during the war make an impressive list: Bartók, Alban
Berg, Ferruccio Busoni, Sergei Rachmaninoff, Erik Satie, Jean Sibelius,
and Igor Stravinsky.

Composers, nonetheless, re-evaluated their role in society and their
feelings about war and its horrors. After World War I, they seldom
composed works like the entertaining keyboard battle pieces that had

flourished in the nineteenth century. The Americans George Chadwick, Mabel Daniels, Heinrich Hammer, and Charles Ives (*He is There!*) (no. 440) continued to write some patriotic, victory-based compositions, as did European composers Max Reger, Florent Schmitt, Charles-Marie Widor, and Cyril Scott. These compositions had an optimistic, "we-will-win" attitude, forecasting the glorious moment of victory. At the end of the war, seven composers in Great Britain composed *Seven Hymns of Thanksgiving for Victory*.[5] These works served their patriotic function but rarely achieved the quality of the more intense lament compositions, to which composers more frequently turned.

The decision to write serious vocal and orchestral laments to express the suffering for those who had lost their lives in wars marks a major change in the compositional history of war-related music. The topos of nineteenth-century American battle pieces, with their habit of quoting "Yankee Doodle," were replaced with something far more serious and noble. Musical laments reached a profound level that could comfort and engage listeners rather than entertain them with a mockery of war. Although only a few laments for the dead were composed prior to the first World War, they became prevalent in war-related compositions during and after World War I. During the war at least four requiems and numerous laments appeared. Alexander Kastal'sky, Joseph Pembaur, Max Reger, and Frederick Delius wrote large-scale requiems specifically dealing with the fighting, although none of them have remained in the contemporary repertory.

The British also turned out a considerable number of smaller lament compositions. In 1915 Cyril Rootham composed his "For the Fallen" (no. 479), and Frank Bridge wrote his *Lament* (no. 465), a work for string orchestra dedicated to the victims who drowned during the sinking of the *Lusitania*. In 1917 Edward Elgar contributed the most significant lament composition of the war, *The Spirit of England* (no. 471), which consists of three songs based on texts written by Laurence Binyon. It begins with "The Fourth of August," which highlights the soprano solo and tends to the heroic, overblown side of Elgar. The music is grand, highly lyrical, and at times borders on the over-exuberant, with its occasional outbursts of brass and timpani. The second section ("To Women") is much more refined and sensitive than the first part, but not as significant as what follows in "For the Fallen." The last section, lasting almost fifteen minutes, has been singled out for its particular effectiveness and became a national memorial played each year on Remembrance Day in Great Britain after the war. Binyon wrote the poem after the first wave of casualties had occurred during World War I. The text itself is a powerful lament mentioning the youth who died for their mother country. Elgar's setting begins with a noble orchestral introduction and continues with pained elegance throughout. Again the soprano is featured, but this time in one of Elgar's most haunting and sublime melodies. This remains one of the most effective laments to originate from World War I. Ernest Newman praised Elgar's work on several occasions. In July 1917 he wrote that

> I cannot speak for others; but of myself I can say that the "Carillon," "To Women," and "For the Fallen" have been the works that more than any others have strengthened and consoled me in these last three desolate years. Alone among our musicians,—alone, as far as I have means of knowing, among the musicians of any of the belligerent nations,—Elgar has seen this terrible and horrible thing *sub specie aeternitatis*.[6]

After the premiere of *The Spirit of England* in its entirety, Newman proclaimed in November 1917 that

> Elgar has expressed the enduring emotions of the war better than anyone else has done or can hope to do either in music or poetry. The general idiom of "The Spirit of England" is just that idealized common speech of the feelings that a truly national work demands. The simplest soul would find itself at home in it; and there would be no better celebration of peace than a performance of it on a truly communal scale.[7]

Elgar was also the most prolific British composer of war-related music. In addition to *The Spirit of England*, he wrote several patriotic works particularly for those suffering in other countries—among them: *Polonia* (1915) (no. 470) for a Polish Victims Relief Fund Concert, and three others to garner support for Belgium: *Carillon* (1914) (no. 467), *Une voix dans le désert* (1915) (no. 472), and *Le drapeau belge* (1917) (no. 469). These last three works all include narrator and orchestra but, while important for their functional use of the time, had little to offer after the war concluded. Ernest Newman believed that "In the 'Carillon' Elgar gave expression to the best that is in us at that time of trial. It was not mere war-music; it was music that transcended the shouting and the trampling, the blood and murk of war."[8]

It is important to remember that even before World War I Elgar composed his famous *Pomp and Circumstance* marches, which stem from Shakespeare's *Othello*, "The pomp and circumstance of glorious war." Elgar wrote these marches to inspire young soldiers to march off to war and die for the glories of their country. It did not take him long to realize how war had changed, however, and his music changed accordingly, most clearly in his last direct war statement "For the Fallen."

A number of composers from other Western countries produced laments as well. In America Ives wrote his *Second Orchestral Set* (1915) (no. 442) in response to the *Lusitania* disaster and Bernard Rogers his dirge *To the Fallen* (1918) (no. 504). The Italians Alfredo Casella and Gian Malipiero contributed elegies to the dead, as did Matthijs Vermeulen in the Netherlands. In Germany, Reger wrote a powerful organ work *Trauerode* (from *Sieben Stücke*, 1916) (no. 460) for those killed during the first two years of fighting, and the Austrian composer Emil Rezniček wrote one of the longest laments: *In Memoriam* (1916) (no. 447). In France Maurice Ravel dedicated individual movements of his *Le tombeau de Couperin* (1917) (no. 453) to soldiers killed in the war, and Claude Debussy wrote two small pieces, *Berceuse héroïque* (1915) (no. 449) and *Noël des enfants qui n'ont plus de maisons* (1915) (no. 451), to lament the destruction in France and Belgium. Many French criticized Debussy's effort in *Berceuse héroïque*, in particular because it seemed to be too insubstantial for a serious work about the war. Ernest Newman joined the criticism with a particularly damning statement: "The utter irrelevance, the too self-conscious egoism of a deliberately super-subtle idiom was shown us some time ago by the 'Berceuse héroïque' that Debussy wrote for King Albert's book."[9]

Although few of these compositions are familiar to us today, they exhibit the radical change in musical consciousness that World War I created. The humor, the heroics, the grandeur was taken out of war and the music portraying it. Composers were unsure how to replace the earlier victory and battle pieces. (By World War II they would feel more at home in the musical depiction of wars and the massive death and devastation for which war was now responsible.) World War I remained an important theme in the war music written before 1939, when World War II replaced it as the most relevant war for which to compose music.

AFTER WORLD WAR I

Immediately following the war, composers continued to write compositions dealing with the first great war. American composers, however, having been involved only a year or so in World War I, did not yield a large number of compositions about the war after it was over.

Frederick Converse and Horatio Parker immediately answered in 1919 with patriotic victory celebrations: *The Answer of the Stars* (no. 510) and *A.D. 1919* (no. 514). Four years later Ernest Schelling composed *A Victory Ball* (1923) (no. 515) to show how war intruded on the dance of peace. In 1929 John Becker wrote his Third Symphony ("Symphonia brevis") (no. 509) in which he lamented the young men killed senselessly in the war. This symphony and Becker's vitriolic comments in his preface together form one of the earliest and harshest protest works to arise out of World War I.

After the war the English, in particular, improved upon the requiem and lament tradition that they had employed so much during the war. John Foulds, Arthur Bliss, and Frank Bridge contributed the most notable successes. Foulds's *A World Requiem* (no. 524) achieved short-lived fame in post-war Britain and received performances each Armistice Day in London between 1923 and 1926. Written for four soloists, boys' choir, organ, chorus, and orchestra, Foulds's requiem includes a large battery of percussion instruments. The text consists mostly of passages from the Bible, but the work also contains an unusual fifth movement in which each nation is called upon to live in peace with one another. Two movements ("Pax" and "Lux Veritatis") specifically request that the boys' choir be placed "in a distant gallery," a device that quite likely influenced Benjamin Britten. Forty years later Britten's *War Requiem* included similar instrumental and vocal forces and specifically marked parts for the boys' choir as "distant."

Bliss had been haunted by recurrent dreams since the end of the war and felt he had to compose his *Morning Heroes* (no. 520) to exorcise these nightmares.[10] Written in 1930 after extensive reflection, Bliss dedicated the composition to his brother, who had been killed at the Battle of the Somme, and to "all my other comrades-in-arms who fell in the Great War of 1914-18." He subtitled the work "Symphony for Orator, Chorus and Orchestra." It contains five movements and uses texts from Homer, Walt Whitman, Wilfred Owen, Robert Nichols, and the Chinese poet Li Tai-Po. Each of the movements deals with a different aspect of war. The orator reads "Hector's Farewell to Andromache" in the first movement, which treats the subject of a husband and wife parting because of war. The second, based on Whitman's "The City Arming," deals with the self-sacrifice young volunteers make as they go off to war. The third deals with the emotions of the young soldiers at the front, their loved ones at home, and the longing they have for one another. The fourth, based on Homer's *Iliad*, illustrates the heroism in battle. In the last movement, Bliss begins with a narration of Owen's "Spring Offensive" before setting Robert Nichols's poem "Dawn on the Somme," which deals specifically with the Battle of the Somme in which Bliss's brother was killed. *Morning Heroes* is one of the earliest large-scale compositions to contain extensive narration, a technique that many subsequent composers of war-related music have employed[11] and was, as well, the first to incorporate the poetry of Wilfred Owen in music. Other composers, most notably Rudolf Escher and Benjamin Britten, followed in setting Owen's poetry to music.

Bridge's thirty-minute *Oration* (no. 521), in nine continuous parts, contains some rather explosive military marches and fanfares, but largely is, as its subtitle "Concerto elegiaco" indicates, highly lyrical and elegiac. Its ominous opening with soft drum rolls sets the stage for the darkness of the work. Most telling, however, is the brief conclusion which Bridge later added to the work and which provides a symbolic gesture with its D-major conclusion, perhaps indicating the need for peace.

Following in the tradition of Foulds's *A World Requiem* and Bliss's *Morning Heroes*, Vaughan Williams selected his own text, combining Biblical passages, the text of the Agnus Dei, and poetry by Walt Whitman for his *Dona nobis pacem* (1936) (no. 400). Since the central three movements are based on Whitman's text depicting the horror of war and the tragedy it brings, it is more than a peace composition the title indicates. For the fourth movement, Vaughan Williams included his earlier setting of Whitman's "Dirge for Two Veterans." The work begins with "Agnus Dei qui tollis peccata mundi, Dona nobis pacem," and ends with the optimistic Biblical phrase, "Glory to God in the highest, and on earth peace, good-will toward men."

The greatest work dealing with World War I is undoubtedly Benjamin Britten's *War Requiem* (1961) (no. 523). Authors of all types, writing in books, journals, and reviews, have referred to this work as one of the monumental masterpieces of the century. It is at times grandiose, but just as often haunting in its simplicity. What makes the composition work so well is the way Britten combines the three different musical sounds into one whole. The tenor and baritone soloists represent a British and German soldier respectively and are accompanied by a chamber orchestra. A soprano solo or full chorus presents the Latin text with a full orchestral accompaniment, and though not used as frequently, a boys' choir sings accompanied by a chamber organ. Only near the end do these three disparate sounds and groups come together. In addition to the requiem text, Britten interpolated several of Owen's poems written during World War I (and before his death as a soldier in 1918). The most powerful of these is the last one Britten set, "Strange Meeting," in which two enemy soldiers who are mortally wounded meet.

To create many of his gripping effects in this work, Britten uses different patterns and types of repetition. He opens and closes with repeated notes, with the chorus chanting the words "Requiem aeternam."

Repeated notes are also called for in the opening fanfare of the Dies Irae. Britten also uses the interval of a tritone conspicuously in this work. The requiem begins with bells and chorus on F-sharps before moving to Cs; later the tritone appears harmonically in the bells themselves. (See example 9.) Near the end of the requiem, the tritone returns in the boys' choir, and the final sound the orchestra makes is the bells a tritone apart.

Example 9: Britten, *War Requiem*, I:
  © Copyright 1962 by Boosey & Hawkes Music Publishers, Ltd. Copyright Renewed. Reprinted by permission.

Although based in part upon World War I poems, Britten's *War Requiem* is as much about World War II as it is World War I. Britten composed the work specifically for the re-opening of Coventry Cathedral, which German bombs destroyed in World War II, and, as well, he selected soloists from three Western countries to symbolize these warring countries coming together as one: Peter Pears from Great Britain, Dietrich Fischer-Dieskau from Germany, and Galina Vishnevskaya from the Soviet Union.

THE RUSSIAN REVOLUTION

During the years after the 1917 Russian Revolution, Soviet composers began a prolific campaign of depicting the revolution in all genres of music. Countless number of composers, the vast majority unknown in the West, contributed to this enormous patriotism and national consciousness—a practice which continued until the last couple of decades. Composers began producing works during and immediately after the revolution. Nicolay Myaskovsky, who fought in World War I and the Russian Revolution, wrote three symphonies between 1917 and 1923 that deal in some way with the war or revolution. Symphony No. 6 (no. 560), in particular, quotes "Dies irae," "Carmagnole," and "Ah ça ira" and is his most substantial symphonic lament and grand heroic symphony to grow out of this period. Prokofiev also responded immediately to the revolution with *Seven, They are Seven* (no. 491) and a brief sketch of war in his *Visions fugitives* (no. 492).[12] Aleksandr Grechaninov composed his *Hymn of Free Russia* (1917) (no. 487) which was one of the earliest compositions written for the Russian Revolution.

Within the first decade after the revolution, Vladimir Deshevov had composed the ballet *The Red Whirlwind* (1924) (no. 574), Arseny Gladkovsky the first Soviet opera on a revolutionary subject *Red Petrograd* (1925) (no. 578), and Konstantin Listov and Mikhail Gnesin had composed oratorios, respectively, *October* (1921) (no. 584) and *1905-1917* (1925) (no. 558). The tenth anniversary inspired numerous composers to celebrate this milestone and started the tradition of celebrating the revolution every ten years with newly composed music. Nearly every Soviet composer wrote at least one work for these celebrations. Prokofiev, for example, composed his massive *Cantata for the 20th Anniversary of the October Revolution* (no. 562) in 1927, and Shostakovich composed works for each anniversary from 1927 to 1967. In 1927 he composed his Symphony No. 2 ("October") (no. 563) concluding with a heroic chorus. In 1937 he rebounded from Stalin's disfavor with his Symphony No. 5 (subtitled "A Soviet Artist's Reply to Just Criticism"). In 1947 he finished his little-known patriotic cantata *Poem of the Motherland*. In 1957 he dedicated his Symphony No. 11 (no. 1101) to the fortieth anniversary of the Revolution, and in 1967 he followed with a new, brash symphonic poem *October* (no. 1269). He also dedicated his Symphony No. 12 (no. 1102) to the revolution and gave each movement an appropriate revolutionary title. In the case of Shostakovich, some of these works transcend their perfunctory roles. With few exceptions, however, these revolutionary works have not outlived their time, particularly now with the recent demise of the Soviet Union.

THE SPANISH CIVIL WAR

During the thirties—the decade of Hitler, Nazi Germany, the Spanish Civil War, and Second Sino-Japanese War (1931-1945)—writers, visual artists, and composers created a large number of war-related works. Maria Jose Montes's bibliography of literature related to the Spanish Civil War *La guerra española en la creación literaria* listed over four hundred novels and numerous plays and poems.[13] Immediate reactions to the Spanish Civil War led Henry Leland Clarke (no. 536), Vít Nejedlý (no. 588), Jaroslav Ježek (no. 580), Wallingford Riegger (no. 539), Paul Dessau (no. 545), and, most importantly, Britten (no. 675) to memorialize this tragedy through their compositions. Later, Clermont Pépin (no. 1072), Luigi Nono (no. 1091), William Penn (no. 1229), Alcides Lanza (no. 1237), Walter Steffens (no. 1250), Leonardo Balada (no. 1270), and Bronislaw Przybilski (no. 1262) contributed major works dealing exclusively with Picasso's famous anti-war painting *Guernica*.

The uneasiness of composers after Hitler's rise led composers such as Hanns Eisler, William Alwyn, and Vaughan Williams to write war-related works out of fear of the future. Vaughan Williams's *Dona nobis pacem* (1936) (no. 400) and Eisler's *Gegen den Krieg* (1936) (no. 547) and *Deustche Sinfonie* (1938) (no. 546) are the most important war-related works of the decade before the beginning of World War II.

ANNOTATED LISTING OF WAR COMPOSITIONS:
1900-1913

America (United States)

Baker, J.L. (20th c.)

411. *The Battle of Manila.* Piano [c. 1902]. #Kansas City, Kan.: J.L.
Baker, 1902.
M25.B
Prefaced with a poem of the same title, this work is one of the
last typical battle pieces looking back to the works that so
dominated war-related music in the eighteenth and nineteenth
centuries. The work is in ten sections, including "Ships sailing in
the bay under cover of darkness," "The gongs sound and the men
rush to their port of duty," and "Drums as they parade the streets of
Manila." Includes the tune "Yankee Doodle" and has a lament in G
minor.

Farwell, Arthur (1872-1952)

412. *Navajo War Dance.* Piano [1904]. #*The Wa-Wan Press 1901-1911*,
ed. Vera Brodsky Lawrence (New York: Arno Press & the New
York Times, 1970), vol. 3, pp. 58-60. Later arranged for
unaccompanied voices as Op. 102 and appears on *New World
213.
M1669.F
A syncopated C-major piece in 9/8 meter uses ostinato bass
Cs and primitive, repeated, dance-like patterns accelerating "with
savage abandon."

413. *Navajo War Dance No. 2,* Op. 29. Piano [1908]. #New York:
Music Press, 1947. *New World Recordings NW 213.
M31.F
A fast, chromatic, and strongly accented work based in E
major, written chiefly in 4/4 but with a middle section alternating
between 6/8 and 9/8. Significant virtuosity is required in its use of
fast open octaves and thick chords.

Loeffler, Charles Martin (1861-1935)

414. *For One Who Fell in Battle.* Chorus [1911]. #New York: G.
Schirmer, 1911. Text by T.W. Parsons.
    M1582.L825F6
    A brief, heroic lament for eight-part chorus, highly
sectionalized and ending in B major. The music is tonal
throughout, with some adventuresome chromaticism. Dedicated to
Major Henry Lee Higginson in memory of his comrades who never
returned from war.

Troyer, Carlos (1837-1920)

415. *Kiowa-Apache War Dance.* Piano [1907]. #*The Wa-Wan Press
1901-1911*, ed. Vera Brodsky Lawrence (New York: Arno Press &
the New York Times, 1970), vol. 4, pp. 73-83.
    M1669.T
    "In a mystic and startling manner," this work is a transcription
of an Apache war dance. It is notated in cut time and is highly
repetitive with heavy accents on the first, third, and fourth beats of
each measure.

Czechoslovakia

Janáček, Leoš (1854-1928)

416. *Mr. Brouček's Excursions to the Moon.* Opera [1908-1917]. 1st:
23 April 1920. *Supraphon 1116 3291.
    M1503.J265V73 1965
    Part II returns to the fifteenth century at the time of the
Hussite Wars. The chorale "Hear ye, the Warriors of God" appears
in the second act and the scene ends with a spectacular victory
celebration.

France

Boulanger, Lili (1893-1918)

417. *Pour les funérailles d'un soldat.* Baritone, chorus, and orchestra
[1912]. #New York: G. Schirmer, 1981. *Festive Classique FC
411. Text by Alfred Musset.
    M1530.B76P5

A poignant lament for the soldiers who died in war. The work, in the style and tempo of a funeral march, uses snippets of the Dies irae theme.

Bruneau, Alfred (1857-1934)

418. *Les quatre journées.* Opera [1908-1916]. 1st: 25 December 1916. #Paris: Choudens, 1916. Libretto after Emile Zola.
    M1503.B899Q3
    The second of four acts, "Summer" contains a vast battle scene with soldiers crying "To death" and later standing over the dead lying in the fields. Full of tremolos and ostinatos built largely around C minor.

Great Britain

Boughton, Rutland (1878-1960)

419. *The Invincible Armada.* Symphonic poem for chorus and orchestra [1901]. 1st: Newcastle-on-Tyne Triennial Music Festival, 1909. #London: Novello, 1909.
    *MP (English) NYPL call number
    Dedicated "To my Brother (at war, 1901)," this is a heroic work in B-flat major illustrating the British victory over the Spanish Armada.

Harty, Hamilton (1879-1941)

420. *With the Wild Geese.* Symphonic poem [1910]. 1st: 1910. #London: Novello, 1912. *Chandos CHAN 8321.
    M1002.H34
    A historical tone-poem dealing with the Wild Geese (the Irish Regiment who fought against the French at Fontenoy in 1745). Two poems by Emily Lavless preface the score. The music is romantic, lush, and mildly programmatic with fanfares and the confusion of battle.

Holbrooke, Josef (1878-1958)

421. *The Song of Gwynn ap Nudd,* Op. 52. Piano and orchestra [1907, revised 1923]. #London: J.B. Cramer, 1909. Text by T.E. Ellis.
    M1011.H72 Op.52

A programmatic work, with text excerpts placed as headings for various sections of the work. The battle section beginning with "Blade that meets blade" (Allegro, molto fuoco) is *ff* and highly chromatic, with bombastic chordal textures in the piano.

Holst, Gustav (1874-1934)

422. *Battle March,* Op. 26, No. 1 in *Choral Hymn from the Rig Veda.* Chorus and orchestra [1908-1909]. #Melville, New York: H.W. Gray, 1912. *EMI CDC 7494092. Text translated from Sanskrit.
        M1531.H76 Op. 26
        A C-minor march in 5/4 with accents on two and four. Serves in some ways as a study for the more elaborate 5/4 "Mars" movement in *The Planets* composed six years later.

MacCunn, Hamish (1868-1916)

423. *The Masque of War and Peace.* Opera [c. 1900]. 1st: London, 13 February 1900. #London: Chappell, 1960. Libretto by Louis N. Parker.
        M1523.M17M4
        A sectionalized, opera-like work with titles such as "Wars and the Rumours of War," "War! and Entry of War," and "Entrance of Victory, Rebellion, The Arts of Peace &c." War is associated with the key of F minor, loud dynamics, brass, and dotted rhythms. The work ends with a call for peace in G major.

Neumann, Mathieu (20th c.)

424. *Sardanapalus,* Op. 51. Baritone, male chorus, and orchestra [c. 1902]. 1st: May 1902. #London: J. Curwen, 1903.
        M1538.N49S3
        A tale of the Emperor Sardanapalus burning his palace because he could not defend Nineveh. Includes cries of battle with dotted rhythms, imitation in contrary motion, and ferocious tremolos.

Parry, Hubert (1848-1918)

425. *War and Peace.* Symphonic ode for soloists, chorus, and orchestra [1903]. #London: Novello, 1930.
        M1533.P26W2
        In ten sections: "Prologue," "War Song," "Recompense," "Comradeship," "The Dirge," "Home-coming," "Peace," "Home,"

"Marching Song of Peace," and "Aspirations." The "War Song" is typically fast and loud, starting in F major and ending in C major.

Speer, Charlton (20th c.)

426. *The Battle of Lake Regillus*. Cantata for chorus and orchestra. [c. 1909]. #London: Breitkopf & Härtel, 1909. Text by Lord Macaulay.
M1533.S74B3
A grandiose retelling of the Roman battle. In three parts: "The Challenge," "The Battle," and "The Twin Brethren." The music is pompous and full of the exhilaration of pride in war.

Stanford, Charles V. (1852-1924)

427. *Ode to Wellington*, Op. 100. Soprano, baritone, chorus, and orchestra [1907]. #London and New York: Boosey & Hawkes, 1907. Text by Alfred, Lord Tennyson.
M1533.S795W3
Not a war composition in the usual sense, but an outmoded, out-of-proportion glorious composition full of praise for a dead military hero.

Taylor, H.J. (20th c.)

428. *The Battle of Inkerman*. Chorus and orchestra [1912]. #London: Weekes, 1912. Text by Charles Mackay.
M1533.T233B3
A heroic ballad reenacting the battle with cries "To arms" when the Russians attack the British. It ends with a victorious praise of France and England and their routing of the Russians. The music is tonal, explosive, and descriptive of the text.

Wood, Charles (1866-1926)

429. *Dirge for Two Veterans*. Bass solo, chorus, and orchestra [1901]. #London: Boosey, 1901. Text by Walt Whitman.
M1533.W874D3
In E-flat major, this work begins in "Dead-march time" with a largely homophonic chorus. Thereafter the soloist alternates with the chorus in various key and tempo changes. The chorus divides into eight parts for the concluding twenty measures ending softly in E-flat major.

Hungary

Bartók, Béla (1881-1945)

430. *Kossuth*. Symphonic poem [1903]. 1st: Budapest, 13 January 1904. #Mainz: B. Schott's Söhne, 1963. *Sefel SE,CD 5008. M1002.B227K7

A ten-part tone-poem telling the life of Kossuth and his role in the 1848 Hungarian Revolution. Parts six through ten illustrate the call to arms, the struggle, and the defeat. Bartók employs minor keys in this section along with the timpani and gong.

The Netherlands

Anrooy, Peter van (1879-1954)

431. *Piet Hein*. Orchestral rhapsody [1901]. #Middelburg [Leipzig]: A. A. Noske, 1902. *Fontana 6530-044. M1002.A6

Piet Hein was an admiral from Holland who was important in the Netherlands' war against Spain (1568-1648). The work is a boisterous C-major composition, highly diatonic, with numerous repeated motives, including the revolutionary tune "Wien Neêrlands bloed" which originated in 1830.

Russia

Grechaninov, Aleksandr [Gretchaninoff, Alexander] (1864-1956) [American citizen 1946]

432. *To the Memory of the Fallen for Freedom*. Chorus [1905].
[No LC number available]

Deals with the massacre on 9 January 1905 in the Winter Palace Square in St. Petersburg. In his autobiography *My Life*, trans. Nicholas Slonimsky (New York: Coleman-Ross, 1952), Grechaninov wrote: "When the news of the massacre reached Moscow, I was indignant and outraged. . . . and I wrote a threnody for the fallen victims" (p. 100).

Rimsky-Korsakov, Nikolay (1844-1908)

433. *Le coq d'or.* Opera [1908]. 1st: Moscow, 7 October 1909. #New
York: Kalmus, 197-. *Gramophone 20148/50. Libretto by
Vladimir Bielsky.
M1503.R577Z6
A satire on war, but also realistic and anti-war at times. The
war beginning in Act II is not successful; however, two sons of
King Dodon are killed and the king sings a tragic lament upon
finding his dead sons.

434. *Legend of the Invisible City of Kitezh.* Opera [1903-1905]. 1st: 20
February 1907. #Leningrad: Muzyka, 1981. *Melodiya 33S-
0377/82. Libretto by Vladimir Bielsky.
M1503.R577S42
Contains a battle piece "The Battle of Kerzhenets" often
extracted as an individual orchestral work. Its driving, repeated
rhythmic patterns anticipate Prokofiev's "Battle on the Ice" in
Alexander Nevsky.

SUPPLEMENT OF WAR COMPOSITIONS:
1900-1913

435. Bantock, Granville (1868-1946). Great Britain. *The Charge of the
Light Brigade.* Male chorus [c. 1911]. #London: J. Curwen, 1911.
Text by Alfred, Lord Tennyson.
436. Bax, Arnold (1883-1953). Great Britain. *A Song of War and
Victory.* Tone poem for orchestra [1905]. Never performed. [Cited
in Lewis Foreman, *Bax: A Composer and His Times* (Cambridge:
University Press, 1987), p. 34ff].
437. ———. *Mircath (Viking Battle Song).* Song [1905]. Text by
Fiona Macleod. [Cited in Foreman, p. 38ff].
438. Kienzl, Wilhelm (1857-1941). Germany. *Geschichtsbilder,* Op. 79.
Cantata for male chorus and orchestra [c. 1908]. #Leipzig: F.E.C.
Leuckart, [c. 1908]. *MP (NYPL call number). Deals with the
Bauernkrieg of 1502.

America (United States)

Homer, Sidney (1864-1953)

439. *The Battle of Blenheim*, Op. 32. Voice and piano [1914]. #New
      York: G. Schirmer, 1914. Text by Robert Southey.
          *MP box (NYPL call number)
          An F-major cynical view of war, undermining what a patriotic
      victory really is. An eight-page song about the Duke of
      Marlborough and Prince Eugen.

Ives, Charles (1874-1954)

440. *He is There!* Voice and piano. [30 May 1917]. #*114 Songs*, pp.
      107-11.
          M1620.I92S6
          Grouped as the second in *Three Songs of the War*, this is the
      most outrageous of Ives's war songs. Includes quotes from
      "Tenting Tonight," "Battle Cry of Freedom," and "Marching
      Through Georgia." More popular in its expanded version *They are
      There!* See also item 443.

441. *In Flanders Fields*. Baritone or male chorus and piano [1917,
      revised 1919]. #*114 Songs*, pp. 104-06. Text by McCrae.
          M1620.I92S6
          An anti-war song quoting fragments of "America" and "La
      marseillaise"; the first of the *Three Songs of the War*.

442. Second Orchestral Set ("From Hanover Square North at the End of
      A Tragic Day the People Again Arose"). Orchestra [1915]. #New
      York: International, 1971. *London SPC 21060 and CBS MK-
      37823.
          M1003.I9407 no. 2
          Dedicated to the victims in the sinking of the *Lusitania*. In
      three movements (Very slowly, Allegro, and [Allegro]) with
      characteristic Ivesian polyrhythms, dissonances, and textural
      confusion.

443. *They are There: A War Song March.* Chorus and orchestra [1917, text revised 1942]. #New York: Peer International, 1961. Text by Ives.

  M1544.I9T5

  An expanded version of *He is There!* The Kronos Quartet plays an arrangement with a recording of Ives singing on Elektra Nonesuch 979242-2.

444. *Tom Sails Away.* Voice and piano [1917]. #*114 Songs*, pp. 112-14. *Etcetera ETC 1020.

  M1620.I92S6

  A poignant, subtle war song, the last of the *Three Songs of the War.*

Ornstein, Leo (b. 1892)

445. *Poems of 1917.* Piano [1918]. #New York: Fischer, 1918.

  [OCLC 21863012]

  Ten piano pieces written during and about World War I: "No Man's Land," "The Sower of Despair," "The Orient in Flanders," "The Wrath of the Despoiled," "Night Brooding Over the Battlefield," "A Dirge of the Trenches," "Song Behind the Lines," "The Battle," "Army at Prayer," and "Dance of the Dead."

Treharne, Bryceson (1879-1948) [Welsh born]

446. *Dirge for a Fallen Soldier.* Voice and piano (and optional chorus) [c. 1917]. #Boston: Boston Music, 1917. Text by George Henry Boker.

  M1621.T

  Begins with a slow funeral march in C minor but ends victoriously on a C-major chord.

Austria

Reznicek, Emil Nikolaus von (1860-1945)

447. *In Memoriam.* Alto, baritone, chorus, and string orchestra (in fourth movement two trumpets and timpani ad libitum) [1916]. 1st: 1916. #Vienna: Universal, 1916. Texts from Jeremiah, Lamentations of Jeremiah, and Psalms.

  *MRHI+ (NYPL call number)

In two parts and seven sections, this is one of the largest
choral laments to be written during the war. The musical language
is chromatic and the string orchestra keeps the death-feeling
appropriate to the reason for its being written.

Czechoslovakia

Janáček, Leoš (1854-1928)

448.   *Taras Bulba*. Orchestra, including organ [1915-1918]. 1st: 9
       October 1921. #Prague: Editio Supraphon, 1980. *London
       410138-2 LH and Angel CDC-47048. Based on text of Gogol.
            M1045.J32T3 1947
            A twenty-five minute, programmatic tone-poem illustrating
       musically the anguish of a besieged seventeenth-century town and
       the death of Taras Bulba. A battle scene erupts at the end of the
       first section ("The Death of Andri"), with fanfares and sinister
       trombone blasts and percussion sounding like swords clashing. The
       second ("The Death of Ostap") also has battle imagery, and the last
       section ("The Prophecy and Death of Taras Bulba") contains a
       heroic vision of the people resisting the enemy.

France

Debussy, Claude (1862-1918)

449.   *Berceuse héroïque*. Piano (Also an orchestral version) [1914]. 1st:
       15 October 1915. #London: Editions Peters, 1975. *Pantheon
       D20929 and Kapp KC 9061-S.
            M25.D (piano); M1060.D28 B5 (orchestra)
            "Inscribed to the King of the Belgians and his soldiers," this
       sixty-eight measure work remains soft throughout except for a
       brief, eight-measure "climax" that leads nowhere. The work centers
       around E-flat minor and often uses a tonic-dominant ostinato in the
       bass.

450.   *En blanc et noir*. Two pianos [1915]. 1st: 21 December 1916.
       #Paris: Durand, 1915. *Elektra/Nonesuch 79161-2 and Harmonia
       Mundi 90957.
            M214.D28E6
            Influenced by the events of war and includes sounds imitating
       gunfire and trumpet fanfares. Debussy dedicated the second

movement to Lieutenant Jacques Charlot who was killed in action in 1915.

451. *Noël des enfants qui n'ont plus de maisons.* Voice and piano (Also a version for children's two-part chorus) [1915]. 1st: 9 April 1916. #Paris: Durand, 1916. *Westminster WL 5336. Text by Debussy.
     M2114.5.D
     A short, simple song in A minor that contains two different ostinatos in the piano. The voice is smooth, diatonic, and not particularly inspired, all packaged together in an ABA form.

Indy, Vincent d' (1851-1931)

452. Symphony No. 3 ("Sinfonia brevis de bello gallico"), Op. 70. Orchestra [1916-1918]. 1st: 14 December 1919. #Paris: Rouart & Lerolle, 1919.
     M1001.I424
     The first movement opens with a slow introduction, followed by a faster section. The second movement is a scherzo in ABA form; the third is a traditional slow movement. The fourth is very lively concluding in D major. It uses a substantial amount of percussion but is not overtly programmatic.

Ravel, Maurice (1875-1937)

453. *Le tombeau de Couperin.* Piano, later orchestrated [1914-1917]. #Paris: Durand, 1918. *Chandos CHAN-8620 (piano) and London 400051-2 LH (orchestra).
     M24.R27T5
     Each movement is dedicated to a soldier killed in World War I, and the work as a whole is an homage to Couperin. Other than the dedication, there is nothing specifically war-like in any of these short movements written in forms of the Baroque suite.

Saint-Saëns, Camille (1835-1921)

454. *Vers la victoire. Pas redoublé pour musique militaire*, Op. 152. [1918]. #Paris: Durand, 1918.
     **M.455.6 (Boston)
     An eleven-page victory work written at the close of the war.

Schmitt, Florent (1870-1958)

455. *Chant du guerre*, Op. 63. Tenor, male chorus, and orchestra [1914].
#Paris: A. Durand, 1916. Text by Léon Tonnelier.
M1540.S344C4
A patriotic battle cry in A-flat major, ending *ff* with
percussion, full orchestra and chorus, and harp glissandi on the
words "victory and liberty."

Widor, Charles-Marie (1845-1937)

456. *Salvum fac populum Tuum*, Op. 84. Three trumpets, three
trombones, drum, and organ [1917]. 1st: Paris, 17 November
1918. #Paris: Heugel, 1917.
**MX+ (NYPL call number)
"Composed for the services in Notre Dame cathedral,
November 17, 1918, celebrating the victory of the Allies in the
European war." Opens *fff* in C minor with considerable dotted
rhythms and concludes in a grandiose *fff* C major.

Germany

Pfitzner, Hans (1869-1949)

457. *Palestrina.* Opera [1917]. 1st: 12 June 1917. #Mainz & New York:
Schott Music, 1951. *Melodram MEL 429 and DG 427 417-2.
Libretto by Pfitzner.
M1500.P529P3 1951
Not related to World War I but composed during it. The end of
Act II contains a brief but highly energetic battle scene, with gun
shots and blasting brass sounds as Madruscht orders the soldiers to
fire upon the servants who are upset over an insult that occurred at
the Council of Trent meetings in 1563.

Reger, Max (1873-1916)

458. *Dankpsalm* from *Sieben Stücke*, Op. 145. Organ [1916]. #*Max
Reger: Sämtliche Werke*, (Wiesbaden: Breitkopf & Härtel), vol.
18.
M3.R42 Bd. 18
Dedicated to "Dem deutschen Heere," this D-major vivace is in
stark contrast to the preceding *Trauerode*. It ends with the chorale
"Lobet den Herren."

459. *Siegesfeier* from *Sieben Stücke*, Op. 145. Organ [1916]. #*Max Reger: Sämtliche Werke*, vol. 18. *Telefunken SAT 22519.
   M3.R42 Bd. 18
   A fast, turbulent, grandiose work full of *ff* chords, rapid thirty-second note passages, and abundant chromaticism concluding in G major.

460. *Trauerode* from *Sieben Stücke*, Op. 145. Organ [1916]. #*Max Reger: Sämtliche Werke*, vol. 18. *Telefunken SAT 22519.
   M3.R42 Bd. 18
   The dedication reads, "Dem Gedenken der im Kriege 1914/15 Gefallen." The D-minor work begins and ends *pppp* and is highly chromatic and expressive, full of minor seconds, and concludes with the chorale "Was Gott tut, das ist wohlgetan."

461. *Eine vaterländischen Ouvertüre*, Op. 140. Orchestra [1914]. 1st: 8 January 1915. #Berlin & Leipzig: N. Simrock, 1914.
   M1004.R333V3
   A fourteen-minute overture dedicated to the German army and includes "Deutschland, Deutschland, über Alles" and ends gloriously (*fff*) on an F-major chord.
   Reger also wrote a war-related work which he failed to complete: Requiem, Op. 145a. Baritone, chorus, and orchestra [1915]. #Vienna: Philharmonischer, 1925. M2023.R333I7.

Great Britain

Bax, Arnold (1883-1953)

462. *In Memoriam*. Cor anglais, harp, and string quartet [1916]. #London: Murdoch & Murdoch, 1935.
   M682.B35I5
   Written as a response to the Easter Rising in Ireland, it begins forcefully in E minor, progressing to F and C minor, before returning to tonic minor and concluding *ppp* in E major. It is predominantly a graceful work and serious lament, but its intensity leads it to a "rough and fierce" outburst before arriving at its concluding E-major section.

463. Violin Sonata No. 2. Violin and piano [1915, revised 1922]. 1st: April 1922. #London: Murdoch & Murdoch, 1923.
   M219.B355

Some writers claim this sonata was influenced by the fighting during World War I and have called the second movement "The Dance of Death." See Lewis Foreman, *Bax: A Composer and His Times*, 2nd ed (Cambridge: Cambridge University Press, 1988), p. 137.

Brian, Havergal (1876-1972)

464. *The Tigers*. A satirical anti-war opera [1916-1919 (Orchestration 1928-1929)]. 1st: 3 May 1983. #London: Cranz, 1932.
      M1503 .B8502 T4
      As a "distraction from war horrors," Brian wrote this opera whose plot includes a law requiring every male under seventy-five years old to serve. He depicts the aerial zeppelin attacks on London during World War I.

Bridge, Frank (1879-1941)

465. *Lament*. String orchestra [1915]. 1st: London, 15 September 1915. #London: Goodwin & Tabb, 1915. *EMI ED 2908681.
      M1145 .B85 L3
      The eight-part string orchestra opens *con sordini* and with descending minor seconds establishing the sorrowful mood of the piece. Dedicated to Catherine, age 9, who died on the *Lusitania*.

Delius, Frederick (1862-1934)

466. Requiem. Soprano, baritone, double chorus, and orchestra with extended percussion and six horns [1914-1916]. 1st: London, 23 March 1922. #London: Boosey & Hawkes, 1965. *Odeon ASD 2397. Texts by Shakespeare, Nietzsche, and from the Bible.
      M2023.D35R3
      Dedicated to "all young artists who lost their lives in the war." A pantheistic view of life that did not receive much attention until after 1965. The English and German text is not based on the liturgical Latin text. The work is in five distinct sections and is in a more dramatic and chromatic style than generally found in Delius's music.

Elgar, Edward (1857-1934)

467. *Carillon*, Op. 75. Narrator and orchestra [1914]. 1st: 7 December 1914. #London: Elkin, 1914. *EMI ESD 7167 and Pearl SHE CD

9602. Text by Emile Cammaerts, English version by Tita Brand
Cammaerts.

M1729.E

In the tradition of the late nineteenth-century melodramas, this
nine-minute composition was quite popular with the warring
public. Rarely do the orchestra and the narrator perform
simultaneously. The music is march-like, bold and uplifting with
singable melodies, traditional harmonies, and bells of lament. The
work expresses outrage at the German invasion of Belgium.

468. *Fringes of the Fleet.* Four baritones and orchestra [1917]. 1st: June
1917. #New York: G. Ricordi, 1917. *Pearl SHE CD 9602. Text
by Rudyard Kipling.

M1554.E

Contains five simple songs on the themes of ships,
submarines, and death that were popular during the war (and before
Kipling announced his disapproval).

469. *Le drapeau belge*, Op. 79 (*The Belgian Flag*). Narrator and
orchestra [1917]. 1st: April 1917. #London: Elkin, 1916. *Pearl
SHE CD 9602. Text by Emile Cammaerts.

M1729.E

A brief, three-minute work in the tradition of his successful
Carillon and dealing with war-torn Belgium.

470. *Polonia*, Op. 76. Symphonic prelude [1915]. 1st: London, 15 July
1915 (at a Polish Victim's Relief Fund concert). #London: Elkin,
1915. *Pearl SHE CD 9602.

M1004.E412P5

A fifteen-minute symphonic poem which incorporates
quotations from Polish composers (Chopin and Paderewski) as
well as the Polish National Hymn into its heroic and martial
wartime atmosphere. Begins in A minor and ends (Grandioso) in F
major.

471. *The Spirit of England*, Op. 80. Soloists, chorus, and orchestra
[1916]. 1st: 24 November 1917. #London: Novello, 1916.
*Chandos CBR 1013. Text by Laurence Binyon.

M1533.E41S7

A thirty-minute composition that consists of three songs:
"The Fourth of August" (dedicated to the "memory of our glorious
men, with a special thought for the Worcesters"), "To Woman,"
and "For the Fallen." Cyril Rootham had also previously set the

last song in this cycle. See pages 135-37 for additional information. Also see item 479 below.

472. *Une voix dans le désert.* Narrator, soprano, and orchestra [1915]. 1st: January 1916. *Pearl SHE CD 9602. Text by Emile Cammaerts, English version by Tita Brand Cammaerts.
M1614.E42V6
A haunting, dark work more effective than the somewhat overblown *Carillon.* Elgar achieves a better balance between orchestra and narrator in this work, and the addition of the soprano fits in beautifully with the drama and the music as well.

Holst, Gustav (1874-1934)

473. *Dirge for Two Veterans.* Male chorus, three trumpets, two bombardons (or trombone and tuba), side drum, and bass drum [1914]. #London: J. Curwen & Sons, 1914. Text by Walt Whitman.
M1540.H77D5
Written before the war started, this setting in C major uses trumpet fanfares, march-like ostinatos on tonic and dominant, and largely homophonic choral writing.

474. *Mars, the Bringer of War,* from *The Planets.* Orchestra and voices [1914-1916]. 1st: 19 October 1919. #London: J. Curwen & Sons, 1921. *London 414657-2 LH and Philips 416456-2 PH.
M1003.H765
In 5/4 meter with repeated-note patterns climaxing on consecutive single note Gs played *fff.* This movement was completed shortly before the war broke out.

Ireland, John (1879-1962)

475. *The Soldier.* Voice and piano [1917]. #London: Winthrop Rogers, 1917. Text by Rupert Brooke.
M1741.I
A traditional G-flat major setting of this text in a straightforward and largely diatonic four-page song.

Miles, Philip Napier (1865-1935)

476. *Battle,* Op. 7. Song cycle for voice and piano [c. 1917]. #London: Sydney Acott, 1917. Text by Wilfred W. Gibson.

M1741.M

A cycle of ten art songs written during 1916. These songs with titles such as "The Bayonet," "The Fear," and "In the Ambulance" are simple and unpretentious.

Parry, Charles Hubert Hastings (1848-1918)

477. *The Chivalry of the Sea.* Naval Ode by Robert Bridges. Five-part chorus and orchestra [c. 1916]. 1st: 12 December 1916. #London: Novello, 1916.

8053.1059 (Boston Public Library call number)

Written "to commemorate the officers and men of His Majesty's Fleet and of the Mercantile Marines who have fallen in the war." A ten-minute patriotic work that speaks of adding new names to the list of heroes past.

478. *From Death to Life.* Symphonic poem [1914]. 1st: 12 November 1914. *Chandos CHAN 8955 and Nimbus NI5296.

[No LC number available]

Written as a direct response to the beginning of World War I, this sensitive, eighteen-minute composition is in two parts, originally entitled "Lament" and "Consolation," but changed to "Via Mortis" and "Via Vitae" after the first performance. The dramatic music contains lush harmonies, featuring soaring strings and stern low brass in the tradition of Liszt and Tchaikovsky.

Rootham, Cyril (1875-1938)

479. *For the Fallen.* Chorus and orchestra [1915]. #London: Novello, 1915. *EMI EL 27 0605 1. Text by Laurence Binyon.

M1533.R795F5

A heroic elegy in D minor for those killed in the early years of the war. It opens in the spirit of a funeral march which is effective and challenges Elgar's setting of the same text in *The Spirit of England.* See also item 471.

Italy

Casella, Alfredo (1883-1947)

480. *Elegia eroica.* Orchestra [1916]. #Vienna: Universal Edition A.G., 1922.

M1045.C34 E5

A powerful, mature work incorporating timpani and tam tam with repeated-note patterns, tremolos, and trills to produce a harrowing cry against war. The work ends on a tritone, softly in a "tempo di berceuse" and is dedicated to those who lost their lives during World War I.

481. *Pagine de guerra*. Piano four-hands (Orchestra in 1922) [1916]. #Milan: Ricordi, 1916.
M203.C32P3
In four movements or "musical films" dealing with the war in four different areas: "Nel Belgio," "In France," "In Russia," and "In Alsazia." The first opens *f* with harsh, dissonant ostinatos in the bass. The second is calm and full of impressionistic plaining. The third returns to the fast, bass ostinato of the first, growing into a ferocious *fff* and ending on a cluster. The last is a "Tempo di berceuse," moderate, soft, and distant.

Malipiero, Gian F. (1882-1973)

482. *Pause del silenzio*. Symphonic expression [1917]. 1st: Rome, 27 January 1918. #London: J.W. Chester, 1917. *Stradivarius STR 13608.
M1045.M295pa 1917
A twelve-minute, seven-part orchestral work of intense lyricism and pain, growing out of World War I. Brilliantly orchestrated, it contains a dirge-like funeral march as well as other martial overtones.

The Netherlands

Vermeulen, Matthijs (1888-1967)

483. *La veille*. Mezzo-soprano and piano [1917. (Orchestral version in 1932)]. #Amsterdam: Donemus, 1951. *Composer's Voice 8384/2 (Orchestral version). *Composer's Voice 8384/1 (Piano version). Text by François Porché.
M1621.V52V4 198-
A poignant eleven-minute anti-war song which takes place in a woman's mind on the eve of a battle.

484. *The Soldier*. Voice and piano [1917]. #Amsterdam: Donemus, 1983. Text by Rupert Brooke.
Music (Sheet) 86-1050 (NYPL call number)

A gracious yet passionate, five-page Mixolydian setting (Appassionata ed Agitato) of this famous war poem in 2/2.

Norway

Lund, Signe (1868-1950)

485. *The Road To France.* Song [1917]. #New York: G. Schirmer, 1917. Text by Daniel M. Henderson.
M1646.L
The text and music were awarded First Prize by the National Arts Club in its War Song Competition in New York on 31 October 1917. The F-major patriotic call to support America's involvement in the war contains text of heroic proportions.

Russia

Cui, César [Kyui, Tzezar'] (1835-1918)

486. *War: A Momentous Song.* Song [1917]. #New York: John Franklin, 1917. Text by Judah A. Joffe.
[No LC number available]
A curious blend of strong anti-war murmurings and praise for righteous war. Beginning in F minor, the text of the first four stanzas is anti-war; however after three similar stanzas, the work ends in F major dealing with the beauty and fairness of war.

Grechaninov, Aleksandr [Gretchaninoff, Alexander] (1864-1956) [American citizen 1946]

487. *Gimn svobodnoi Rossii (The Hymn of Free Russia).* Chorus [1917]. #New York: Schirmer, 1917. Text by Konstantin Balmont.
M1258.C
A brief three-page, diatonic song in A major. One of earliest works to grow out of the Russian Revolution.

Kastal'sky, Aleksandr [Kastalsky, Alexander] (1856-1926)

488. *Requiem for the Fallen Heroes of the Allied Armies.* Chorus and large orchestra with percussion [1916]. 1st: Moscow, Spring 1916. Also performed in Birmingham, England, 22 November 1917.
[No LC number available]

A large-scale requiem in twelve sections. In her article ("A Requiem for the Aerial Heroes," *Musical Times* 58 (1917), pp. 496-97), Rose Newmarch described sections of this requiem: "The Divine Office is attended by representative groups of soldiers from the allied armies; funeral chants are heard, now from the Russians, now from the Roman Catholics, now from the Serbs, now from the English. One language alternates with another. Sometimes the trumpet calls of the different armies resound—the beat of the drum and the cannonade; more distantly the lamentations of wives, mothers and orphans are audible" (p. 497).

Myaskovsky, Nikolay (1881-1950)

489.   Symphony No. 4 in E minor, Op. 17. Orchestra [1917-1918].
           M1001.M597 Op. 17
           A three-movement work in E minor depicting Myaskovsky's war years. The first movement begins with a slow introduction which leads to an Allegro appassionata in E minor. The second movement (Largo, freddo e senza espressione) is in A-flat major. The last is a fast movement full of ostinatos ending *ffff*.

490.   Symphony No. 5 in D major, Op. 18. Orchestra [1918]. 1st: 18 July 1920. #Moscow: Gos. Muz. Izd-Vo, 1923. *Melodiya C10-08829-30.
           M1001.M594 Op. 18 1964
           A four-movement symphony in D major that uses folk tunes Myaskovsky collected during the war.

Prokofiev, Sergey (1891-1953)

491.   *Seven, They Are Seven*, Op. 30. Cantata for declamatory tenor solo, mixed chorus, huge orchestra [1917-1918, revised 1933]. 1st: Paris, 29 May 1924. #Berlin: Edition Russe de Musique, 1933. *Quintessence P4C-7196. Text by Konstantin Balmont which he based on Chaldean cuneiform writings.
           *MP (Russian) (NYPL call number)
           Prokofiev's response to the 1917 Russian Revolution, this work indicates his feeling of exultation at the revolution. It remains one of Prokofiev's least known and performed works and requires monumental forces, particularly the brass and percussion.

492.   *Visions fugitives*, Op. 22, no. 19. Piano [1915-1917]. #Moscow: A. Gutheil, 1922. *Ex Libris CD-6024.

M25.P

In his biography of Prokofiev, Robinson claimed this brief, thirty-second piece was in part Prokofiev's musical response to the February Revolution (p. 129).

SUPPLEMENT OF WORLD WAR I MUSIC: 1914-1918

493. Aim, Vojtech Borivoy (1886-1972). Czechoslovakia. *From the Years of War*. Male chorus [1915].

494. Axman, Emil (1887-1949). Czechoslovakia. *Z vojny (From the Army)*. Male chorus [1916]. #Prague: Hudební matice Umělecké besedy, 1921.

495. Bax, Arnold (1883-1953). Great Britain. *In Memoriam, Pádraig Pearse*. Piano score, never orchestrated. Unperformed. [Cited in Foreman, p. 139ff]. Written as a response to the Easter Rising in Ireland.

496. Fiala, Jirí Julius (1892-1967). Czechoslovakia. *War and Peace* [1917, revised 1944].

497. Krohn, Felix (1898-1963). Finland. *Sotarukous (War Prayer)*. Orchestra [1918]. [Cited in BAKER, p. 971].

498. Madetoja, Leevi (1887-1947). Finland. Symphony No. 2, Op. 35. Orchestra [1918]. #Helsinki: Fazerin Musikk i Kauppa, 1939. *Finlandia FACD 011. M1001.M16 Op. 35. A four-movement symphony which grew out of Finland's war of independence, in no way programmatic.

499. Maryon, Edward (1867-1954). Great Britain. *Armageddon Requiem*. Symphonic poem [1916]. [Cited in BAKER, p. 1156]. Dedicated to the dead of World War I.

500. Novák, Vitězslav (1870-1949). Czechoslovakia. *Síla a vzdor (Power and Defiance)*, Op. 51. Six male choruses and orchestra [1916-1917]. [Cited in NEW GROVE, vol. 13, p. 437]. Expresses his hatred toward war.

501. _____. *Karlštejn*, Op. 50. Opera [1914-1915]. #Vienna: Universal Editions, 1916. Based on work of Emil Bohuslav Frida. M1503.N93K2. An early anti-war work.

502.   Parker, Horatio (1863-1919). America. *An Allegory of War and Peace*. Mixed chorus and band [1916]. #Manuscript at Yale Library.

503.   Pembaur, Joseph Sr. (1848-1923). Austria. *Requiem*. Chorus and orchestra [1916]. [Cited in BAKER, p. 1741]. Composed in memory of the Tyrolese fallen in World War I.

504.   Rogers, Bernard (1893-1968). America. *To the Fallen: A Dirge*. Orchestra [1918]. 1st: New York, 13 November 1919. [Cited in BAKER, p. 1527].

505.   Scott, Cyril (1879-1970). Great Britain. *Britain's War March*. Piano [c. 1914]. #London: Schott, 1914. M28.S. A pompous C-major work with tremolos and lyrics praising the king. The profits went to the National Relief Fund. "Dedicated, by gracious permission, to H.R.H. The Prince of Wales."

506.   Skilton, Charles S. (1868-1941). America. *War Dance. Cheyenne Tribal Melody* from *Suite Primeval on Indian Melodies*. Orchestra [1915]. 1st: Minneapolis, 29 October 1916. #New York: Carl Fischer, 1917-1921. M1003.S65.

507.   Vomáčka, Boleslav (1887-1965). Czechoslovakia. *Outcries*. Male chorus [1918]. #Prague: Hudební matice Umělecké besedy, 1929.

508.   Vycpálek, Ladislav (1882-1969). Czechoslovakia. *Vojna (War)*. Song cycle [1915]. #Lipsko: Hudební matice Umělecké besedy, 1919.

ANNOTATED LISTING OF WORLD WAR I MUSIC
COMPOSED AFTER 1918

America (United States)

Becker, John Joseph (1886-1961)

509. Symphony No. 3 ("Symphonia brevis"). Orchestra [1929]. 1st: Minneapolis, 20 May 1937. #New York: C.F. Peters, 1972. *Louisville LS 721.
      M1001.B387 no. 3
      The second movement is entitled, "Memories of War—Sorrow—Struggle—A Protest!" On the title page of this fifteen-minute symphony, Becker indicates the work is a protest against the so-called civilized nations who starve its citizens in times of peace and murder them in times of war.

Converse, Frederick (1871-1940)

510. *The Answer of the Stars*. Chorus, soprano, and orchestra [1919]. 1st: 19 June 1919. #Boston: C.C. Birchard, 1919. Text by M.A. De Wolfe Howe.
      M1659.W38C
      An eighteen-page work written in honor of American soldiers and sailors who served during World War I, celebrating America's victory over the Germans and cadencing in A major (*fff*<*ffff*) with "where the fight was won."

Foote, Arthur William (1853-1937)

511. *Three Songs. 1914-1918*, Op. 79. Voice and piano. #Boston: Arthur P. Schmidt, 1919. Texts by John McCrae, Rupert Brooke, and C.A. Richmond.
      M1621.F667S66 Op. 79
      Eleven pages in the following order: "In Flander's Fields," "The Soldier," and "Oh, Red is the English Rose."

Gardner, Samuel (1891-1984)

512. Quintet in F Minor, Op. 16. Piano, violins, viola, and cello.
      #Boston: Oliver Ditson, 1926.
          *MX (NYPL call number)
          Includes "Prologue," "La vie - Capriccio - Dans la foret," and
      "La mort - Epilogue." Written in memory of David Hochstein who
      was killed in action in France. The first movement is quite frenetic
      with polyrhythms, extreme chromaticism, and full of repeated
      patterns. The third movement is a Marche funèbre in 4/4 with
      highly expressive outbursts and some syncopation.

Noon, David (b. 1946)

513. *Star Captains*. Orchestra [1981]. 1st: 5 December 1981.
          [No LC number available]
          Prefaced with James Elroy Flecker's poem "The Dying
      Patriot" about World War I. The composition, with recurring
      motives, is a musical elegy capturing the composer's feelings on
      the futility of war and fear that war will be taken into new frontiers
      in space.

Parker, Horatio (1863-1919)

514. *A.D. 1919*, Op. 84. Chorus and piano [1919]. #New Haven: Yale
      University Press, 1919. *Carillon Productions K80P-6126, private
      recording. Text by Brian Hooker.
          **M.455.7 (Boston Public Library call number)
          Written in memory of the Yale graduates who lost their lives
      in World War I. A lengthy celebration of the cause for which these
      young men died, replete with "Taps" and martial figurations in the
      heroic key of E-flat major.

Schelling, Ernest H. (1876-1939)

515. *A Victory Ball*. Symphonic poem [1922]. 1st: 23 February 1923.
      #Leipzig: F.E.C. Leuckart, 1925. Prefaced by a poem by Alfred
      Noyes.
          M1002.S323V4
          Dedicated to the memory of an American soldier, it
      incorporates various dances heard during the twenties (such as the
      waltz and the polonaise), which are interrupted with bugle calls and
      war-like responses. Concludes with an afterthought, a slow section

of only twelve measures with an off-stage, solo trumpet playing
"Taps" over the sound of drums.

France

Dupré, Marcel (1886-1971)

516. *De profundis.* Chorus, tenor, organ, and orchestra [c. 1921].
#Paris: Leduc, 1921.
      M2023.D86D3
      A nine-movement work highly expressive of the "De
profundis" text and serving as a deeply felt requiem to the dead
soldiers. "Pour les soldats morts pour la patrie."

Germany

Butting, Max (1888-1976)

517. *Trauermusik für Orchester* [1933]. #Leipzig: F.E.C. Leuckart,
1933.
      *MTO (NYPL call number)
      A ten-minute, very slow, lyrical work that is highly charged
with intense chromaticism. Dedicated to "dem Gefallenen des
Weltkrieges."

Schüler, Karl (b. 1894)

518. *Langemarck*, Op. 26. Four-part male chorus. #Berlin-Lichterfelde:
C.F. Vieweg, 193-? Text by Herbert Boehme.
      *MP (German) NYPL call number
      A ten-minute lament about World War I, moving from D
minor to D major. In four stanzas, each ending with cries of
"Deutschland."

Great Britain

Alwyn, William (1905-1985)

519. *Tragic Interlude.* Two horns, timpani, and string orchestra [1936].
      *Chandos CHAN 9065.
      [No LC number available]
      Prefaced with a World War I poem by Richard Addington
("Death of a Hero"), this eight-minute work of noble intensity and

passion looks back at World War I with the threat of World War II coming. The music is dark and contains a ferocious repetitive-pattern climax with ominous timpani and shimmering strings.

Bliss, Arthur (1891-1975)

520.   *Morning Heroes*. Symphony for narrator, chorus, and orchestra [1930]. 1st: 22 October 1930. #London: Novello, 1930. *EMI Classics CDM 7 63906 2. Texts by Homer, Li Tai-Po, Wilfred Owen, Robert Nichols, and Walt Whitman.
         M1533.B646M5
         Dedicated to his brother and to "all my other comrades-in-arms who fell in the Great War of 1914-18." See pages 138 to 139 for additional information.

Bridge, Frank (1879-1941)

521.   *Oration: Concerto elegiaco*. Cello and orchestra [29 June 1930]. 1st: London, 17 January 1936. #London: Faber Music, 1979. *Lyrita SRCS 104.
         M1016.B84 O7
         Written for those who lost their lives between 1914 and 1918, this concerto is not overtly programmatic; rather, it uses its dissonance and polytonality in a fitting tribute to the dead of World War I.

522.   Piano Sonata. Piano [1921-1924]. 1st: 15 October 1925. #London: Augener, 1925. *Conifer CDCF 186.
         M23.B85 1925
         Dedicated "To the memory of Ernest Bristowe Farrar who was killed in World War I," this thirty-minute, three-movement work is adventurous for Bridge in both its harmonies and its virtuosity. After its bell-like opening, the work grows dissonant and angry at times with some startling dissonances and polytonality.

Britten, Benjamin (1913-1976)

523.   *War Requiem*, Op. 66. Soloists, chorus, and orchestra [1961]. 1st: City of Birmingham Orchestra, 30 May 1962. #London: Boosey & Hawkes, 1962. *Angel CDC-47033 and Telarc CD80157. Texts by Wilfred Owen and from the requiem.
         M2010 .B838 Op.66

Perhaps the best known war-related work of the century. A poignant combination of texts and musical styles ranging from its haunting tritone relationships in the beginning to its asymmetrical outbursts in the Dies irae. In the English tradition established by John Foulds and Vaughan Williams. See Alec Robertson, *Requiem: Music of Mourning and Consolation* (New York: Praeger, 1968), pp. 265-85. See pages 139-40 above for additional information.

Foulds, John Herbert (1880-1939)

524.   *A World Requiem.* Four soloists, youth's chorus, boy's chorus, mixed chorus, and orchestra [1919-1921]. 1st: London, 11 November 1923. #London: Paxton, 1923.
M2023.F755W5
A tribute to the memory of the dead, a message of consolation to the bereaved of all countries. An immensely popular work for the first years after its composition and performed each Armistice night from 1923 to 1926. In two parts, each subdivided into ten further sections interwoven with non-religious sections containing references to war and peace. The fifth section of Part I lists the names of various countries and religions from the north, south, east, and west to make peace with one another. Fanfares from different parts of the cathedral sound in the direction called out after each geographical area. The sixth movement ("Pax") includes youths and boy's choir, and the work concludes on the text "Alleluia" and with the ringing of bells. Fould's requiem is a mixture of sacred and secular texts within a context of war and undoubtedly later influenced Vaughan Williams's *Dona nobis pacem* and Britten's *War Requiem.*

Italy

Santoliquido, Francesco (1883-1971)

525.   *La sagro dei morti.* Orchestra [1929]. #Florence: A. Forlivesi, 1956.
M1045.S229S3
A forceful C-minor lament that also demonstrates the heroic and grandiose side of war's spirit. The music is virtuosic, chromatic, and contains numerous descending two-note slurs, often of a second. Dedication: "Elegia per gli Eroi Italiani caduti nella grande guerra."

The Netherlands

Escher, Rudolf (1912-1980)

526. *Strange Meeting*. Baritone and piano [1952]. #Amsterdam: Donemus, 1984. Text by Wilfred Owen.
      M1621.E74 S7
      A slow song (Largo) emphasizing the low register of the keyboard with stark chords containing only tonics and fifths. The vocal line is highly chromatic, and the text is set syllabically. Third relationships dominate, and the work ends on a C-major chord.

SUPPLEMENT OF WORLD WAR I MUSIC COMPOSED AFTER 1918

527. Bruneau, Alfred (1857-1934). France. *Le tambour. Poème lyrique de Saint-Georges de Bouhélier*. Chorus and piano. #Paris. Choudens, 1915. No. 1 in **M.450.84 (Boston Public Library call number). "Occasioned by the European War of 1914-1918."

528. Gould, Morton (b. 1913). America. *World War I*. Orchestral score for television. Incidental music for television arranged for concert band by Louis Brunelli [1964-65]. #New York: G. & C. Music, 1965 (excerpts). *RCA Victor LSC 2791. M1527.7.G64W7 (complete score) M1255.G (arr.).

529. Kienzl, Wilhelm (1857-1941). Germany. *Im Schlachtendonner*, Op. 92. Six war songs for male chorus [1914-1917]. #Leipzig: Zimmerman, 1917. **M.455.10 (Boston Public Library call number).

530. Pentland, Barbara (b. 1912). Canada. *Ruins (Ypres, 1917)*. Voice and piano [1932]. 1st: Winnipeg, 21 September 1936. #Unpublished. Text by George H. Clarke. [Cited in Sheila Eastman and Timothy McGee, *Barbara Pentland* (Toronto: University of Toronto Press, 1983), p. 98]. Pentland's first composition dealing with her reactions and horror of war. Approximately four minutes.

531. _____. *Lament*. Voice and string quartet [1932]. Text by Wilfred Wilson Gibson. [Cited in Eastman and McGee, p. 98]. A musical summation of Pentland's horror of war.

532. Sousa, John Philip (1854-1932). America. *The Last Crusade.* Ballad for mixed quartet and chorus. Text by Anne Higginson Spicer. #Cincinnati: John Church, 1920. **M.435.86 (Boston Public Library call number).
533. Spross, Charles Gilbert (1874-1961). America. *In Flanders Fields.* Piano and voice. Text by John McCrae. #Cincinnati: John Church, 1918. 8058.409 (Boston Public Library call number).
534. Villa-Lobos, Heitor (1887-1959). Brazil. Symphony No. 3 ("A guerra"). Orchestra [1919]. 1st: Rio de Janeiro, 30 July 1919. [Cited in BAKER, p. 1965].
535. ____. Symphony No. 4 ("A vitória"). Orchestra [1919]. *Angel (Laser) 6-CDZF-67229. [Cited in BAKER, p. 1965].

America (United States)

Clarke, Henry Leland (b. 1907)

536. *Danza de la muerte.* Oboe and piano [1937]. 1st: 13 August 1937.
  #New York: Composer Facsimile Edition, 1952.
    AMC M246.C598D2
    Dedicated to the memory of the Americans who died fighting
    fascism during the Spanish Civil War. A slow, dark lament with
    dissonance and occasional clusters.

Cross, Henry P. (20th c.)

537. *Braddock's Defeat.* A patriotic cantata for soprano, alto, and bass
  chorus. #Boston: Oliver Ditson, 1929. Text by Frederich H.
  Martins.
    JNF 74-57 (NYPL call number)
    Retells how America defeated the British in the American
    Revolution. The music (in eight sections) is lively and diatonic
    with a clear narrative of events including a "War Dance at Du
    Quesne" and the battle at Monogahola Ford.

Koutzen, Boris (1901-1966) [Russian born]

538. *Valley Forge.* Symphonic poem [1931]. 1st: 19 February 1940.
  #New York: American Music Center, 1946.
    M1002.K9V3
    A twelve-minute full orchestral work in which the composer
    tries to capture what people think about the events so long ago
    when they visit the present-day Valley Forge. The work is
    sectionalized, tonal, and parallels the historic despair that
    eventually turned into triumph.

Riegger, Wallingford (1885-1961)

539. Symphony No. 4, Op. 63. Orchestra [1936-1957]. 1st: 12 April
  1957. #New York: Associated Music, 1960.

M1001.R543 Op. 63 1960
The symphony as a whole was dedicated to the memory of Riegger's wife. The second movement, however, deals with the Spanish Civil War and was composed in 1936.

Czechoslovakia

Martinů, Bohuslav (1890-1959)

540. *Comedy of the Bridge.* Radio-opera [1935, revised 1950]. 1st: 18 March 1937. #London: Boosey & Hawkes, 1952. *Supraphon 1116 3314.
M1503.M3843C6 1951
A farcical parody of war with people caught on a bridge and whom the patrols on each side will not allow to pass. A battle breaks out, the people can pass, and there is a great victory celebration with a triumphant march.

541. *Double Concerto.* Two string orchestras, piano, and timpani [1938]. #New York: Boosey & Hawkes. 1946. *Panton 8110 0022.
M1110.M379D7
An extraordinary three-movement work written concurrently with the conference in Munich which tried to appease Hitler by giving him Martinů's homeland.

Novák, Vítězslav (1870-1949)

542. *Jihočeská svita (South Bohemian Suite),* Op. 64. Orchestra [1936-1937]. #Leipzig: Breitkopf & Härtel, 1940. *Supraphon 1110 2486 G.
M1003.N93 op 64
In four movements ("Pastorale," "Träumerei," "Einst," and "Epilog"), the third of which is a march using the Hussite battle song "Ye Who Are Warriors of God" and dark, ostinato patterns climaxing in a victorious celebration.

Vomáčka, Boleslav (1887-1965)

543. *1914.* Cycle of five songs for voice and piano [1919-1920]. #Prague: Hudební matice Umělecké besedy, 1923. Texts by Rudolf Medek, Fráňa Šrámek, St. Hanuš, and Otakar Theer.
M1614.V6

Highly expressive, chromatic songs dealing with the dead and wounded of World War I: "1914," "Voják v poli" ("The Soldier at the Front"), "Raněny" ("The Wounded"), "Kmotra smrt" ("Goodman Death"), and "Za mrtvými" ("The Dead").

France

Ravel, Maurice (1875-1937)

544. *Méfiez-vous des blancs* from *Chansons madécasses*. Soprano, flute, cello, and piano. [1925-1926]. #Paris: Durand, 1926. *CBS MK-39023 and Philips 420778-2 PM. Text by Evariste Parny.
      M1613.3.R25C4
      The second of three songs, this powerful depiction of the bloodshed and wars that the white man brought to the natives before the white man was defeated and driven from the shores. The work includes piercing war cries and dramatic dissonances, and in the Allegro feroce Ravel uses a pungent ostinato over twenty measures to illustrate the expulsion of the white man.

Germany

Dessau, Paul (1894-1979)

545. *Guernica: Klavierstück nach Picasso*. Piano [1937]. #Leipzig: Breitkopf & Härtel, 1979.
      M22.D47 I6 1979
      A four-page work, not particularly programmatic but full of loud, dissonant passages and tempo changes creating a chaotic and desperate aura.

Eisler, Hanns (1898-1962)

546. *Deutsche Sinfonie*, Op. 50. Cantata for soloists, two speakers, chorus, and orchestra [1935-1943]. 1st: 25 June 1937, revised performance Berlin, 24 April 1959. *Nova 8 85 061/2 and Ars Vivendi 2100235. Texts by Bertolt Brecht, Ignazio Silone, and Julius Bittner.
      [No LC number available]
      In eleven sections, this hour-long work includes "An die Kämpfer in den Konzentrationslagern" ("To the Fighters in the Concentration Camps"). More of a political work than a war work, it remains an anti-fascist lament for the destruction that war

brought to Germany during Hitler's reign. See Thomas Phelps, *Hanns Eislers "Deutsche Sinfonie": ein Beitrag zur Asthetik des Widerstands* (Kassel/New York: Bärenreiter, 1988).

547. *Gegen den Krieg.* Mixed chorus [1936]. #Leipzig: Deutscher Verlag für Musik, 1972. *Nova 885 091. Text by Bertolt Brecht.
    M1610.E5G4
    A theme with twenty-three variations and a coda protesting war; includes statements against the fighting (e.g., "Dieser Krieg ist nicht unser Krieg").

548. *Kriegskantate,* Op. 65. Voice, two clarinets, viola, and cello [1937]. #Vienna: Universal, 1972. *Nova 885183. Text by Ignazio Silone.
    M1613.3.E34K7
    An anti-war, anti-government text sung in a direct, syllabic manner. The brief work is often chromatic, with sparse accompaniment that does not distract from the text.

Strauss, Richard (1864-1949)

549. *Friedenstag.* Opera [1938]. 1st: 24 July 1938. #Berlin: J. Oerter, 1938. *Koch 3-7111-2H1. Libretto originally by Stefan Zweig, taken over by Joseph Gregor.
    M1503.S916F7 1938
    Dealing with the besieged city of Bada at the end of the Thirty Years War, Strauss created an anti-war composition by showing the folly of war and how it is waged for the soldiers and against the citizens' will. The chorus plays an atypically large role for a Straussian opera.

Weill, Kurt (1900-1950)

550. *Das Berliner Requiem.* Cantata for tenor, baritone, male chorus, winds, and percussion [1927]. 1st: 22 May 1929. #Vienna: Universal Edition, 1967. *Koch Schwann 314050. Text by Bertolt Brecht.
    M1539.W4B5
    A seven-part, twenty-minute cantata including two poignant laments about unknown soldiers. Weill's strongest anti-war composition was influenced by Bach's passions.

551. *Legende vom toten Soldaten.* Chorus [1929]. #[S.l.: s.n.], 1929?
     *Koch Schwann 314050. Text by Bertolt Brecht.
          M1584.W
          A haunting 6/8 march based on a ghastly, cynical text.

552. *Zu Potsdam unter den Eichen.* Male chorus [1928]. #Vienna:
     Universal, 1930. *Koch Schwann 314050. Text by Bertolt Brecht.
          M1532.W39B46
          A brief, cynical lament for a soldier and an accusation of the
     military that was previously part of *Das Berliner Requiem.*

Great Britain

Vaughan Williams, Ralph (1872-1958)

•   *Dona nobis pacem.* See item number 400 above.

Hungary

Kodály, Zoltán (1882-1967)

553. *Budavári Te Deum.* Chorus, organ, and orchestra [1936]. 1st: 2
     September 1936. #Vienna & London: Universal Edition, 1937.
     *Hungaroton HCD 11397-2.
          M2020.K73T3
          Celebrates Buda's defending the city from the Turks and in
     honor of the 250th anniversary of Buda's liberation. The work
     itself is a powerful, yet non-programmatic Te Deum.

554. *Háry János.* Singspiel. Also arranged as a six-movement orchestral
     suite [1926]. 1st: Budapest, 16 October 1926. #London: Universal
     Edition, 1927. *CBS MY 38527. Libretto based on the poem by
     János Garay.
          M1503.K763 H33 1983
          The third adventure in the Singspiel takes place on a battlefield
     where Háry takes Napoleon prisoner. This scene, known in the
     suite as "The Battle and Defeat of Napoleon," ends with a funeral
     march.

Italy

Casella, Alfredo (1883-1947)

555. *Il deserto tentato*. One-act opera [1937]. 1st: 6 May 1937. #Milan:
     Ricordi, 1937.
         M1503.C339D4
         Deals positively with Mussolini's invasion of Ethiopia. In the
     third episode, Casella writes a battaglia in C minor with repeated
     notes and motives. The following episode begins with the men
     crying out "Vittoria!" several times.

Romania

Enesco, Georges (1881-1955)

556. Symphony No. 3, Op. 21. Orchestra, organ, piano, and wordless
     chorus [c. 1919]. 1st: 25 May 1919. #Bucuresti: Editura Muzicala
     a Uniunii Compozitorilor, 1968. *Marco Polo 8.223143.
         JMD 80-146 (NYPL call number)
         Attempts to portray the cycles of peace, war, and peace that
     have taken place in the twentieth century up to 1919. This fifty-
     minute work in C major contains three movements in a slow—
     fast—slow format.

Soviet Union

Glière, Reinhold [Glier, Reingol'd] (1875-1956). Ukraine

557. *Solemn Overture*, Op. 72. Orchestra [1937]. #Moscow: Editions de
     musique de l'U.R.S.S., 1941. *Melodiya S10 21717 004.
         M1060.G452 Op. 72 1941
         Written for the twentieth anniversary of the October
     Revolution; begins with heroic trumpet fanfares on B-flat major
     and continues through extensive ostinatos and various climaxes
     until the last one *fff* in G major is achieved.

Gnesin, Mikhail (1883-1957). Russia

558. *1905-1917* ("Symphonic Monument"), Op. 40. Chorus, soloists,
     and orchestra [1925]. #Moscow: Gosudarstvennogo Izdatelsvta,
     1926 (Piano four-hands arrangement).
         M208.G648 N4

A large-scale work with a choral finale; evolves around quartal harmonies and modal melodies while capturing the spirit of the heroic and tragic times between the two revolutions. Includes funeral marches and a closing triumphal march.

Kabalevsky, Dmitry (1904-1987). Russia

559. Symphony No. 1, Op. 18. Orchestra [1932]. #Melville, N.Y.: Belwin Mills, 1980? *Olympia OCD 268.

    M1001.K23 no. 1

    A programmatic symphony in two movements dealing with the gloom of pre-revolutionary days. Dedicated to the October Revolution in celebration of its fifteenth anniversary. Cited in Stanley D. Krebs, *Soviet Composers and the Development of Soviet Music* (New York. W.W. Norton, 1970), p. 237.

Myaskovsky, Nikolay (1881-1950). Russia

560. Symphony No. 6 in E-flat minor, Op. 23. Orchestra (with optional choral ending) [1921-1923]. 1st: 4 May 1924. #Vienna: Universal, 1925. *Olympia OCD 510.

    **MTA (NYPL call number)

    In four movements, this is an early symphony dealing with the Russian Revolution and including several revolutionary songs before concluding with a Russian folksong. A highly extroverted, virtuosic work with numerous mood and tempo changes moving from E-flat minor to E-flat major.

561. Symphony No. 18, Op. 42. Orchestra [1937]. 1st: 1 October 1937. #Moscow: Gos. Muz. Izd-vo, 1940.

    [No LC number available]

    A three-movement symphony which celebrates the twentieth anniversary of the Russian Revolution. Cited in HO, p. 369.

Prokofiev, Sergey (1891-1953). Russia

562. *Cantata for the 20th Anniversary of the October Revolution*, Op. 74. Chorus and orchestra [1936-1937]. 1st: May 1966. *Chandos CHAN 9095. Texts by Marx, Feuerbach, Stalin, and Lenin.

    [No LC number available]

    A forty-six minute, ten movement work with the largest orchestra Prokofiev ever used (quadruple winds and an enormous number of strings, brass, and percussion). Titles include "Revolution," "Victory," "The Oath," and "The Constitution."

Shostakovich, Dmitry (1906-1975). Russia

563. Symphony No. 2 ("October"), Op. 14. Orchestra and final chorus [1927]. 1st: Leningrad, 5 November 1927. *Melodiya MCD 200. Text by Alexander Bozymyensky.
      M1001.S567 Op. 14
      Composed for the tenth anniversary of the October Revolution—the first of many anniversary works for Shostakovich. A twenty-two minute symphony in one movement with a choral finale. The music is darker than it is heroic until the end. The choral finale weakens the work with its major-key glorification of the revolution.
      In his childhood Shostakovich wrote other war-related works: *Revolutionary Symphony, Funeral March in Memory of the Victims of the Revolution,* and *Hymn to Liberty.* See *Testimony: The Memoirs of Dmitri Shostakovich,* ed. Solomon Volkov (New York: Harper & Row, 1979), p. xxii.

Sweden

Alfvén, Hugo (1872-1960)

564. *Gustav II Adolf,* Op. 49. Orchestra [1932]. #Carl Gehrman's Musikförlag, 1938 and 1941 (excerpts). *Swedish Society Discofil SCD 1013.
      M1003.A347G8
      A thirty-five minute orchestral suite based on the life of Gustavus Adolphus who was killed during the Thirty Years War. The last and most extended movement in the suite is the eleven-minute "Battle of Breitenfeld" which includes fanfares, drum rolls, and a delightful, engaging military march brilliantly orchestrated.

SUPPLEMENT OF WAR COMPOSITIONS:
1919 to 1938

565. Aav, Evald (1900-1939). Estonia. *Vikings*. Opera [1928]. 1st: Tallinn, 8 September 1928. Melodiya 33D 08021-22. [Cited in HO, p. 1]. Deals with a 1198 campaign against the Vikings.
566. Absil, Jean (1893-1974). Belgium. *La guerre*. Cantata [1922]. Won the Prix de Rome. [Cited in BAKER, p. 5].
567. Alemshah, Kourkene M. (1907-1947). Armenia. *La bataille d'avarayr*. Symphonic poem [1934]. 1st: 2 June 1934. [Cited in BAKER, p. 23].
568. Asaf'yev, Boris (1884-1949). Russia. Symphony No. 2 in F-sharp minor ("From the Age of the Peasant Uprisings"). Orchestra [1938]. [Cited in NEW GROVE, vol. 1, p. 649].
569. Barraine, Elsa (b. 1910). France. *Pogroms*. Symphonic poem [1933]. 1st: Paris, 11 March 1939. [Cited in SLONIMSKY, p. 689]. Anti-Semitic persecutions in Tsarist Russia.
570. Bartevian, Aka. (20th c.). Armenia? *Mass-Oratorio in F minor*. Mass-oratorio. *Contrepoint 43001. In memory of the victims of the Armenian Genocide of 1915.
571. Brian, Havergal (1876-1972). Great Britain. Symphony No. 2 in E minor (with "Battle Scherzo"). Orchestra, including sixteen horns, two pianos, and three timpani [1930-1931]. 1st: 19 May 1973. M1001.B83 no. 2.
572. Cheryomukhin, Mikhail (b. 1900). Russia. *Red Army*. Cantata [1932]. [Cited in HO, p. 93].
573. Deshevov, Vladimir (1889-1955). Russia. *Ice and Steel*. Opera [1930]. 1st: 5 May 1930. [Cited in HO, p. 114]. Deals with the 1921 Kronstadt Rebellion.
574. _____. *The Red Whirlwind, Bolsheviki*. Ballet [c. 1924]. 1st: 29 October 1924. [Cited in HO, p. 114]. Based on a story about the 1919 Russian Revolution.
575. Elmore, Robert (1913-1985). America. *Valley Forge, 1777*. Symphonic poem [1937]. 1st: Philadelphia Orchestra, 9 April 1937. [Cited in BAKER, p. 492].
576. Erdlen, Hermann (1893-1972). Germany. *Requiem für die Gefallen*. Chorus [1931].
577. Femeldi, Vladimir (1905-1931). Soviet. *Anniversary Symphony*. Orchestra [1927].

578. Gladkovsky, Arseny (1894-1945). Russia. *1919* or *Red Petrograd* (with Eugene Prussak). Opera [1925]. [Cited in HO, p. 170]. First Soviet opera on a revolutionary subject.
579. Gundry, Inglis (b. 1905). Great Britain. *Naaman, The Leprosy of War.* Opera [1938]. [Cited in BAKER, p. 685].
580. Ježek, Jaroslav (1906-1942). Czechoslovakia. *Symphonic Poem.* Orchestra [1936]. 1st: 25 March 1936. *Panton 8110 0254. [Cited in BAKER, p. 852.] Deals with the Spanish Civil War.
581. Khrennikov, Tikhon (b. 1913). Russia. *A Soldier Returns from the Front.* Incidental music [1938].
582. Korchmaryov, Klimenty (1889-1958). Ukraine. *Ten Days That Shook the World.* Opera [1929-1931]. [Cited in HO, p. 276]. Deals with the 1917 Russian Revolution.
583. Krein, Aleksandr (1883-1951). Russia. *Zagmuk.* Opera [1930]. 1st: Moscow, 29 May 1930. #Moscow: Staatsmusikverlag, 1931. After a play by A. Glebov. 782.1.K92z (Mills College, Oakland call number). A story about the Jewish insurrection set in the eighth century B.C.E.
584. Listov, Konstantin (1900-1983). Russia. *October.* Oratorio [1921]. [Cited in HO, p. 311].
585. Mengelberg, Karel (1902-1984). The Netherlands. *Bataille.* Ballet [1922]. [Cited in BAKER, p. 1196].
586. Mokrousov, Boris (1909-1968). Russia. *Anti-Fascist Symphony.* Chorus and military band [1936]. 1st: Moscow, 1 August 1937. [Cited in HO, p. 354].
587. Moreno, Segundo Luis (1882-1972). Ecuador. *9 de Julio.* Overture [1925]. [Cited in BAKER, p. 1583].
588. Nejedlý, Vít (1912-1945). Czechoslovakia. Symphony No. 3 ("Spanish"). Orchestra [1937-1938]. [Cited in BAKER, p. 1294]. Dedicated to the Spanish defenders of democracy and freedom during the Spanish Civil War.
589. Quinet, Fernand (1898-1971). Belgium. *La guerre*, Op. 2. Cantata [1921]. Text by Valère Gilles. [Cited in BAKER, p. 1461]. Received the Belgian Grande Prix de Rome.
590. Rechmensky, Nikolay (1897-1963). Russia. *Battleship Potemkin.* Opera [1933]. [Cited in HO, p. 439].
591. Schillinger, Joseph (1895-1943). Ukraine [American citizen 1936]. *October.* Symphonic rhapsody for piano and orchestra [1927]. [Cited in HO, p. 471].
592. Schulhoff, Erwín (1894-1942). Czechoslovakia. *1917.* Cycle of twelve songs [1933]. [Cited in BAKER, p. 1651].
593. Skalkottas, Nikos (1904-1949). Greece. *The Unknown Soldier.* Chorus and orchestra [1929].

594. Suk, Josef (1874-1935). Czechoslovakia. *Legend of the Victorious Dead*. Orchestra [1919-1920]. #Prague: Hudební Matice, 1937. *Supraphon 50476. M0145.S95 Op. 35b.
595. Tomilin, Viktor (1908-1941). Ukraine. *Episodes of Civil War*. Symphonic suite [1936]. [Cited in HO, p. 554].
596. _____. *Year 1905*. Opera (written with Valery Zhelobinsky, Yury Kochurov, and Iona Tuskiya) [1931]. [Cited in HO, p. 554].
597. Verikovsky, Mikhail (1896-1962). Ukraine. *1905 god* (*The Year 1905*). Chorus [1925].
598. Zhelobinsky, Valery (1913-1946). Russia. Symphony No. 2 ("To the Memory of Revolutionary Victims"). Orchestra [1932]. [Cited in HO, p. 618].

NOTES

1. See J.G. Prod'homme, "Music and Musicians in Paris During the First Two Seasons of the War," *The Musical Quarterly* (1918), pp. 135-60; Barbara L. Tischler, "World War I and the Challenge of 100% Americanism" *An American Music* (New York & Oxford: Oxford University Press, 1986), pp. 68-91.

2. Prod'homme, pp. 142, 148. American orchestras also raised funds for the Red Cross. See Tischler, p. 76.

3. "The Music in War-Time Committee: Hospital Concerts," *Musical Times* (1 August 1917), p. 372.

4. Ernest Krauss, *Richard Strauss: The Man and His Work*, trans. John Coombs (London: Collet's Publishers, 1964), p. 62.

5. The seven composers were J. Barnby, J.F. Bridge, J. Langran, G.C. Martin, W. Parratt, C.H.H. Parry, and J.E. West.

6. Ernest Newman, "Elgar's 'Fourth of August,'" *Musical Times* (1 July 1917), p. 295.

7. Ernest Newman, "The Spirit of England," *Musical Times* (1 November 1917), p. 506.

8. Ernest Newman, "'The Spirit of England': Edward Elgar's New Choral Work," *Musical Times* (1 May 1916), p. 235.

9. Newman, "Elgar's 'Fourth of August,'" p. 297.

10. Arthur Bliss, *As I Remember* (London: Faber & Faber, 1970), p. 96.

11. The war-related works by the following composers contain narration: Michael Adamis, Leonard Bernstein, Darijan Bozicâ, Hanns Eisler, Lou Harrison, Arthur Hills, Aram Khachaturyan, Václav Kučera, Daniel Lentz, Robert Lombardo, William Mayer, Witold Rudziński, R. Murray Schafer, Arnold Schoenberg, Ben Steinberg, Georgy Sviridov, and Ilja Zeljenka.

12. Harold Robinson, *Sergei Prokofiev* (New York: Viking, 1987), p. 129

13. Maria Jose Montes, *La guerra española en la creación literaria: Cuadernos bibliograficos de la guerra de españa (1936-1939)* (Madrid: Universidad de Madrid, 1970).

14. W.R. Whittlesey, Acting Chief of the Division of Music at the Library of Congress, compiled a partial listing of songs that originated during World War I. See *A Check List of the Literature and Other Material in the Library of Congress on the European War.* Compiled under the direction of Herman H.B. Meyer, chief bibliographer, with the cooperation of members of the library staff (Washington: Government Printing Office, 1918), pp. 211-93. Whittlesey's list includes

approximately 3,000 American songs and approximately 1,300 songs from fourteen additional countries. While an occasional song by Debussy or Elgar appears in the listing, the overwhelming majority were popular songs written by popular song writers.

VI. WORLD WAR II: PATRIOTISM AND THE HORRORS OF WAR: 1939-1945

World War II was truly a world war. By 1941 every great power was actively involved, and by 1945, the last year of the war, all but six of the world's independent countries had joined the fighting.[1] When the last bombs were dropped and the casualty lists compiled, over forty million people were estimated to have been killed. Unlike World War I, a significant number of those forty million dead were civilians. Increased mechanization allowed cities to be destroyed within hours, sometimes within minutes. Defenseless women, children, and elderly people also fell victim in this war.

During the Second World War, composers from over twenty-five countries produced more than 200 war-related compositions—the greatest amount of war-related music in the history of music. In 1943 alone, over sixty war compositions appeared. Some composers attempted to portray the reality and horror of World War II as never before; however, the majority of composers concerned themselves more with propagating political values rather than achieving high artistic standards.

In spite of this outpouring of propaganda and functional war compositions, war-related music of World War II rose to unprecedented artistic heights. Unlike those in World War I, composers during World War II produced a number of compositions that are masterpieces of twentieth-century music. Roy Harris, Paul Hindemith, Arthur Honegger, Bohuslav Martinů, Oliver Messiaen, Walter Piston, Sergey Prokofiev, Arnold Schoenberg, Dmitry Shostakovich, Richard Strauss, Igor Stravinsky, Michael Tippett, and Ralph Vaughan Williams contributed important works to this repertory.

The Soviet composers wrote the greatest number of war compositions during the war not only because they were more organized, but also because the government was striving to create a new Soviet war music. In addition to the many art compositions composed during that period, the Soviets composed over one thousand songs, many written by major composers. On 22 June 1941, the Moscow Composer's Club agreed to contribute to the war effort by writing songs.[2] This club consisted of prestigious members such as Reinhold Glière, Dmitry Kabalevsky, Tikhon Khrennikov, Aram Khachaturyan, Lev Knipper, Nikolay Myaskovsky, Sergey Prokofiev, and Dmitry Shostakovich, as well as popular song writers like Alexander Alexandrov, Matvei Blanter, Isaak Dunayevsky, and Konstantin Listov. In *Soviet Wartime Music*, Sidonie Lederer pointed out that in the Moscow club there was "no line of demarcation between so-called 'popular' and 'classic' composers. Popular war songs seem to spring from the pens of the most 'classic' composers."[3] Glière clearly stated, "We Soviet composers are employing the medium of our art to help the Red Army wage its struggle against the brutal enemy. . . . When we write these songs we are forging weapons for the front, weapons that make it easier for the Red Army to fight and win."[4]

The musical war effort reached heroic proportions during the siege of Leningrad. Lederer suggests that "Leningrad composers had created some 150 symphonies, overtures, cantatas, and songs during the seventeen months the city was cut off from the rest of the nation."[5] This is all the more remarkable considering the circumstances under which the people were living. From September 1941 to February 1943, when the Germans lay siege to the city, water became contaminated, diseases rampant, and fires widespread. Masses of people froze and starved to death. Conditions were so severe and food so scarce that some people resorted to cannibalism.[6] Harrison Salisbury reasonably estimated the death toll to be between 1,300,000 and 1,500,000. Even though the official Soviet account was 632,253, some writers have estimated up to 2,000,000 casualties.[7] Nonetheless, even during such devastating times, Boris Schwarz reports that "theatres struggled to function, musicians continued to play, composers managed to write music. Actors appeared in overcoats and felt boots, musicians played in wool gloves with cut-out finger tips."[8]

Although the United States' security was never directly threatened as was that of the Soviets, American composers still wrote a considerable number of war works to support America's involvement in the war. In the early years of the war, however, composers received little direct support from the government. In the spring of 1942 when speaking at the annual meeting of the League of Composers' Board, Aaron Copland commented on the lack of affiliation between composers and government: "We have offered Washington the services of the composer to write background music for war films, to arrange music for army band, to write songs or production numbers for the entertainment of troops—yet to date very little effort has come of it. The composers want to help in the war effort."[9] By 1943 the government had become more involved with music. In his article "Music in America," R.D. Welsh reports that the United

States government was supporting music "unprecedented in American history" through commissions for education, war bonds, and recruitment.[10]

Hollywood composers were actively supplying war music for the film industry, and the distinguished composer Gail Kubik, serving as Director of Music for the Office of War Information, also composed music for several films, including *World at War*. Several other composers wrote music while serving in the military, and the Army Air Corps commissioned large-scale compositions from Samuel Barber and Marc Blitzstein, who were serving as enlisted men. Also, the League of Composers commissioned eighteen short compositions, based on a war-associated theme, which the New York Philharmonic premiered between 1943 and 1945.[11] Eugene Goosens and the Cincinnati Symphony Orchestra invited composers to compose short fanfares to be performed after the national anthem, and twenty composers participated in this project.[12]

The American government also recognized the value of music to servicemen abroad. The military spent over one million dollars to send eight million V-Discs to servicemen overseas between 1943 and 1947.[13] V-Discs were twelve-inch, seventy-eight rpm recordings produced by the military to provide musical entertainment and a feeling of "home" to the soldiers stationed overseas. Only a few of these recordings contained recently composed art music. The majority were not classical, but those that were consisted of standard, well-known literature written largely by non-American composers (Tchaikovsky's *1812 Overture*, Rachmaninoff's *Rhapsody on a Theme of Paganini*, Wagner's *Liebestod*, and Grofé's *Grand Canyon Suite*).

The majority of compositions serious American composers wrote during the war were independently created and resulted from the composers' own feelings about the war. Although the government participated to some degree, the best compositions were composed without direct government assistance. Through the widespread efforts of patriotic American conductors, composers, and performers, however, "more new American art music was heard in concert halls during these years than ever before in the United States."[14]

American popular-song writers were also quite active in creating war songs during the war. Twenty-seven popular war songs reached the top ten popular charts. In 1942, America's first full year of fighting, seventeen percent of all popular songs reaching the top ten were war songs.[15] Some of the most popular songs were "Comin' in on a Wing and a Prayer," "Der Fuehrer's Face," and "Praise the Lord and Pass the Ammunition." Unlike the Soviets, no "serious" American composers wrote songs that became popular at home or the front. In addition, community singing organizations were prevalent throughout the states. The Department of Public Instruction in the State of Indiana, for example, published a booklet entitled *Music and Morale in Wartime*, which contained lists of patriotic songs (usually old-time favorites) to sing for various group participation.

Little serious art music related to war came from Germany during World War II. While the Soviets were actively producing new music to establish Soviet patriotic music, Germany largely looked back to its glorious musical past for its serious music. With Hitler's coming to power, contemporary art music that was in the least innovative was discredited, and composers such as Hindemith and Schoenberg were forced to flee to the United States. Richard Strauss, who was 75 at the beginning of the war, remained in Germany; with the exception of the *Metamorphosen* (no. 672) written upon Germany's defeat, however, his music from the war years seems to be little affected by the turmoil of war.

With the rise of Hitler, new German music was most active in the political songs, the "politische Kampflieder." These songs were major instruments in Nazi propaganda, and their influence is not to be underestimated. Hans Bajer asserts that the political songs of Nazi Germany were "the most effective propaganda tool for the SA. . . . Not with their polished weapons do the SA draw out a country and its entire population; rather they succeed with their *Kampflieder* which they sing promising victory as they march in the city and the country."[16] According to Richard Haug, these songs "are a single way [used] to bring about a further union between people and art. One can not contemplatively hum them to oneself. . . . For the first time there are songs which bring together the entire Reich."[17]

Many of the more famous Kampflieder paired pre-existing melodies with poems such as "Die Rache wird kommen," "Was unser Führer uns gebracht," and "Wir sind des Hitlers braune Sturmkolonnen." Perhaps the most famous political song was the "Horst Wessel Lied," which has been called "the barometer for the forward motion of [the Nazi] movement,"[18] and which later took its "place alongside 'Deutschland über Alles' as one of the two national anthems" of Nazi Germany.[19]

In *Music and Society*, Paul Honigsheim argues that the function of music in the Third Reich was chiefly propagandistic and had little to do with entertainment. He suggests the music was written "to express a national enthusiasm for the Nietzschian theory of the superrace adopted by the Nazis. Musical practice was to promote audience awareness of and pride in belonging to the Aryan Race."[20] Consequently, the music of the Third Reich was largely based on earlier art music (mainly compositions by Wagner, Bruckner, and Beethoven) politicized through use at Nazi functions. Hitler required that a performance of Wagner's *Die Meistersinger* open the Nazi's Party Rally each year,[21] and that a movement from a Bruckner symphony be played before each of his "cultural speeches" at the Nuremberg party rallies.[22] After the Soviets had defeated the Germans at the Battle of Stalingrad in February of 1943, Hitler ordered the radio announcement to be followed by the Andante of Beethoven's Fifth Symphony.[23] No contemporary works with the stature of Shostakovich's Seventh Symphony or Harris's Fifth Symphony came from the pen of a German composer during the war.

Nonetheless, concert life in Germany remained active. Wilhelm Furtwängler conducted the Berlin Philharmonic Orchestra in regular concerts throughout the war until 12 April 1945. The compositions played at this "farewell" concert were the finale from Wagner's *Götterdämmerung*, Beethoven's Violin Concerto, and Bruckner's Fourth Symphony.[24] Soon after the end of the war, on 14 July 1945, "Allied Occupation Authorities in Germany issued an order forbidding playing military music or singing Nazi songs."[25]

Early in the war composers from around the world showed a heroic, patriotic side to war. Even if war was tragic, even if people suffered, in the end their side would be victorious. Much of the music is optimistic, even defiant; the outcome was not in doubt. These characteristics cross national boundaries, but appear particularly in works of those opposing the German aggressors: Soviet, Czech, Yugoslavian, Polish, and American composers.

Shostakovich's Seventh Symphony (no. 717) became enormously popular during World War II as an optimistic, patriotic work to show the defense of the Soviets against the invading Nazis. Solomon Volkov suggests that "this was probably the first time in musical history that a symphony played so political a role."[26] In the first movement the "invasion theme" plunges forward step by step for over ten minutes and 280 measures, with virtually no major changes except for the orchestration and dynamics. The unrelenting nature of the march continues until it reaches a harsh, prolonged climax. This symphony, which begins darkly in C minor, closes triumphantly with a highly defiant and exhilarating ending in C major.

Like the Shostakovich Seventh Symphony, the majority of the symphonies written during the early years of the war may contain movements that depict war and its horrors or an expression of grief over the dead, but they end triumphantly to illustrate the strength of people to overcome adversity in war. Khachaturyan's Second Symphony (no. 704) quotes the "Dies irae" in its third movement to express grief for those who were killed by the Nazis, but the work ends triumphantly. George Antheil's Fourth Symphony (no. 600), completed soon after the allied victory at Stalingrad, concludes heroically with an exuberant E-flat major chord. Roy Harris's Fifth Symphony (no. 616), originally dedicated to the U.S.S.R., became America's symbol of alliance and was broadcast on short-wave radio to the armed forces eleven times during the war.[27] Harris's Sixth Symphony ("Gettysburg") (no. 617), written in the middle of World War II, ends triumphantly with a triple fugue—no doubt with World War II in mind instead of the pyrrhic victory at Gettysburg. Paul Ben-Haim's First Symphony (no. 689) begins as a lament for the dead, but turns to a heroic, defiant ending. Arthur Honegger's (no. 722), and Piston's Second (no. 631) Symphonies, and Myaskovsky's Twenty-Second Symphony (no. 704), Stravinsky's *Symphony in Three Movements* (no. 638), and Vermeulen's Fourth Symphony (no. 692) all end triumphantly. Prokofiev's Fifth Symphony (no. 711) displays an optimistic, almost indomitable spirit throughout, and Vermeulen, in his Fourth Symphony (no. 692), written in 1940 and 1941, expressed intense belief that the Germans would be defeated. Several of the optimistic symphonies in addition to Harris's Sixth (no. 617) culminate in fugues: the Barber Second (no. 602), Egge First (no. 694), Harris Fifth (no. 616), and Stravinsky *Symphony in Three Movements* (no. 638). Not a single peace symphony appeared between 1939 and 1945. The defiance also clearly appeared in Panufnik's *Tragic Overture* (no. 698) Schoenberg's *Ode to Napoleon* (no. 644) (ending in E-flat major), and Miloslav Kabeláč's *Neustupujte (Do Not Yield!)* (no. 651), written in 1939, calling for his people to never give in to Nazi aggression.

Prokofiev composed a number of defiant works during the war as well. His oratorio *Ivan the Terrible* (no. 707) (based on his score for a film of the same name and written in the midst of the war) contains scenes that have direct relevance on the events that surrounded Prokofiev as he composed the music. The section entitled "Over the Dead Bodies of the Enemy" was as pertinent in the time of Ivan the Terrible as it was during World War II, perhaps more so. Prokofiev also wrote a little-known symphonic cantata (*Ballad of a Boy Who Remained Unknown*) (no. 706) in an attempt to illustrate through heroic music the sufferings children undergo in times of war. The work is a triumphant one, in a style similar to *Alexander Nevsky* and *Ivan the Terrible*.

During the war years, the Soviets composed over two dozen war-related operas, which either dealt with heroic victories of the past or anticipated the Nazi defeat in World War II. These Soviet operas were mostly functional compositions which were never published; they nevertheless account for the majority of all World War II war operas. (In America, for example, where there was no strong indigenous opera, not a single American composed a war opera during the war.) In explaining the reasons for the overall poor quality of these works written during the war in the Soviet Union, Boris Schwarz writes that "current events cannot be transferred to the stage like a newsreel; they need artistic distillation and reflection. . . . Of all the war operas [written during the war], only the titles have remained—like memorial plaques commemorating sincere but futile efforts."[28]

The only two significant war-related operas to come from World War II were Prokofiev's *War and Peace* (1941-1953) (no. 713) and von Einem's *Dantons Tod* (1944-1946) (no. 642), both of which were completed after the war. The subjects of these works were historical rather than current, the Napoleonic wars and the French Revolution, respectively. Composers wrote considerably more war operas about historical victories than about World War II itself. Fewer than ten operas written between 1939 and 1945 derived their subjects from the Second World War, and none of these has been performed since the war. These operas set in World War II are virtually unknown today: Ivan Dzerzhinsky's *The Blood of the People* (no. 747), Dmitry Kabalevsky's *V'ogne* (no. 756), Vasily Dekhteryov's *Tania* (no. 744), Yevgeny Tikotsty's *Alesia*, Viktor Voloshinov's *Stronger Than Death*, and Dag Wirén's *Blåutt, gult, rött* (no. 796). The chief function of much of this music was to "console and uplift, to encourage and exhort; nothing else mattered. . . . Only the survival of body and soul mattered, and the essential element of music was its morale-building force. In detached retrospect one finds occasional shallowness, posturing, hollow heroics; but under fire it all seemed real and very vital."[29]

From 1943 until near the end of the war, the optimism faded in much of the music. For composers who wrote two war symphonies during the war, their second was rarely as optimistic as the first. Myaskovsky's Twenty-Fourth, Prokofiev's Sixth (no. 712), Vermeulen's Fifth (no. 693), and Shostakovich's Eighth (no. 718) symphonies were all darker, more austere and pessimistic than their predecessors. None of these later war symphonies ended triumphantly. Prokofiev's Sixth is darker and evokes the tragedy of the war when the bells have stopped ringing and the victors see that war is horrible even in winning.

To create this dark atmosphere of war, composers often relied upon the idea of repetition. For example, Shostakovich's Eighth Symphony (1943) (no. 718) particularly acknowledges the "terrible tragedy of the war" and requires extended use of repetition, along with an intense rhythmic propulsion unprecedented in war music to create this horror. The symphony has five movements, of which the third is an incessant scherzando march consisting of a simple theme built on triadic and stepwise motion, which he develops through various repetitions and chromatic transformations. By using this idea, Shostakovich repeats the quarter-note pulse four times every measure for each of its 506 measures.

It does not stop until it reaches the terrifying climax at the beginning of the fourth movement. As well, Shostakovich depicts the sounds of bombs with sudden *sforzando* blasts in the low brass and timpani.

The lament tradition from World War I continued in Douglas Moore's *In Memoriam* (no. 629), William Schuman's *Prayer in Time of War* (no. 636), William Grant Still's *In Memoriam* (no. 637), and Samuel Adler's *Epitaph for the Young American Soldier* (no. 729), which he wrote when he was sixteen and later withdrew. Early in the war Paul Creston composed his *Chant of 1942* (no. 609), which combines the idea of a funeral march with a defiant tone to show that these deaths had not been in vain. Immediately after the war, Paul Hindemith, then living in America, composed his *When Lilacs Last Bloom'd* (no. 375) dedicated in part to the American soldiers who died during the war. Emil Hlobil dedicated his *Commemoration of the Martyrs* (no. 649) to the victims of the Nazi occupation of Czechoslovakia. Guillaume Landré composed his *Pia memoriae pro patria mortuorum* (no. 767) in remembrance of those killed in the 1940 German invasion of the Netherlands, and Henri Sauguet dedicated his *Symphonie expiatoire* (no. 670) to the innocent victims of the war. Strauss's *Metamorphosen* (no. 672), written during the last months of Germany's collapse, uses the funeral march from Beethoven's "Eroica" Symphony to mourn the suffering of the German people. Goffredo Petrassi contributed a poignant elegy during the war with his *Coro di morti* (no. 691).

The Czechs were outraged and grief-strucken by the tragedy of Lidice. During the war and after, the destruction of the Czech village led numerous composers to write memorial music for this horror. Most of these compositions are not known today and only a couple have been recorded, largely because this theme was taken up chiefly by Czech composers whose music has not been widely distributed. Most important of these is Bohuslav Martinů's *Memorial to Lidice* (no. 654) and the second and third movements of Antheil's Symphony No. 4 (no. 600). In addition are Antonín Balatka's *Lidice* (no. 991), Miroslav Barvík's *Lidice* (no. 732), Miloš Vacek's *Lidice* (no. 1052), Rudolf Forst's *Threnody: In Memory of Lidice* (no. 612), Miloslav Ištvan's *The Lidice Odyssey* (no. 901), Karel Janeček's *Tema con variazioni* (no. 650), Václav Kučera's *Lidice* (no. 905), Martinů's Symphony No. 1 (no. 655), Theodor Schaefer's *Love Ballads* (no. 782), Klement Slavicky's *Lidice* (no. 659), and Vaclav Lidl's *Balada o cervnovem ranu. Lidice* (no. 907).

At the same time composers recognized the horrors of war, their hope of victory also began to strengthen as seen in a number of compositions. The Soviets were particularly engaged in writing victory compositions at the end of the war and even forecasting the victory before the war had ended. Kangro's *Glory to Victors* (no. 971), Glière's *Victory Overture* (no. 703), Grechaninov's *Towards Victory* (no. 701), Boris Maizel's Third Symphony (no. 770), Aleksander Mosolov's *Glory to the Soviet Army* (no. 1028), Vano Muradeli's *The Path of Victory* (no. 1133), and Gavriil Popov's *To Victory* (no. 777) are all works that either anticipate or celebrate the glorious Soviet triumph over the Nazis.

These Soviet victory compositions were almost formulaic. The composers called for prominent use of brass and percussion instruments, especially at loud dynamic levels and fairly rapid tempos. Major tonalities were frequent and dissonance was used sparingly. All victory compositions included large amounts of repetition and are usually in a duple meter. They occasionally included text, but were most frequently written for a large orchestra without chorus or soloists. Unlike most war works, victory compositions were not particularly programmatic. All that was required for victory music was that the music express an optimistic mood through its attractive melody, euphonious harmony, and lively tempo without attempting to portray a particular event.

Prokofiev's *Ode to the End of the War* (no. 708) was the most noted of the victory celebrations at war's end. Prokofiev calls for an exceptionally large orchestra (excluding strings) in this work, specifying an additional eight harps and four pianos. Although history has passed unfavorable judgement on the work, it admirably captures the nationalistic pride and the relief that the citizens must have felt to have saved their country. In England, Vaughan Williams composed and recorded his *Thanksgiving for Victory* (no. 685) before the end of the war in order for it to be broadcast the day the allies defeated the Germans. Bernard Stevens's *Symphony of Liberation* (no. 681), composed during the German bombing of London, won first prize in a Victory Music competition the British sponsored.

Of the vast amount of music World War II produced, only a small portion remains important today. Nonetheless, several of the most significant works of the century appeared between 1939 and 1945 and dealt specifically with the war. Shostakovich's Seventh and Eighth Symphonies (nos. 717, 718), Prokofiev's Fifth and Sixth Symphonies (nos. 711, 712), Stravinsky's *Symphony in Three Movements* (no. 638), Honegger's Second Symphony (no. 720), Martinů's *Double Concerto*, and Strauss's *Metamorphosen* (no. 672) are all major works. Schoenberg's *Ode To Napoleon* (no. 644), Messiaen's *Quartet to the End of Time* (no. 664), and Prokofiev's Piano Sonata No. 7 (no. 710) are also important contributions to the chamber literature of the time. Two great operas emerged from the Second World War, Prokofiev's *War and Peace* (no. 713) and von Einem's *Dantons Tod* (no. 642), as did two major choral works, Tippett's *Child of our Time* (no. 682) and Hindemith's *When Lilacs Last Bloom'd* (no. 375).

America (United States)

Antheil, George (1900-1959)

599. *Campaign.* Symphonic suite in four movements for orchestra
   [1943]. #Unpublished manuscript in LC.
       ML96.A723 no. 13 Case
       In four movements: "Tunisia," "Sicily" (with oriental hand
   drum), "Interlude" (including a "Marcia alla Turk"), and "Invasion."
   The last movement is presto, with driving rhythms and heavy use
   of brass and percussion. Some of the rhythmic syncopation and
   primitivism shows the influence of Stravinsky.

600. Symphony No. 4 ("1942"). Orchestra [1942]. 1st: New York, 13
   February 1944. #London: Boosey & Hawkes, 1947. *Everest
   KOBR 6013.
       M1001.A64 no. 4
       A four-movement martial symphony played without pause and
   with cyclic elements (the opening brass theme returns in the other
   movements). Influenced by the war, particularly the second and
   third movements written during the time in which the composer
   learned of the tragedies of Lidice. The first movement is extremely
   martial with its incessant driving rhythms and repetitions in the
   brass and percussion. The fourth movement, composed as Antheil
   learned of the allied victories at Stalingrad, ends explosively with a
   crashing E-flat major chord.

Barber, Samuel (1910-1981)

601. *A Stopwatch and an Ordinance Map.* Male chorus, brass, and
   kettledrums [1940]. 1st: 16 December 1945. #New York: G
   Schirmer, 1954. *Vanguard VRS 1065 or VSD 2083. Text by
   Stephen Spender.
       M1539.B235S8 1942
       A brief martial composition with almost continuous use of
   the kettledrums effectively capturing the subtleties and seriousness
   of the text. Inspired by the Spanish Civil War.

602. Symphony No. 2, Op. 19. Orchestra [1944, revised 1947]. 1st:
     Boston, 3 March 1944. #New York: G. Schirmer, 1950. *Everest
     SDBR 3282.
     M1001.B23 Op. 19
     Commissioned by the Army Air Force while Barber was a
     corporal in the Army. Although Barber denied this work had any
     programmatic connotation, David Ewen in his *Complete Book of
     20th Century Music* (Englewood Cliffs, N.J.: Prentice Hall, 1959)
     suggests that it was written to commemorate the Air Force because
     of the instrumentation in the second movement simulating the
     sounds of aircraft signals (p. 11).

Becker, John Joseph (1886-1961)

603. Symphony No. 6 ("Out of Bondage"). Narrator, chorus, and
     orchestra [1941-1942]. #Holograph in NYPL. Text by Abraham
     Lincoln.
     MNZ-Amer. (NYPL call number)
     The movements include "Ballad of Fallen France," "Lincoln's
     Gettysburg Address," and "Victory March." The *Gettysburg
     Address* is narrated over sustained chords and with brief orchestral
     interludes often consisting of various dotted rhythms. The
     movement concludes with the chorus singing the word "America"
     over and over again.

Bernstein, Leonard (1918-1991)

604. Symphony No. 1 ("Lamentation of Jeremiah"). Mezzo-soprano and
     orchestra [1939-1942]. 1st: Pittsburgh, 28 January 1944. #New
     York: Hauns, 1943. *DG 415964-2 GH. Text from the *Book of
     Lamentations*.
     M1001.B533 no. 1 1943
     Contains three movements, "Prophecy," "Profanation," and
     "Lamentation," the last of which laments the destruction of
     Jerusalem by the Babylonians. The intense opening movement
     with its repeated motives and brilliant orchestration sets the tone
     for this urgent and tragic composition.

Blitzstein, Marc (1905-1964)

605. *Freedom Morning*. Symphonic poem for orchestra [1943]. 1st: 28
     September 1943. #Unpublished facsimile in NYPL. *Supraphon
     H-18130.

MTO-Amer. (NYPL call number)

Dedicated to the United States Army Negro Troops, this work is syncopated, sectionalized, and not particularly programmatic.

606. *Symphony: The Airborne.* Narrator, male chorus, and orchestra [1944]. 1st: New York City, 11 April 1946. #New York: Chappell. *Columbia M34136. Text by Blitzstein.

M1533.3.B55A5

In three movements and twelve sections depicting the history of aviation from mythology to World War II. Subtitles of the sections include "The Enemy," "Threat of Approach," and "Ballad of the Bombardier."

Copland, Aaron (1900-1990)

607. *A Lincoln Portrait.* Speaker and orchestra [1942]. 1st: 14 May 1942. #New York: Boosey & Hawkes, 1943. *CBS MK-42431. Text by Abraham Lincoln.

M1625.C76L5

A fourteen-minute patriotic work that concludes with a section from Lincoln's *Gettysburg Address* to honor the war-dead of World War II. The work is noble, heroic, and ends brilliantly on a *fortissimo* C-major chord.

608. Sonata for Violin and Piano [1943]. #New York: Boosey & Hawkes, 1944. *Crystal S-631 and Desto 6439.

M219.C77S6

Dedicated to "Lt. Harry H. Durham (1910-1943), a friend of mine who lost his life while on duty in the South Pacific." In Copland's highly attractive American style and in three movements: Andante semplice, Lento, and Allegretto giusto.

Creston, Paul (1906-1985)

609. *Chant of 1942,* Op. 33 [1943]. 1st: New York, 3 May 1943. #New York: G. Schirmer. *Crystal Records CD508.

[No LC number available]

An eleven-minute work in two parts dealing with the despair as well as the hope during the year 1942. The first section is a somber lament, followed by a second section built upon a ground bass which develops into a strong, defiant march.

Damrosch, Walter (1862-1950) [German born]

610. *Dunkirk.* Ballad-poem for baritone, chorus, and small orchestra [1943]. 1st: 2 May 1943, NBC Radio Network. #New York: G. Schirmer, 1943.
M1609.D
A war ballad about a boy named Will. Tonal with much parallel chromaticism in C and E major.

Diamond, David (b. 1915)

611. *Epitaph (On the Graves of a Young Cavalry Officer Killed in the Valley of Virginia).* Voice and piano [1945]. #New York: Associated Music, 1946. Text by Herman Melville.
*MP box (NYPL call number)
A serene, two-page, diatonic setting in G major with a prominent four-note motive.

Forst, Rudolf (b. 1900)

612. *Threnody: In Memory to Lidice.* String orchestra [1944]. #New York: Editio Musicus, 1944.
M1145.F76T5
A sixty-six-measure Adagio lamentoso, consisting of numerous two-note ascending slurs of major and minor seconds, sustained pedal points, and increasingly complex chromaticism, ends on a F-sharp major chord (*morendo*).

Gould, Morton (b. 1913)

613. *Jericho.* Wind ensemble [c. 1941]. #New York: Mills Music, 1941. *RCA LM-2308.
M1245.G
An eleven-minute work based on four programmatic ideas: "March and Battle," "Joshua's Trumpets," "The Walls Came Tumblin' Down," and "Hallelujah." The work contains an enormous climax to depict the falling walls.

614. Symphony No. 1. Orchestra [1943]. #New York: G. & C. Music. *RCA Victor LM 2893.
M1001.G67 no. 1
Dedicated to "My three brothers in the armed forces of the U.S. and their fellow fighters." In four movements, "Epitaph,"

"Dances," "Pastoral and Battle Music," and "Resolution." The pastoral music is marked "slowly moving, flowing and songlike," and has muted strings and soft dynamics. The battle music begins with a bass drum roll which interrupts the pastoral section. Soon the music breaks away into a ferocious, intense battle movement.

Harris, Roy (1898-1979)

615. *March in Time of War*. Orchestra [1943]. #Unpublished, controlled by Mills Music.
      *MTO-Amer. (NYPL call number)
      Dedicated to the American composers in the Armed Services. A substantial, hard-hitting work with considerable percussion and strong cross-relations; not particularly programmatic.

616. Symphony No. 5. Orchestra [1942]. 1st: Boston, 26 February 1943. #New York: Mills Music, 1961. *Louisville Orchestra LOU 655.
      M1001.H3 no. 5
      "Dedicated to the heroic and freedom-loving people of our great ally, the Union of Soviet Socialist Republics as a tribute to their strength in war, their staunch idealism for world peace, their ability to cope with stark materialistic problems of world order without losing a passionate belief in the fundamental importance of the arts." (The dedication was later removed.) A three-movement symphony ("Prelude," "Chorale," and "Fugue") in the heroic manner of its dedication. The chorale is a dark, funeral march with winds and strings playing over an ostinato punctuated with steady pulses.

617. Symphony No. 6 ("Gettysburg"). Orchestra [1943-1944]. 1st: Boston, 14 April 1944. #New York: Mills Music. *Andante AD 72402.
      M785.11.H31555
      Based upon the text of Lincoln's *Gettysburg Address*, in four movements: "Awakening" ("Fourscore and seven years ago"); "Conflict" ("Now we are engaged in a great civil war"); "Dedication" ("We are met on a great battlefield of that war"); "Affirmation" ("That we here highly resolve that these dead shall not have died in vain"). An adventuresome work for Harris in its use of polychords and particularly the furor created in the second movement. The symphony, based upon material from his earlier *American Creed*, ends in a spirit of triumph with a triple fugue.

Herrmann, Bernard (1911-1975)

618. *For the Fallen.* Symphonic poem [1943]. 1st: 16 December 1943.
     #New York: Broude Brothers, 1955.
     M1045.H55F6
          "A berceuse for those who lie asleep on the many alien
     battlefields of this war." A slow, six-minute work in 6/8
     beginning on Es and concluding a tritone away on a B-flat major
     triad. Herrmann frequently uses two-note slurs and repeated
     rhythms building to a huge climax, before once again subsiding
     and ending *ppp*. Includes a quotation from Handel's *Messiah* ("He
     shall feed His flock like a shepherd").

Howe, Mary (1882-1964)

619. *To the Unknown Soldier.* Song for voice and orchestra [1945]. 1st:
     Washington, D.C., 1946. #New York: G. Schirmer, 1945.
     *WCFM 13. Text by Nicholas G. Lély, trans. Joseph Auslander.
     ML96.H857 Case
          A heroic, patriotic song ending victoriously on high *sforzando*
     Gs.

Johansen, Gunnar (1906-1991) [Dutch born]

620. *Pearl Harbor Sonata.* Piano [1941]. *Artist Direct.
     [No LC number available]
          Johansen finished this work the night before the attack on Pearl
     Harbor and claimed he had a premonition of the event (See letter to
     author, 26 December 1984). In three movements, the sonata
     contains jazz-like "victory motives" and the Dies irae theme.

Kahn, Erich Itor (1905-1956) [Czech born]

621. *Ciaccona dei tempi di guerra.* Piano [1943]. #New York: Bomart
     Music, 1951. *CRI SD-188.
     M25.K
          A highly complex and dissonant piano work written in a
     fantastical manner with many sudden juxtapositions of styles and
     moods.

Kennan, Kent (b. 1913)

622. *The Unknown Warrior Speaks*. Male chorus [1944]. 1st: National
      Gallery of Art, 1944. #New York: H.W. Gray, 1948. Text by
      Margery Smith.
         M1594.K
         Written for William Strickland and the Army Music School
      Chorus, this patriotic work opens on a D-major chord and closes
      on a G-sharp major chord a tritone away. The text glorifies finding
      life in death, and the largely homophonic setting expressively
      treats this mixed feeling of despair and affirmation.

Krenek, Ernst (b. 1900) [Austrian born]

623. *Cantata for Wartime*, Op. 95. Cantata for soprano, women's
      chorus, and orchestra [1943]. 1st: 24 March 1944. #Mainz: B.
      Schott's Söhne, 1943. Text by Herman Melville.
         M1528q.K745, Op. 95
         A fifteen-minute work based upon five Melville poems,
      including "A Utilitarian View of the Monitor's Fight" and "A
      Requiem for Soldiers Lost in Ocean Transports." The work opens
      with spoken text, but soon the extensive chromaticism enters and
      the work intensifies dramatically with frequent tempo and textural
      changes.

Kubik, Gail (1914-1984)

624. *A Litany and Prayer*. Cantata for male chorus, brass, and
      percussion [1943-1945]. 1st: Washington, D.C., 2 April 1944.
      #New York: Southern Music, 1953. Two alternate texts taken
      from the *Episcopal Book of Common Prayer*: 1) A service of
      intercession for the war and 2) A supplication for deliverance from
      sin and guidance in the ways of peace.
         M2029.K85L5
         An eighteen-minute work in two parts, the *Litany* (originally
      entitled *A War-Time Litany*) and a *Prayer* (written later in memory
      of Franklin D. Roosevelt). The *Litany* is a slow, somewhat
      chromatic, patriotic dirge. After a brief introduction, the *Prayer*
      itself is little more than a drum beat which provides a background
      for extended narration.

Lee, Dai Keong (b. 1915)

625. *Pacific Prayer.* Orchestra [1943]. 1st: New York City, 12 March 1944.
   [No LC number available]
   "I wanted this composition to express the hopes of the fighting men in the Pacific for a just end to the war and a better postwar world" (Cited in David Ewen, *American Composers: A Biographical Dictionary* [New York: G.P. Putnam, 1982], p. 408).

McDonald, Harl (1899-1955)

626. *Bataan.* Symphonic poem [1942]. 1st: 3 July 1942. #Philadelphia: Elkan-Vogel, 1942.
   M1045.M13B4
   Prefaced with MacArthur's words, "No Army has ever done so much with so little," and dedicated to "General MacArthur and the American and Philippine troops whose monumental courage and heroism will remain a bright spot in our history." Composed during the climactic events on the Bataan Peninsula in the spring of 1942. A brief, 109-measure work, essentially a C-minor march that achieves an enormous climax with trumpets and drums before subsiding to wind solos over sustained strings.

627. *Dirge for Two Veterans.* Women's chorus and piano [c. 1940]. #Philadelphia: Elkan-Vogel, 1940. Text by Walt Whitman.
   M1574.M
   A dramatic tonal setting, highly sectionalized with an extensive piano introduction.

628. *Elegy and Battle Hymn.* Baritone and orchestra [1943]. #Philadelphia: Elkan-Vogel, 1943. Text by Edward Gilson.
   M1613.M13E4
   The *Elegy* is an anti-war text, poignantly set with considerable chromaticism and a variety of moods and tempo changes. The *Battle Hymn* is bombastic and evolves into the "Battle Hymn of the Republic" with which the work heroically closes.

Moore, Douglas Stewart (1893-1969)

629. *In Memoriam.* Orchestra [1943]. 1st: Rochester, 27 April 1944. #Philadelphia: Elkan-Vogel, 1946. *Bay Cities BCD 1017 and CRI 127.

M1045.M82I6

"Dedicated to those who die young and speak of the bitterness of youth cut down in its prime, the irreconcilable loss to us and to them." A ten-minute dirge in three sections with the middle movement using a muted trumpet and serving as a soliloquy on the dirges that come before and after it.

Piston, Walter (1894-1976)

630. *Passacaglia.* Piano [1943]. 1st: 23 October 1944. #New York: Mercury Music, 1943. *3-Vox SVBX 5303.
       M25.P
       In his biography *Walter Piston* (Ann Arbor: UMI Research Press, 1982), Howard Pollack argues that this four-minute work is also an expression of war displaying anger and mournfulness (p. 82).

631. Symphony No. 2. Orchestra [1943]. 1st: National Symphony Orchestra, 5 March 1944. #New York: Associated Music, 1944. *Desto DC 6410.
       M1001.P62 no. 2
       Pollack claimed this symphony was a result of America's involvement in World War II and thought it equal to wartime symphonies of the Soviet Union: Prokofiev's Fifth Symphony and Shostakovich's Seventh Symphony (pp. 82-83).

Reisfeld, Bert (b. 1906) [Austrian born]

632. *Stalingrad.* Tone poem for piano [1942]. #New York: Mutual Music Society, 1942.
       *MYD box (NYPL call number)
       A three-page piano work in D minor with a fugal opening and building to a pretentious and majestic climax.

Richardson, Clive (20th c.)

633. *London Fantasia: A Musical Picture of the Battle of Britain.* Orchestra (Piano arranged by Henry Geehl) [c. 1940]. #New York: Chappell, 1945.
       *MYD (NYPL call number)
       A ten-minute, old-fashioned, programmatic work in clear sections, with subtitles such as "Machinery," "London Street Cries," "Siren," and "All Clear." While serving in London during

the war, the composer wrote the work which contains numerous tremolos and chromatic scales.

Robinson, Earl (b. 1910)

634. *Battle Hymn.* Cantata for chorus, soloists, narration, and piano [1942]. #New York: Chappel, 1943. Texts by John Latouche and the composer, based on President Roosevelt's State of the Union Address, 6 January 1942.
M1533.R67B3
Over sounds imitating a telegraph, voices call out information about the Fascists taking over various places and countries, and that their aim is to conquer the world. The composer suggests at one point that the "headline slogans to be shouted by soloist, should be considered as only temporary and should be changed with each new evidence of attack of the U. S. and United Nations." This tonal work was propaganda to get the U.S. citizens even more involved in the war.

Schuman, William (1910-1992)

635. *A Free Song.* Secular cantata for mixed chorus and orchestra [16 October 1942]. 1st: Boston, 26 March 1943. #New York: G. Schirmer, 1943. Text by Walt Whitman.
M1533.S386F7
Written in two parts. The first consists of "Long, too long, America" and "Look down, fair moon," the latter containing the graphic texts of the wounded with outstretched arms looking up at the moon. Schuman sets this section with two-note, descending major seconds typical of lament compositions. Part two ("Song of the Banner") opens with a fugue and is more optimistic, concluding *fortissimo* with the word "Liberty" set in D major. Won the Pulitzer Prize in 1943.

636. *Prayer in Time of War.* Orchestra [1943]. 1st: Pittsburgh, 26 February 1943. #New York: G. Schirmer, 1950. *Louisville LOU S721.
M1045.S396P7 1950a
A slow, non-programmatic work describing the composer's feelings during the war. The work is highlighted by an explosive middle section beginning at measure 231 and climaxing at measure 340.

Still, William Grant (1895-1978)

637. *In Memoriam: The Colored Soldiers Who Died for Democracy.*
Symphonic paragraph [1943]. 1st: New York, 5 January 1944.
#Los Angeles: Delkas Music, 1943.
    M1045.S855I5
    One of his most popular works written to support the war
    effort, this B-flat minor lament is full of repeated notes, tempo
    fluctuations, and muted brass. It remains in 4/4 throughout and
    climaxes at the end with a *ffff* outburst on a B-flat minor chord.

Stravinsky, Igor (1882-1971) [Russian born]

638. *Symphony in Three Movements.* Orchestra [1942-1945]. 1st: 24
January 1946. #New York: Associated Music, 1946. *Columbia
MS 6331 and DG 415128-2 GH.
    M1001.S915S9 1946
    An important war-related symphony in three movements.
    Stravinsky wrote that "[This] Symphony was written under the
    impression of world events. I will not say that it expresses my
    feelings about them, but only that without participation of what I
    think of as my will, they excited my musical imagination. . . .
    The *finale* even contains the genesis of a war plot, though I
    accepted it as such only after the composition was completed. The
    beginning of the movement is partly and in some inexplicable way
    a musical reaction to the newsreels and documentaries I had seen of
    goose-stepping soldiers. The square march beat, the brass-band
    instrumentation, the grotesque *crescendo* in the tuba, these are all
    related to those abhorrent pictures" (Notes to phonodisc Columbia
    MS 6331).

Weinberger, Jaromir (1896-1967) [Czech born]

639. *A Lincoln Symphony.* Orchestra [c. 1941]. 1st: 17 October 1941.
#New York: Carl Fischer, 1941.
    M1001.W41L5
    A forty-five minute work for large orchestra with organ;
    contains four separate movements: "The Hand on the Plough,"
    "Scherzo Heroique," "O Captain! My Captain!: Recitativo and
    Marcia funèbre," and "Deep River." The movements are in standard
    forms and are all tonal. The third specifically is a lament for the
    assassinated Lincoln.

Weisgall, Hugo David (b. 1912) [Czech born]

640. *Soldier Songs*. Baritone and orchestra [1944-1946, revised 1965]. 1st: New York, 26 April 1954. #New York: Mercury Music, 1953. Texts by e.e. cummings, Robert Graves, John Manifold, Herman Melville, Wilfred Owen, Isaac Rosenberg, Siegfried Sassoon, and Karl Shapiro.
      M1621.W
      A powerful evocation of war in this setting of nine wide-ranging poems, using a dissonant but tonal musical language.

Wolpe, Stefan (1902-1972) [German born]

641. *Battle Piece* (from *Encouragements*). Piano [1943-1947]. #Toronto: Sound Way, 1983. *New World NW 354-2.
      M25.W64E527
      A twenty-minute dissonant work in seven sections written to oppose fascism during World War II.

Austria

Einem, Gottfried von (b. 1918)

642. *Dantons Tod*. Opera [1944-1946]. 1st: 6 August 1947. #Vienna: Universal Edition, 1947. *Orfeo S102 842H. Libretto by Boris Blacher and the composer, based on the Georg Büchner drama.
      M1500.E32D44 1961 Case
      This largely traditional opera about Danton and the French Revolution is the only war-related opera after World War II to find a place in the active opera repertory. The last scenes at the Tribunal in scene v and the execution in scene vi create the furor of the revolutionary times—the thrill, the intensity, the tragedy, and the grief.

Rubin, Marcel (b. 1905)

643. Symphony No. 4 ("Dies irae"). Orchestra [1943-1945, revised 1971]. #Vienna-Munich: Ludwig Doblinger. *Preiser SPR 137. Text by Bertolt Brecht.
      [No LC number available]
      Contains three movements, "Kinderkreuzzug 1939" (Children's Crusade 1939), "Dies irae," and "Pastorale." The first tells of the effect the war had on the children in Poland.

Schoenberg, Arnold (1874-1951)

644. *Ode to Napoleon*, Op. 41. Narrator, piano, and string quartet
      [1942]. 1st: New York, 23 November 1944. #New York: G.
      Schirmer, 1945. *DG 415982-2 GH. Text by Byron.
         M1625.S26 Op. 41 1944
         Written at the height of World War II to illustrate the
      similarities between Hitler and Napoleon. A forceful, narrated,
      twelve-tone work that alludes to the heroic key of E-flat major.

Ullmann, Viktor (1898-1944)

645. *The Emperor of Atlantis*. Opera [1944]. 1st: Amsterdam 1975.
      #London: British Broadcasting, 1974. Libretto by Peter Kien.
         M1503.U56 Op. 49 1974
         A fifty-minute opera composed in the Terézin concentration
      camp; it was so anti-Hitler and anti-war that it was never performed
      in the camp.

Canada

Pentland, Barbara (b. 1912)

646. *Rhapsody 1939: The World on the March to War Again*. Piano
      [1939]. 1st: Winnipeg, 12 March 1941. #Unpublished manuscript
      at NYPL.
         *MYD (NYPL call number)
         Opens with a long trill in the right hand and marcato bass
      octaves in jagged rhythms establishing an angry, disruptive mood
      which is intensified with chromatic thirty-second notes. The five-
      minute work is not overtly programmatic, but it creates an
      atmosphere of agitation and despair that expresses the composer's
      outrage and fear that world war was once again breaking out.

Czechoslovakia

Dobiás, Václav (1909-1978)

647. *Stalingrad*. Cantata [1945]. #Prague: Nakladatelství Národní
      Osvéta, 1945. Text by Jirí Novák.
         782.2 D653s1 (Free Library of Philadelphia call number)

A heroic work using modal harmonies, interesting cross-relations, and considerable march-like patterns, ending with a strong *fff* cadence in B major.

Foerster, Joseph Bohuslav (1859-1951)

648. *Kantáta 1945*, Op. 187. Soprano, baritone, and mixed chorus [1943-1945]. #Prague: Foerstrova spolecnost, 1946. Texts by Marie Rafajová and Bohumil Mathesius.
M1533.F64 Op. 187
A highly contrasting tonal work with frequent key changes; opens with dark, foreboding colors, but offers hope with its *ppp* ending on a C-major chord.

Hlobil, Emil (1901-1987)

649. *Tryzna mučedníkům*, Op. 25 (*Commemoration of the Martyrs*). Symphonic fresco for large orchestra [1944-1945]. *Panton 8110 0508.
[No LC number available]
A thirty-minute work with a frenetic, militaristic middle section although the beginning and ending are dark, solemn, and somewhat austere. Dedicated to the victims of the Nazi occupation.

Janeček, Karel (1903-1974)

650. *Tema con variazioni*, Op. 23. Piano [1942]. #Prague: Hudební matice Umělecké besedy, 1944.
M27.J35 T4
A non-programmatic work inspired by the tragedy of Lidice after the reprisals for the assassination of Heydrich.

Kabeláč, Miloslav (1908-1979)

651. *Neustupujte* (*Do Not Yield*), Op. 7. Cantata of resistance for male chorus, band, and percussion [1939]. 1st: Prague, 28 October 1945. #Prague: Editio Supraphon, 1968. *Supraphon DV 5682.
M1576.K32 N4 1968
A nine-minute patriotic cantata written to encourage the Czech people never to give up but to defend their country and as a protest against the 1938 Munich Agreement. Uses folk tunes and a portion of the Hussite chorale "Ye Warriors of God." The music is martial, full of major and minor seconds, and forceful.

652. Symphony No. 2. Orchestra [1942-1946]. 1st: 17 April 1947.
#Prague: Panton, 1960.
M1101.K116 Op. 15
A three-movement, thirty-six minute work expressing
resistance against the Nazi occupation of Czechoslovakia. The
second movement is an elegy and the third a rousing, optimistic
finale beginning with extensive percussion and ending with a
triumphant fugue played *ff* in the brass.

Martinů, Bohuslav (1890-1959)

653. *Field Mass.* Male chorus, baritone, and orchestra [1939]. 1st:
Prague, 28 February 1946. #London: Boosey & Hawkes.
*Supraphon C37-7735 and 1112 3576 ZA. Text by Jirí Mucha
with quotes from the Psalms.
M2010.M383F5
Written as a tribute to volunteers in Czechoslovakia fighting
the Nazis, this work, composed during the terror of the Nazi
invasion, captures the fears and intensity of the horrible events to
come.

654. *Memorial to Lidice.* Orchestra [1943]. 1st: New York, 2 October
1943. #Moscow: State Music, 1966. *Unicorn RHS 309.
M1045.M383L5
A brief, brooding work written quickly upon the composer's
learning of the Nazi massacre in Lidice.

655. Symphony No. 1. Orchestra [1942]. 1st: Boston, 13 November
1942. #New York: Boosey & Hawkes, 1947. *RCA Victor Red
Seal RD60154-2RC.
M1001.M387 no. 1
The intense third movement of this thirty-five minute, four-
movement traditional symphony with its pungent chromaticisms
and periodic timpani blasts displays Martinů's first reaction to
Lidice. It begins in E-flat minor and ends in E minor.

656. Symphony No. 2. Orchestra [1943]. 1st: Cleveland, 28 October
1943. #New York: Boosey & Hawkes, 1966. *BIS CD-362 and
RCA Victor Red Seal RD60154-2RC.
M1001.M387 no. 2 1966
A four-movement, twenty-four minute symphony written to
support Martinů's fellow citizens in Czechoslovakia during the
war. It ends triumphantly on a D-major chord.

Novák, Víteslav (1870-1949)

657. *De profundis,* Op. 67. Symphonic poem for organ and orchestra [1941]. 1st: 9 October 1941. #Prague: Hudební matice Umělecké besedy, 1945.

M1002.N93 Op. 67

With movements such as Largo lugubre and Appassionata doloroso, this intense twenty-seven minute work illustrates Novák's despair at the beginning of the war. It begins in A minor and ends softly in B major with a feeling of resigned hope.

658. *Majova Symphonie,* Op. 73. Soloists, chorus, and orchestra [1943]. 1st: 5 December 1945. #Prague: Státni hudebni vydavatelstvi, 1962. Texts by K.H. Macha, V. Hálek, and František Branislav.

M1001.N93 Op. 73

The first two movements were composed when news of Hitler's defeats in 1943 were circulating. The last movement, however, was composed after the Battle of Stalingrad and the composer chose to show the horrors of war and the suffering it caused. Novák quotes parts of the Nazi anthem and a victorious Russian song "Ej, uchnem!." The work concludes with a feeling of national unity by quoting the Czech National Anthem.

Slavický, Klement (b. 1910)

659. *Lidice.* Double chorus for male voices [1945]. *Panton 81100508. Text by František Halas.

[No LC number available]

Dedicated "to the memory of the Lidice martyrs," this nine-minute work contains sudden dramatic shifts and displays of intense anger and grief.

Denmark

Tarp, Svend Erik (b. 1908)

660. *Pro defunctis.* Orchestra [1945]. 1st: 20 August 1945. #Copenhagen: Skandinavisk Musikforlag, 1946.

*MTO (NYPL call number)

A four-and-one-half minute lyrical yet highly chromatic work written as a lament for those who died during World War II.

France

Jolivet, André (1905-1974)

661. *Les trois complaintes du soldat.* Voice and orchestra (or piano)
    [1940]. 1st: 28 February 1943. #Paris: Durand, 1942.
    *MP (French) (NYPL call number)
    Contains three songs: "La complainte du soldat vaincu 'Me
    voici donc sans armes'"; "La complainte du pont de Gien 'Et voici
    le soldat sur la route'"; and "La complainte à Dieu 'Mon Dieu,
    c'est plain des larmes.'"

Martinon, Jean (1910-1976)

662. *Musique d'exil ou Stalag IX.* Orchestra. [1941]. 1st: Paris, 11
    January 1941. #Paris: Choudens, 1947.
    M1045.M38 Op. 31
    A thirteen-minute orchestral work full of jazz idioms. Written
    during Marinon's detention in a Nazi labor camp.

663. *Psaume 136 (Chant du captifs),* Op. 33. Soprano, tenor, chorus,
    and orchestra [1940-1942]. #Paris: Lucien de Lacour, 1946.
    M2023.M383P8
    In five sections in a highly expressive, foreboding and
    chromatic language. Also written while Martinon was detained in a
    Nazi labor camp.

Messiaen, Oliver (1908-1992)

664. *Quartet to the End of Time.* Violin, clarinet, cello, and piano
    [1941]. 1st: Stalag 8A, Gorlitz, Silesia, 15 January 1941. #Paris:
    Durand. *DG 423247-2 GC and Delos CD-3043.
    M422.M48Q3
    Messiaen wrote this apocalyptic work while a prisoner during
    World War II.

Milhaud, Darius (1892-1974)

665. *Cantate de la guerre.* Chorus [1940]. #New York: G. Schirmer,
    1942. Text by Paul Claudel.
    M2092.5.M
    Consists of four tonal songs, including "Chorus of the Guilty"
    and "Chorus of the Martyrs."

666. *La liberation des Antilles.* Voice and piano [1944]. 1st: 6 December 1945. #New York: Leeds Music, 1949. Text from two Creole texts.
      M1621.M
      A celebration song of the French West Indies.

667. *Suite française.* In two versions: for winds and for orchestra [1944]. 1st: Wind version, New York, 13 June 1945. 1st: Orchestra version, 29 July 1945. #New York: Leeds Music, 1947. *EMI/Angel DS-38121.
      M1203.M
      Not a war composition in the traditional sense, but a depiction of the areas in France where the Allies supported the French underground during World War II. In five movements named after these areas, the work includes folk melodies associated with each place.

668. *Two Marches.* Orchestra [1945]. 1st: CBS Symphony Orchestra, 16 December 1945. #New York: G. Schirmer, 1947.
      *MTK (NYPL call number)
      Two brief marches, loud and triumphant, combined for approximately six minutes: "In memoriam (Pearl Harbor)" and "Gloria victoribus."

Poulenc, Francis (1899-1965)

669. *Figure humaine (The Face of Man).* Cantata for double chorus [1943]. 1st: 25 March 1945. #Paris: Rouart & Lerolle, 1945. *Supraphon 11-12-3359 and Erato STU 70924. Text by Paul Éluard.
      M1610.P6F5
      Poulenc wrote this work so that it would be performed as soon as possible after liberation. It consists of eight separate sections discussing man's stupidity in war, but ends with the idea of liberty *ffff* on an E-major chord with the soprano solo singing a high E.
      Poulenc also composed a war song entitled *C.* Song for voice and piano [1940]. #Paris: Rouart & Lerolle, 1949. Text by Louis Aragon.

Sauguet, Henri (1901-1989)

670. *Symphonie expiatoire.* Orchestra [1944-1946]. 1st: 8 February 1948. #Paris: Editions Salabert, 1948.

M1001.S26S9

In four movements, this large work is dedicated to the innocent victims of war 1939-1945. The movements are tonal in E minor, E major, A minor (a ferocious march), and E major/minor (an elegiac, slow movement).

Germany

Brautigam, Helmut (1914-1942)

671. *Der Krieg stosst in sein Horn.* Soldier cantata for male chorus and band [c. 1942]. #Potsdam: L. Voggenreiter, 1942. Texts by Max Barthel and Oskar Wohrle.
    M1540.B842K7
    An introduction and five songs beginning and ending in B-flat major. The music is diatonic, militaristic with dotted rhythms, triplets, and predominantly in duple meters.

Strauss, Richard (1864-1949)

672. *Metamorphosen.* Twenty-three string instruments [1945]. 1st: 25 January 1946. #New York: Boosey & Hawkes, 1946. *DG 423888-2 GGA and Angel CDC-47992.
    M1145.S888M4
    Written as Germany lay in the chaos of defeat, this work sums up the despair associated with war as well as any. Ends with a reference to the funeral march from Beethoven's "Eroica" Symphony.

Weill, Kurt (1900-1950)

673. *Walt Whitman Cycle.* Baritone and small orchestra [1942-1947]. #Valley Forge: European American Music, 1986. *Arabesque Z6579 or Koch Schwann 314050. Text by Walt Whitman.
    M1621.W
    Contains settings of "O Captain! My Captain," "Beat! Beat! Drums!," "Dirge for Two Veterans," and "Come Up From the Fields, Father." The works are attractive and tonal. The second is the most martial with its continuous march pulse and the sound of the bugles.

Great Britain

Bax, Arnold (1893-1953)

674. *Malta G.C.* Film music for orchestra [1942]. 1st: December 1942.
      #London: Chappell, 1949.
         M1003.B38M3
         A suite of over twenty minutes in length, including numerous
      orchestral descriptions of war events indicated by headings:
      "Ruins," "Air Raid," "Quick March," and "Ruins and sorrows after
      the raid." Bax also made a revision of the final march (*Victory
      March*) from this film in 1945.

Britten, Benjamin (1913-1976)

675. *Ballad of Heroes.* Tenor (or soprano), chorus, and orchestra [1939].
      1st: London, 5 April 1939. #London: Boosey & Hawkes, 1939.
      *Chandos 8983-8984. Texts by W.H. Auden and Randall
      Swingler.
         M1533.B865B3
         A lament that grew out of the Spanish Civil War. In three
      parts ("Funeral March," Scherzo: "Dance of Death," and
      "Recitation and Choral.") The work concludes with an epilogue
      returning the opening material from the funeral march. Three
      trumpets and a side drum perform in a gallery or somewhere behind
      the scenes.

Bush, Alan (b. 1900)

676. *Meditation on a German Song of 1848*, Op. 22. Violin, piano, and
      strings [1941]. 1st: 6 December 1941. #London: J. Williams,
      1948.
         M223.B
         A nine-minute, dissonant virtuoso work based upon a poem
      by Georg Herwegh about a German conscript fighting in the army
      of the Holy Roman Empire.

Finzi, Gerald (1901-1956)

677. *Farewell to Arms*, Op. 9. Tenor and small orchestra [1921 and
      1941]. 1st: Manchester, England, 30 March 1945. #London:
      Boosey & Hawkes, 1945. *Lyrita SRCS 93. Texts by Ralph
      Knevet and George Peele.

M1614.F45F3

In two parts on poems by two poets, this lyrical work emphasizes the lush sounds of the strings and looks for a time without weapons and war.

678. *June on Castle Hill*, Op. posth. Voice and piano [1940]. #London: Boosey, 1965. Text by J. Lucas.

[No LC number available]

A brief, two-minute song in G minor telling of the inevitability of future war.

Heming, Michael (1920-1942)

679. *A Threnody for a Soldier Killed in Action*. Orchestra. Based on a sketch left by Michael Heming who was killed in action at El Alamein. Completed by Anthony Collins [1942]. 1st: Sheffeld, England, 14 January 1943, Halle Orchestra. #London: Keith Prowse, 1944. *HMV C3427. An arrangement for piano also exists: #London: Keith Prowse, 1945.

M1045.H5T4 (orchestra); M35.H (piano)

A six-minute, highly chromatic lament in C minor. The sensitive writing and the circumstances surrounding this work, make it a unique example of war-related music.

Searle, Humphrey (1915-1982)

680. *Vigil (France 1940-1944)*, Op. 3. Piano [1944]. #London: A. Lengnick, 1949.

**MYD (NYPL call number)

A five-page work with an opening section similar to Satie's *Gymnopédie No. 2*. This slow composition is calm, with a more agitated and extended middle section but not specifically programmatic. Dedicated "To my friends of the Fighting French Forces."

Stevens, Bernard (1916-1983)

681. Concerto for Violin and Orchestra, Op. 4. Violin and orchestra [1943]. *Meridian CDE84174.

M1013.S833C66

A traditional work in three movements of which the second is a slow, funeral-like march and the third contains martial elements in its optimistic conclusion.

Tippett, Michael (b. 1905)

682. *A Child of Our Time*. Oratorio [1939-1941]. 1st: London, 19
March 1944. #London: Schott, 1944. *Philips 6500985.
M2003.T63C5 1944
The idea for this work grew out of the "general situation" of the
world before World War II and was composed as the war
progressed. The opening lines set the tone for this examination of
war and peace, evil and good, oppression and freedom. Includes
Negro spirituals.

Vaughan Williams, Ralph (1872-1958)

683. *Five Wartime Hymns*. Voice and piano (or organ). (Revised as
Songs of Faith) [1942]. #London: Oxford University Press, 1945.
Text by Canon G.W. Briggs.
*MRA (NYPL call number)
Written in conjunction with Martin Shaw and Ivor Atkins,
Vaughan Williams set only two of these hymns: "A hymn of
freedom," and "A call to the free nations."

684. *Six Choral Songs to be Sung in Time of War*. Chorus and piano
(or organ) [1940]. #London: Oxford University Press, 1940. Text
by Shelly.
*MP (English) (NYPL call number)
Includes songs on courage, liberty, healing, victory (which ends
ff in C major), "Pity, Peace, and Love," and "The New Age."

685. *Thanksgiving for Victory* (later renamed *A Song of Thanksgiving*).
Narrator, soprano, chorus, children's voices, and orchestra [1944].
1st: 13 May 1945. #London: Oxford University Press, 1945.
*HMV ED 2902581. Texts from Shakespeare, the Bible, and
Kipling.
M1530.3.V35T5
A fifteen-minute work written and recorded before the war's end
so that it could be broadcast on the day the Allies defeated the
Germans. In B-flat major, largely diatonic, and easy to sing, this
piece admirably fulfills its patriotic duty.

686. *The Story of a Flemish Farmer*. Orchestral suite (taken from film
music of the same title) [1943]. 1st: London Symphony Orchestra,
31 July 1945. #London: Oxford University Press.
[No LC number available]

Cited in Michael Kennedy, *The Works of Ralph Vaughan Williams* (London: Oxford University Press, 1980), p. 259.

Wood, Thomas (1892-1950)

687. *The Rainbow. A Tale of Dunkirk.* Set to music for tenor and baritone, men's voices and brass band [c. 1951]. #London: Stainer & Bell, 1951. Text by Christopher Hassall.
M1533.W85R3
An hour-long work "commissioned for the festival of Britain 1951."

Hungary

Kodály, Zoltán (1882-1967)

688. *Csatádal (Battle Song).* Double chorus [1943]. #London: Boosey & Hawkes, 1959. Text by Sándor Petöfi.
M1582.K63 C8
An excellent example of a descriptive battle song: loud throughout, highly energetic with repeated rhythms, and ending on an A-major chord.

Israel

Ben-Haim, Paul (1897-1984) [German born]

689. Symphony No. 1. Orchestra [1940]. 1st: 5 June 1941. #New York: Leeds, 1957. *CBS S72629.
*MTA (NYPL call number)
Influenced by the war years, this symphony laments the destruction and death caused by the Nazis, but ends heroically with the conviction that they will be defeated.

Italy

Malipiero, Gian F. (1882-1973)

690. Symphony No. 3 ("Delle Campane"). Orchestra [1945]. 1st: 4 November 1945. #Milan: Suvini Zerboni, 1947.
M1001.M25 no. 3 1947a
A four-movement symphony relating to the day when the Nazis rescued Mussolini. Malipiero discussed this day of 8 September

1943: "The bells of San Marco in Venice rang at sunset but they could not deceive those who knew their true voice. They tolled not for peace but for new torments, new horrors" (Cited in SLONIMSKY, p. 805).

Petrassi, Goffredo (b. 1904)

691. *Coro di morti.* Dramatic madrigal for male chorus, brass, double basses, three pianos, and percussion [1940-1941]. 1st: Venice, 28 September 1941. #Milan: Suvini Zerboni, 1953. *MHS MHC 5783 or Westminster XWN 18539. Text by Giacomo Léopardi.
     M1533.P46C6
     A seventeen-minute dramatic elegy in five sections with emphasis on low brass and timpani. The repetitive, march/lament of the pianos haunts this striking wartime work.

The Netherlands

Vermeulen, Matthijs (1888-1967)

692. Symphony No. 4 ("Les victories"). Orchestra [1940-1941]. 1st: Rotterdam, 30 September 1949. #Amsterdam: Donemus, 198-?. *Composer's Voice 8384/2.
     M1001.V516 no. 4 1980z
     A continuous symphony which includes a battle march, a funeral march, a fanfare, and a war song written with the firm belief that victory would prevail and that the Germans would be defeated.

693. Symphony No. 5 ("Les lendemains chantants"). Orchestra [1941-1945]. 1st: Amsterdam, 12 October 1949. #New York: Henmar. *Composer's Voice 8384/2.
     [No LC number available]
     The title of this three-movement symphony is "taken from a letter written by one of the great leaders of the French Resistance as a goodbye and farewell before he was shot, having already been tortured" (See note to phonodisc Composer's Voice 8384/2). Vermeulen attempts here to capture the darkness and despair of the war.

Norway

Egge, Klaus (1906-1979)

694.   Symphony No. 1, Op. 17. Orchestra [1942]. 1st: 4 October 1945.
        #Drammen, Norway: H. Lyche, 1946. *Philips 6507 049.
           M1001.E32 Op. 17 1948a
           Dedicated to the "Norwegians who served at sea during the
           Second World War," this three-movement, forty-five minute tonal
           symphony does not depict the war in any programmatic manner.

Saeverud, Harald (b. 1897)

695.   *Kjempevise-slåtten (The Ballad of Revolt)*. Piano (Later arranged
        for orchestra) [1943]. #Oslo: Musikk Huset, 1946. *Norwegian
        Composers NC 4913.
           M1060.S13 Op. 22a no. 5
           A six-minute work dedicated to the homefront's great and small
           fighters.

696.   Symphony No. 6 ("Sinfonia dolorosa"), Op. 19. Orchestra [1942].
        1st: Bergen, Norway, 27 May 1943. #Oslo: Musikk Huset, 1945.
           M1001.S223 Op. 19
           A fourteen-minute symphony that, in spite of its title, seems
           more like an optimistic work certain of victory. Its spirited
           conclusion employs bells and tremolos, ending *fff* on a B-flat
           major chord.

Poland

Maklakiewicz, Jan (1899-1954)

697.   *Grunwald*. Symphonic poem [1939-1944]. 1st: 1 September 1945.
        #Warsaw: Polskie Wydawnictwo Muzyczne, 1960.
           M1002.M238G8
           Written during the war years, this work depicts the Battle of
           Grunewald in 1410. It relies on frenetic repetitions, dotted
           rhythms, and intense chromaticism to depict the ferociousness of
           war.

Panufnik, Andrzej (1914-1991)

698. *Uwertura tragiczna (Tragic Overture)*. Orchestra [1942, 1945, revised 1955]. 1st: Warsaw, 1942. Revised version: 1st: London, 20 May 1955. #Cracow: Polskie wydawnictwo muzyczne, 1948. *Unicorn RHS 306.
M1004.P18U9
Dedicated to his brother who died fighting for the Polish Underground Army, this seven-minute work captures in three parts the suffering and the heroism of the people in Poland during the horrors of World War II.

Woytowicz, Bolesław (1899-1980)

699. Symphony No. 2 ("Warszawska"). Orchestra [1945]. 1st: 27 September 1946. #Crakow: Polskie wydawnictwo muzyczne, 1958.
M1001.W938 no. 2 1958
Dedicated to his stepson killed in the 1944 Warsaw Uprising and contains four programmatic movements in traditional symphonic form: "Disaster," "Insurrection," "Contra spem spero," and "Jubilation." Forty minutes.

Soviet Union

Glière, Reinhold [Glier, Reingol'd] (1875-1956). Ukraine

700. *Pobeda (Victory Overture)*, Op. 86. Orchestra [1945]. 1st: 30 October 1945. #Moscow: State Music, 1946.
M1004.G56V65
A multi-sectioned overture full of largely-diatonic, repeated-note patterns in winds and brass. Begins with a slow introduction and concludes triumphantly and *ff* in B-flat major (Marziale maestoso e molto animato).

Grechaninov, Aleksandr [Gretchaninoff, Alexander] (1864-1956). Russia

701. *Poème élégiaque*, Op. 175. Grand orchestra [1945]. 1st: 29 March 1946. #Holograph at NYPL.
*MNZ Mus. Res. (NYPL call number)
A passionate, tonal lament with sudden mood swings from triumph to despair. Composed in memory of those who gave their lives for freedom.

702. *Towards Victory.* Male chorus and orchestra [1943]. #Photostatic copy of autograph, NYPL. Text by Pushkin.

    *MNZ (NYPL call number)

    Dedicated to the "valiant heroes of the second patriotic war," this work begins Andante ("In Russia all is quiet") in D minor. "Suddenly the enemy invades" appears in C minor leading to the chorus's entrance singing "Running as at Spring a torrent to Russian fields the foes invade." Highly chromatic with considerable sixteenth-notes, repeated notes, and text painting, ending with the triumphant energy indicated by the title.

Khachaturyan, Aram (1903-1978). Georgia

703. Symphony No. 2. Orchestra [1943]. 1st: Moscow, 30 December 1943. #Moscow: State Music, 1969. *London 414169-1LE.

    M1001.K45 no. 2

    A significant war work in four movements. The first contains its noted bell motive; the explosive second movement has incessant rhythmic drive; the tragic third portrays (according to the composer) "superhuman sufferings caused to the Soviet people by the Nazi monsters" (Cited in Ewen, *Complete Book of 20th Century Music*, p. 205) and includes the "Dies irae" theme; the fourth concludes with a grandiose triumph.

Myaskovsky, Nikolay (1881-1950). Russia

704. Symphony No. 22 in B minor, Op. 54 ("Symphonic Ballad"). Orchestra [1941]. 1st: 12 January 1942. #New York: Leeds Music, 1945. *Melodiya CM 03157-58.

    M1001.M597 Op. 54 1944

    A three-movement symphony written early in the war. The first movement is dark and brooding in B minor, but the last movement opens with fanfares and resolves triumphantly to B major symbolizing the victory that the Soviets would win.

Prokofiev, Sergei [Prokof'yev, Sergey] (1891-1953). Russia

705. *Alexander Nevsky*, Op. 78. Cantata (taken from 1938 film score) [1939]. 1st: Moscow 17 May 1939. #New York: Leeds Music, 1945. *Telarc CD-80143 and RCA 5606-2-RC.

    M1530.P85 Op. 78 1941

    A seven-movement cantata about the Russian defense of Novgorod in 1242 against the invasion of the Teutonic Knights.

The last four scenes are particularly relevant to war music and present Prokofiev at the height of his powers: 4) "Arise, Ye Russian people"; 5) "The Battle on the Ice"; 6) "Field of the Dead"; and 7) "Alexander's Entry Into Pskov"—the last a triumphant victory celebration.

706. *Ballad of a Boy Who Remained Unknown*, Op. 93. Cantata [1942-1943]. 1st: 21 February 1944. #Moscow: Izd. Musica, 1975. *Ricordi-Melodiya RCL 27077. Text by Pavel Antokolsky.
    M1530.P85B37
    Prokofiev wrote: "I wanted the cantata to be impetuous and dramatic, and the music to reflect the dramatic mood of the text. As I wrote it, I saw before me images of a broken childhood, of [a] cruel enemy, inflexible bravery and an approaching bright victory" (Cited in Vladimir Blok, compiler, *Sergei Prokofiev: Materials, Articles, Interviews* [U.S.S.R: Progress, 1978], p. 42). The music operates on two levels, that of the inhuman march of the invaders and the gentle lyricism of the unknown boy.

707. *Ivan the Terrible*, Op. 116. Oratorio (arranged by A. Stasevich, 1961) [1942-1945]. #New York: Belwin Mills, 1979. *Forlane UCD 16530 and Melodiya S4103.
    M2003.P85I92 1962
    Contains several scenes that are war-related, particularly the overture, "Over the Dead Bodies of the Enemy," "The Tartars," and "The Gunners."

708. *Ode to the End of the War*, Op. 105. Orchestra [1945]. 1st: 10 November 1945. #New York: Belwin Mills, 1979. *Melodiya A10 00083005.
    JMG 76-1265 (NYPL call number)
    A pompous, loud, grandiose victory celebration replete with four pianos, eight harps, sixteen string basses and dominated by brass, woodwinds, and percussion. Prokofiev found no need to include violins, violas, or cellos.

709. *Semyon Kotko*, Op. 81. Opera [1939]. 1st: 23 June 1940. #Moscow: State Music, 1947. *Urania URLP 7135.
    M1503.P969S47 1960
    About the war in the Ukraine in 1918.

710. Sonata No. 7, Op. 83. Piano [1939-1942]. 1st: 18 January 1943.
      #Moscow: State Music, 1943. *DG 419202-2 GH and CBS M3K-
      42150.

      M23.P93 Op. 82 1968
      Considered by Israel Nestyev and Glenn Gould to be a war
      piece. Gould wrote, "The finale, in 7/8 time, is one of those 'just
      as our lines are beginning to crumble comes another column of our
      impregnable tanks even if they do happen to be Sherman and to
      have arrived lend-lease at Murmansk last week' toccatas." See Tim
      Page, ed. *The Glenn Gould Reader* (Toronto: Lester & Orpen
      Dennys, 1984), p. 166.

711. Symphony No. 5, Op. 100. Orchestra [1944]. 1st: Moscow, 13
      January 1945. #New York: Kalmus, 1944. *CBS MK-35877.

      M1001.P96 Op. 100 1946a
      Boris Yarustovsky, David Ewen, and others considered this a
      war symphony particularly with its dynamic outbursts in the
      scherzo and the intense lament of the third movement.

712. Symphony No. 6, Op. 111. Orchestra [1944-1947]. 1st:
      Leningrad, 10 October 1947. #New York: MCA Music, 1949.
      *Erato ECD-75462.

      M1001.P96 Op. 111 1949a
      Darker than the victorious-ending Fifth, Nestyev believed this
      work to be a war-related work as well. See Israel V. Nestyev,
      Prokofiev, trans. Florence Jonas (Stanford: Stanford University
      Press, 1960), p. 399.

713. *War and Peace*, Op. 91. Opera [1943-1952]. 1st: Leningrad, 12
      June 1946. #Moscow: Gosudarstvennoe Musykalnoe Izdatelstvo,
      1958. *Columbia/Melodiya M4 33111 and Erato ECD-75480.
      Libretto by the composer and Mira Mendelson-Prokofieva.

      M1503.P969W47 1973
      A three-hour opera in five acts (and thirteen scenes) based on
      Tolstoy's famous novel of Napoleon's invasion of Russia. A
      magnificent work and one of the few operas conceived and
      primarily written during the war that is still performed today.
      Scenes viii-xi show in part the Battle of Borodino with Napoleon
      as one of the main characters. The battle proper beginning in scene
      ix uses repeated-note patterns, disjunct fragments in the winds, and
      steady drum blasts.

714. *The Year 1941*, Op. 90. Symphonic suite [c. 1943]. 1st: 21 January 1943. #Moscow: State Music, 1973. *Chandos ABRD 1122.
     JMF 77-218 (NYPL call number)
     Deals with the Nazi invasion of Russia in three movements: "In Battle," "Night," and "For the Brotherhood of Nations." The battle movement (Allegro tempestuoso) is in D minor, ending heroically (*ff*) in D major. Predominantly in 6/8 with numerous ostinatos and repeated notes. From rehearsal numbers 13 to 17, Prokofiev builds to a heroic climax with repeated martial rhythms and extensive brass and percussion.

Shaporin, Yury (1887-1966). Glukhov

715. *A Tale of the Battle for the Russian Land*, Op. 17. Oratorio [1944]. 1st: Moscow, 18 April 1944. #Moscow: Soviet Kompozitor, 1969. *Melodiya SO1421-4.
     M2000.S495S62
     Similar in structure to *On the Field of Kulikovo*; refers to past wars to represent the present in a symbolic fashion. Awarded a Stalin Prize.

716. *On the Field of Kulikovo*, Op. 14. Symphonic cantata [1918-1939]. 1st: 18 November 1939. #Moscow: State Music, 1946. *Melodiya DO24817-20. Text by Alexander Blok with additions and supplements by Mikhael Lozinsky. Awarded a Stalin Prize.
     M1530.S53 Op. 14
     Deals with the Russian victory over the invading Mongols in 1380 and is in seven movements with a prologue and epilogue. In the "Chorus of Tartars" Shaporin presents a ferocious battle scene at rehearsal numbers 146 and 147, using glissandi in the strings and rapid chromatic scales in the winds. The work ends with a victory celebration in C major.

Shostakovich, Dmitry (1906-1975). Russia

717. Symphony No. 7, Op. 60. Orchestra [1941]. 1st: Kuibyshev, 5 March 1942. #New York: Leeds Music, 1945. *London 417392-2 and CBS MK-44855.
     M1001.S554 Op. 60
     The most performed and most famous war symphony written during the war. This four-movement symphony begins with an incredible repetitive march that grows more harrowing with every

musical footstep (which the Soviets took to be the Germans invading the Soviet Union).

718. Symphony No. 8, Op. 65. Orchestra [1943]. 1st: Moscow, 4 November 1943. #Leipzig: Breitkopf & Härtel, 1947. *London 411616-2 LH.
      M1001.S554 Op. 65
      A much darker work than the previous Seventh and the high point of Shostakovich's war-related compositions. See pages 190 to 191 for additional information.

719. Symphony No. 9, Op. 70. Orchestra [1945]. 1st: Moscow, 3 November 1945. #New York: Leeds Music, 1946. *London 414677-2 LH.
      M1001.S554 Op. 70 1946
      A war symphony by default. Stalin wanted a grand, heroic symphony in the tradition of Beethoven's Ninth to celebrate the Soviet's victory over the Nazis. Instead, Shostakovich wrote a five-movement neoclassic work for which Shostakovich feared Stalin would have him executed.

Switzerland

Honegger, Arthur (1892-1955)

720. Symphony No. 2. String orchestra with optional trumpet [1941]. 1st: Basel, 23 May 1942. #Paris: Salabert, 1942. *DG 2543805.
      M1101.H75 no. 2 1968
      A less than overt war symphony that Willi Reich believed caught "much of the mood of occupied Paris." (See Ewen, *Complete Book of 20th Century Music*, p. 186.) A twenty-four minute symphony in three movements: Molto moderato - Allegro; Adagio mesto (a tremendous lament); and Vivace, non troppo.

Martin, Frank (1890-1974)

721. *In Terra Pax*. Oratorio [1944]. 1st: Radio broadcast, 7 May 1945. #Vienna: Universal Edition, 1953. *London OS 25847. Text from the Old and New Testaments.
      M2003.M38I5
      Commissioned by Radio Genève for Armistice Day of World War II, this work is in four sections and incorporates some twelve-tone technique. The first section deals with the warlike

characteristics of mankind and the last section calls for peace on earth.

Yugoslavia

Vukdragović, Mihailo (b. 1900)

722. *Put u pobedu* (*The Road to Victory*). Symphonic poem [1944]. 1st: 14 October 1945. #Belgrade: Srpska Akademija Nauka i umetnosti, 1979.
JMG 82-66 (NYPL call number)
Dedicated to the memory of Vojislav Vucković, this work opens darkly in G minor and, through its various tempi and character changes, builds to a defiant, diatonic close in G major.

SUPPLEMENT OF WORLD WAR II MUSIC:
1939-1945

723. Adler, Samuel Hans (b. 1928). America [German born]. *Epitaph for the Young American Soldier* [1945]. #New York: Booscy & Hawkes. Written when Adler was only sixteen; he later withdrew the work, and it no longer exists. See letter to author, 21 January 1985.
724. Amirov, Fikret (1922-1984). Born in Kirovabad. *To the Memory of the Heroes of the Great Nation War*. Symphonic poem [1944].
725. Arnell, Richard (b. 1917). Great Britain. *The War God*. Cantata [1944]. Text by Stephen Spender. ML96.A91 case.
726. Arnič, Blaž (1901-1970). Slovenia. *The Whirlwind of War*. Orchestra [1941]. [Cited in BAKER, p. 56].
727. Ashrafi, Mukhtar (1912-1975). Bukhara. *Buran*. Opera [c. 1939]. 1st: 11 June 1939. Orchestrated and organized by Vasilenko. Deals with the Uzbek Rebellion in 1916.
728. _____. *Heroic Symphony*. Orchestra [1942]. [Cited in HO, p. 31].
729. Balanchivadze, Andrey (b. 1906). Georgia. *Kartsanissky Battle*. Symphonic picture [1943]. [Cited in HO, p. 44].

730. Barkhudaryan, Sergey (1887-1972). Georgia. *1942*. Overture [1943]. [Cited in HO, p. 48].
731. Bartoš, Josef (b. 1902). Czechoslovakia. *The Unknown Soldier.* Cantata [1940].
732. Barvík, Miroslav (b. 1919). Czechoslovakia. *Lidice*. Piano sonata [1943].
733. Becker, John Joseph (1886-1961). America. *The Snow Goose: A Legend of World War II.* Orchestra [1944]. [Cited in BAKER, p. 131].
734. Berlinsky, Pavel (b. 1900). Irkutsk. *Alexander Nevsky*. Cantata [1942]. [Cited in HO, p. 55].
735. Blatný, Josef (1891-1980). Czechoslovakia. *Te Deum and Alleluia.* Organ [1942]. Inspired by Blatný's "unshakeable faith in the liberation of his people."
736. Blumenfeld, Harold (b. 1923). America. *See Here the Fallen.* Chorus and orchestra [1943]. 1st: Rochester, 1945. [Cited in *New Grove Dictionary of American Music*, vol. 1, p. 249].
737. Bogatiryov, Anatoly (b. 1913). Vitebsk. *Drygva (Woodland Thicket)*. Opera [c. 1939]. 1st: Minsk, 28 August 1939. [Cited in HO, p. 62]. Deals with the Byelorussian peasant's rebellion against Polish occupation in 1919.
738. Brott, Alexander (b. 1915). Canada. *War and Peace.* Ballet for orchestra [1944]. [Cited in BAKER, p. 252].
739. Carpenter, John (1876-1981). America. *War Lullaby*. Orchestra [1942]. 1st: Seattle, 1942.
740. Cerník, Vilém (b. 1909). Czechoslovakia. *May 1945*. Incidental music.
741. Chevreuille, Raymond (1901-1976). Belgium. *Prière pour les condamnes à mort.* Narrator and orchestra [1944]. 1st: 14 October 1945. [Cited in BAKER, p. 324].
742. Chlubna, Osvald (1893-1971). Czechoslovakia. *Eulogies on Liberation*. Song cycle [1945].
743. Cikker, Ján (1911-1989). Czechoslovakia. *Vojak a matka (Soldier and Mother)*. Symphonic poem [1943]. #Prague: Slovensky hudobny fond. *Opus 9010 0366-9.
744. Dekhteryov, Vasily (1910-1987). Born in Orenburg. *Tania*. Opera [c. 1943]. 1st: 23 February 1943. [Cited in HO, p. 111]. Deals with the Nazi invasion of 1941.
745. Dobiás, Václav (1909-1978). Czechoslovakia. Symphony No. 1. Orchestra [1943]. [Cited in BAKER, p. 439]. Deals with the Nazi occupation of Czechoslovakia.

746. Doubrava, Jaroslav (1909-1960). Czechoslovakia. Symphony No. 2 ("Stalingradska"). Orchestra [1943-1944]. [Cited in BAKER, p. 451].
747. Dzerzhinsky, Ivan (1909-1978). Tambov. *The Blood of the People.* Opera [c. 1942]. 1st: Leningrad, 21 January 1942. [Cited in BAKER, p. 473]. Deals with the Nazi invasion of the Soviet Union.
748. Eisler, Hanns (1898-1962). Germany. *Schweyk in zweiten Weltkrieg.* Soloists, chorus, and orchestra [1943-1959]. #Henschelverlag Kunst und Gesellschaft in Lieder und Kantaten, vol. 8. Text by Bertolt Brecht. [Cited in BAKER, p. 485].
749. Glière, Reinhold (1875-1956). Russia. *Rachel.* Opera [1942]. 1st: 19 April 1942. [Cited in HO, p. 174]. Deals with the 1871 Franco-Prussian War.
750. Gnesin, Mikhail (1883-1957). Russia. *Trio in Memory of Our Perished Children.* Trio [1943].
751. Goh, Taijiro (1907-1970). Japan. *Otakebi (War Cry).* Overture [1939]. [Cited in BAKER, p. 642].
752. Harris, Roy (1898-1979). America. *Ballet on the Subject of War* (or) *Walt Whitman Suite* [1944]. #New York: Mills Music; *Conflict.* Winds and percussion. (Reworking of Symphony No. 6) [1944]. #New York: Belwin Mills.
753. Hartmann, Karl Amadeus (1905-1963). Germany. *China kämpft (China at War).* Symphonic overture [1942]. 1st: Darmstadt, July 1947. [Cited in BAKER, p. 724].
754. Honegger, Arthur (1892-1955). Switzerland. *Chant de liberation.* Baritone, chorus, and orchestra [1942]. 1st: 22 October 1944. #Paris: Salabert. [Cited in BAKER, p. 795].
755. Kabalevsky, Dmitry (1904-1987). Russia. *At Moscow.* 1st: Moscow, 28 November 1943. #Moscow, 1955. Revised as *Into the Fire,* 7 November 1947. [Cited in BAKER, p. 875].
756. _____. *V'ogne (Into the Fire).* Opera. Revision of *At Moscow* [1942]. 1st: 7 November 1947. Revised and incorporated into *The Taras Family.* [Cited in BAKER, p. 875]. The story is based on the Red Army's defense of Moscow.
757. Kalomiris, Manolis (1883-1962). Greece. *Symphony of the Brave Young Men.* Orchestra [c. 1945]. 1st: 26 March 1945. [Cited in SLONIMSKY, p. 798].
758. Kaminski, Heinrich (1886-1946). Germany. *Dem Gedächtnis einer verwundeten Soldaten.* Two sopranos and piano [1941]. [Cited in BAKER, p. 883].
759. Kapp, Eugen (b. 1908). Estonia. *Tasuleegid (Flames of Vengeance).* Opera [1945]. 1st: 21 June 1945. #Moscow: Riiklik

muusika kirjastus, 1958. *Melodiya D17649-56. M33.5.K. Deals
with the Estonian Rebellion in 1343.
760. Khrennikov, Tikhon (b. 1913). Yelets. *At Six P.M. after the War*.
Film. Orchestra [1944]. [Cited in HO, p. 259].
761. Knipper, Lev (1898-1974). Georgia. Overture ("Liberation").
Orchestra [1939]. 1st: 31 October 1939. [Cited in SLONIMSKY,
p. 701].
762. Koval', Marian (1907-1971). Russia. *The People's Holy War of
1941*. Oratorio [1942]. [Cited in BAKER, p. 955].
763. Kubik, Gail (1914-1984). America. *Memphis Belle: A War Time
Episode*. Narrator and orchestra [1944]. 1st: Culver City, 8 October
1944. #New York: Property of G. Schirmer. Text by Lester
Koenig. *MNZ-Amer.++ (NYPL call number).
764. _____. *The World at War*. Orchestra. Film score [1942]. #New
York: 1942. *MSI-Amer. (NYPL call number).
765. Kvapil, Jaroslav (1892-1958). Czechoslovakia. *Symphonic
Variations ("From Difficult Times")*. Orchestra [1939]. #London:
Boosey & Hawkes. *Panton 8110 0003. [Cited in BAKER, p.
988].
766. _____. Symphony No. 4 ("Vítézná"). Orchestra [1943]. [Cited in
BAKER, p. 988].
767. Landré, Guillaume (1905-1968). The Netherlands. *Piae memoriae
pro patria mortuorum*. Chorus and orchestra [1942]. #New York:
Henmar. [Cited in BAKER, p. 1004].
768. Latham, William P. (b. 1917). America. *Prayer after World War*.
Chorus [1945]. [Cited in BAKER, p. 1014].
769. Levitin, Yury (b. 1912). Poltava. *Sacred War*. Voice and orchestra
[1942]. [Cited in HO, p. 308].
770. Maizel', Boris (b. 1907). Russia. Symphony No. 3 ("Victoriously
Triumphant"). Orchestra [1945]. [Cited in HO, p. 330].
771. McDonald, Harl (1899-1955). America. *My Country at War*.
Symphonic suite [1943].
772. Müller, Gottfried (b. 1914). Germany. *Führerwörte*. Oratorio [c.
1944]. 1st: 14 April 1944. [Cited in SLONIMSKY, p. 784].
773. Niyazi, Tagi-zade-Gazhibekov (1912-1984). Georgia. *Battle
Reminiscences*. Orchestra [1944]. [Cited in HO, p. 380].
774. Pipkov, Lubomir (1904-1974). Bulgaria. *Momchil*. Opera [1939-
1944]. 1st: 24 April 1948. #Sofia: Nauka i iskustvo, 1952.
*Balkaton BOA 1231/33. M1503.P663M67 1957. Deals with a
fourteenth-century rebellion in the Balkans.
775. Podešva, Jaromír (b. 1927). Czechoslovakia. *V krajvešla Rudá
armáda (The Red Army Enters the Country)*. Symphonic poem

from *The Path of the Homeland* [1942-1943]. [Cited in BAKER, p. 1422].

776. Popov, Gavriil (1904-1972). Russia. *Alexander Nevsky.* Incomplete opera [1941]. [Cited in HO, p. 412].

777. _____. *To Victory.* Overture-cantata [1944]. [Cited in HO, p. 412].

778. Pylkkänen, Tauno (1918-1980). Finland. *Kullervon sotaanlahto (Kullervo Leaves for War).* Orchestra [1942]. [Cited in BAKER, p. 1458].

779. Ristič, Milan (1908-1982). Serbia. *Covet i rat (Man and War).* Symphonic poem [1942].

780. Rogers, Bernard (1893-1968). America. *The Colors of War.* Orchestra [1939]. 1st: Rochester, 25 October 1939. #Philadelphia: Elkan-Vogel. [Cited in BAKER, p. 1528].

781. _____. *Invasion.* Orchestra [1943]. 1st: New York, 17 October 1943. [Cited in BAKER, p. 1528].

782. Schaefer, Theodor (1904-1969). Czechoslovakia. *Love Ballads.* Vocal [1943]. [Cited in BAKER, p. 1602]. In memory of the Lidice tragedy.

783. Shishov, Ivan (1888-1947). Russia. *Song of Victory.* Overture. Orchestra [1942]. Anticipating victory during World War II. [Cited in HO, p. 487].

784. Spilka, František (1877-1960). Czechoslovakia. *Panychida (The Service for the Dead).* Chorus [1945].

785. Stanislav, Josef (1897-1971). Czechoslovakia. *The Red Army Symphony.* Orchestra [1942-1944]. #Prague: Národni hudebni vydavatelstui orbis, 1951. [Cited in BAKER, p. 1767].

786. Starokadomsky, Mikhail (1901-1954). Russia. *Victory March.* Orchestra [1942]. *HMV CSD 3782. [Cited in HO, p. 519].

787. Taranov, Gleb (b. 1904). Ukraine. *Ice Battle.* Opera [1943-1979]. [Cited in HO, p. 544].

788. Tigranyan, Vartan (1906-1974). Armenia. *Cantata for the 25th Anniversary of the October Revolution.* Cantata [1942]. [Cited in HO, p. 548].

789. Tikhomirov, Georgy (1913-1967). Russia. *Year 1812.* Suite-cantata [1944]. [Cited in HO, p. 548]. Set during the Napoleonic Wars.

790. Tilicheyeva, Yelena (b. 1909). Soviet. *Oratorio in Memory of Dead Heroes.* Oratorio [1942].

791. Umr-Shat, Vagan (b. 1890). Soviet. *To Stalingrad.* Piano concerto [1943].

792. Van Vactor, David (b. 1906). America. Symphony No. 2 ("Music for the Marines"). Orchestra [1943]. 1st: Indianapolis, 27 March

1943. #Roger Rhoads Music. *Composer Recordings CRI 169. [Cited in BAKER, p. 1940].

793. Válek, Jiří (b. 1923). Czechoslovakia. *The Year 1942*. Piano [1942].

794. Veprik, Aleksandr (1899-1958). Balta, Odessa district. *Fascism be Cursed*. Chorus and orchestra [1944]. [Cited in HO, p. 575].

795. Wagenaar, Bernard (1894-1971). America [Dutch born]. *Song of Mourning for the Dutch Patriots*. Orchestra [1944]. #New York: Carl Fischer.

796. Wirén, Dag Ivar (1905-1986). Sweden. *Blåutt, gult, rött*. Radio opera [1940]. [Cited in BAKER, p. 2062].

797. Yevlakhov, Orest (1912-1973). Russia [Polish born]. *Leningrad*. Voice and orchestra [1944]. [Cited in HO, p. 607].

NOTES

1. Gwynne Dyer, *War* (New York: Crown, 1985), p. 160.
2. Sidonie K. Lederer, *Soviet Wartime Music: A Russian War Relief Report* (New York: Russian War Relief, 1948), p. 6.
3. Lederer, p. 7.
4. Lederer, p. 8.
5. Lederer, p. 16.
6. Harrison Salisbury, *The 900 Days: The Siege of Leningrad* (New York: Harper & Row, 1969), pp. 544-56.
7. Salisbury, p. 594.
8. Boris Schwarz, *Music and Musical Life in Soviet Russia* (Bloomington: Indiana University Press, 1983), p. 177.
9. Claire R. Reis, *Composers, Conductors, and Critics* (New York: Oxford University Press, 1955), p. 167.
10. R.D. Welsh, "Music in America," *Music Review* 4 (1943), pp. 32-33.
11. See Barbara A. Zuck, *A History of Musical Americanism.* Studies in Musicology, no. 19 (Ann Arbor: UMI Research Press, 1980), p. 194, for a list of commissioned works.
12. See Zuck, p. 196, for a list of fanfares.
13. Richard S. Sears, *V-Discs: A History and Discography* (Westport, Conn.: Greenwood, 1980), p. lxxxvii.
14. Zuck, p. 197.
15. Peter Hesbacher and Les Waffen, "War Recordings: Incidence and Change (1940-1980)," *Popular Music and Society* 8 (1982), p. 78.
16. Hans Bajer, "Lieder machen Geschichte," in *Musik im Dritten Reich: Eine Dokumentation*, ed. by Joseph Wulf (Gütersloh: Sigbert Mohn, 1963), p. 244. ["Das wirkungsvollste Propagandamittel für die SA war das Kampflied. . . . Nicht mit der blanken Waffe zog die SA aus, ein Land und ein ganzes Volk zu gewinnen, sondern mit ihren siegverhissenden Kampfliedern auf den Lippen marschierte sie in Stadt und Land."]
17. Richard Haug, "Unser Dank—unsere Pflicht," in *Musik im Dritten Reich*, p. 243. ["Sie sind der einzige Weg, um wieder eine Verbindung zwischen Volk und Kunst zu schaffen. Diese Lieder kann man nicht besinnlich vor sich hinsummen. . . . Es ist das erste Mal, dass es Lieder gibt, die das ganze Reich zusammenfassen."]
18. Hans Bajer, "Lieder machen Geschichte," in *Musik im Dritten Reich*, p. 245. ["Das Kampflied war der Gradmesser für das Vorwärtsstürmen der Bewegung."]

19. William Shirer, *The Rise and Fall of the Third Reich* (New York: Simon & Schuster, 1959), p. 278.

20. K. Peter Etzkorn, ed., *Music and Society: The Later Writings of Paul Honigsheim* (New York: John Wiley & Sons, 1973), p. 187.

21. Albert Speer, *Inside the Third Reich,* trans. Richard and Clara Winston (New York: Macmillan, 1970), pp. 98-99.

22. Speer, p. 185.

23. Shirer, p. 1219.

24. Speer, p. 585.

25. Nicholas Slonimsky, *Music Since 1900*, 4th ed. (New York: Charles Scribner's Sons, 1971), p. 801.

26. *Testimony: The Memoirs of Dmitry Shostakovich*, ed. Solomon Volkov. Trans. Antonina W. Bours (New York: Harper & Row, 1979), p. 136. According to Volkov, Shostakovich also claimed he started composing this symphony before Hitler attacked the Soviet Union and that it was as much, if not more, to do with those Stalin had killed in the purges (Volkov, p. 159).

27. David Ewen, *Complete Book of 20th Century Music* (Englewood Cliffs, N.J.: Prentice Hall, 1959), p. 169.

28. Schwarz, p. 182.

29. Schwarz, p. 180.

VII. THE AFTERMATH OF WORLD WAR II

THE KOREAN WAR

Largely because of its brevity and limited number of countries involved, the Korean War failed to inspire many composers. No major composers specifically wrote works dealing with the war, and only a handful of compositions about the Korean war have appeared since 1953 (unlike in the mediums of films, books, and television). Although the number of works written during the Korean War increased slightly compared to the years immediately preceding it, only four rather obscure composers (Fikret Amirov, Miroslav Barvík, Lowndes Maury, and Miloš Vacek) composed works about the Korean War during the war. Only Maury's *In Memory of the Korean War Dead* (no. 1067) for violin and piano was ever recorded. Since then, Donald Erb and Un Yung La have written works on the Korean War theme (nos. 1062, 1092). Erb's work is particularly graphic, in one spot having the chorus scream the word "kill" numerous times within a ten-second period of time.

WORLD WAR II MUSIC: 1946-1990

World War II continued to be the focal point of much war-related music. Immediately after the war, Aaron Copland, Jan Cikker, Emil Hlobil, Darius Milhaud, Milan Ristić, and others wrote optimistic, life-affirming symphonies clearly illustrating their relief that the Nazis had been defeated. The lament tradition intensified in the works of Paul Hindemith, Jean Coulthard, Louis-François-Marie Aubert, and Gian

Malipiero. Andrzej Panufnik and Nancy Van de Vate wrote strong works about the massacre at Katyń. One of the most important laments growing out of the post-war era was Roman Maciejewski's *Missa pro defunctis* (no. 959) started in 1945 and completed in 1959. It is a massive two-hour requiem dedicated "to the victims of the wars of all time, victims of tyrants of human ignorance, victims of broken divine laws." Outside of the Britten *War Requiem*, no other requiem of the century so powerfully laments those lost in war.

　　The dark, horrific compositions continued as well. The second movement of Shostakovich's Eighth String Quartet (no. 981), written against fascism, is similar to the scherzo of the Eighth Symphony (no. 718). The same intense rhythmic drive is present in the melodic pattern which is structurally similar to the eight-bar theme from his Eighth Symphony. For nearly 350 measures various musical ideas are repeated over and over, never cadencing until arriving attaca at the next movement. Other composers looked back with a new musical language and created some experimental music dealing with World War II. Daniel Bukvich's Symphony No. 1 (no. 875) and Gordon Mumma's electronic *Dresden Interleaf 13 February 1945* (no. 887) are both highly individualistic accounts of the firebombing of Dresden. Siegfried Matthus's opera *Die Weise von Liebe und Tod den Cornets Christopher Rilke* (no. 925) deals with the destruction of Dresden as well and was based on poems of Rilke that soldiers carried to the front in both world wars. Georg Katzer's *Aide Memoire* (subtitled "Seven nightmares from the thousand year night") (no. 833) is a powerful composition written in 1983 for the fiftieth anniversary of Hitler's rise to power in 1933. Katzer based this electronic work on what he calls "acoustic fragments from the biggest garbage pile of history,"[1] and he took various fragments from original recordings dating from Hitler's rise of power in 1933 to his demise in 1945. Katzer claimed that the only way that made sense to him in writing about Hitler's Germany was to consider it all a great and terrible nightmare. To do this he resorted to a collage of items taken from Nazi documents of the time and created seven scenes in which the dreamer tosses restlessly among these nightmares.

THE ATOM BOMB

Two themes concerned with the Second World War clearly began to emerge in the late 1950s, however, and grew to dominate music dealing with World War II: compositions about dropping the atom bomb on Japan, and the Holocaust. While composers wrote only three compositions about the bombing of Hiroshima and Nagaski before 1956, at least eleven appeared in the following decade between 1957 and 1967. A similar pattern can be seen with the Holocaust. Only a few composers wrote compositions dealing with the concentration camps before 1956; however, the decade from 1957 to 1967 witnessed the composition of over twenty works dealing directly with the Holocaust. The dropping of the atom bomb on the cities of Hiroshima and Nagasaki and the revelations of the concentration camps shook humanity to such a degree that it was a considerable time before composers turned to these tragedies in their music.

Over forty years after the events now, composers from eleven countries have written musical compositions about the destruction of Hiroshima and Nagasaki. The Finnish composer Erkki Aaltonen wrote one of the earliest works about Hiroshima in 1949, his Symphony No. 2 ("Hiroshima") (no. 989). In the early fifties, Masao Ohki composed two symphonic works dealing with the theme and neither are known today: Symphony No. 5 ("Atomic Bomb") (no. 1033) and *Hiroshima* (no. 951). The latter work, inspired by the paintings *Pictures of the Atom Bomb* of Iri Maruki and Thshiko Akamatsu, is a graphic portrayal of and a polemic about the event. The history of compositions dealing with Hiroshima, however, changed dramatically with widespread attention given to Krzysztof Penderecki's *Threnody to the Victims of Hiroshima* (no. 963), the most famous work on the effects of the atom bomb and one of the most famous works of the century. First performed in 1961, this work for strings only has received hundreds of performances and has been anthologized in numerous twentieth-century texts and anthologies. It is an extraordinary and innovative work using experimental string sounds to make the sounds of bombs dropping, the roar of air-plane engines, and a rugged, horrific atmosphere of dissonance through the use of sound-mass, glissandi, and piercing high notes. The textural changes of the composition create four distinct sections one of which includes some twelve-tone writing. The sounds in conjunction with the impact of the title have produced an extraordinary and tragic war composition.

Penderecki's composition highly influenced R. Murray Schafer's *Threnody* (no. 895), written for five young narrators, youth chorus, voices, orchestra, and tape in 1966. *Threnody* is a powerful evocation of the tragedy at Nagasaki. Schafer parodies in outrageous ways the scientific thought behind the dropping of the bomb juxtaposed with the suffering of the children who experienced first-hand the results of that decision and planning. To get this effect, he has men speaking on a tape about the success of the bombing and how delighted the politicians were. The children, on the other hand, recite gory texts taken from eyewitnesses of the event. Schafer also uses a graphic score, experimental effects, and some improvisation in his attempt to overwhelm the listener with a dissonant, chaotic re-enaction of the event.

Years after Ohki's pioneering efforts, the Japanese contributed highly poignant and imaginative works on these tragedies. Most important are Toshiya Sukegawa's *the eternal morning 1945.8.6* (no. 952) and Masaaki Hayakawa's *Inori for Hiroshima* (no. 948) for soprano, contra-bass, and percussion. Sukegawa's work is the more adventurous, using electronic sounds combined with piano and string orchestra. Hayakawa's work, based on the poem *Lamentation* by Kazuok Yamada, depicts a mother looking for her lost sons separated after the atomic blast. The expression in the soprano's voice makes this dramatic work heartbreaking, particularly in the eleventh part of the poem in which she repeatedly yells for her children: "Hey Shoji! Hey Yasushi! Hey Shoji! Hey Yasushi!" Tomiko Kojiba's *Hiroshima Requiem* (1979) (no. 949) for string orchestra and antique cymbals is a highly effective memorial for those who died during the blast. Written in graphic notation, Mayako Kubo's *Iterum meditemur for Hiroshima* (1978) (no. 950) for trombone and tape is an angry work, including sounds of oriental wind chimes and a voice reading clips from an American newspaper in the 1940s. Yori-Aki Matsudaira's *Dark Mirror: Young Orpheus on a Theme of the Atomic Bomb* (no. 1022), first performed in Osaka in 1962, is virtually unknown in the West.

European composers have been quite prolific in writing about these themes as well. Siegfried Behrend's *Requiem auf Hiroshima* (1973) (no. 921) is a nightmarish work for voice, mandoline, guitarre, percussion, and plucked string instruments, and also includes vocal groans and shrieks and instrumental cacophony and outbursts. Paul Dessau's *Einstein* (1973) (no. 922) at one point, after counting down from ten to zero, includes boys' chorus singing "Hiroshima" and "Nagasaki" and leads to Einstein's descriptions of the cities destroyed. Gaetano Giuffrè's *Hiroshima* (1965) (no. 941) is a dramatic setting in Greek, employing speaking and frequent changes in tempo and meter in a precisely notated lament. Luigi Nono's *Sul Ponte di Hiroshima* (no. 945) for soprano, tenor, and orchestra premiered in 1963, and Carmen Petra-Basacopol's *Pro pace* (c. 1973) (no. 964) is a cycle of three songs dealing with the dropping of the bomb on

Hiroshima: "Meeting Hiroshima," "Choir of the Killed Children," and "The Voices of the Birds of Hiroshima." William Mathias's *Ceremony After a Fire Raid* (1973) (no. 934) is an erratic, explosive twenty-minute work with graphic texts and a chorus that yells, whispers, and speaks in addition to singing in its depiction of the bombing of Hiroshima during World War II. Gérard Condé's *Memorial* (c. 1980) (no. 919) for narrator and string quintet is an experimental portrayal of the bombing of Nagasaki. Michael Berkeley's *Or Shall We Die?* (1982) (no. 927) includes a section depicting a survivor from Hiroshima looking for her lost daughter. Two German operas are based on the theme of Hiroshima: Jean Kurt Forest's *Die Blumen von Hiroshima* (1967) (no. 1002) and Udo Zimmerman's *Wenn ich an Hiroschima denke* (1982) (no. 1057).

The Soviet composer Yury Levitin uses clusters, glissandos, Sprechstimme, and other dramatic effects in his *Hiroshima Must Not Be Repeated* (1967) (no. 975) to produce a protest against dropping this bomb on innocent people. In these six movements, Levitin makes particular use of children's chorus in the fourth and sixth movements. Titles of movements include "Children of Hiroshima are drawing," "The girl Sakaya is dying," and the last, "Hiroshima must not be repeated." The only American composition specifically about Hiroshima or Nagasaki that I have found is Jackson Hill's *Toro Nagashi* (1977) (no. 882) about the ceremonial lighting of candles each year in memory of those who died in the blast at Nagasaki.

The continued detonation of nuclear bombs in the Pacific Ocean led Lou Harrison and Brenton Broadstock to compose their respective compositions *Pacifka Rondo* (1963) (no. 881) and *Beast from Air* (1985) (no. 893) to protest against this continued nuclear testing in the Pacific. Herbert Eimert's *Epitaph für Aikichi Kuboyama* (1962) (no. 923) is a harsh electronic protest against the deadly effects the testing of the hydrogen bomb had on a poor fisherman Aikichi Kuboyama who died shortly after a test explosion in the Pacific.

While these laments for those killed during the bombing of Hiroshima and Nagasaki have captured the attention of composers throughout the world, a new theme also has emerged: the end of the world through mankind's own stupidity. While apocalyptic compositions based upon the Bible have increased tremendously in this century and particularly after World War II, the theme of us destroying ourselves through our own means is relatively unheard of before the dropping of the atom bombs.

Numerous composers composed works to protest the nuclear age and the overwhelming threat of nuclear destruction of the world. Hans Werner Henze's *Nachstücke und Arien* (1957) (no. 924) was one of the earliest purely protest works. Michael Berkeley's *Or Shall We Die?* (no. 927) goes beyond the Hiroshima theme to be a polemic against nuclear war, even though the music is rather non-descriptive. Karel Husa's *Apotheosis of This Earth* (no. 883) is one of the most performed end-of-the-world compositions. In the second movement Husa employs ingenious rhythmic devices to illustrate the earth breaking apart after a possible nuclear explosion. His hope in this work is that what he has done musically and fictionally is terrible enough to prevent it from ever occurring in reality. Tony Biggin's *The Gates of Greenham* (no. 928), a blend of popular elements within a classical context, protests against nuclear war and in particular against the installation of cruise missiles at the American Air Force Base near Newbury, England. In the third movement ("Dies irae") of Donald Swann's *Requiem for the Living* (no. 938) he attempts to create the trauma of the aftereffects of a nuclear bomb explosion.

Three operas by European composers attempt to demonstrate the hopelessness and ultimate destruction of the world by atomic bombs: Giacomo Manzoni's *Atomtod* (no. 1021), Karl-Birger Blomdahl's *Aniara* (no. 983), and György Ránki's *The Tragedy of Man* (no. 1038). Niels Bentzon's oratorio *Torquilla* (no. 994) is based upon Nevil Shute's popular novel *On the Beach* about Australia's final days of earth as the wave of radioactive materials closes in on the last survivors of a nuclear war between China and the Soviet Union.

Several American composers have dealt with this theme as well. In his multi-media work *Testimony* (1985-1987) (no. 879), Kenneth Gaburo based his work on interviews in which he asked people to answer his question about being indispensable in the event of nuclear war. Barton McLean's *The Last Ten Minutes* (no. 886) goes to the heart of the matter and attempts to share the experience of the last ten minutes on earth, with the audience listening in a darkened hall as computer-generated sounds of groaning, growling, and roaring pour forth from monolithic speakers on a stage. John Rahn selected the idea of the Indian goddess Kali for his computer composition *Kali* depicting the end of time and the world (no. 888). The American bombing raid on Libya in the 1980s led him to compose the work.

THE HOLOCAUST

The second and most prolific single theme to grow out of World War II is the Holocaust. Art compositions written about the Holocaust have appeared regularly since 1959. Composers from fifteen countries and composing in styles ranging from serialism to minimalism, traditional to collage, have written works dealing in some way with the Holocaust.[2] Their music may sound different and their methods may conflict, but these composers in their individual ways have expressed their innermost feelings on this tragedy.

For some it was a catharsis, a time of healing; for others an attempt at social responsibility. For Karl Amadeus Hartmann, his Sonata "April 27, 1945" (no. 832) was "not a sonata alone—it was a testimony. . . . a composite reaction to a terrible confrontation on April 27, 1945, expressed by a deeply emotional eyewitness."[3] The inscription at the head of the work depicts this eyewitness account: "On April 27 and 28, 1945, a throng of Dachau concentration camp 'inmates' dragged itself past us—unending was the horde—unending was the misery—unending was the suffering."[4]

For Francis Schwartz, his Holocaust compositions, *Auschwitz* (no. 868) and *Caligula* (no. 817) represented his grappling "with the injustices inflicted upon innocent human beings."[5] He based *Caligula* "upon political realities in a troubled world" and dedicated the composition "to the victims of massacres," including those at Auschwitz.[6] For Srul Irving Glick, his Holocaust composition *I Never Saw Another Butterfly* (no. 824), based on poems by children of the Holocaust, resulted from "the emotional impact caused . . . [by reading these poems]."

For Tera de Marez Oyens, her *Charon's Gift* (no. 844) was written after a close friend of hers, who had long been haunted by his memories as an inmate at Auschwitz, tried to commit suicide. For four days he lay in a coma. De Marez Oyens wrote, "Like Orpheus, I descended into Hades there to plead with Charon. As he released . . . [m]y dear one to me, *Charon's Gift* was written in gratitude."[7]

In order for music to express the emotions released by this terrible historical event, composers have often turned to novel methods of composition—to different techniques and styles. While composers call for conventional instrumental forces in traditional ways in a number of these compositions (e.g., Edel's *Suite in Memoriam* [no. 840], Partos's *Yizkor,* [no. 841] Morawetz's *The Diary of Anne Frank* [no. 825]), the best of these works, as well as the best known, use unusual forces and methods to depict the tragedy.

In one of the earliest Holocaust compositions, Arnold Schoenberg took perhaps the most successful approach to wed music and text together psychologically. *A Survivor From Warsaw*[8] (1947) (no. 822), scored for narrator, chorus, and orchestra, is a highly structured composition strictly employing twelve-tone technique. The text, which Schoenberg presents virtually verbatim in his composition, is taken from a true story of a survivor from the Warsaw Ghetto. A speaker narrates the story using Sprechstimme, which enables every word to be clearly discernible through speaking, shouting, and singing. The orchestra accompanies the speaker, setting the moods indicated by the text itself. The most dramatic moment of the work takes place when the sergeant orders the group of prisoners who are to be taken to the gas chamber to count off. The counting started—"one, two, three, four . . . became faster and faster so fast that it finally sounded like a stampede of wild horses . . . and all of a sudden in the middle of it they begin singing Shema Yisroel." The music during these moments becomes increasingly faster and more complex; the rhythms depict the "stampede of wild horses" with its syncopation and two against three, and the chorus, making its only appearance, actually begins singing *Shema Yisroel* as the narrator indicates. Leibowitz, who conducted the first performance of this work, has written:

> Schoenberg's work most acutely comprehends and reflects the particular tragedy that is its subject. . . . It is a work that achieves the highest synthesis of extramusical and purely musical elements. . . . It would be wrong to say that Schoenberg's starting point . . . was 'purely human' or 'purely musical'; both sources contributed simultaneously to his inspiration.[9]

In his biography of Schoenberg, Reich reported one of the audience's reactions to hearing Schoenberg's work: "Whole volumes, long essays, many articles have been written about this problem [the Holocaust], but in eight minutes Schoenberg has said far more than anyone has been able to do before."[10]

The first movement of Shostakovich's Thirteenth Symphony (1962) (no. 850) is a searing setting of Yevgeny Yevtushenko's poem *Babi Yar*. The Nazis slaughtered over 70,000 Jews and "buried" them in the deep ravine outside Kiev known as Babi Yar. Shostakovich's music in this movement is dark and foreboding, consisting of men's choir and bass soloists in addition to five-string double basses and tolling bells.

Wilfred Joseph's *Requiem* (1963) (no. 836), one of the most moving and quietly disturbing of these works, follows an unusual organization.

This work, which commemorates the Jews who died during World War II, is extraordinary for its formal organization. While it is a setting of Kaddish (Prayer for the Dead), the chorus sings the text in only six of the ten movements. The other four movements, all slow, serve as instrumental dirges for the dead—one, five, and nine are for string quintet and the orchestra alone performs the seventh movement. The predominant tempo is quite slow; the dynamic levels are soft. Only the third movement (*Yehey Sh'mey Raba* for double chorus and orchestra) is fast (Allegro ritmico) and loud, ending with a dissonant *fortissimo* cluster.

The first work to incorporate electronic means into a Holocaust composition appeared in 1965. Luigi Nono's *Ricorda cosa ti hanno fatto in Auschwitz* (no. 842) uses a soprano and a children's chorus with electronic manipulations of sound to create a haunting and oppressive atmosphere of sorrow. The music in conjunction with the title is effective, but without the specificity of the title, the work is so abstract it could be about most anything. For the most part, the sounds, both vocal and electronic, are quite high; they are rarely piercing, however. With the exception of a few brief electronic outbursts, the sounds remain soft, almost a whimper or a light groan, interspersed with silence and emptiness. At most this work seems to be a psychological portrayal of the aftermath of the Holocaust: the disbelief, the sorrow, and the uncertainty.

Penderecki's *Dies Irae* (1967) (no. 847), "dedicated to the memory of those murdered at Auschwitz," was first performed on the grounds of Auschwitz in 1967. In the first movement, "Lamentation," Penderecki includes texts from the Psalms and from contemporary Polish poetry which he translated into Latin to achieve an overall unity. These texts in conjunction with the disturbing music create an artistic world of anguish and despair. The opening words, in translation, set the mood for the entire composition. Penderecki's treatment of these texts is a highly dissonant one. He often has the choir singing a cluster of chromatic pitches simultaneously. He uses glissandos, high tessituras, and indeterminate chanting to convey the despair indicated by the texts, although he does not engage in actual tone painting of specific words.

Henryk Górecki's Symphony No. 3 ("The Symphony of Sorrowful Songs") (1977) (no. 845) includes soprano solo in each of its three movements. The second movement is based upon a brief four-line text scribbled by an eighteen-year-old girl on the wall of her cell in a prison at Zakopane. The eight-and-a-half-minute movement is minimal in the truest sense of the word. Górecki calls for only a few bare chords, but this sparsity of texture establishes a rare and ethereal atmosphere. Malgorzata Gasiorowska wrote about this symphony, "No other piece by a Polish composer, written in the past few years, has provoked so much argument and discussion, brought so many contradictory judgments and a clash of aesthetics and critical views."[11] Górecki's most ambitious work on the Holocaust, *The Barbaric Mass* (no. 846), however, is still incomplete. He conceived the project in 1960, but now, over thirty years later, he has never brought the work to completion.

Francis Schwartz molded his unusual composition around the idea of single words. He based *Caligula* (1975) (no. 817) on names of concentration camps and massacre sites: Auschwitz, Mylai, Maalot, Katyń, Ponce, etc. In an eerie, pell-mell atmosphere created by prepared piano, electronic elements, and concrete sounds, human voices groan and howl as they chant these familiar words that were once just geographical locations but have acquired horrific connotations in this century.

One of the more extreme portraits of the Holocaust is the fourth section of Georg Katzer's *Aide Memoire* (1983) (no. 833). This section combines condescending texts about Jews ("not people of a normal kind, parasites and spongers un-human form") with the sounds of an ancient Jewish song, sickening sounds of gas, and children singing a *Miserere*. Tape-splicing, mixing, and electronic distortions manipulate these sounds to create a horrifying Holocaust composition.

One of the most recent Holocaust works, Steve Reich's *Different Trains* (1988) (no. 815) illustrates many of the characteristics of Holocaust works that we have already seen. It is a novel work written for unusual instrumental combinations used in unusual ways; and it, too, is a controversial work. In the program notes, Reich makes the claim that the work "begins a new musical direction"—one that he expects "will lead to a new kind of documentary music video theater in the not too distant future." He discusses the novelty of the work and his method of recording voices in this documentary and using their speech fragments to "generate the musical material for musical instruments."[12]

In its three movements, *Different Trains* depicts Reich's autobiographical train journeys from New York to Los Angeles during the years 1939-1942, a train journey to the gas chamber that he, as a Jew, might have taken if he had lived in Europe at that time, and train rides from New York to Los Angeles after the war but without the innocence of pre-war days. In the section dealing with the Holocaust, Reich uses sirens almost continuously and loud train sounds as the background under the fragments of taped voices of two Holocaust survivors Paul and Rachel. The tempo increases at the text "Germans invaded Hungary" and again at the words "and he said, 'Don't breathe!'" The music becomes more frenetic and hysterical at the words "into those cattle wagons," where loud piercing whistles of the train join in the frenzy of the train's sounds and the sirens. This second movement ends with a surrealism of text and music, "flames going up to the sky—it was smoking."

Works related to the events of World War II continue to be written with considerable frequency, especially works about the atomic bomb and the Holocaust. Between 1980 and 1990 nearly thirty works dealt with the bomb, the Holocaust, or some other aspect of World War II. World War II compositions tended to be more explicit in their depiction of war and were the first to effectively display the horror of war. The difference between the war compositions written from World War II to the present day compared with those written before 1939 clearly illustrates the change of consciousness that our civilization in general has undergone in this century.

ANNOTATED LISTING OF HOLOCAUST MUSIC:
1946-1990

America (United States)

Adler, Samuel (b. 1928)

798. Symphony No. 5 ("We are the Echoes"). Mezzo-soprano and
      orchestra [1974-1975]. 1st: Fort Worth, 10 November 1975. #New
      York: Boosey & Hawkes, 1986. Texts by Karl Wolfskehl, Muriel
      Rukeyser, James Oppenheimer, Carol Adler, and Abraham J.
      Heschel.
         M1613.A25S95 1986
         A twenty-two minute symphony based on five texts, dealing
      with the Jewish experience throughout history. The work only
      tangentially is about the Holocaust, but Adler sets a poem written
      durlng World War II, "Even During War." This movement begins
      slowly with two-note descending slurs and incorporates glissandi
      and string harmonics before breaking into a faster, contrasting B
      section with changing meters. The opening theme and tempo
      return to quietly close the movement.

Blumenfeld, Aaron (b. 1932)

799. *Holocaust Memorial Cantata for Friday Evening Sacred Service.*
      Cantor, mezzo-soprano, child's voice, chorus, and orchestra [1985].
      1st: Oakland, 26 April 1987. #Holograph at AMC.
         AMC M2020.H6585H7
         Includes chanting, an active piano part, some Sprechstimme,
      and repetitive instrumental patterns.

Davidson, Charles S. (b. 1929)

800. *I Never Saw Another Butterfly.* Chorus and piano [c. 1974].
      #Elkins Park, Pa: Ashbourne Music, 1971. *Ashbourne Records C
      ARC 1576. Songs based on poems of children in the Terezín
      concentration camp.
         M1621.4.D
         Dedicated to Congregation Beth Sholom, Long Beach, New
      York, Solomon Mendelson, Cantor. Contains nine simple, tonal,

and sincere songs. Unlike the others, "Terezín" is the most striking, written in a highly chromatic and intense manner. Davidson prefaces this song with the remarks "With an air of tragic resignation." The other songs include "It All Depends on How You Look at It," "Man Proposes, God Disposes," "The Butterfly," "The Garden," "The Little Mouse," "On a Sunny Evening," "Yes, That's the Way Things Are," and "Birdsong."

Derr, Ellwood (b. 1932)

801.   *I Never Saw Another Butterfly.* Soprano, alto sax, and piano [1966]. #Islington, Mass: Dorn Production, 1977.

JNF 82-139 (NYPL call number)

Dedicated "To the everlasting memory of the children who suffered and made these poems." Contains five movements based upon selected poems from the publication of the same title: "Terezín," "The Butterfly," "The Old Man," "Fear," and "The Garden." The dramatic climax comes in "Fear" with the use of *fortissimo* clusters in the piano and flutter-tonguing in the extreme registers on the alto sax. The work also includes a brief quotation from "Deutschland, Deutschland über Alles."

Foss, Lukas (b. 1922) [German born]

802.   *Elegy for Anne Frank.* Orchestra and piano obbligato [1989]. 1st: 12 June 1989. #New York: Carl Fischer, 1989.

[Available from publisher on rental]

Written for the sixtieth anniversary of the birth of Anne Frank and for a memorial service at St. John the Divine, this five-minute elegy uses a child-like melody to represent Anne's innocence and interrupts it with a militant, Nazi hymn. Foss later incorporated this independent work into his Symphony No. 3. See item 803 below.

803.   Symphony No. 3 ("Symphony of Sorrows"). Orchestra with organ [1991].

[No LC number available]

Commissioned by the AT&T Foundation for the centennial of the Chicago Symphony Orchestra. The work contains four movements: "Fugue of Strife and Struggle," "Elegy for Anne Frank," "Wasteland" (including five quotations from T.S. Eliot's poem of the same title), and "Prayer." The music is dissonant, but traditional, using augmented octaves, almost inaudible sounds at times, explosive organ passages, and ends with a chorale representing resignation or despair. See item 802 above.

Gould, Morton (b. 1913)

804. *Holocaust Suite.* Wind band or orchestra [1978]. 1st: April 1978.
     #New York: G. Schirmer, 1978. *RCA ARL1 2785.
          M1380.G (selections)
          Written originally for television, this extended suite follows
     the narrative of the film. Gould uses references to the "Horst
     Wessel Song" and "Die Lorelei" and provides background music for
     the events of *Kristallnacht*, Buchenwald, and Babi Yar.

Hardyk, Joel M. (20th c.)

805. *I Never Saw Another Butterfly.* Chorus of young voices and oboe
     [c. 1980]. #New York: G. Schirmer, 1980. Poems by children of
     the Holocaust.
          M1577.H27 1980
          Consists of settings of five poems written by children who
     were held prisoners in Terezín concentration camp: "At Terezín,"
     "I'd Like to Go Alone," "The Little Mouse," "The Garden," and
     "The Butterfly." Voices speak in addition to singing in primarily a
     two-voice texture (although some places call for four parts). The
     oboe plays chiefly in introductions, transitions, and codas and is
     silent in the third song.

Heifetz, Vladimir (b. 1893) [Russian born]

806. *Babi Yar*, Op. 81. Soloists, chorus, and orchestra [c. 196-?].
     #Unpublished manuscript. Based on Yevgeny Yevtushenko's poem
     of the same title in Yiddish translation.
          JMG 76-882 (NYPL call number)
          Begins with a brief march in E minor, followed by a faster
     choral section. The middle part entitled "Anne Frank" is in D
     minor with four-part contrapuntal writing. During the G-minor
     soprano solo, Heifetz writes for her to scream on two occasions.
     The work ends with an extended *a cappella* chorus in F major.

807. *Lerern mire. Ghetto cantata.* Cantata [c. 194-?]. #Unpublished
     manuscript. Text by A. Sutzkever
          JNG 76-282 (NYPL call number)

A tonal lament beginning in E minor and leading to an optimistic ending in E major (*ff*). An expressive, traditional work.

Holliday, Kent (b. 1940)

808. *In Memoriam: Karlrobert Kreiten.* Piano trio [1988]. 1st: Blacksburg, Va., 16 April 1989.
     [No LC number available]
     In one movement and written in remembrance of the pianist Karlrobert Kreiten who was killed by the Nazis at Plötzensee on 7 September 1943. The music is meticulously notated and includes frequently changing meters, glissandos, *col legno* effects, and numerous ostinatos. It concludes with a *pianissimo*, elegiac coda.

Isaacson, Michael (b. 1946)

809. *Cradle of Fire.* Women's chorus and orchestra [1988]. #New York: Transcontinental Music, 1988.
     M1544.I8C7
     An arrangement of five songs of the Holocaust: "Shtiler, Shtiler," "S'Brent," "Zog nit keyn mol," "Babi yar," and "Ani Maamin." These works are all tonal and expressive arrangements that make an effective suite.

Janowski, Maxim Dubrow (b. 1943)

810. *And They Shall Not Learn War Any More.* A Hebrew cantata for cantor, chorus, and keyboard [1963]. #Chicago: Friends of Jewish Music, 1963.
     M2023.J35A5
     Contains three songs in Hebrew with some melismatic vocal writing and traditional harmony: "Shirus Ladonai," "Shima Yisraeyl," and "V'hayah B'acharit Hayamim."

Kahn, Erich (1905-1956) [German born]

811. *Nenia judaeis qui hac aetate perierunt (In Memory of the Jews Who Perished in the Holocaust).* Piano and cello [1940-1943]. #New York: American Composers Alliance, 1955. *CRI CD563.
     JPB 90-52 (NYPL call number)
     In two movements, Andante molto sostenuto and Allegro moderato, ma con molto fuoco. Not specifically programmatic, but

an electrifying, dissonant, angry work, with considerable virtuosity and thick textures ending *fff*.

Lees, Benjamin (b. 1924)

812. Symphony No. 4 ("Memorial Candles"). Mezzo-soprano and orchestra with solo violin [1985]. 1st: Dallas, 1985. #New York: Boosey & Hawkes, 1986. Text by Nelly Sachs.
    M1001.L533 no. 4 1986
    An hour-long work written to commemorate the fortieth anniversary of the Holocaust's end. Lees traveled to Israel to find background information for the symphony.

Lichtin, J. Leon (b. 1924)

813. *Zichronot No. 1 (Remembrances No. 1)*. Violin and narrator [c. 1973]. #J. Leon Lichtin, 1973. Texts by Yehuda Shamir and Mrs. Herbert Mengel with excerpts from Nelly Sachs and the Book of Job.
    M1625.L65Z5
    In three parts: "These were the ones who were murdered" (a theme and four variations on a song "Olen Pripetshiki"); "The murderers" (which opens with a fragment from Haydn's "Emperor" Quartet and includes Sach's poem "O Ye Chimneys"); and "Finale: I Believe."

Ran, Shulamit (b. 1949) [Israeli born]

814. *O, The Chimneys*. Mezzo-soprano, flute, clarinet, cello, percussion, and piano [1969]. #New York: Carl Fischer, 1975. *Turnabout TV-S 34492. Text by Nelly Sachs.
    M1613.3.R184O2
    A setting of five poems: "A dead child speaks," "Already embraced by the arm of heavenly solace," "Fleeing," "Someone comes," and "Hell is naked." The first poems deal with the death of a child, but the last one broadens the horror to the end of the world. In this last song, the composer adds a pre-taped excerpt containing metallic sirens and tolling bells to assist in depicting the death of all.

Reich, Steve (b. 1936)

815. *Different Trains*. String quartet and tape [1988]. 1st: 1988 New Music Festival in Miami. *Elektra/Nonesuch 79176.
    [No LC number available]
    A twenty-five minute minimalistic work using melodic fragments based upon spoken (and recorded) text taken from Holocaust survivors. The three movements represent various train rides, but three highly different journeys: Reich's boyhood journey between New York and Los Angeles before World War II; the journey to the death camps that he as a Jew would have likely taken had he lived in central Europe during the war; and the journey back in the states after the war. Awarded the Lucien Wilson Award for Best New Music (1989) from National Public Radio— Performance Today.

Rosner, Arnold (b. 1945)

816. *From the Diaries of Adam Czerniakow*. Narrator and orchestra [1985-86]. #Unpublished score available at the AMC, 198-?. Text by Adam Czerniakow, trans. into English.
    AMC M1625.R822F9
    A twenty-minute composition based upon the graphic diaries that discuss the hunger, the killing, the suicides, and the epidemics. The music is often romantic, with intense interludes following after a dramatic statement. The music is tonal, chromatic, and highly expressive.

Schwartz, Francis (b. 1940)

817. *Caligula*. Voices, prepared piano, concrete sounds and tape [1975]. 1st: New York, 3 March 1975. #New York: Peer-Southern International. *Serie Musica Contemporanea ICPC17.
    [No LC number available]
    An unique work noted for its ugliness of sound in attempting to portray the devastation of those who lived and died during unbelievable wartime conditions. Dedicated to the victims of the massacres including those at Auschwitz and Mylai.

Secunda, Sholom (1894-1974) [Russian born—U.S. citizen 1923]

818. *Yiskor in Memory of the Six Million*. Oratorio. #Carlstadt, N.J.: Ethnic Music, 1967. Text by Samuel Rosenbaum.

M2003.S43Y62

A rather direct, large-scale attack on humankind and a plea not to forget the Holocaust. Through considerable narration and chanting from the chorus, the message is loud and clear.

Stern, Robert (b. 1934)

819. *Terezín*. Soprano, cello, and piano [1967]. 1st: University of Massachusetts, February 1968. *CRI SD264. Text from *I Never Saw Another Butterfly*.

[No LC number available]

A twenty-one minute setting of six songs: "At Terezín," "The Butterfly," "Yes, That's the Way Things Are," "The Little Mouse," "To Olga," and "I'd Like to Go Alone." The settings are controlled, not overly emotional in order to let the text carry the weight. Three inserted instrumental interludes based on three of the drawings provide time for the listener to reflect upon the poems and the tragedy which they represent.

Subotnik, Morton (b. 1933)

820. *Jacob's Room*. Monodrama for performers and digital sound synthesis [1985-1986]. 1st: Philadelphia, Autumn 1988. *Wergo WER 2014-50 (includes first and last sections for amplified voice, cello, and Yamaha Computer-Assisted Music System). Texts by Plato, Virginia Woolf, and Nicholas Gage.

[No LC number available]

Part II "Eleni" is a setting in which a young boy discovers the death of his mother at the end of World War II, and Part III "Night" hauntingly depicts a train journey to the concentration camps. The soprano speaks dramatically and sings with a wide range, using falsetto, extended trills, glissandos, and other unusual special vocal techniques. The music is often minimalistic, but always driving toward a musical goal urged on by the clarity of the text.

Waxman, Franz (1906-1967) [German born]

821. *Song of Terezín*. Children's chorus, mixed chorus, mezzo-soprano, and orchestra [1964-1965]. 1st: 22 May 1965. #Bryn Mawr: Presser, 1966. Based on *I Never Saw Another Butterfly*.

M1533.W337S62

An extensive, forty-five minute setting of eight texts in a relatively dissonant language: "On a Sunny Evening," "Forgotten,"

"The Little Mouse," "Bird Song," "Now It's Time," "Concert in the Old School Garret," "The Garden," and "Finale." Dedicated to "the memory of the thousands of children who have passed through the concentration camp of Terezín, but particularly to those whose poems I have set to music. Their eloquence and imagination have been a great source of inspiration, and their courage shall be an eternal beacon to all mankind."

Austria

Schoenberg, Arnold (1874-1951)

822. *A Survivor from Warsaw*, Op. 46. Narrator, orchestra, and male chorus [1947]. 1st: 4 November 1948. #New York: Bomart Music, 1949. *Columbia M2S-679. Text based on writings of a Holocaust survivor from Warsaw.

    M1538.3.S387S9 1979

    An eight-minute serial work that sets the standard for all other Holocaust works—one of the first works on the subject and remains among the most forceful and honest approaches to the Holocaust. See Christian Martin Schmidt "Arnold Schoenberg Kantate 'Ein Überlebender aus Warschau,' Op. 46," *Archiv für Musikwissenschaft* 33 (1976), pp. 174-88.

Ullmann, Viktor (1898-1944)

823. Sonata No. 7. Piano [1944]. *Koch 3-7109-2H1.

    [No LC number available]

    The last of several piano sonatas written while he was in the Terezín concentration camp; Ullmann alludes to the Czech national anthem and quotes the Hussite hymn "Ye who are God's Warriors" in the fifth movement. Ullmann was the most prolific composer in the concentration camps before his death at Auschwitz. See also item 645 above.

Canada

Glick, Srul Irving (b. 1934)

824. *I Never Saw Another Butterfly*. Song cycle for contralto and piano (or orchestra) [1968]. #Willowdale, Ontario: Leeds Music (Canada), 1972. *Canadian Broadcasting CSC 122. Texts selected from poems collected in *I Never Saw Another Butterfly*.

M1621.4.G
Written for Maureen Forrester and commissioned by the
Canadian Broadcasting Corporation. Subtle, evocative music
accompanies the selected poems: "To Olga," "Yes, That's the Way
Things Are," "The Little Mouse," "On A Sunny Evening," "The
Narrative," and "The Butterfly."

Morawetz, Oskar (b. 1917) [Czech born]

825. *From the Diary of Anne Frank.* Soprano and orchestra [1970]. 1st:
Toronto, 26 May 1970. *Radio Canada International RCI 601.
Text by Anne Frank.
[No LC number available]
A dramatic narrative about the horror and despair of the
concentration camps displayed in this large-scale, tonal
composition.
Morawetz also created an excerpt from this work called *Who
Has Allowed Us To Suffer.* Chorus [1970, revised 1972].
"Dedicated to Anne Frank's father, Otto, the only member of the
Frank family to survive the Nazi death camp." Cited in BAKER,
p. 1248.

Chile

Schidlowsky, León (b. 1931)

826. *La noche de cristal.* Symphony for male chorus, tenor, and
orchestra [1961].
M1001.S33S6
Deals with the martyrdom of the Jews during World War II. In
the preface to his *Koloth* (JMH 74-13), there is mention of four
other Holocaust works by Schidlowsky: *Memento, Kadish, Babi
Yar,* and *Lamentation.*

Czechoslovakia

Berman, Karel (b. 1919)

827. *Suite for Piano Solo (1939-1945).* Piano [1944, revised 1984].
*Channel Classics CCS 3191.
[No LC number available]
In eight movements, Berman started this work in the Terezín
concentration camp and originally entitled it *Suite Terezín.*

Starting with "Youth" and "Family—Home," the movements outline Berman's life and also include "15 March 1939 Occupation," "Auschwitz—Corpse factory" (originally named "Horror"), "Typhus in the Kauffering concentration camp," "Alone—alone," and "New Life." The music opens lively, light, and delicate, growing more ominous in the occupation section with some louder, lower dissonant notes. The other music is slower and lament-like, except for sudden outbursts of dissonant sounds.

Mácha, Otmar (b. 1922)

828. *Noc a Naděje (Night and Hope)*. Symphonic poem [1959]. 1st: Prague, 26 May 1960, Symphony Orchestra of the Czechoslovak Radio. #Prague: Státní hudební vydavatelství, 1961.
M1002.M139N6
Awarded Honorable Mention at the Jubilee Contest in Czechoslovakia (1960), this twelve-minute work attempts to capture the horror and terror of the Terezín ghetto with its monothematic obsession and dramatic tension. The music is often sparse, dark, and intense in a traditional harmonic language.

Podešva, Jaromír (b. 1927)

829. *Kounicovy kolejie (Kounic College)*. Symphonic poem [1956]. #Prague: Státní i nakladatelství, 1957.
M1002.P62K68
A twelve-minute lament dealing with a concentration camp at Brno.

Reiner, Karel (1910-1979)

830. *Motýli tady nežijí (Butterflies Don't Live Here Anymore)*. Orchestral suite [1959-1960]. #Prague: Cesky Hudební Fond, 1962.
M1003.R4
A fourteen-minute excerpt from a film depicting the tragedy of children in Terezín presented in six orchestral pictures, several strung together without pause. The music is in duple meter throughout, tonal, full of ostinato rhythmic patterns, highly motivic, and somewhat dependent upon the use of the harp and celeste.

Zeljenka, Ilja (b. 1932)

831. *Oswieczym*. Melodrama for two narrators, two choruses, and orchestra [1960]. 1st: Bratislava, 29 April 1965. #Bratislava: Supraphon. *Supraphon SUA 18753.
      [No LC number available]
      An extended work dealing with the tragedy of Auschwitz. Cited in BAKER, p. 2102.

Germany

Hartmann, Karl Amadeus (1905-1963)

832. Sonata ("April 27, 1945"). Piano [c. 1946?]. #Mainz: Schott Edition 6879, 1983. *Virgin Classics VC7 91170-2.
      M23.H334 S6 1983
      A four-movement work with two versions of the last movement (both recorded on disk). The central point is the lengthy third movement, a slow, solemn funeral march. Hartmann composed this work upon seeing some of the inmates at Dachau.

Katzer, Georg (b. 1935)

833. *Aide Memoire*. Electronic collage [1983]. *Recommended Records RRP22. "Seven Nightmares from the thousand year night."
      [No LC number available]
      A graphically horrifying collage of materials collected from the Nazi period between 1933 and 1945 that succeeds in its own excess. The fourth section deals specifically with the Holocaust and includes sounds of suffocating gas, fragments of Hitler's speeches, and musical quotations that announced Hitler's broadcasts or other Nazi bulletins.

Great Britain

Frankel, Benjamin (1906-1973)

834. Violin Concerto, Op. 24. Violin and orchestra [1951]. 1st: 10 June 1956. #London: Augener, 1952. *Rococo (RR) 2101.
      M1012.F89 Op. 24 1952a
      A four-movement concerto written in highly chromatic language and dedicated to the memory of the six million Jews who

lost their lives during World War II. The third movement (Andante mesto) is highly lyrical and intensely expressive.

Hamilton, Iain (b. 1922)

835. *Threnos - In Time of War*. Organ [1966]. #Bryn Mawr: Theodore Presser, 1970. *Crystal S-180
M9.H264T5
In four movements, the second is entitled "Holocaust" (with *ff* use of clusters and tremolos) and the last "Purgatory and Requiem."

Josephs, Wilfred (b. 1927)

836. *Requiem*. Bass, baritone, chorus, string quintet, and orchestra [1963]. 1st: Milan, 28 October 1965. #London: Josef Weinberger, 1965. *Unicorn-Kanchana DKP 9032.
M2017.6.J68 Op.39
A ten-movement composition in four sections based on "Kaddish," the Hebrew Prayer for the Dead. The unusual format includes a string quintet performing without any text in movements 1, 5, and 9, although the other movements are for orchestra with soloists or chorus. A solemn composition with nine of the ten movements in a slow tempo. It won the International Competition for Symphonic Composition of the City of Milan and La Scala and serves as a memorial to Jews slain by the Nazis.
Josephs' earlier quintet was added to the *Requiem: Requiescant pro defunctis iudaies*. String quintet [1961]. #London: J. Weinberger, 1965. M552.J66 Op. 32 1965.

Martland, Steve (b. 1958)

837. *Babi Yar*. Orchestra and electric guitar [1983].#London & New York: Schott, 1989. *Factory Classical Record Fact 266.
M1045.M38652B11 1989
A thirty-five minute work which divides the orchestra into three groups, each with its own rhythms synchronized with only its own members. Each group spends much of its time hammering away with extensive amounts of non-melodic percussive writing, displayed in metallic and disjointed repetitive patterns until bell-like chords end this highly angular work.

Greece

Theodorakis, Mikis (b. 1925)

838. *Liturgie. Den Kindern, getötet in Kriegen.* Mixed chorus [1982].
1st: Dresden Music Festival, 1983. #Leipzig: Deutscher Verlag für
Musik, 1983. Texts by Tasos Livadhitis and the composer.
M1579.T44L5 1983
Contains fourteen unaccompanied songs ranging from
"Abendgebet" and "Die heilige Mutter" to "Anne Frank—
Ibrahim—Emilano," "Der Tag der Apokalypse," "Der heilige Che
[Gueverra]," and "Totem Sohne." The music is tonal (using key
signatures), simple, and most frequently in four parts. Several of
the songs are strophic and all are quite brief.

Hungary

Ránki, György (b. 1921)

839. *Elegiac Variations.* Orchestra [c. 1964]. 1st: Vienna, 25 June
1964. #Zurich: Universal Editions, 1966. *First Edition LS-715.
M1003.R27E4
A fourteen-minute, tonal lament dedicated to a victim of the
Nazi gas chambers.

Israel

Edel, Yitzhak (b. 1896)

840. *Suite in Memoriam.* Piano trio [1947]. *CBS S-72839.
[No LC number available]
In five movements played without pause and contains
melodies and hymns sung by the Jews in Poland. Dedicated to the
Polish victims of the Holocaust.

Partos, Oedoen (1907-1977) [Hungarian born]

841. *Yizkor (In Memoriam).* Viola and string orchestra [1946]. #Israeli
Music Publications, 1951. *Music Masters 2055.
M1112.P35Y6
A ten-minute lament written in memory of the victims of war
and originally for a mimic dance conceived by Deborah Bertonoff.

The rather traditional work won the "Yoel Engle Prize" of the Tel-Aviv Municipality in 1948.

Italy

Nono, Luigi (1924-1990)

842. *Ricorda cosa ti hanno fatto in Auschwitz.* Soprano, children's chorus, and tape [1965]. *Wergo WER 60038.
    [No LC number available]
    A twelve-minute experimental portrayal of anguish in seemingly indistinguishable waves of dissonant sounds.

The Netherlands

Kox, Hans (b. 1930)

843. *Anne Frank Cantata: A Child of Light.* Symphonic cantata for soprano, contralto, bass, mixed chorus, and orchestra [1985]. 1st: 4 May 1985. #Amsterdam: Donemus, 1985. *Composers' Voice Special 1987/4. Texts from the Bible, Augustine, Rilke, Kaléko, Blake, Celan, and sayings of the SS and Hitler.
    M1530.K84 A5 1985
    An intense, forty-minute cantata using texts in Latin, German, and English. The bass represents evil and sings passages based on sayings of the SS and Hitler. The soprano represents Anne Frank, and the chorus represents those who can only ask how something so terrible could possibly occur.

Marez Oyens, Tera de (b. 1932)

844. *Charon's Gift.* Piano and tape [1982]. *Composers' Voice 8702.
    [No LC number available]
    The other-worldly, glass-like opening sets the stage for this haunting, often hypnotic and pointillistic work awarded a distinction at the tenth International Electro-acoustic Music Competition in Bourges, France in 1982.

Poland

Górecki, Henryk Mikolaj (b. 1933)

845. Symphony No. 3 ("Symphony of Sorrowful Songs"), Op. 36.
      Soprano and orchestra [1977]. 1st: Baden-Baden, 4 April 1977.
      #Kracow: Polskie wydawnictwo muzyczne, 1977. *Schwann
      Musica Mundi VMS 1615.
         M1613.G66 Op. 36
         A symphony in three movements with the soprano solo
      singing in each of the movements. The second movement (Lento e
      largo), based upon a brief four-line text scribbled by an eighteen-
      year-old girl on the wall of her cell in a prison at Zakopane, is
      noteworthy in its simplicity and understatement, consisting of
      only a few static chords repeated and sustained throughout the
      movement.

846. *Barbaric Mass.* Planned for five sopranos, chorus, and orchestra
      [1960- (incomplete)]. Based on texts from and about the Holocaust.
         [No LC number available]
         Górecki planned to write a massive work in memory of the
      millions who died at Auschwitz, but the composition remains
      unfinished. See Tadeusz Marek and David Drew, "Górecki in
      Interview (1968)—And 20 Years After," *Tempo* 168 (March 1988),
      p. 26.

Penderecki, Krzysztof (b. 1933)

847. *Dies irae.* Oratorio [1967]. 1st: Auschwitz, 16 April 1967. #Celle:
      Moeck, 1967. *Philips 839701. Texts all translated into Latin
      from the Bible, ancient Greek drama, and contemporary French and
      Polish poets.
         M2000.P323D5
         An overpowering three-movement work composed in a highly
      dissonant, austere manner with clusters, quarter tones, unspecified
      pitches, sirens, chains, bells, and glissandi produced from a
      graphically notated score. Dedicated to the memory of those
      murdered at Auschwitz and provides an extraordinarily disturbing
      contribution to the Holocaust music literature. See Wolfram
      Schwinger, *Krzysztof Penderecki: His Life and Work*, trans.
      William Mann (London: Schott, 1989), pp. 214-17.

Soviet Union

Finko, David (b. 1936). Russia

848. *Holocaust: An uprising in the ghetto.* Symphonic poem for
   orchestra [1965, revised 1983]. #Philadelphia: Dako, 1985.
       M1002.F532 H6 1985
       A ten-minute, loud, biting work with dissonant, disjunct
   writing combined with faster sixteenth-note passages and stark
   syncopations.

Frid, [Fried] Grigory (b. 1915)

849. *Anne Frank's Diary,* Op. 60. Mono opera for soprano and twenty-
   six instruments [1969]. 1st: Moscow, 18 May 1972. #Moscow:
   Soviet Composers, 1976. *Harmonia Mundi LDC 288045. Text
   by Anne Frank.
       M1503.F898D6 1976
       In two parts and twenty-one separate numbers, this work
   examines the life of Anne Frank. The music uses clusters and
   selected aleatoric devices along with the traditional notation that
   prevails. The soprano cries, whispers, shouts, and hums to portray
   the various emotions Anne displays in her diary.

Shostakovich, Dmitry (1906-1975). Russia

850. Symphony No. 13 ("Babi Yar"), Op. 113. Male chorus and
   orchestra [1962]. 1st: 18 December 1962. #New York: Leeds
   Music, 1970. *London 417261-2 LH2. Text by Yevgeny
   Yevtushenko.
       M1538.S53 Op. 113
       The title of symphony comes from Yevtushenko's poem of
   the same name which is set in the first movement of this five-
   movement symphony. The dark, somber colors of low strings and
   male chorus describing the fate of the Jews at Babi Yar make it
   among Shostakovich's most brooding works.

851. Piano Trio in E minor, Op. 67. Violin, cello, and piano [1944].
   *Philips 432079-2PH.
       M312.55 Op. 67
       A tribute to those murdered by the SS troops in the Ukraine
   and one of the most haunting war-related works of Shostakovich,

particularly the sounds of the opening muted cello. The third movement is a dark passacaglia based on an eight-measure theme.

§

Persecution of the Jews before the Holocaust of World War II has been the subject of several additional compositions. Four are listed here:

Berlinski, Herman (b. 1910). America [German born]

852. *Litanies for the Persecuted.* Alto, narrator, and organ [1990]. 1st: York, May 1990. Texts from the Psalms, Ibn Gabriol, and *Eleh Eskereh,* a seventeenth-century litany.
      [No LC number available]
      Written for the Clifford's Tower 800th-Anniversary Commemoration in 1990. See a review of the concert: Malcolm Miller, "Clifford's Tower: A Commemoration at York," *The Musical Times* 131 (May 1990), p. 278.

Dana, Walter (b. 1902). America

853. *The Wailing Wall.* Orchestra [1971]. #Miami Beach: Dana Publishing, 1971.
      AMC M1045.D171W2
      A slow, orchestral work with repetitive patterns but not programmatic even though it deals with the ancient Jews' fight for freedom.

Lipkin, Malcolm (b. 1932). Great Britain

854. *Clifford's Tower.* Wind quintet and string trio [1977]. #Sussex: Lipkin, 1977. *Hyperion A66164.
      M862.L57C6 1977
      This mildly dissonant work is in three sections: "Into Darkness," "Threnody," and "Hymn of Peace." Written for the Clifford's Tower 800th-Anniversary Commemoration in 1990. See a review of the concert: Malcolm Miller, "Clifford's Tower: A Commemoration at York," *The Musical Times* 131 (May 1990), p. 278.

Marescotti, André-François (b. 1902). France

855. *Massada from Ittocseram*. Piano [c. 1983]. #Paris: Joubert, 1983. M25.M3I82x
Deals with the Roman persecution of the Jews during the early days of Christianity.

SUPPLEMENT OF HOLOCAUST MUSIC: 1946-1990

856. Adomián, Lan (1905-1979). America. *Auschwitz*. Baritone and instruments [1970]. [Cited in BAKER, p. 12].
857. Amram, David (b. 1930). America. *The Final Ingredient*. Opera [1965]. 1st: ABC TV, 11 April 1965. *AMRAM FI 200. Libretto by Arnold Weinstein. [Cited in BAKER, p. 35]. The story is set in a Nazi concentration camp.
858. Finko, David (b. 1936). Russia. *In a Torture Chamber of the Gestapo*. Opera [1970]. [Cited in BAKER, p. 541].
859. Flosman, Oldřich (b. 1925). Czechoslovakia. *Motýli zde nežijí (Butterflies Do Not Live Here)*. Piano sonata [1961]. [Cited in BAKER, p. 943]. Inspired by a film based on the drawings of children in the concentration camp.
860. Gelbrun, Artur (b. 1913). Israel [Polish born]. *Holocaust and Revival*. Narrator, chorus, and orchestra [1977-1978]. [Cited in BAKER, p. 609].
861. _____. *Lament for the Victims of the Warsaw Ghetto*. Voice and orchestra. *Everest SD 3273.
862. Halpern, Eddie (b. 1921). Israel. *Music for the Holocaust Day*. Orchestra [1982].
863. _____. *To Remember It All: Prayer for the Holocaust Day*. Soprano, narrator, chorus, piano, organ, percussion, and string orchestra [1982].
864. Kolman, Petr (b. 1937). Czechoslovakia. *Monumento per 6,000,000*. Orchestra [1964]. *Supraphon 0120472. [Cited in BAKER, p. 943].
865. Křivinka, Gustav (b. 1928). Czechoslovakia. *Butterflies Do Not Live Here*. Oratorio for soprano, baritone, children's chorus, and

orchestra [1960-1962]. Poems of Jewish children who died at Terezín.

866. Mitrea-Celarianu, Mihai (b. 1935). Romania. *Piano de matin "Ecouté pour Anne Frank."* "Action" for 5 instruments, electro-acoustical devices and projectors [1972]. [Cited in BAKER, p. 1229].

867. Ridout, Godfrey (1918-1984). Canada. *In Memoriam Anne Frank.* Soprano and orchestra [c. 1965]. 1st: Toronto, 14 March 1965. [Cited in BAKER, p. 1510].

868. Schwartz, Francis (b. 1940). America. *Auschwitz.* Tape, dancers, aromas, lights, and slide projector [1968]. 1st: San Juan, 15 May 1968. #New York: Peer Southern International. [Cited in BAKER, p. 1667].

869. Senator, Ronald (20th c.). America. *Kaddish for Terezín.* Uses texts from children's poems as well as from the liturgy.

870. Šesták, Zdeněk (b. 1925). Czechoslovakia. *Auschwitz.* Melodrama [1959]. Text by Quasimodo. [Cited in BAKER, p. 1689].

871. Steinberg, Ben (b. 1930). Canada. *Echoes of Children.* Soloists, narrator, chorus, tape, and orchestra [1978]. 1st: March 1979. Dedicated to the 1-1/2 million children who perished in the Holocaust.

872. Weiner, Lazar (1897-1982). America [Russian born]. *Songs of the Concentration Camps.* Voice and piano [1948]. #New York: Schulsing, 1948. M1850.W4S64.

873. White, Michael (b. 1931). America. *The Diary of Anne Frank.* Soprano and orchestra [1960].

ANNOTATED LISTING OF WORLD WAR II
MUSIC AFTER 1945

America (United States)

Benjamin, Thomas (b. 1940)

874. *The Young Dead Soldiers.* Narrator, chorus, and piano [1988].
#Holograph at NYPL. Text by Archibald MacLeish.
AMC M1626.B468Y8
A simple, five-minute, tonal lament in D minor for those who
lost their lives in war. Commissioned by Peace Odyssey.

Bukvich, Daniel J. (20th c.)

875. Symphony No. 1. Winds and percussion [1981]. *(at Indiana
University: Program, 1987-1988, no. 520).
[No LC number available]
A ten-minute work in four movements: "Prologue," "Seeds in
the Wind," "Ave Maria," and "Fire Storm," vividly depicting the
night of 13 February 1945 and the fire-bombing of Dresden. The
music starts dark, with the sounds of roaring engines, beginning a
march-like section with heavy use of percussion and brass. The
texture is often thick and quite dissonant, and near the end includes
screaming and wild *fff* improvisation.

Copland, Aaron (1900-1990)

876. Symphony No. 3. Orchestra [1946]. 1st: Boston, 18 October
1946. #New York: Boosey & Hawkes, 1947. *[DG 419170-2
GH].
M1001.C78 no. 3
Celebrates the end of World War II; incorporates *A Fanfare for
the Common Man* into the fourth movement.

Dello Joio, Norman (b. 1913)

877. *Air Power.* Orchestral suite from film score [1957]. *Columbia
ML 5214.
M1527.8.D

An introduction and three movements, in which the second ("Mission in the Sky") deals with the bombing of Germany, and the last is called "War Scenes."

Foss, Lukas (b. 1922) [German born]

878. *Exeunt.* Orchestra [1980-1982]. Based on an early version entitled *Dissertation.* 1st: Indiana, 2 July 1981.
      M1045.F733E9 1982
      "Refers to the vision of human annihilation, the possibility of which cannot be ignored today." Foss prefaces each of the sections with a quotation from T.S. Eliot's *Waste Land.* An eighteen-minute serial composition.

Gaburo, Kenneth (b. 1926)

879. *Testimony.* Multi-media production including video, music, and interviews [1985-1987].
      [No LC number available]
      A video project in which Gaburo has taped numerous individuals as they respond to his questions about being expendable during a nuclear war.

Harrison, Lou (b. 1917)

880. *Novo Odo.* Male chorus, reciting chorus, occidental orchestra, percussion, and assimilated oriental instruments [1961-1963]. 1st: Seoul Korea, 1963.
      [No LC number available]
      A highly lyrical work in three parts written in the manner of an outrageous protest against war, with memorable phrases from the children: "Does fallout hurt?" or "What are you going to be when you blow up?"

881. *Pacifka Rondo.* Chorus and Asian instruments [1963]. *Desto DC 6478.
      [No LC number available]
      The sixth movement protests atomic testing in the Pacific Ocean and ends with a scream.

Hill, Jackson (b. 1941)

882. *Toro Nagashi (Lanterns of Hiroshima)*. Two pianos [1977]. #Wolverhampton, PA: Faircloth House, 1977.
AMC M214.H646T6
Written for the ceremony "Toro Nagashi" where lighted candles are placed on small rafts each year on 6 August as a memorial to the victims of the American bombing of Hiroshima. Commissioned by the Pennsylvania Music Teachers Association, it is a brief, sensitive work of 150 measures with imitation and some limited improvisation, but is chiefly traditional in its notation and diatonicism and full of repeated notes and irregular rhythms.

Hindemith, Paul (1895-1963) [German born]

• *When Lilacs Last Bloom'd: A Requiem for Those We Love.* Soloists, chorus, and orchestra [1946]. See item number 375.

Husa, Karel (b. 1921) [Czech born]

883. *Apotheosis of This Earth.* Wind band (chorus and orchestra version 1973) [1970]. 1st: Ann Arbor, 1 April 1971. #New York: Associated Music, 1970. *Golden Crest 4134.
M1530.H95 A6
A serial composition (based on four sets of three-note motives) which ends with members of the orchestra chanting "This beautiful earth." The second movement, with its elaborate, syncopated rhythmic structure, shows the earth disintegrating, possibly from a nuclear attack.

Litkei, Ervin (b. 1924) [Hungarian born]

884. *Peace and Remembrance.* Concerto for piano and orchestra [1963]. *Mercury SRM 1 1198.
[No LC number available]
A five-movement, tonal concerto providing a reflection of the war with programmatic titles: "Home," "Peace Before War," "War and the Prison Camp," "Liberation," and "New Horizons." The work concludes with "The Liberation March" in the fashion of film music.

London, Edwin (b. 1929)

885. *Day of Desolation.* Chorus, soloists, two male speakers, and bells
      [1970-1971]. #Hackensack, N.J.: J. Boonin, 1971. *Ubres CS-
      302.
           M2092.7.L654
           An experimental work with considerable whispering,
      proportional notation, indeterminacy, climaxing with an eight-part
      chorus repeatedly calling for and finally screaming for help.

McLean, Barton (b. 1938)

886. *The Last Ten Minutes: Reflections on the Human Agony of the
      Last Nuclear War.* Computer music produced on a Fairlight
      Computer Music Instrument [1982]. *Folkway Records FSS
      37465.
           [No LC number available]
           An eleven-minute study in anti-beauty containing groans,
      darkness, and ugliness in many variations. No recognizable
      instrumental sounds are heard. Sounds, such as door squeaks or
      human cries, are externally generated and digitally sampled creating
      material for the composition.

Mumma, Gordon (b. 1935)

887. *Dresden Interleaf 13 February 1945.* Tape [1965]. *Lovely
      Music/Vital Records VR 1091.
           [No LC number available]
           A twelve-minute, electronic work with pulsating sections of
      white noise leading to a terrifyingly loud mass of sound similar to
      a continuous air-raid siren.

Rahn, John (b. 1944)

888. *Kali.* Computer-generated tape [1986].
           [No LC number available]
           Deals with the Indian goddess Kali who brings about the end
      of time. The events that led to the American attack on Libya
      inspired Rahn to compose this intense, at times painful, work. It
      is sectionalized, incorporating the sounds of sirens, airplanes
      roaring, stalled motors, loud white noise, and sudden
      juxtapositions of silence.

Schifrin, Lalo (Boris) (b. 1932) [Argentine born]

889. *Cantata from the Rise and Fall of the Third Reich.* Oratorio for soloists, chorus, narrator, orchestra, and tape [1967]. 1st: 3 August 1967. #New York: Hastings Music, 1967. *MGM1SE 12ST. Text by Alfred Perry.
     M1530.3.S35R6
     In fifteen sections, including "Following the First World War," "The Creation of Hitler," "Bonfires were Built," "The War," "The Fall," etc. Most numbers use text, and several of Hitler's speeches appear in between some of the sections followed by the chorus screaming "Heil. Heil. Siegheil." "The War" is purely orchestral, with an extensive piano cadenza and wildly fluctuating dynamics. Everything is clearly notated throughout, with frequently changing meters.

Schuman, William (1910-1992)

890. *The Young Dead Soldiers.* Soprano and 17 instruments [1975]. 1st: 6 April 1976. #Bryn Mawr: Merion Music, 1976. *CRI SD 439. Text by Archibald MacLeish.
     M1613.3S395Y7
     A fifteen-minute lamentation, remarkable for its sensitive text-setting and for its orchestration featuring the soprano and horn.

Van de Vate, Nancy (b. 1930)

891. *Kracow Concerto (Katyń).* Percussion and orchestra [1989]. 1st: Kracow, 28 November 1989. *Conifer CDCF185.
     [No LC number available]
     A twenty-five minute work in five movements which uses quotations from Polish folk songs and Renaissance composers coupled with dissonances and gun shots. Dedicated to the victims of the Katyń forest massacre.

Weisgall, Hugo David (b. 1912) [Czech born]

892. *Nine Rivers from Jordon.* Opera [1964-1968]. 1st: New York, 9 October 1968. #Bryn Mawr: Theodore Presser, 1968. Libretto by Dennis Johnston.
     [No LC number available]
     Set on several fronts of World War II including in a concentration camp, the work uses various settings of war and

popular songs in several languages and portrays a ghastly picture of what humans do to other humans in the name of war.

Australia

Broadstock, Brenton (20th c.)

893.   *Beast From Air.* Trombone and percussion [1985].
          [No LC number available]
          A protest composition written because of the composer's anger over nuclear devices being detonated in the Pacific Ocean.

Canada

Coulthard, Jean (b. 1908)

894.   String Quartet No. 2 ("Threnody"). [1953, revised 1969]. 1st: Cheltenham Festival, 1972. #Toronto: Berandol Music, 1975.
          M452.C7994 no. 2 1975
          Written as a "musical requiem or an expression of sorrow for our war century," this brooding quartet (25'30") is in three movements and is a synthesis of many twentieth-century techniques and languages. In the preface the composer wrote that the second movement is about "sorrow" and the third is about "the wind of war over the land." The last movement is full of tempo and stylistic changes, relatively dissonant and jagged.

Schafer, R. Murray (b. 1933)

895.   *Threnody.* Five young narrators, youth chorus, voices, orchestra, and tape [1966]. #Toronto: Berandol Music, 1970. *Melbourne SMLP 4017.
          M1996.S36T5
          Influenced by Penderecki's *Threnody* (no. 963), this graphically notated score is a powerful evocation of the tragedy at Nagasaki. Schafer parodies in outrageous ways the scientific thought behind the dropping of the bomb juxtaposed with the suffering of the children who experienced first hand the results of that decision and planning. See Schafer, "Threnody: A Religious Piece for Our Time," *American Organist* (May 1970), pp. 33-37.

Czechoslovakia

Báchorek, Milan (b. 1939)

896. *Lidice*. Melodramatic tableau for solos, narrator, chorus, percussion, and orchestra [1973].
[No LC number available]
A significant, thirty-minute composition lamenting the tragedy of Lidice's destruction during World War II. Cited in "Milan Báchorek," CZECH.

Chlubna, Osvald (1893-1971)

897. *Eupyros*. Opera [1962]. #Unpublished. Libretto by the composer.
[No LC number available]
Deals with a possible atomic holocaust. Cited in "Osvald Chlubna," CZECH.

Cikker, Ján (1911-1990)

898. *Symphony 1945*. Orchestra [1974-1975]. 1st: Bratislava, 22 May 1975. #Prague: Slovensky hudobny fond, 1976. *Opus 9110 0412.
[No LC number available]
A four-movement symphony which is a reflection upon the end of fighting in 1945. Uses traditional forms and tonality as it attempts to depict the pain and suffering during the war years and the hope for a better future.

Felix, Václav (b. 1928)

899. Symphony No. 1, Op. 39. Female voice and orchestra [1974]. *Panton 110605-11606. Text by Marie Kuderiková.
[No LC number available]
A fifty-five minute work based upon texts of a Czech anti-fascist leader. Cited in "Václav Felix," CZECH.

Hlobil, Emil (1901-1987)

900. Symphony No. 2 ("The Day of Victory"), Op. 38. Orchestra [1951]. #Prague: Panton, 1978.
M1001.H67 Op. 38

A twenty-five minute symphony celebrating the Czechoslovakian triumph over Nazi oppression.

Ištvan, Miloslav (1928-1990)

901. *The Lidice Odyssey.* Piano [1963]. 1st: Brno, 12 May 1963. #Prague: Státni hudebni vydavatelstvi, 1966.
     M786.4.I870 (Multnomah County Library, Portland, Oregon)
     In the preface to the score, the composer wrote that the work was inspired by the children of Lidice who "were torn from their homes and after long years of wandering were returned to their families." The five-minute work emphasizes the treble ranges (and extremes of the keyboard), frequently changes meters, and is partially modal and partially serial.

Janeček, Karel (1903-1974)

902. *To the Fallen,* Op. 26. Male chorus [1950-1951]. Text by František Halas.
     [No LC number available]
     A seventeen-minute composition in commemoration of those who died during the Nazi occupation of Czechoslovakia. Cited in BAKER, p. 842.

Kardoš, Dezider (b. 1914)

903. Symphony No. 6, Op. 45. Orchestra [1974-1975]. #Bratislava: Opus, 1977. *Opus 9110 0880.
     [No LC number available]
     A four-movement traditional symphony attempting to capture the hard times before the end of the war and the euphoria upon liberation. Written on the occasion of the thirtieth anniversary of liberation of Czechoslovakia. Cited in BAKER, p. 888.

Kubín, Rudolph (1909-1973)

904. *Ostrava.* Cycle of five symphonic poems [1951].
     [No LC number available]
     Deals with the liberation of Ostrava by the Red Army during World War II. Consists of *Vítězství (Victory), Maryčka Magdónova, Ostrava, V Beskydách (In the Beskid Mountains),* and *Ocelové srdce (Heart of Steel).* Cited in BAKER, p. 976.

Kučera, Václav (b. 1929)

905. *Lidice.* A wireless musical-dramatic fresco for narrators, soprano, instrumental ensemble, and tape [1972].
[No LC number available]
A forty-minute work written for the twenty-fifth anniversary of the liberation of Czechoslovakia at the end of World War II and to commemorate the destruction of Lidice. Won the Italian Radio Prix d'Italie in 1972. Cited in BAKER, p. 976.

906. *Manifest jara. Na pamět' pražského Května 1945 (Spring Manifesto. In the Memory of Prague, May 1945).* Chamber cycle for four players [1974]. *Panton 110392.
[No LC number available]
Cited in "Václav Kučera," CZECH.

Lidl, Vaclav (b. 1922)

907. *Balada o červnovém ránu. Lidice 1942 (Ballad about a morning in June. Lidice 1942).* Orchestra [1982]. #Prague: Panton, 1986.
JMG 92-527 (NYPL call number)
A fifteen-minute work dealing with the destruction of Lidice in 1942.

Rak, Stcpán (b. 1945)

908. *Hiroshima.* Guitar; later arranged and expanded for orchestra. [1973]. *Chandos ABRD 1310 (guitar version).
[No LC number available]
The guitar version lasting nearly thirteen minutes attempts to convey the confusion that the immediate survivors felt after the atomic blast through its experimental use of extended tremolos and plucked sounds. The orchestral version, in two parts lasting twenty minutes, won the Silver Medal in the Czech National Competition for Young Composers in 1974.

Seidel, Ján (b. 1908)

909. *Polnice slávy (The Bugle of Glory).* Male chorus [1946]. *Supraphon EDS 112 1327. Text by František Halas.
[No LC number available]

A massive, fifty-minute composition illustrating the Czech struggle against the invading Nazis. Cited in "Jan Seidel," CZECH.

Tausinger, Jan (1921-1980)

910. Symphony No. 1 ("Liberation"). Orchestra [1952].
[No LC number available]
A twenty-three minute symphony written to celebrate the defeat of the Nazis. Cited in BAKER, p. 1855.

Trojan, Václav (1907-1983)

911. *The Ruined Cathedral.* Solo accordion [1958].
[No LC number available]
Composed after the composer saw the ruined cathedral in Dresden that was destroyed during World War II. Cited in "Václav Trojan," CZECH.

Vacek, Miloš (b. 1928)

912. *Poéma o padlých hrdinech (Poem of Fallen Heroes).* Alto solo and orchestra [1974].*Panton 11 0528
[No LC number available]
A twenty-five minute composition used as background music for the Hrabyne Memorial of the Ostrava Operation. Cited in BAKER, p. 1928.

913. *Svědomi světa (World's Conscience).* Symphonic poem [1981].
[No LC number available]
A twelve-minute composition written to commemorate the fortieth anniversary of the razing of Lidice and Ležáky. Cited in BAKER, p. 1928.

Válek, Jiří (b. 1923)

914. Symphony No. 14 ("Triofale"). Two pianos and orchestra [1983]. *Panton 8110 0517.
[No LC number available]
A twenty-five minute symphony written to celebrate the fortieth anniversary of the end of World War II. Cited in BAKER, p. 1931.

Denmark

Koppel, Herman (b. 1908)

915. *Three Psalms of King David*, Op. 48. Tenor, chorus, boys'
     chorus, and orchestra [1949]. 1st: 28 June 1951. #Copenhagen:
     Scandanavia Musikforlag, 1951. Text from Psalms 13, 23, and
     150.
     M2020.K77D4 1951
     A twenty-six minute setting of three psalms "composed in
     memory of the sufferings of mankind in World War II." The
     opening psalm is an urgent lament that is intense and very
     chromatic. The last psalm is an Alleluia symbolizing the post-war
     hope for humankind.

Finland

Englund, Einar (b. 1916)

916. Symphony No. 1. Orchestra [1946]. *Finlandia FA 304.
     [No LC number available]
     A four-movement work cited as the first Finnish war
     symphony (See notes to Finlandia Records FA 304, 1979). A
     victorious, optimistic work with heavy percussion and full
     orchestra, often *ff*. Cited in BAKER, p. 497.

France

Ancelin, Pierre (b. 1934)

917. *Poèmes de guerre*. Baritone and orchestra [c. 1958-1959]. 1st:
     Stockholm, January 1961. #Paris: Societe des Editions Jobert,
     1966. Text by Henri de Montherlant.
     M1614.A536P6
     Three brief songs employing frequently changing meters,
     ostinatos, fast repeated notes and sections, and strong dissonances.
     Dedicated "à la mémoire de toutes les victimes de toutes les
     guerres."

Aubert, Louis-François-Marie (1877-1968)

918. *Offrande*. Orchestra [1947]. #Paris: Durand, 1952. *Columbia
     FCX 597.

M1045.A85O3

A slow, expressive work opening and concluding with trumpet fanfares in D minor and D major respectively. Dedicated "à la mémoire des héros et de toutes les victimes de la guerre."

Condé, Gérard (20th c.)

919. *Memorial.* Baritone narrator and string quintet [c. 1980]. #Paris: Editions musicales transatlantiques, 1980. Text is adapted from Takaski Nagai.

JMG 83-257 (NYPL call number)

Rhythms are notated, but rarely are pitches in this portrayal of the tragedy of Nagasaki in 1945.

Milhaud, Darius (1892-1974)

920. Symphony No. 3 ("Hymnus Ambrosianus"). Chorus and orchestra [1946]. 1st: Paris, 30 October 1947. #Paris: Heugel, 1951. *Westminster XWN 19101.

M1001.M65 no. 3 1951a

Commissioned by the French government to commemorate the liberation of France from the Nazis. The four movements of this thirty-one minute symphony are "Fièrement," "Très recueilli," "Pastorale," and "Hymnus Ambrosianus—Te Deum." The second and fourth movements use chorus, but only the last contains text. The music is largely traditional and tonal.

Germany

Behrend, Siegfried (1933-1990)

921. *Requiem auf Hiroshima.* Voice, mandoline, guitar, percussion, and plucked string instruments [1973]. #Cologne: Musikverlag H. Gerig, 1976. *Capella Thorofon CTH 2026.

M1613.3.B394R5

Dedicated to Dr. Hisao Itoh, the pioneer of the plucked string instruments, this work creates a nightmare account of the tragedy of Hiroshima with its vocal groans and shrieks, and the instrumental cacophony and outbursts. It is indeed an eerie work of more than eleven minutes and, like McLean's *The Last Ten Minutes* (no. 886), a study in anti-beauty. In four sections, the score is proportional and filled with dots, squiggles, sustained blocks, remarkable graphics, and no standard musical notation.

Dessau, Paul (1894-1979)

922. *Einstein.* Opera [1971-1973]. 1st: 16 February 1984. #Berlin: Henschelverlag Kunst & Gesellschaft, 1973. Libretto by Karl Mickel.

M1503.D475 .E4 1973

An opera with a brief prologue, three acts, and two interludes, recounting the life of Einstein and his discoveries in a somewhat experimental musical style of intense chromaticism, aleatoric passages, and clusters. At one point, after counting down from ten to zero, boys' chorus sings the words "Hiroshima" and "Nagasaki," leading to Einstein's descriptions of the cities destroyed. Other parts include sayings such as "Make love not war."

Eimert, Herbert (1897-1972)

923. *Epitaph für Aikichi Kuboyama.* Narrator and Sprachklange [1960-1962]. *Wergo 60014.

[No LC number available]

Written about the first victim who died after being near the H-Bomb test explosion in the Pacific Ocean and related to war because the test explosion of the H-bomb was possibly planned to be used for mass destruction. Eimert captures the tragedy of this event responsible for Aikichi Kuboyama's death through horrific, grinding electronic sounds that accompany the narration.

Henze, Hans Werner (b. 1926)

924. *Nachstücke und Arien.* Soprano and orchestra [1957]. 1st: 20 October 1957. #Mainz: B Schott's Söhne, 1958. Text by Ingeborg Bachmann.

M1613.H54N3

A twenty-three minute polemic against war and nuclear bombs divided into "Nachtstück I," "Aria I," "Nachtstück II," "Aria II," and "Nachtstück III." The night pieces are without text but highly expressive, particularly the last with its *ff*, vivace sixteenth-note unisons.

Matthus, Siegfried (b. 1934)

925. *Die Weise von Liebe und Tod des Cornets Christoph Rilke.* Opera [1986]. #Leipzig: Deutscher Verlag für Musik, 1986. Libretto based on poems of Rainer Maria Rilke.

M1503.M4467W44 1986

Evokes the destruction of Dresden and written to reopen the Dresden Opera House which had been bombed during the war. During both world wars, the poems on which the opera is based were well-known to German soldiers who carried the poems with them to the front.

Schröder, Hanning (1896-1987)

926. *Musik für vier Instrumente in memoriam: Lied der Moorsoldaten.*
    String quartet [1952]. #Leipzig: Breitkopf & Härtel, 1962.
    *Thorofon Capella 76.23970.
        M452.S375M9
        In three sections, the work was inspired by the "Song of the Soldiers of the Moors" that was sung in the concentration camp at Börgermoor and that moved the composer through the sheer determination of the inmates to survive.

Great Britain

Berkeley, Michael (b. 1948)

927. *Or Shall We Die?* Oratorio [1982]. 1st: London, 6 February 1983.
    #London: Oxford University Press, 1982. *EMI ASD 2700581.
    Texts by Ian McEwan and William Blake.
        M1533.B492 O7 1984
        A fifty-minute, traditional and propagandistic oratorio with a considerable anti-war and often anti-science message. The central part deals with the destruction of Hiroshima and a woman in search of her lost daughter. A polemic against nuclear war.

Biggin, Tony (20th c.)

928. *The Gates of Greenham.* Musical comedy for soloists, narrator, chorus, electric guitars, drum-kit, and orchestra [1985]. 1st: London, 8 April 1985. #London: Leaveners, 1985. *Sain/D Sharp 1352R.
        [No LC number available]
        Subtitled "A peace passion for today," this work of propagandistic significance combines classically influenced music with rock music in the tradition of Leonard Bernstein. Emphasis is on protest of nuclear proliferation.

Britten, Benjamin (1913-1976)

929. *Canticle No. 3*, Op. 55. Tenor, horn, and piano [1954]. 1st: 28 January 1955. #London: Boosey & Hawkes, 1956. *Argo ZRG 946. Text by Edith Sitwell.
M1613.3.B86C33
A setting of "Still Falls the Rain"—a World War II poem in two parts: "The Raids, 1940" and "Night and Dawn." The music creates an atmosphere of lament with its mournful, repetitive melodic phrases. Structurally it alternates with variations and free, recitative-like verses.

Lloyd, George (b. 1913)

930. Piano Concerto No. 1 ("Scapegoat"). Piano and orchestra [c. 1965]. *Albany TROY 037-2.
[No LC number available]
Lloyd was shell-shocked during World War II, and several of his compositions that he wrote during the sixties are reflections upon the war. Each of these concerti is tonal for the most part, but contains angry, dissonant outbursts landing somewhere between Rachmaninoff and Bartók. This concerto is twenty-five minutes long and in one movement.

931. Piano Concerto No. 2. Piano and orchestra [c. 1966]. 1st: London, May 1984. *Albany TROY 037-2.
[No LC number available]
Lloyd based his principal theme of this one-movement concerto on a newspaper clipping he saw of Hitler dancing a victory jig. Thirty-three minutes of tonal and virtuosic music.

932. Piano Concerto No. 3. Piano and orchestra [c. 1968] *Albany TROY 019-2.
[No LC number available]
The slow movement was inspired by the terrorism the composer felt resulted from Hitler's occupation of many places in Europe.

933. Symphony No. 4. Orchestra [1946]. *Lyrita SRCS 129.
[No LC number available]
With a superscription "A world of darkness, storms, strange colours and a far-away peacefulness," the first movement of this

work is Lloyd's reflection upon World War II; his first work after Lloyd was shell-shocked during the war.

Mathias, William (b. 1934)

934. *Ceremony After a Fire Raid*, Op. 63. Voice, piano, and percussion [1973]. 1st: London, 19 September 1973. #London: Oxford University Press, 1975. Text by Dylan Thomas.
M1531.M35C5
An erratic, explosive twenty-minute work with graphic texts and a chorus that yells, whispers, and speaks in addition to singing in its depiction of the bombing of Hiroshima during World War II. All pitches and rhythms are precisely and traditionally notated. The composer wrote that the poem had special meaning to him, reflecting events close to the time of writing rather than specifically and exclusively dealing with World War II. Commissioned by and dedicated to The Scholars.

McCartney, Paul (b. 1942) and Davis, Carl [America]

935. *Liverpool Oratorio.* Chorus and orchestra [1991]. 1st: 28 June 1991. *EMI Classics CDS 7543712.
[No LC number available]
A ninety-minute work consisting of a curious blend of pop lyrics and tunes in an art-music, full-orchestra-and-chorus format. In eight sections based on the life of Paul McCartney; the first is called "War," because he was born during the middle of World War II. The last movement ("Peace") is about our living in peace together symbolized by the love of Mary Dee and Shanty.

Stevens, Bernard (1916-1983)

936. *Symphony of Liberation*, Op. 7. Orchestra [1940-1945]. 1st: London, 7 June 1946. *Meridian CDE 84124.
[No LC number available]
In three movements ("Enslavement," "Resistance," and "Liberation") this symphony was composed chiefly during the German blitz of World War II and won first prize in a Victory Music contest sponsored by the *Daily Express* during the war. The work is dedicated to Clive Branson who was killed in battle in 1944. The music is tonal and shows influences of Bartók and Vaughan Williams. See Bertha Stevens, ed., *Bernard Stevens and His Music* (London: Kahn & Averill, 1989), pp. 81-85.

Still, Robert (1910-1971)

937. Symphony No. 3. Orchestra [1960]. *Lyrita SRCS 46.
     [No LC number available]
     Malcolm Macdonald suggested this symphony is reflective of
     World War II, especially the second movement which is a lament
     for those who never made it back from the front. (See notes to
     phonodisc Lyrita SRCS 46.)

Swann, Donald (20th c.)

938. *Requiem for the Living.* Narrator, bass, chorus, piano, cimbalom,
     and percussion [1971]. 1st: "A Concert in Search of Peace," 1971.
     *Planet Life PLR061. Text by C. Day Lewis.
     [No LC number available]
     A nine-section pop requiem dealing with the earth, peace, and
     the end of the world. The third movement ("Dies irae") attempts to
     depict the destruction of the world after a nuclear bomb has been
     dropped.

Vaughan Williams, Ralph (1872-1958)

939. Symphony No. 6. Orchestra [1948, revised 1950]. 1st: London, 21
     April 1948. #London: Oxford University Press, 1948. *Angel
     CDC-47215 and RCA 6779-2 RG.
     M1001.V38 no. 6 1983
     A four-movement work in E minor that Frank Howes claimed
     dealt with war. See Howes, *The Music of Ralph Vaughan
     Williams* (London: Oxford University Press, 1954), p. 53.
     Vaughan Williams never conceded that it was about war, if it was,
     although the second movement—in particular its martial use of
     percussion and trumpets—would indicate that the war influenced
     the work to some degree.

Hungary

Ránki, György (b. 1907)

940. *Nineteen Forty-four.* Oratorio for chorus, strings, and percussion
     [1966, revised 1969]. 1st: Budapest, 24 April 1967. #Budapest:
     Editio Musica, 1970.
     M1531.R185N5

"Commissioned by the Executive Committee of the Council of Budapest for the 20th Anniversary of the liberation of the city." The work is more subdued than most "liberation" works, but it does have the mandatory big ending. Ránki's style is relatively dissonant, but straightforward rhythmically.

Italy

Giuffrè, Gaetano (b. 1918)

941. *Hiroshima*. Bass, chorus, and orchestra [1964-1965]. 1st: Tokyo, 6 August 1967. #New York: Seesaw Music, 1979. Text by I.M. Panayotopoulos.
    M1530.G5H5
    A dramatic setting in Greek, calling upon speaking, primitivism, and frequent tempo and meter changes in a precisely notated, considerably dissonant lament.

Malipiero, Gian Francesco (1882-1973)

942. Symphony No. 4 ("In Memoriam"). Orchestra [1946]. 1st: 27 February 1948. #Milan: G. Ricordi, 1948.
    M1001.M25 no.4 1948a
    A four-movement, twenty-five minute symphony written as a memorial to those lost in the war. The second movement is a funeral march and the last a set of variations.

Nono, Luigi (1924-1990)

943. *Il canto sospeso* (*Broken Song*). Three voices, chorus, and orchestra [1956]. 1st: 24 October 1956. #Mainz: Ars Viva, 1956.
    M1530.N85C3
    A twenty-eight minute work breaking up syllables and based on letters from resistance leaders who were killed in World War II.

944. *Intolleranza*. Opera/oratorio [1960-1961]. 1st: 13 April 1961. #Mainz: Ars Viva, 1962. *Reel tape at Indiana University. Libretto by Bertolt Brecht, Paul Eluard, and Vladimir Mayakovsky.
    M1500.N85I6 Case
    Includes seven scenes in the first part and four in the second which present an outrageous political parody. Scene vi in Part I takes place in a concentration camp.

945. *Sul ponte di Hiroshima* (from *Canti di vita e d'amore*). Soprano, tenor, and orchestra [1962]. 1st: 22 August 1963. #Mainz: Ars Viva, 1963. *Wergo 60067. Text by Günther Anders, trans. into Italian by Renato Solmi.

   M1528.N65C3 1963

   A somewhat pointillistic, dissonant setting that is meticulously notated with tempi that change almost in each measure. The work reaches an enormous climax at its end that leads directly to the next song in the cycle "Djamila Boupachà." Commissioned by the Edinburgh International Festival.

Rossellini, Renzo (1908-1982)

946. *La guerra*. Opera [1956]. 1st: Rome, 25 February 1956. #Milan: Ricordi, 1956. *Impresario Editions IE 3003.

   M1503.R813G8 1956

   A dramatic, tonal work set during World War II and includes strong timpani rolls and the sounds of sirens and bombers flying overhead.

Zafred, Mario (1922-1987)

947. Symphony No. 4 ("In onore della resistenza"). Orchestra [1950]. #Milan and New York: G. Ricordi, 1952.

   *MTA (NYPL call number)

   A twenty-four minute, four-movement work with intense and somewhat angry first and second movements with considerable use of brass. The last movement begins with a fugue and a rather severe, slow introduction.

Japan

Hayakawa, Masaaki (b. 1934)

948. *Inori for Hiroshima*. Soprano, contra-bass, and percussion [after 1945]. *Fontec RFO-1043. Text by Kazuko Yamada.

   [No LC number available]

   A wonderfully expressive lament for those who died in the tragedy of Hiroshima. From its dark, resonating opening with slow but steady drum beats, it holds the listener throughout with its imaginative use of percussion, the sustaining power of the bass, and the dramatic soprano part.

Kojiba, Tomiko (b. 1952)

949. *Hiroshima Requiem.* String orchestra with divided sections and antique cymbals [1979]. 1st: Athens, August 1985.
      [No LC number available]
      A slow, brooding, lyrical work which climaxes a couple of times with accelerating, repeated rhythmic patterns of increasing dissonance and intensity. A twelve-minute composition in the tradition of Strauss's *Metamorphosen* (no. 672).

Kubo, Mayako (20th c.)

950. *Iterum meditemur for Hiroshima.* Trombone and tape (or taperecorder) [1978]. #Vienna: Ariadne, 1979.
      JMF 83-225 (NYPL call number)
      Over fourteen minutes in two different versions, with or without tape recorder-feedback. In graphic score with timed sections, the trombonist plays along with a tape which includes sounds of oriental wind chimes and a voice reading clippings about the war from an American newspaper in the 1940s.

Ohki, Masao (1901-1971)

951. *Hiroshima.* Symphonic fantasy [1953]. #Tokyo: Zen-On Music, 1956.
      M1002.44H5 1956
      Inspired by the paintings *Pictures of the Atom Bomb* created by Iri Maruki and Toshiko Akamatsu. The work is divided into a prelude and seven programmatic sections: 1) "Ghosts: It was a procession of ghosts"; 2) "Fire: Next moment fire burst into flames"; 3) "Water: People wandered around seeking for water"; 4) "Rainbow: People were suffering without [a] word. All of a sudden black rain poured over them and then appeared a beautiful rainbow"; 5) "Boys and Girls: Boys and girls died without knowing any joy of human life and calling for their parents"; 6) "Atomic desert: Boundless desert with skulls"; 7) "Elegy." The preface printed in five languages (Japanese, English, French, German, and Russian) is a polemic claiming that the Japanese had to report the conditions of the aftereffects of the bombing because other countries were attempting to keep the conditions secret. The music itself is highly chromatic, rather dissonant, often densely textured with cross-rhythms, and contains numerous pictographic

devices (string harmonics in the desert section, rapid Wagnerian chromaticism, and string glissandos to depict fire, etc.)

Sukegawa, Toshiya (b. 1930)

952. *the eternal morning 1945.8.6.* Piano, string orchestra, and electronic tape [1983]. *Vienna Modern Masters VMM 3006.
[No LC number available]
A twenty-minute, highly successful composition providing a graphic portrayal and re-enactment of the bombing of Hiroshima in August 1945. The roaring of engines, sirens, and knocking sounds on tape combine with Penderecki-sounding strings and an out-of-tune piano that was damaged during the bombing to create an imaginative and poignant composition.

The Netherlands

Delden, Lex Van (1919-1988)

953. Symphony No. 1 ("De Stroom Mei 1940") ("The Torrent, May 1940"). Soprano, chorus, eight instruments, and percussion [1952]. #Amsterdam: Donemus.
[No LC number available]
Describes the destruction of Rotterdam during World War II. Cited in BAKER, p. 411.

Henkemans, Hans (b. 1913)

954. *Bericht aan de levenden* (*Message to the Living*). Speaker, mixed chorus, and orchestra [1964]. 1st: 4 May 1965. Text by H.M. van Randwijk.
[No LC number available]
Written for the twentieth anniversary of the liberation of Holland from the Nazis and to commemorate the war dead. Begins with the horrors of war and was inspired by the monument at the Erebegraafplaats at Bloemendaal. Cited in BAKER, p. 755.

Kox, Hans (b. 1930)

955. *Requiem for Europe.* Four choruses with instrumental groups and two organs [1971]. 1st: 6 July 1971. #Amsterdam: Donemus, 1971. Texts by Paul Celan, the composer, and from Psalms, Proverbs, and the "Canticum Moysis."

M1531.K69 R37

A forty-minute work in two parts: "Fugue of Death" and "For the Lost Hopes of Humanity."

Lier, Bertus Van (1906-1972)

956. *5 Mei: Zij (5th of May and Them)*. Oratorio for boy's chorus, chorus, and orchestra [1962]. 1st: 5 May 1963. #Amsterdam: Donemus, 1962. Text by K.H.R. de Joselinde Jong.
      *MP (Netherlands) (NYPL call number)
      An extended work which deals with the liberation of Holland from Nazi occupation. It ends in C major using dotted rhythms and cries of freedom.

Marez Oyens, Tera de (b. 1932)

957. *Litany of the Victims of War*. Orchestra [1985]. #Amsterdam: Donemus, 1987. *Composers' Voice 8702.
      M1045.M34L5 1987
      An eleven-minute, self-proclaimed "anti-war manifesto" lamenting those who have died in all wars throughout history. While combining elements of the funeral march and militaristic touches of orchestration, the work remains otherwise quite conventional.

Norway

Nordheim, Arne (b. 1931)

958. *Eco*. Soprano, boy's and mixed chorus, and orchestra [1967-1968]. 1st: 27 June 1969. #Copenhagen: W. Hansen Musikforlag, 1972. *Edition Wilhelm Hansen WH29617. Text by Salvatore Quasimodo.
      M1530.N856E3
      Dedicated to Karl-Birger Blomdahl in memoriam and based on two poems "I morti" and "Alle fronde dei salici." The work opens with a thirty-second horrific cry (*fff*) in the strings and the winds, gradually diminishing to *p*. Numerous aleatoric devices are used, including highest-lowest pitches, rapid, non-pitched figurations, clusters, and glissandos. It requires six large batteries of percussion instruments. The chorus often speaks in addition to singing. All rhythms are notated proportionally.

Poland

Maciejewski, Roman (b. 1910)

959. *Missa pro defunctis.* Chorus, soloists, and orchestra [1945-1959].
    1st: Warsaw, 1960. *Polskie Nagrania PNCD 039 A & B.
    [No LC number available]
    A little-known masterpiece over two hours long, dedicated "to
    the victims of the wars of all time, victims of tyrants of human
    ignorance, victims of broken divine laws." The Dies irae (nearly
    ninety minutes itself) contains moments of immense power and
    subtlety. This work does not depict war in any way, but
    emotionally it grew out of the war, and that intensity is apparent
    in every bar of the composition.

Panufnik, Andrzej (1914-1991)

960. *Heroic Overture.* Orchestra [1952, revised 1969]. 1st: Helsinki-
    1952, Finnish Radio Orchestra. #Kracow: Polskie wydawnictwo
    muzycene, 1953. *Unicorn RHS 306.
    M1004.P18U9
    A six-minute work, originating from the German attack upon
    Poland and the heroism displayed by the Polish citizens; it
    includes references to the patriotic song "Warszawianki."

961. *Katyń Epitaph.* Orchestra [1967, revised 1969]. 1st: New York, 17
    November 1968. #London: Boosey & Hawkes, 1972. *Unicorn-
    Kanchana DKP 9016.
    M1045.P19K3
    An eight-minute work written to express the composer's
    outrage that the Katyń atrocity has largely been forgotten and
    dedicated to the memory of the 15,000 Poles who were killed
    defending their own country. The work is based upon a three-note
    cell that gradually develops into a huge crescendo.

Penderecki, Krzysztof (b. 1933)

962. *Polish Requiem.* Soloists, chorus, and orchestra [1983]. 1st:
    Stuggart, 28 September 1984. #Mainz: B. Schott's Söhne, 1984.
    [No LC number available]
    In Penderecki's more romantic style, this enormous work has
    various connections to war and the suffering it creates. The Dies
    irae commemorates the Warsaw uprising against the Nazis in

1944, and the Recordare, Jesu pie was written in response to a victim of Auschwitz. See Wolfram Schwinger, *Krzysztof Penderecki: His Life and Work*, trans. William Mann (London: Schott, 1989), pp. 233-49.

963. *Tren pamieci ofiarom Hiroszimy (Threnody to the Victims of Hiroshima)*. Fifty-two string instruments [1959-1960]. 1st: 31 May 1961. #Warsaw: Polskie wydawnictwo muzyczene, 1961. *Philips 412 0301 and EMI C605-02484.

M1145.P4T6

An extraordinary and innovative sectionalized work using experimental string sounds to imitate bombs dropping and airplane engines; creates a rugged, horrific atmosphere of dissonance through the use of clusters, glissandi, and piercing high notes. See Schwinger, *Krzysztof Penderecki*, pp. 124-28.

Romania

Petra-Basacopol, Carmen (b. 1926)

964. *Pro pace*. Soprano, flute, and piano [c. 1973]. #Editura muzicala a uniunii compozitoriler, 1973.

JMF 81-831 (NYPL call number)

A cycle of three songs dealing with the dropping of the bomb on Hiroshima: "Meeting Hiroshima," "Choir of the Killed Children," and "The Voices of the Birds of Hiroshima."

Serbia

Ristić, Milan (1908-1982)

965. Symphony No. 3. Orchestra [1961]. 1st: Belgrade, 17 October 1961. #Belgrad: Naucno delo, 1965.

M1001.R63 no. 3

A four-movement, twenty-eight minute symphony illustrating the events in Yugoslavia around the time of World War II: "Youth," "Political Struggle," "Nazi Occupation," and "Liberation."

Soviet Union

Boiko, Rostislav (b. 1931). Russia

966.   Symphony No. 2. Orchestra [1978]. #Moscow: Muzyka, 1982.
       *Melodiya 249 016.
              M1001.B697 no. 2 1982
              A twenty-one minute work in three movements (Adagio,
       Allegro, and Andante cantabile). Inspired by the heroic struggle of
       the Leningrad citizens during the siege, it remains a grandiose
       work, tonal, rhythmically energetic, and in the end almost too
       much like film music.

Eshpay, Andrey (b. 1925). Russia

967.   Symphony No. 4. Orchestra [1982]. #Moskva: Vses. izd-vo Sov.
       kompozitor, 1985.
              M1001.E765 no. 4 1985
              Dedicated in memory of the composer's brother who was
       killed in 1941.

Firtich, Georgy (b. 1938)

968.   *Leningrad.* Cantata for soprano, baritone, chorus, and orchestra. [c.
       1976]. #Leningrad: Soviet Kompozitor, 1976
              M1533.F53L4
              In six sections, the music is tonal, dramatic, and ends *fff* in A
       major. The choral parts are simple to sing and obviously meant for
       amateur choirs.

Geviksman, Vitaly (b. 1924)

969.   *The Great Patriotic War.* Orchestra. Incidental music to television
       series [c. 1985]. #Moscow: Muzyka, 1985.
              M1527.2 .G
              Includes sections entitled "The Battle of Kursk," "The Brest
       Fortress," and "The Banner of Victory."

Kabalevsky, Dmitry (1904-1987). Russia

970.   *War Requiem.* Chorus, children's chorus, and orchestra [1962].
       1st: Moscow, 9 February 1963. #New York: Kalmus, 1974.
       *Melodiya SRB 4101. Text by Rozhdestvensky.

M2013.K11R57
Not based upon the requiem mass, the work was written in memory of those who died during World War II. Uses the key of B-flat minor for lament passages.

Kangro, Raimo (b. 1949)

971. *Glory to Victors.* Oratorio [1975]. *Melodiya C10 09239-40.
[No LC number available]
A three-movement work influenced by Stravinsky; celebrates a victorious conclusion to World War II.

Kapp, Eugen (b. 1908). Estonia

972. *Leningrad Symphonic Suite.* Orchestra. #Moscow, 1959. *Melodiya D05906-07.
M1003.K147L4
A six-movement suite depicting scenes from Leningrad. The fifth movement ("Peter and Paul Fortress") is a funeral march in B-flat minor, and the sixth movement ("Square of Revolt") depicts the beginning of the October Revolution in a whirlwind of ostinatos.

Khachaturyan, Aram (1903-1978). Georgia

973. *In Memory of the Heroes.* Cantata. Taken from *the Battle of Stalingrad* [1976]. *Hungaroton SLPX 11922. Text by Gábor Garai added between the movements after Khachaturyan composed the music.
[No LC number available]
A propagandistic cantata in eight sections, including "The City is in Flames," "Fight for the Homeland," "Eternal Glory to the Heroes," and "Forward to Victory." See item 974.

974. *Suite from Battle of Stalingrad.* Film music for orchestra [1952]. 1st: Moscow, film performance, 9 December 1949. #Moscow: 1951. *Melodiya CM 04377-78.
M1003.K45S8
In eight distinct sections, the music was later used in the cantata *In Memory of the Heroes.* See item 973.

Levitin, Yury (b. 1912)

975. *Hiroshima Must Not Be Repeated.* Oratorio for orchestra, narrator, soprano, children's chorus, and mixed chorus [1967]. #Moscow: Soviet Kompositor, 1972. Text by M. Matussovsky.
JMG 76-491 (NYPL call number)
Uses clusters, glissandos, Sprechstimme, and other effects to produce a protest against dropping the bomb on innocent people. In these six movements, Levitin makes particular use of children's chorus in the fourth and sixth movements. Titles of movements include "Children of Hiroshima are drawing," "The girl Sakaya is dying," and the last, "Hiroshima must not be repeated."

Myaskovsky, Nikolay (1881-1950). Russia

976. Symphony No. 25, Op. 69. Orchestra [1946]. #Moscow, 1949.
M209.M63 Op. 69 (Four-hands piano arrangement)
A three-movement symphony in D-flat major reflecting on World War II experiences.

Pärt, Arvo (b. 1935). Estonia

977. *Nekrolog*, Op. 5. Orchestra, including piano and xylophone [1960]. #Frankfurt: M.P. Belaieff, 1990.
M1045.P133 Op. 5 1990
A powerful, full-orchestral work in three continuous sections with considerable repetition and dedicated to the victims of fascism.

Petrov, Andrey (b. 1930). Russia

978. *To the Memory of the dead during the Years of the Siege of Leningrad.* Symphonic poem for strings, organ, and 4 trumpets [1966]. 1st: 28 September 1968. *Columbia/Melodiya M-34526.
[No LC number available]
An austere fifteen-minute work in five sections with considerable dissonance written to convey the agony of the dead during 1941.

Prokofiev, Sergei [Prokof'yev, Sergey] (1891-1953). Russia

979.   *Story of a Real Man*. Opera [1947-1948]. 1st: Leningrad, 3
       December 1948 (only a private run-through). #Berlin: Henschel,
       1962. *Westminster 8317.
          M1503.P969S87 1962
          Illustrates the life of a fighter pilot who is shot down by the
       Germans in World War II: he hears sounds of the continued
       fighting and comes to a burned village; he is on the verge of total
       depression before he is inspired through stories of the Civil War to
       return to action and bring victory to the Motherland.

Shaporin, Yury (1887-1966). Ukraine

980.   *Dokole Korshunu Kruzhit?* Op. 20 (*How Long Shall the Kite
       Soar?*). Oratorio for baritone, mezzo-soprano, chorus, and orchestra
       [1945-1947, revised 1963]. #Moscow: Muyzka, 1966. *Melodiya
       MLD-32118. Texts by Aleksandr Blok and Konstantin Simonov.
          M2000.S495D67
          A setting of texts from both world wars, this six-part oratorio
       is a lament describing the destruction of war; uses traditional
       nineteenth-century harmonies and techniques.

Shostakovich, Dmitry (1906-1975). Russia

981.   String Quartet No. 8, Op. 110 [1960]. 1st: Leningrad, 2 October
       1960. #New York: Kalmus v. 2. *Angel CDC-47507.
          M452.S556 Op. 110
          In memory of victims of fascism and war, these five
       continuous movements use Shostakovich's musical initials
       frequently. The second movement is graphic in its portrayal of war
       with sudden *sfff* outbursts in the lower strings similar to the
       scherzo of his Eighth Symphony.

Zhubanova, Gaziza (b. 1927)

982.   *Hiroshima*. Suite from the ballet for full orchestra [1966].
       #Moscow: Soviet Kompozitor, 1972.
          M1003.Z63H6
          A suite in eight sections with programmatic headings, such as
       "Fiery Tornado" and "Tojo on the Bottom of the Sea." The suite
       opens and closes with marches in D minor and B-flat minor,

respectively two of the prominent keys within the work. The music is conventionally notated and tonal throughout.

Sweden

Blomdahl, Karl-Birger (1916-1968)

983. *Aniara.* Opera [1959]. 1st: 31 May 1959. #New York: Associated Music, 1959. *Caprice CAP 20161-2.
    JMG 81-190 (NYPL call number)
    A science-fiction approach to opera, depicting a bleak future of atomic war.

Tubin, Eduard (1905-1982) [Estonian born]

984. *Requiem for the Fallen Soldiers.* Alto, male chorus, trumpet, percussion, and organ [1950-1979]. 1st: Stockholm, 17 May 1981. *BIS CD297. Texts by Jenrik Visnapuu and Marie Under.
    [No LC number avaiable]
    A five-movement, forty-five minute, non-liturgical setting of poems from the Estonian War of Independence in 1919 and World War II. Includes "Be hailed, be hailed!," "A Soldier's Funeral," "The Soldier's Mother," and "Lilac." The opening distant melody and the steady drum beat set the tone for this dark and deeply moving austere work.

Werle, Lars Johan (b. 1926)

985. *Animalen.* Music Fable in two acts for soloists, strings, accordion, mandolin, electric guitar, and bass [1979]. 1st: Gothenburg Opera, 19 May 1979. #Stockholm: Edition Suecia, 1984. Libretto by Tage Danielsson.
    M1621.W415A55 1984
    Deals with the cold war and the "Balance of Terror."

Switzerland

Honegger, Arthur (1892-1955)

986. Symphony No. 3 ("Liturgique"). Orchestra [1946]. 1st: Zurich, 17 August 1946. #Paris: Salabert, 1946. *DG 423242-2 GC.
    M1001.H78L5

In three movements: "Dies irae," "De profundis clamavi," and "Dona nobis pacem." A significant war-related symphony depicting the horror of war as well as the optimistic hope for peace. The agitated opening is brilliantly orchestrated and immediately establishes the alarm of war.

Liebermann, Rolf (b. 1910)

987. *Leonore 40/45.* Opera [1952]. 1st: 25 March 1952. #Vienna: Universal Editions, 1952. *(at Indiana University). Libretto by Heinrich Strobel.
    M1503.L7174L4 1952
    In two acts and seven scenes, this opera deals with the years 1939 and 1947, particularly with the Nazi occupation of Paris and the aftermath of this event. The music is dissonant and bitonal.

Yugoslavia

Hristić, Zoran (b. 1938)

988. *Darinkin dar (Darinka's Gift).* A ballet for chorus and orchestra [c. 1974]. 1st: Belgrade, 1974. #Belgrade, 1974. *RTB LP 2583. Text by Božidar Božović.
    [No LC number available]
    A forty-five minute experimental work in the tradition of Penderecki. It is a graphic portrayal of a woman in a Serbian village where enemy soldiers killed her two daughters in front of her and then the woman herself because she saved a wounded and unknown Serbian soldier. The first of the eight movements, "Nozevi" ("Knives"), is a horrifying picture of war, murder, and suffering depicted with glissandos, tremolos, and loud clusters.

SUPPLEMENT OF WORLD WAR II MUSIC
AFTER 1945

989. Aaltonen, Erkki (b. 1910). Finland. Symphony No. 2
      ("Hiroshima"). Orchestra [1949]. [Cited in BAKER, p. 1].
990. Aleksandrov, Yury (b. 1914). Russia. *Caucasus*. Symphonic
      cantata [1947]. [Cited in HO, p. 14]. Dedicated to the memory of
      the liberators of the Caucasus during World War II.
991. Balatka, Antonín (1895-1958). Czechoslovakia. *Lidice*. Male
      chorus [1955].
992. Bandur, Joran (1899-1956). Yugoslavia. *Poem 1941*. Chorus,
      bass, and orchestra [c. 1948]. 1st: 9 May 1948. [Cited in
      SLONIMSKY, p. 854]. Deals with the Nazi massacre of
      Yugoslavian schoolboys.
993. Basner, Veniamin (b. 1925). Russia. *Poem of the Besieged
      Leningrad*. Symphonic poem [1957]. [Cited in HO, p. 50].
994. Bentzon, Niels Viggo (b. 1919). Denmark. *Torquilla*. Oratorio
      [1961]. 1st: Denmark, 23 October 1961. [Cited in
      SLONIMSKY, p. 1126]. Portrays a fictional atomic war
      between Russia and China after Nevil Shute's novel *On the
      Beach*.
995. Bruči, Rudolf (b. 1917). Yugoslavia. *A Man is a Horizon
      Without End*. Cantata [1961]. 1st: 21 December 1961. [Cited in
      BAKER, p. 256]. Deals with World War II.
996. Cossetto, Emil (b. 1918). Yugoslavia. *Borbena Kantata (Cantata
      of the Struggle)*. Cantata [1947]. [Cited in BAKER, p. 363].
      Inspired by wartime resistance in Yugoslavia during the war.
997. Deshevov, Vladimir (1889-1955). Russia. *In Memory of the
      Martial Glory of the Russian People*. Orchestra [1947]. [Cited in
      HO, p. 114].
998. Dolukhanyan, Aleksandr (1910-1968). Georgia. *Sevastopol
      Heroes*. Cantata [1948]. [Cited in HO, p. 118].
999. Dzegelyonak, Aleksandr (1891-1969). Russia. *Stalingradskaya
      bitva (The Battle of Stalingrad)*. Wind band [1950].
1000. Feld, Jindřich (b. 1925). Czechoslovakia. *May 1945*. Dramatic
      overture [1959-1960]. [Cited in BAKER, p. 525].
1001. _____. *Vojna (War)*. Male chorus [1954]. Text by Fráni
      Srámek.
1002. Forest, Jean Kurt (1909-1975). Germany. *Die Blumen von
      Hiroshima*. Opera [1967]. *Nova 8 85 069 (excerpts).

1003. Glodeanu, Liviu (1938-1978). Romania. *The Young Dead Soldiers*. Cantata [1958]. 1st: Cluj, 21 March 1962. Text by Archibald MacLeish. [Cited in BAKER, p. 636].

1004. Golubev, Yevgeny (b. 1910). Russia. *Heroes are Immortal*. Oratorio [1946]. [Cited in HO, p. 185].

1005. Halpern, Eddie (b. 1921). Israel. *Katyń*. Cantata for female voice, narrator, instruments, and tape [1978].

1006. Hemel, Oscar van (1892-1981). The Netherlands. *Herdenkingshymne 1940-1945 (Memorial Hymn 1940-1945)*. Mixed chorus, children's chorus, brass, and percussion [1955 (orchestra version 1970)]. #New York: Henmar. [Cited in BAKER, p. 752].

1007. Holoubek, Ladislav (b. 1913). Czechoslovakia. *Professor Mamlock*. Opera [1966]. 1st: 21 May 1966. [Cited in BAKER, p. 791]. Based on a subject dealing with World War II.

1008. Hrušovský, Ivan (b. 1927). Czechoslovakia. *Against Death, Part I ("Hiroshima")*. Cantata [1961-1962]. [Cited in BAKER, p. 806].

1009. Ištvan, Miloslav (1928-1990). Czechoslovakia. *Blacked Out Landscape*. String quartet [1975]. [Cited in BAKER, p. 830]. Written in memory of those who died in World War II.

1010. Kabalevsky, Dmitry (1904-1987). Russia. *The Family of Taras*. Opera [1947]. 1st: Leningrad, 7 November 1950. #Moscow, 1955. *Classic Editions CE 3004 (Excerpts). Based on B. Gorbatov's *The Unsubdued*. M71507.K14F3. The subject is the Nazis in the Ukraine in 1942. Won a Stalin Prize.

1011. _____. *In Memory of Heroes of Gorlovka*. Symphonic poem [1965]. Deals with World War II.

1012. Kostić, Dušan (b. 1925). Croatia. *Kragujevac*. Orchestra and chorus [1962]. 1st: Belgrade, 5 February 1962. [Cited in BAKER, p. 952]. Deals with the Nazis in Yugoslavia.

1013. Koval', Marian (1907-1971). Russia. *Sevastopoltzy*. Opera [1946]. 1st: 28 November 1946. #Moscow: Soiuz sovetskikh kompozitorov, 1947. Libretto by N. Braun and Sergei Dmitrievich Spasski. M1508 (selections). Deals with the Nazi invasion of the Crimea.

1014. Kox, Hans (b. 1930). The Netherlands. *In Those Days*. Orchestra [1969]. Deals with World War II and the Battle of Arnhem.

1015. Kučera, Václav (b. 1929). Czechoslovakia. *Lidice*. Narrator, two reporters, announcer, soprano, chorus, instrumental ensemble, and tape [1972]. [Cited in BAKER, p. 976].

1016. Landré, Guillaume (1905-1968). The Netherlands. *Sinfonia sacra in memoriam patris* [1948]. 1st: Rotterdam, 7 November 1948.

#Amsterdam: Donemus, 1948. [Cited in BAKER, p. 1004].
Uses musical motives from his father's requiem.

1017. Levitin, Yury (b. 1912). Russia. *Requiem in Memory of Fallen Heroes*. Voice and orchestra [1946]. [Cited in HO, p. 308].

1018. Logar, Mihovil (b. 1902). Yugoslavia. *1941*. Opera [c. 1961]. 1st: 10 February 1961. [Cited in BAKER, p. 1076]. Deals with the Nazis in occupied Belgrade.

1019. Magne, Michel (1930-1984). France. *La symphonie humaine*. 150 performers [1955]. 1st: Paris, 26 May 1955. M1671.M (excerpt). For the victims of World War II.

1020. Maiboroda, Georgi (b. 1913). Ukraine. *Milana*. Opera [1957]. 1st: 26 October 1957. #Moscow: Sovetski i kompozitor, 1960. *Melodiya D06863/4 (selections). Libretto by Ahata Turchinska. M1503.M216M. [Cited in BAKER, p. 1117]. Deals with the Nazis in Transcarpathia.

1021. Manzoni, Giacomo (b. 1932). Italy. *Atomtod*. Opera [1964]. 1st. Milan, 25 March 1965. #Milan: Edizioni Suvini Zerboni, 1964. Depicts the destructive power of an atomic war.

1022. Matsudaira, Yori-Aki (b. 1931). Japan. *Dark Mirror: Young Orpheus on a Theme of the Atomic Bomb*. Opera [c. 1962]. 1st: Osaka, Japan, 16 April 1962. [Cited in SLONIMSKY, p. 1134].

1023. Matys, Jiří (b. 1927). Czechoslovakia. *To Those Fallen in May 1945*. Symphonic poem [1949]. [Cited in BAKER, p. 1168].

1024. Meitus, Yuly (b. 1903). Ukraine. *The Young Guard*. Opera [1947, revised 1950]. 1st: 7 November 1947. [Cited in BAKER, p. 1186]. Deals with World War II.

1025. Mihály, András (b. 1917). Hungary. *Sinfonia da requiem*. Orchestra [1946]. [Cited in BAKER, p. 1218]. "In memory of those killed as a result of war and persecution."

1026. Molchanov, Kirill (1922-1982). Russia. *Stronger Than Death*. Opera. 1st: 23 March 1967. [Cited in SLONIMSKY, p. 1026]. Deals with the fighting in Brest-Litovsk in 1941.

1027. _____. *Zori zdes tikhie (The Dawns are Quiet Here)*. Opera [1973]. 1st: 1 April 1975. #Moscow: Soviet Kompozitor, 1978. *Melodiya C10-07901-6. M1503.M717.Z67 1978. Deals with the Nazis in Russia.

1028. Mosolov, Aleksandr (1900-1973). Ukraine. *Glory to the Soviet Army*. Oratorio [1947]. [Cited in HO, p. 357].

1029. Moyzes, Alexander (1906-1984). Czechoslovakia. Symphony No. 4 in E-Flat. Orchestra [1947]. #Prague: Státne hydobné vydavatel'stov, 1963. [Cited in BAKER, p. 1260]. Deals with World War II.

1030. Nono, Luigi (1924-1990). Italy. *Die Ermittelung (the Inquest)*. Oratorio, electronic [1965]. 1st: Berlin, 18 October 1965. [Cited in BAKER, p. 1314]. Deals with World War II.
1031. Obrovská, Jana (b. 1930). Czechoslovakia. *In Memory of Hiroshima*. Symphonic poem [1962].
1032. Očenáš, Andrey (b. 1911). Czechoslovakia. *The Monuments of Glory*. Symphonic tetralogy for tenor, children's chorus, mixed chorus, and orchestra [1963]. Depicts the struggle of his people for freedom during World War II.
1033. Ohki, Masao (1901-1971). Japan. Symphony No. 5 ("Atomic Bomb"). Orchestra [c. 1953]. 1st: Tokyo, 6 November 1953. [Cited in SLONIMSKY, p. 967].
1034. Papandopulo, Boris (b. 1906). Croatia. *Legend of Comrade Tito*. Cantata for soprano, mezzo-soprano, alto, baritone, bass, narrator, chorus, two flutes, three trumpets, and percussion [1960]. 1st: 10 May 1962. #Yugoslavia: Akademija Znanosti Umjetnosti, 1968. Text by Vladimir Nazor. M1531.P24L4. Depicts Tito leading the Yugoslavs against the Nazis.
1035. Petrovics, Emil (b. 1930). Hungary [Serbian born]. *C'est la guerre*. Opera [1961]. 1st: 17 August 1961. *Hungaroton LPX 1208. Libretto by Miklos Hubay. Libretto ML50.P449C33. Deals with the Nazis in Hungary.
1036. Podéšt, Ludvík (1921-1968). Czechoslovakia. *Raymonde Dien*. Symphonic poem [1950-1951]. [Cited in BAKER, p. 1422]. In honor of the French fighters for peace during World War II.
1037. Raichev, Alexander (b. 1922). Bulgaria. *The Bridge*. Opera [1964]. 1st: Bulgaria, 2 October 1965. [Cited in BAKER, p. 1467]. Deals with the liberation from the Nazis.
1038. Ránki, György (b. 1907). Hungary. *The Tragedy of Man*. Opera [c. 1970]. 1st: 4 December 1970. *Hungaroton SLPX 11714. Includes a vision of a nuclear holocaust.
1039. Rota, Nino (1911-1979). Italy. *Napoli milionaria*. Opera [c. 1977]. 1st: Spoleto, 22 June 1977. [Cited in BAKER, p. 1548]. Deals with the American occupation of Naples in 1945.
1040. Różycki, Ludomir (1884-1953). Poland. *Warszawa wyzwolona (Warsaw liberated)*. Symphonic poem [1950]. [Cited in BAKER, p. 1555].
1041. Rupnik, Ivan (b. 1911). Slovak. *Song of the Dead Proletarians*. Cantata [c. 1947]. 1st: Belgrade, 14 December 1947. [Cited in BAKER, p. 1562]. Deals with occupied Yugoslavia.
1042. Sakač, Branimir (1918-1979). Croatia. *Simfonija o mrtvom vojniku (Symphony of the Dead Soldiers)*. Orchestra [1951]. [Cited in BAKER, p. 1576].

1043.   Schnittke, Alfred [Shnitke, Al'fred] (b. 1934). Russia. *Nagasaki.*
        Six-part oratorio [1958]. [Cited in HO, p. 488]. Dedicated to
        victims of the atom bomb.
1044.   _____. *Songs of War and Peace.* Oratorio [1959]. [Cited in HO,
        p. 488].
1045.   Schreiber, Josef (b. 1900). Czechoslovakia. *Maple Tree.* Female
        chorus [1962]. In commemoration of the partisans killed in
        World War II.
1046.   Seidel, Ján (b. 1908). Czechoslovakia. *Vyzva k boji (Call to
        Battle).* Cantata for mixed chorus and orchestra. [1946]. Text by
        Jan Zizka. [Cited in BAKER, p. 1680].
1047.   Smol'sky, Dmitry (b. 1937). Russia. *Songs of Hiroshima.*
        Chamber oratorio [1966]. [Cited in HO, p. 512].
1048.   Stasevich, Abram (1906-1971). Soviet. *Tale of the Great
        Patriotic War: Russian Soldier.* Oratorio [1965]. [Cited in HO,
        p. 520].
1049.   Šesták, Zdeněk (b. 1925). Czechoslovakia. *To Fallen Warriors.*
        Symphonic prelude [1949]. [Cited in BAKER, p. 1689].
1050.   Štědroň, Miloš (b. 1942). Czechoslovakia. *Kolo* (Wheel).
        Orchestra [1971-1972]. [Cited in BAKER, p. 1770]. Deals with
        World War II.
1051.   Toyama, Yuzo (b. 1931). Japan. *Toki (War Cry) Nos. 1 and 2.*
        Orchestra [1965]. [Cited in BAKER, p. 1901].
1052.   Vacek, Miloš (b. 1928). Czechoslovakia. *Lidice.* Chorus [1977].
        Text by Jaroslav Holoubek.
1053.   Válek, Jiří (b. 1923). Czechoslovakia. Symphony No. 11
        ("Revolutionary"). Piano trio, wind quintet, and orchestra
        [1974]. *Panton 11 0528. [Cited in BAKER, p. 1931].
        Commemorates the thirtieth anniversary of Czech liberation.
1054.   Walter, Arnold (1902-1973). Canada [Moravian born]. *For the
        Fallen.* Cantata [1949]. #Canadian Music Centre. [Cited in
        BAKER, p. 2003].
1055.   Wolff, Hellmuth Christian (1906-1988). Germany. *Inferno
        1944.* Oratorio [1946]. 1st: 15 March 1965. [Cited in
        SLONIMSKY, p. 1198].
1056.   Zechlin, Ruth (b. 1926). Germany. *Lidice.* Cantata. #Berlin:
        Neue Musik, [n.d.]. *Etern 720080.
1057.   Zimmerman, Udo (b. 1943). Germany. *Wenn ich an Hiroschima
        denke.* Opera [1982].
1058.   Znosko-Borovsky, Aleksandr (1908-1983). Russia. *Our Victory.*
        Cantata [1946]. 1st: Kiev, 8 May 1981. [Cited in HO, p. 627].

America (United States)

Antheil, George (1900-1959)

1059.   Symphony No. 6. Orchestra [1947-1948]. 1st: 10 February
         1949. #New York: Weintraub Music, 1954.
              M1001.A64 no. 6 1954a
              The first movement of this three-movement symphony
         depicts the battle as represented by Delacroix's painting *Liberty
         Leading the People*. The work ends on an optimistic note to
         symbolize the triumph over war.

Cowell, Henry (1897-1965)

1060.   Symphony No. 11 ("7 Rituals of Music"). Orchestra [1953-
         1954]. 1st: 29 May 1954, Louisville. #New York: Associated
         Music, 1955. *Louisville First Edition.
              M1001.C86 no. 11 1955
              A seven-movement symphony with the sixth movement
         subtitled "War" and written with many repeated patterns in a 5/4
         meter.

Dello Joio, Norman (b. 1913)

1061.   *Meditations on Ecclesiastes*. String orchestra [1956]. 1st: 17
         December 1957. #New York: Fischer, 1956. *CRI 110 and Bay
         City BCD 1017. Text from the third chapter of Ecclesiastes.
              M1103.D333M4
              A twenty-seven minute work in eleven sections based upon
         the text beginning with "To everything there is a
         season . . . and a time to every purpose under heaven." The
         last two sections ("A time of hate and of war" and "A time of
         love and a time of peace") illustrate music's ability to express
         peace and war without the use of text within the composition.
         The war section is fast and more dissonant throughout with
         repeated notes that reach *fff*. The peace section is slower, much
         softer, and ends *ppp* on a C-major chord, resolving any

dissonance that may have preceded it. Winner of the Pulitzer Prize.

Erb, Donald (b. 1927)

1062. *God Love You Now.* Chorus, tape, and unusual instruments, including four Marine band harmonicas, four plastic slide whistles, bongos, maraca, claves, castanets, tambourine, and four large pop bottles, partially filled with water [1971]. #Bryn Mawr: Merion Music, 1973. Text from Thomas McGrath's poem "Ode for the American Dead in Korea."
    M1531.E68G6
    A wild work with its unusual instrumentation and its various techniques. The music depends greatly on clusters, vocal glissandos, nonsense syllables ("wa wa" etc.), and has a ten-second improvisatory section with glissandos on the word "kill" repeatedly. See illustration no. 5.

Gillis, Don (1912-1978)

1063. *The Alamo.* Orchestra [1947]. #New York: Chapell, 1950. *London LPS 177.
    M1045.G47A4
    A thirteen-minute, pro-war work written "to portray musically the deep feelings of emotion that arise in the contemplation of the heroism and courage expressed by the defenders as they gave their lives in their defence of freedom." Dedicated to "the people of the state of Texas."

Krenek, Ernst (1900-1991) [Austrian born]

1064. *Pallas Athene weint.* Opera [1952-1955]. 1st: Hamburg, 17 October 1955. #Mainz: Schott, 1955. *(at Indiana University).
    M1503.K919P3 1955
    Deals with Athens' loss of the Peloponnesian War in 404 B.C.E.

1065. Symphonie ("Pallas Athene"). Orchestra [1954]. #Mainz: Schott, 1959.
    M1001.K88P3
    Krenek extracted this symphony from his opera. See item 1064 above.

Kurka, Robert (1921-1957)

1066. *Good Soldier Schweik*. Opera [1957]. 1st: 23 April 1958. #New
       York: Weintraub Music, 1962. *Koch International Classics
       370912H1 and Candide CE 31089 (Suite). Libretto by Lewis
       Allan after the novel by Jaroslav Hašek.
       M1503.K968G62 1962
       The suite is more often performed and recorded than the
       entire opera and consists of six movements. The "Lament" with
       its slow, lugubrious repeated patterns and pungent drum blasts
       represent the sadness related to war and killing. The fourth
       movement ("War Dance") is a frenetic, pompous dance with
       strong jazz-like ostinatos and syncopations relying heavily on
       brass and percussion. The swinging "Finale" represents
       Schweik's indestructibleness and the common person's victory
       over those who are stupid enough to wage war.

Maury, Lowndes (1911-1975)

1067. *Sonata in Memory of the Korean War Dead*. Violin and piano
       [1952]. #Hollywood: Protone Music, [n.d.]. *Crystal S-631.
       [No LC number available]
       In four movements: Allegro moderato; "Slowly with Slight
       Rhythmic Swing"; "Military!"; and "Elegy." The first is in
       sonata form and the second contains blues-like characteristics,
       but also serves as a lament. The third is a sardonic military
       march with double stops and pizzicati, and the fourth is a highly
       lyrical and expressive dirge. The music is tonal, well-organized,
       and attractive.

Phillips, Burrill (b. 1907)

1068. *The Return of Odysseus*. Baritone, speaker, chorus, and orchestra
       [1956]. #New York: Galaxy Music, 1967. *Illini Union
       Bookstore CRS-5. Text by Alberta Phillips.
       M1530.3.P5R52
       A set battle piece occurs between pages 66 and 79 in which
       the orchestra opens Molto feroce and remains *forte* to the end
       with the chorus shouting "Death to all."

Smith, Julia (b. 1911)

1069. *Remember the Alamo.* Wind orchestra, with optional narrator and chorus [1964]. #Bryn Mawr: Theodore Presser, 1965. Text based on a letter written by Lt. Col. William Barret Travis while under siege at the Alamo. Co-composed with Cecile Vashaw.
       M1245.S
       A twelve-minute programmatic work based on the events that led to Texas's independence from Mexico. The preface to the score contains a narrative program leading from sounds of "mission-fort, bells and an old Spanish hymn" to the Mexican "Deguello" and no mercy shown to the victorious Texans. Numerous folk and patriotic songs are included, e.g., "Will You Come to the Bower," "Oh Bury Me Not on the Lone Prairie," "Texas Hymn," and "America." The music is undistinguished, diatonic throughout, and tuneful.

Argentina

Ginastera, Alberto (1916-1983)

1070. *Cantata para America magica.* Cantata for fifty-three percussion instruments and dramatic soprano [1960]. 1st: 30 April 1961. #Buenos Aries: Barry Editorial, 1961. *Columbia AMS 6447. Based on pre-Columbian texts.
       M1613.3.G48C27
       A six-movement work with the third specifically about war: "Song of the Warriors' Departure." This movement is a frenetic, primitive dance of enormous energy unleashed by a full battery of percussion and a near-hysterical soprano lamenting the warriors heading off to war.

Belgium

Brenta, Gaston (1902-1969)

1071. *Le soldat fonfaron (The Boastful Soldiers).* Suite for Wind Quintet after music for the comedy of Plaute [1952]. #Antwerp: Edition Metropolis, 1956. *Alpha DB 47.
       M557.B825 S65
       A ten-minute work in seven brief sections with descriptive titles, including "Fanfaronnades," "Défilé militaire," and "Marche

des mercenaires ivres"; also contains humor, military marches, and fanfares.

Canada

Pépin, Clermont (b. 1926)

1072.   *Guernica.* Symphonic poem [1951-1952]. 1st: 17 May 1953.
        #Toronto: Canadian Music Centre, 1952.
            M1002.P4G8
            A seventeen-minute work opening with turbulent, repeated
        chords played *ff* and continuing its outrage and despair in various
        instrumental combinations and effects throughout the work. In
        three movements: "Poem symphonique," "Marche funèbre," and
        "Marche militaire."

Czechoslovakia

Barvík, Miroslav (b. 1919)

1073.   *Ruky prec od Koreje!* (*Hands off Korea!*). Baritone, chorus, and
        orchestra [1951]. #Prague: Orbis, 1951.
            M1530.B35R8
            A five-minute, glorious, heroic cantata protesting U.S.
        involvement in Korea. A Marxist-Leninist work ending, "Long
        live Stalin! Long live the peace all over the world!" in A major.
        The poem is printed as a preface in Czech, Russian, English, and
        French. The work is sectionalized and highly diatonic, largely in
        D major or D minor.

France

Barraud, Henry (b. 1900)

1074.   *Numance.* Opera [1949-1952]. 1st: Paris, 15 April 1955.
        #London: Boosey & Hawkes, 1970. *Columbia FCX 597.
        Libretto by Salvador de Madariaga.
            Libretto: JMD 72-265 (NYPL call number)
            Deals with the Spanish town of the title which revolted
        against the Roman consuls.
            Barraud also arranged a symphony from the opera before the
        opera was finished: *Symphonie de Numance.* Orchestra [1950].
        1st: Baden-Baden, 3 December 1950. #Paris: Salabert, 1951.

  *Columbia FCX 597. M1003.B25S94. A twenty-seven minute symphony in three movements: "Overture," "Nocturne," and "Interludes dramatiques."

Milhaud, Darius (1892-1974)

1075.   Symphony No. 4 ("1848"). Orchestra [1947]. 1st: 20 May 1948. #Paris: Salabert, 1948. *Erato STU 70452.
        M1001.M65 no. 4 1948
        This celebration of the 1848 Revolution against King Louis Phillipe contains four programmatic movements: "Insurrection," "To the Dead of the Republic," "The Peaceful Joys of Liberty Regained," and "Commemoration, 1948."

Poulenc, Francis (1899-1963)

1076.   *Dialogues des Carmélites.* Opera [1953-1955]. 1st: Milan, La Scala, 26 January 1957. #New York: Ricordi, 1959. *Angel 2 - CDCB-49331.
        M1503.P873D52 1959
        A powerful opera dealing with the execution of nuns during the French Revolution. The ending march and guillotine scene is one of the most chilling in operas written since World War II.

Germany

Dessau, Paul (1894-1979)

1077.   *Das Verurteilung des Lukullus.* Opera [1949, revised 1951, 1960]. 1st: 17 March 1951. #Berlin: Henschelverlag, Kunst & Gesellschaft, 1961. *Telefunken BLE 43096/7. Libretto by Bertolt Brecht.
        M1503.D475V5 1951
        Written in twelve scenes, this opera deals with a war in Rome before the time of Christ, using narration and chorus extensively. Using considerable dissonance and inflammatory text, the work was disapproved of by the East German government and subsequently withdrawn.

Eisler, Hanns (1898-1962)

1078.   *Winterschlacht-Suite*. Narrator and orchestra [1955]. #Berlin:
        Neue Musik, 1962. *Nova 885088. Text by Johannes R.
        Becher.
            M1003.G39 W55
            Contains eight movements with an introductory prelude for
        strings only. The narrator speaks in movements 4, 6, and 8.
        Movement 7, subtitled "Der Schrecken des Krieges" ("The
        Horrors of War"), includes a funeral march, but the entire scene
        sounds more like easy-to-listen-to movie music.

Henze, Hans Werner (b. 1926)

1079.   *Der Prinz vom Hamburg* (scene iii). Opera [1958]. 1st: 22 May
        1960. #Mainz: B Schott's Söhne, 1960. *(at Indiana
        University). Libretto by Ingeborg Bachman after Heinrich von
        Kleist.
            M1503.H528 P7 1960
            An opera in three acts; in Act I, scene iii the battle is re-
        enacted through cries of "Schießt" and fast repeated notes in the
        instrumental transition from daylight to the dark of evening and
        again to morning. Henze employs cross-rhythms, saxophone
        solos, and considerable dissonances in this section.

1080.   *Los caprichos*. Fantasia for orchestra [1963]. 1st: 6 April 1967.
        #Mainz: B. Schott's Söhne, 1967.
            M1045.H529 C4
            A twenty-minute, rather dissonant work based upon nine
        paintings of Goya: "Nadie se conoce," "Tal para qual," "El sueño
        de la razon produce monstrous," "Quien mas rendido?," "El si
        pronuncian y la mano alargan al primero quel llega," "De que
        mal morira?," "A quellos polvos. . .", "No hubo remedio," and
        "Linda maestra!"

Kelkel, Manfred (b. 1929)

1081.   *Musique funèbre: In Memory of the Innocent Victims of War*,
        Op. 5. Oboe and orchestra [1957; new version 1961 arranged for
        orchestra]. 1st: 21 October 1961. #Paris: Ricordi, 1957.
            M1002.K4T7 and M1060.K28 Op. 5
            A sixteen-minute, multi-sectional funeral composition
        incorporating sections of adagio-like laments with a stern

language. Considerable use of piano and percussion in the new version.

Great Britain

Britten, Benjamin (1913-1976)

1082.   *Billy Budd*, Op. 50. Opera [1951, revised 1960]. 1st: 1 December 1951. #London: Boosey & Hawkes, 1952. *London OSA 1390. Libretto by E.M. Forster and Eric Crozier, based on Herman Melville's novel.
         M1503.B8608B5 1952
         Act II, scene i contains a powerful, although aborted battle scene with raging chorus, repeated drum and brass blasts, and an explosive cannon shot.

Duncan, Trevor (b. 1924)

1083.   *War Front.* Orchestra [1950]. #London: Hawkes & Son, 1951.
         M1045.D86W3
         A three-minute march with changing meters, low strings, dissonant trills, harp glissandos and piano tremolos and attempts to suggest "quasi aeroplane, tanks, etc."

Griffiths, Vernon (b. 1894)

1084.   *Peace and War.* Chorus and brass band [c. 1952]. 1st: New Zealand, Anzac Day 1952. #New York: Boosey & Hawkes, 1956. Text by Bernard O'Brien.
         M1533.G843P4
         A twelve-minute, C-major work which is traditional, simple, and commemorates those who died in war.

Tippett, Michael (b. 1905)

1085.   *King Priam.* Opera [1958-1961]. 1st: 29 May 1962. #London: Schott, 1962. *London 414 241-2 LH2. Libretto by the composer, based upon Homer's *Iliad*.
         M1503.T595K52 1962
         Act II contains some of Tippett's most violent music as the battle rages and the chorus repeatedly cries out "War, War."

Greece

Theodorakis, Mikis (b. 1925)

1086. *Images d'Antigone*. Orchestra from ballet Antigone [c. 1961]. #London: Boosey & Hawkes, 1961.
M1003.T417I4
Sets a "danse de guerre" with driving repeated rhythms, dominating percussion, and high trills in the winds, all in changing meters.

Hungary

Arma, Paul (b. 1904)

1087. *Chant funèbre pour un guerrier* (from *Chants du silence*). Voice and piano [c. 1953]. #Paris: Heugel, 1953. Text by Claude Aveline.
M1621.4.A
A simple, two-minute song with a syllabic text setting in F minor and F-Phrygian.

Ránki, György (b. 1907)

1088. *1514*. Fantasy for piano and orchestra [1959]. (Version for two pianos and percussion completed in 1962). #London: Boosey & Hawkes.
M1011.R2E9
A twenty-one minute fantasy in five movements which depicts the Hungarian Peasant Revolt. The work includes descriptive titles over certain sections depicting the program (e.g., "On the March," "Peasant Sharpening his Scythe," "Breaking Down the Gates," and "Peasant Rebel"). For the section entitled "Defeat" Ránki uses polytonality in highly imaginative and emotional ways.

Szabó, Ferenc (1902-1969)

1089. *Föltámadott à tenger* (*The Sea is Rising*). Oratorio [1955]. 1st: Budapest, 15 June 1955. #Budapest: Zeneműkiadó Vállalat, 1960. *Hungaroton SLPX 11386.
M1533.S9854F64

In eight sections, the fifth ("Es kam der Tod") deals with a burning village and cries for help. The music is thick in texture, chromatic, and urgent in this passage. The sixth section in C major is entitled "Ungarn hört vom Siege," and the eighth is a heroic "Schlachtlied." Deals with the 1848 revolutions.

Italy

Ghedini, Giorgio Federico (1892-1965)

1090.	*Studi per un affresco di battaglia.* Orchestra [1961]. #Milan: Ricordi, 1962.
	M1045.G415S9
	A twenty-minute symphonic poem full of rhythmic ostinatos and jagged, dotted rhythms often at loud dynamic levels to establish the turmoil of war in music. The musical language is chromatic but tonal.

Nono, Luigi (1924-1990)

1091.	*La victoire de Guernica.* Chorus and orchestra [1954]. 1st: Darmstadt, 25 August 1954. #Mainz: Ars Viva, 1954. Text by Paul Eluard.
	M1530.N85V53x
	A thirteen-minute pointillistic work lamenting the destruction of Guernica; uses short but decisive crescendos, refined dissonances, and extensive brass and percussion.

Korea

La, Un Yung (b. 1922)

1092.	Symphony No. 1 ("Korean War"). Orchestra [before 1986]. #Unpublished.
	M1001.N115 no. 1 1950z
	In four movements: "Dawn" (full of ostinatos and highly tonal), "Sufferings" (in A minor), "Lamentation" (in A minor with repeated sections, simple, and sparse), and "Joy" (in C major, exhilarating with dotted rhythms).

Poland

Malawski, Artur (1904-1957)

1093. *Hungaria 1956.* Symphonic poem [1956]. 1st: Warsaw, 14 February 1958. #Warsaw: Przedstawicielstwo Wydawnictw Polskich, 1961.
M1003.M23H8
Deals with the Hungarian insurrection of 1956 and is in five movements: "Allegro barbaro," "Improvisazione," "Quasi rondo," "Notturno," and "Appassionato."

Panufnik, Andrzej (1914-1991)

1094. *Sinfonia sacra.* Symphony [1963]. 1st: Monte Carlo, 12 August 1964. #London: Boosey & Hawkes, 1967. *Unicorn UNS257.
M1001.P2S53
Composed as a tribute to Poland's Millennium of Christianity and Statehood, this twenty-two minute symphony includes the Polish hymn "Bogurodzica," which was often sung on the battlefields by Polish knights.

1095. *Sinfonia elegiaca.* Symphony [1957, revised 1966]. 1st: Houston, 21 January 1957. #London: Boosey & Hawkes, 1972. *Louisville LOU 624.
M1001.P2S45 1972
A twenty-four minute work expressing deep sorrow "for *all* the war victims of *all* nationalities, religions and races" through its three-part organization of lament—protest—lament.

Romania

Mendelssohn, Alfred (1910-1966)

1096. *1907 O mie noua sute si sapte.* Oratorio [1957]. 1st: Bucharest, 21 March 1957. #Bucharest: Editura Muzicala, 1959. Text by Tudor Arghezi.
M2003.M53O265
Written for the fiftieth anniversary of the Romanian Rebellion in 1907, it is in three parts: "La révolte," "L'Embrasement," and "La rançon." The music is often modal and uses irregular meters and subdivisions.

Soviet Union

Muradeli, Vano (1908-1970). Georgia

1097.   *October.* Opera [1961]. 1st: Moscow, 22 April 1964. #Moscow:
        Muzyka, 1967. Libretto by V. Lugovskoi.
        M1503.M986O48 1967
        A heroic opera in three acts, eight scenes with a prologue
        which celebrates the 1917 Russian Revolution.

Petrov, Andrey (b. 1930). Russia

1098.   *Songs of Our Days.* Symphonic cycle [1964].
        *Columbia/Melodiya M-34526.
        M1003.P488S6
        A bravura, thirty-minute work with a snarling, grotesque
        march that dominates a couple of its nine sections; includes
        titles such as "About War," "About Those Who Died in Action,"
        and "About the Revolution."

Shaporin, Yury (1887-1966). Russia

1099.   *The Decembrists.* Opera [1920-1953]. 1st: 23 June 1953.
        #Moscow: 1956. *Melodiya DO16867-72.
        *MS (NYPL call number)
        A monumental opera in thirty-six sections dealing with the
        December rebellion in Russia in 1825 and containing a ferocious
        battle scene. The music is tonal throughout and often in major
        keys.

Shostakovich, Dmitry (1906-1975). Russia

1100.   *Song of the Forests*, Op. 81. Oratorio [1949]. 1st: Leningrad, 15
        December 1949. #Moscow State Music, 1983. *Melodiya CM
        02699-700. Text by Evgeny Dolmatovsky.
        M2003.S54S67a
        In seven movements with boy's chorus as well as a mixed
        chorus, Shostakovich begins with the sorrows of the war that
        has just ended and builds movement by movement into the
        glorious future ending with the last movement "Glory."

1101.   Symphony No. 11 ("The Year 1905"), Op. 103. Orchestra
         [1957]. 1st: 30 October 1957. #New York: Leeds Music, 1958.
         *London 411939-2 LH2 and JVC/Melodiya VDC-1042.
              M1001.S567 Op. 103
              Commissioned for the fortieth anniversary of the Bolshevik
         Revolution and treats the events of Bloody Sunday. The
         movements are "Palace Square," "Ninth of January," "Eternal
         Memory," and "Alarm." Most graphic here is the second
         depicting the slaughter of innocent victims on Bloody Sunday.
         The work ends with bells ringing indicating the wonderful
         victory.

1102.   Symphony No. 12 ("The Year 1917"), Op. 112. Orchestra
         [1961]. 1st: Leningrad, 1 October 1961. #Leipzig: Breitkopf &
         Härtel, 1962. *London 417392-2 LH2 and JVC/Melodiya VDC-
         1044.
              M1001.S567, Op. 112
              Dedicated to the memory of Lenin, this forty-two minute
         symphony is in four continuous movements: "Revolutionary
         Petrograd," "Rasliv," "Aurora," and "The Dawn of Mankind."
         Brass and percussion invade much of the musical texture
         throughout the symphony. The opening of the second movement
         in particular depicts the civil war itself in its frenetic use of
         repeated notes, brass, and overpowering drums. The third
         movement opens ominously but soon erupts into a victory
         celebration.

Sviridov, Georgy (b. 1915). Russia

1103.   *Oratorio pathétique.* Oratorio for narrator, chorus, and orchestra
         [1959]. #Moscow: State Music, 1970. *Melodiya S65878.
              M2000.S95O72 1964
              In seven parts to be performed without pause, this
         remarkable, tonal oratorio contains one movement ("To the
         Heroes of Perekop") that directly portrays the glory of victorious
         battle.

SUPPLEMENT OF WAR MUSIC:
1946-1964

1104.   Amirov, Fikret (1922-1984). Azerbaijan. *The Pledge of the Korean Guerilla Fighter.* Voice and orchestra [1951]. [Cited in BAKER, p. 34].
1105.   Ardévol, José (1911-1981). Cuba. *Cantos de la revolución* [1962]. [Cited in BAKER, p. 51].
1106.   Arnič, Blaž (1901-1970). Slovenia. Symphony No. 9 ("War and Peace"). Orchestra [1960]. #Hans Gerig. [Cited in BAKER, p. 56].
1107.   Bagdasaryan, Eduard (1922-1987). Armenia. *1905.* Vocal symphony (with Dzherbashyan) [1956]. [Cited in HO, p. 39].
1108.   Blacher, Boris (1903-1975). Germany. *Krieg und Frieden.* Incidental music (after Tolstoy) [1955]. Texts by A. Neumann, E. Piscator, and G. Prüfer. [Cited in NEW GROVE, vol. 2, p. 767].
1109.   Blomdahl, Karl-Birger (1916-1968). Sweden. *Anabase.* Cantata for narrator, baritone, chorus, and orchestra [1955-1956]. 1st: Stockholm, 14 December 1956. #New York: Associated Music, 1958. Text by Saint-John Perse. M1533.3.B57A5. Deals with the retreat of the ten thousand from Persia around 399 B.C.E.
1110.   Brenta, Gaston (1902-1969). Belgium. *War Music.* Orchestra [1946]. [Cited in BAKER, p. 241].
1111.   Chaikovsky, Boris (b. 1925). Russia. *Overture on the 40th Anniversary of the October Revolution.* Orchestra [1957].
1112.   Chishko, Oles' (1895-1976). Russia. *Battleship Potyomkin.* Opera [1937-1955]. #Leningrad: Gos. izd-vo "Iskusstvo," 1938. M1503.C537 B7 1938.
1113.   Chugayev, Aleksandr (b. 1924). Russia. *Year 1905.* Symphonic poem [1955]. [Cited in HO, p. 97].
1114.   Ding, Shan de (Shan Te Ting) (b. 1911). China. *Long March Symphony.* Orchestra [1959-1962]. *Hong Kong HK1004 or 8.240292. Commemorates the Red Army's march from Hunan to Shansi between 1934 and 1935.
1115.   Dumitrescu, Gheorghe (b. 1914). Romania. *Tudor Vladimirescu.* Oratorio [1950]. 1st: Bucharest, 23 January 1955. *Electrecord ECE 035. M2003.D85&865. Deals with the nineteenth-century Romanian War of Independence.
1116.   Evans, Patricia (b. 1935). Great Britain. *Song Cycle for the Battle of Hastings.* Song cycle [1962].

1117. Fleming, Robert (1921-1976). Canada. *Hymn to War*. Baritone
       and strings [1954]. [Cited in BAKER, p. 550].
1118. Flyarkovsky, Aleksandr (b. 1931). Russia. *In the Civil War*.
       Oratorio. *Melodiya 33C10-0967780. [Cited in HO, p. 49].
1119. Forest, Jean Kurt (1909-1975). Germany. *Der arme Konrad*.
       Opera [1957]. 1st: 4 October 1958. [Cited in NEW GROVE,
       vol. 6, p. 706]. Deals with the German Peasant Rebellion in
       1514.
1120. Goleminov, Marin (b. 1908). Bulgaria. *Ivailo*. Opera [1958].
       1st: 13 February 1959. #Sofia: Nauka i Izkustvo, 1960. *Tape
       at Indiana University. [Cited in BAKER, p. 646]. Deals with the
       thirteenth-century Bulgarian uprising against the Mongolians.
1121. Hamilton, Iain (b. 1922). Great Britain. *A Testament of War*.
       Baritone and small ensemble [1961]. Text by Lucan. [Cited in
       NEW GROVE, vol. 8, p. 72].
1122. Humble, Keith (b. 1927). Australia. *Fragments of War Poems*.
       Soprano and instruments [1959]. [Cited in BAKER, p. 811].
1123. Kabalevsky, Dmitry (1904-1987). Russia. *Nikita Vershinin*.
       Opera [1954-1955]. 1st: 26 November 1955. *Melodiya 33ND,
       03876/7 (excerpts). [Cited in HO, p. 227]. Examines the Civil
       War in Russia's Far East.
1124. Khrennikov, Tikhon (b. 1913). Russia. *The Mother*. Opera
       [1952]. 1st: 26 October 1957. *Melodiya D-04420/1. [Cited in
       HO, p. 258]. Deals with the 1905 Russian Revolution.
1125. Kiyose, Yasuji (1900-1981). Japan. *Unknown Soldier*. Requiem
       [1963]. [Cited in BAKER, p. 923].
1126. Kodály, Zoltán (1882-1967). Hungary. *Czinka Panna*. Opera
       [1948]. 1st: 15 March 1948. Deals with the Hungarian struggle
       against the Austrians in 1703. See László Eösze, *Zoltán Kodály:
       His Life and Work* (London: Collet's, 1962), p. 43.
1127. Kohoutek, Ctirad (b. 1929). Czechoslovakia. *Ballads from the
       Rebellion*. Two cantatas [1960]. [Cited in BAKER, p. 940].
1128. _____. *Velky prelom (The Great Revolution)*. Symphony
       [1960]. [Cited in BAKER, p. 940].
1129. Kravchenko, Boris (1929-1979). Russia. *The Year 1917*.
       Oratorio [1959]. [Cited in HO, p. 285].
1130. Maiboroda, Platon (b. 1918). Ukraine. *Heroic Overture on the
       30th Anniversary for the October Revolution*. Orchestra [1947].
1131. Molchanov, Kirill (1922-1982). Russia. *Zaria*. Opera [1956].
       1st: Perm, 14 February 1956. #Moscow: Sovetskii Kompozitor,
       1959. Libretto by Sergei Severtsev. M1503.M7177a. About the
       Russian Revolution.

1132. Mosolov, Aleksandr A. (1900-1973). Ukraine. *Glory to the Soviet Army*. Oratorio [1947]. [Cited in HO, p. 357].
1133. Muradeli, Vano (1908-1970). Georgia. *The Path of Victory*. Symphonic poem. Chorus and orchestra [1950]. [Cited in HO, p. 360].
1134. Nikolayev, Aleksey (b. 1931). Russia. *October* [1957]. Deals with the 1917 Russian Revolution.
1135. Partos, Oedoen (1907-1977). Israel. *Ein Geb*. Symphonic fantasy [1952]. 1st: 1 October 1953. #New York: Leeds Music, 1954. M1045.P257E3. Deals with the fighting between Jews and Arabs.
1136. Popov, Alexander (b. 1927). Bulgaria. *Cantata about the April Uprising*. Cantata [1952]. [Cited in BAKER, p. 1430].
1137. Ránki, György (b. 1907). Hungary. *Battle in Peace*. Cantata [1951]. [Cited in NEW GROVE, vol. 15, p. 585].
1138. _____. *In the Year 1848*. Cantata [1948].
1139. Reif, Paul (1910-1978). America [Czech born]. *Requiem to War*. Chorus and percussion [c. 1963]. 1st: New York, 20 May 1963. [Cited in BAKER, p. 1493].
1140. Rice, William (b. 1921). America. *In Memoriam, The Alamo*. Orchestra [1953]. 1st: Houston Orchestra, 1953.
1141. Rodgers, Richard (1902-1979). America. *Victory at Sea*. Symphonic suite [1952]. 1st: Television broadcast, 1952. #New York: Williamson Music, 1955. *RCA Red Seal 66602 RC. M1527.8.R.
1142. Shaverzashvili, Aleksandr (b. 1919). Georgia. *Glory to October*. Voice and orchestra [1957]. [Cited in HO, p. 480]. Celebrates the 1917 Russian Revolution.
1143. Shebalin, Vissarion (1902-1963). Russia. *The Sun over the Steppe*. Opera [1958]. 1st: Moscow, 9 June 1958. #Moscow: Soviet Kompozitor, 1961. [Cited in HO, p. 483]. Deals with the 1919 Civil War.
1144. Simai, Pavol (b. 1930). Czechoslovakia. *Combattimenti*. Symphonic picture [1963].
1145. _____. *Victory*. Symphonic picture [1964]. [Cited in BAKER, p. 174].
1146. Tarp, Svend (b. 1908). Denmark. *The Battle of Jericho*. Symphonic poem [1949]. #Copenhagen: Engstrøm and Sødring, 1949. M1045.T18 Op. 5.
1147. Trudič, Božidar (b. 1911). Serbia. *1804*. Cantata [c. 1956]. 1st: 26 December 1956. Cited in BAKER, p. 1908]. Deals with a Serbian uprising against Turks.

1148.   Vacek, Miloš (b. 1928). Czechoslovakia. *Stop War!* Cantata
        [1953]. Deals with the Korean War.
1149.   Veselov, Vadim (b. 1931). Russia. *On Field Kulikovov.* Cantata
        [1963].*Melodiya C10-21023006. [Cited in HO, p. 579].

NOTES

1. Georg Katzer, notes to phonodisc *Aide Memoire*, Recommended Records RR 22.

2. Nationalities represented include: American, Austrian, Canadian, Czech, Dutch, German, English, Hungarian, Italian, Israeli, Polish, Rumanian, Scottish, Soviet, and Yugoslavian.

3. *Piano Quarterly* 33 (Summer 1985), p. 8.

4. *Piano Quarterly*, p. 8.

5. Notes to phonodisc, Serie Música Contemporánea ICP-C 17 Estéreo.

6. Notes to phonodisc, Serie Música Contemporánea ICP-C 17 Estéreo.

7. Notes to phonodisc, Composers' Voice 8702.

8. For a detailed analysis of Schoenberg's work, see Christian Martin Schmidt, "Arnold Schoenberg Kantate 'Ein Überlebender aus Warschau,' Op. 46." *Archiv für Musikwissenschaft* 33 (1976), pp. 174-88.

9. Willi Reich, *Schoenberg: A Critical Biography*, trans. Leo Black (Vienna: Fritz Molden, 1968), p. 222.

10. Reich, p. 222.

11. Malgorzata Gasiorowska, notes to phonodisc Schwann Musica Mundi VMS 1615, 1983.

12. Steve Reich, notes to phonodisc Nonesuch 9 79176-2.

VIII. THE U.S. AND VIETNAM CONFLICT:
AN ERA OF PROTEST

The Vietnam conflict was a new age war, a war with a culture of protest. Composers no longer wrote compositions to support war as had Aaron Copland, Samuel Barber, Roy Harris, Gail Kubik, and dozens of others during World War II; they openly protested the war and expressed anti-government sentiments directly and to a degree unprecedented in history.

In the spring of 1965 the majority of American citizens and composers supported their country's involvement in Vietnam.[1] As in both world wars, the American soldiers leaving to fight in Vietnam were eager to serve their country. The U.S. public, however, became disillusioned as the war grew increasingly unpopular. Nightly on the television news, the public observed for itself the horrors taking place on a continent far away. The civilian population felt directly involved. In *War and Peace in the Global Village,* Marshall McLuhan wrote: "We are now in the midst of our first television war. . . . The television war has meant the end of the dichotomy between civilian and military. The public is now participant in every phase of the war, and the main actions of the war are now being fought in the American home itself."[2]

A growing number of American composers of art music became active participants in this televised war. American composers significantly increased their war-related art compositions in the decade from 1965 to 1975, and these works exhibited an overt attempt to express political ideology. Roger Hannay, Lou Harrison, Gail Kubik, William Mayer, Elie Siegmeister, Robert Fink, David Noon, Richard Wernick, and John Downey wrote compositions directly protesting the fighting in Vietnam.

Mayer composed his *Letters Home* (no. 1176) "specifically as a protest to U. S. involvement in the Vietnam War and generally as a reminder of the tragic folly of all wars . . . [I wanted] to raise our consciousness . . . [to] the personal anguish war brings to such very young men on both sides and how hollow, slick and obscene the propaganda clichés sound when measured against the staggering price these young men must pay."[3] Although Kubik actively supported the United States during World War II, he opposed the Vietnam conflict. In 1970 he composed *A Record of Our Time* (no. 1168), in which he clearly indicated his vehement feelings about the war and "our time" in the seventies. "[This composition is] a protest piece [that] sums up my feelings about some aspects of the 20th century which put in doubt . . . the values of contemporary Western civilization: the Jewish Holocaust, our lack of concern about social injustices in America, our tragic involvement in Vietnam, the cancerous racism . . . which helped to tear the country apart."[4]

In writing about his *Peace Pieces* (nos. 1164, 1165), Harrison noted, "My personal reasons for composing the works that I have of the 'war/peace' kind are that there are some times when one wants to stand and scream aloud—'This is not right' . . . or 'This is all wrong' and personal frustration led me to express my rage in music."[5] Fink labeled his 1967 opera *Lysistrata and the War* (no. 1161) "an anti-war, anti-administration and anti-capitalist satire,"[6] and Wernick repeated this theme in *Kaddish-Requiem* (no. 1189) about which he said, "[T]he reasons were not complex [for writing my *Kaddish-Requiem*]; the war was wrong and immoral; it still is even with 20/20 hindsight, and it is the only way I have of protesting."[7] Charlie Morrow wrote, "At the time of composition [of *The Birth of the War God* (no. 1177)], the United States was waging an undeclared war in Vietnam. I chose to score the story of the Aztec war god because of the scale and sad irony of viewing the terrible war of the Aztec people who were wiped out by invading Europeans—us."[8] Siegmeister optimistically added, "Obviously, I hoped that [my composition] *The Face of War* (no. 1185) would shorten the miserable Vietnam disgrace by at least one minute—maybe it did!"[9]

Composers outside the United States contributed to the protest movement. Composers from Cuba, Germany, Italy, Canada, Japan, the Netherlands, France, Finland, and Australia wrote music about the Vietnam conflict. The Canadian composer Barbara Pentland suggested that her *News* (no. 1190) was

> an expression of disgust and protest against man's endless violence to himself and the environment. I started the work in 1968 when war atrocities appeared regularly as 'accepted' items of news, riots and violence broke out in cities and the devastation of pollution was being revealed everywhere. The only way I could 're-act' musically was by facing these now frequent reports with satire, scorn and in some cases flippancy.[10]

Many pop singers actively protested the war as well, and not only in their music, but through their arrests during peace marches and public protests. Popular protest songs gained momentum as the war continued. Phil Ochs, Joan Baez, Joe MacDonald, Bob Dylan, and many others actively protested the war. In France during 1966, Peter, Paul, and Mary revived "The Deserter," an anti-war folksong written in 1955. It immediately rose to the top five on the French hit parade before French authorities banned it.[11]

Unlike art composers, however, popular musicians could write a simple song in a matter of minutes, record it, and reach millions in a relatively short time. The text, however, was what made it war music— not the music itself. Popular music could better disseminate the words to a wide audience through radio, recordings, and live concerts, but music served only as a vehicle to spread the message of the text.

Some popular singers and song writers wrote pro-war songs early in the war. Near the beginning of the war, "Ballad of the Green Berets" and "Wish You Were Here, Buddy" had tremendous success, and Red Buttons made a recording of the "Pledge of Allegiance" to support the war. In 1971, after the massacre at Mylai and the trial of Lieutenant William Calley, Terry Nelson sang "The Ballad of Lt. Calley" to the tune of "The Battle Hymn of the Republic" to garner support for Lt. Calley, whom many viewed as a scapegoat. The song was immensely popular and sold over a million copies within the first week of its release. This support for the war and its soldiers as a whole, however, was negligible at best. As Gene Lees noted, "For the first time in U. S. history nearly all the songs were anti-war songs."[12]

Protest songs also arose in Vietnam. In Saigon, Trinh Cong Son protested the war with hundreds of anti-war songs. Thousands flocked to his concerts and purchased tapes and copies of his sheet music until the Saigon government banned his music in 1969. He wrote his songs because "I want to describe the war . . . I want to describe the absurdity of death in my country. . . . I sing what is on the minds of my listeners . . . I'm describing their sadness, their grief at the war."[13] Bernard Weinraub wrote in the *New York Times*, "Trinh Cong Son sings only of war and death—a mother weeping for her lost children, a young woman yearning for her dead lover, a brother hating and killing a brother."[14] One of his songs begins with the following lines: "One thousand years of slavery under China aggressors, 100 years of domination under the Western invaders, 20 years of ceaseless civil war; the fortune a mother bequeaths her children is a sad Vietnam, the mother's fortune is a mound full of graves, the mother's fortune is a brood of rootless bastards and a gang of faithless traitors."[15] One of his songs ends, "piles of flesh and bones are my mother and my brother."[16]

While no major art composers suffered incarceration during the war (as did some of the pop and folk singers), some did openly protest the war. On 24 May 1968, several composers held a "Composers and Musicians for Peace" concert at New York in which war-related compositions, such as Siegmeister's *The Face of War* (no. 1185), Mayer's *A Letter Home* (no. 1176), and David Diamond's *Prayer for Peace* were performed. Near the end of the war, Leonard Bernstein conducted an Inaugural Day Peace Concert in the Washington Cathedral. This event occurred on the same night and in direct competition with the concert held at Kennedy Center as part of President Nixon's inauguration ceremonies. The program at Kennedy Center included heroic, optimistic works: Tchaikovsky's *1812 Overture*, Copland's *Fanfare for the Common Man*, Beethoven's Fifth Symphony, and Grieg's Piano Concerto. For the "Plea for Peace" concert in the Washington Cathedral, Bernstein conducted Haydn's *Mass in Time of War* as "a counterpoint to the '1812 Overture,' the contrast with what's being played at the other concert."[17]

Even though some seats remained empty at the $250-per-person event at the Kennedy Center, thousands attended the peace event at the cathedral:

> People started lining up for the 9 p.m. concert at about 4:30 p.m. as rain was falling. The police estimated about an hour before the concert that there were 10,000 people waiting for admission to the cathedral, and a church spokesman said shortly before the concert began that there were 3,000 persons inside the structure and 'conservatively' 12,000 to 15,000 outside standing in the damp, misty night.[18]

The withdrawal of Vincent Persichetti's *A Lincoln Address* (no. 384), which had been commissioned to parallel the second inaugural address by President Nixon, also marred the inaugural concert. Because of the references to the Civil War and fears that "the text of the work might embarrass President Nixon," the Presidential Inaugural Committee deleted the Persichetti work from the program.[19]

The Vietnam conflict produced a new vision of war among nations. Henry Kissinger wrote, "Vietnam is still with us. It has created doubts about American judgment, about American credibility, about American power—not only at home, but throughout the world."[20] And Philip P. Beidler argued, "Vietnam was always, in a single moment, dreadful, funny, nightmarish, ecstatic. In its moments of highest drama, it was always its own best and worst parody."[21]

The complexity and surreality of this war inspired a different type of war-related musical composition. The rhetoric of war music changed because the war itself was so different. Gilbert Adair's remarks about Vietnam films illustrate the musical parallels as well: "In general the subject matter proved too complex, too multilayered to be comfortably confined within the closed plot structures—a beginning, middle and end in that order—that were natural to the American cinema."[22] Traditional structures of nineteenth-century and conservative twentieth-century music did not create the proper atmosphere for the hallucinatory nightmare of Vietnam, and most composers did not attempt to impose conservative styles on this vision of the war. The notable exceptions to this are Arnold Rosner's *A Mylai Elegy* (no. 1182) and Gregg Smith's *Beware of the Soldier* (no. 1186).

To deal with the Vietnam conflict in music, composers intensified the horror in the musical portrayal of war. Composers used electronic machine-gun fire, sounds of bombs exploding, indeterminate sections with singers shouting and screaming, and other realistic sounds. In *Letters Home,* Mayer asked that his soloist attempt to sing the highest notes that he had written even if his voice strained, "for whatever strain shows up in the voice would fit in well with the words at this point . . . [which are] 'It was me or her, but what in hell right did I have to kill a little child?'"[23] To approach the climax of his *Sayings for Our Time* (no. 1163), Hannay instructed the voices to sing "K.B.A." or "Killed by Air" seventeen consecutive times before breaking into a fully indeterminate section with all instruments and voices increasing to an unbearably loud dynamic level replete with screams and shrieks. In his *America Sing!* (no. 1162), Hannay used the sounds of bombs and machine guns to illustrate that the type of "song" America was singing was a song of war and destruction. In Frederic Rzewski's *Lost and Found* (no. 1204), the solo percussionist was instructed to perform stark naked or "nearly so" to portray a battered and dehumanized Vietnam veteran.

In part four of Kubik's *A Record of Our Time* (no. 1168), eight choral groups chanted and screamed various slogans such as "Better Dead than Red," "Kill the Krauts," "Zap the Japs," or "Hey, Hey, L.B.J., How many kids did you kill today?" at the same time.[24] As he wrote in the score, the "desired effect is that of a real pandemonium. . . . I would even prefer that the last 6 or 8 phrases be quite unintelligible and that one had the impression of a civilized chorus having gradually been converted into a raging, unreasoning and howling mob."[25] Hannay began the third movement of his *Sayings for Our Time* (no. 1163) with unaccompanied voices shouting "Kill for Peace." In Arthur Hills's *A Requiem for Vietnam* (no. 1167), an eclectic composition including church hymns, art chorales, and minimalism, the composer used an ostinato pattern on the text "Rice N' Lice" to parody the American soldiers marching through the rice fields in Vietnam.

Prior to the Vietnam conflict, composers used cynical or satirical texts almost exclusively in popular songs, such as "Der Fuerher's Face," making fun of the enemy. During Vietnam, however, numerous popular and art composers satirized their own troops. Hannay ended his *America Sing!* (no. 1162) with American soldiers counting off "one, two, three, four," speeding up the tape to make them sound like silly ducks marching off to war. According to Mark Behm, John Downey's *Almost 12* (no. 1160) makes the repeated use of the tune "'America' beneath a scattered and fragmentary musical texture . . . more a parody than a cry of indignation."[26] In Daniel Lentz's *Anti Bass Music* (no. 1172), the composer provided four optional endings that include "a reading of a list of American composers not killed in Viet Nam . . . [or] twenty-five to one hundred laughing machines."[27] In Salvatore Martirano's *L'sGA* (no. 1175), based on the Lincoln's *Gettysburg Address* and written during the height of the Vietnam War, an actor inhales helium gas "to change the sounds of a normal voice into a thin, high-pitched parody of speech . . . [which] is combined with films of war and near-deafening prerecorded sounds."[28] In his discussion of this work, Edwin London wrote, "Within this sound and visual setting, the text, one of the monuments of American political literature, seems like empty rhetoric."[29] Joseph Byrd's *The Defense of the American Continent from Viet Cong Invasion* (no. 1154), a "patriotic octet" performed from a one-page map showing Vietnam and America, contains no standard or even decipherable musical notation. He presents no instructions on how to perform the work. The title and the map were only making statements that, according to Byrd, were what the war compositions of the time were all about.[30]

This cynicism found in art music appeared frequently in popular music as well, as seen in Ralph Dale's and Ian Boydn's "Prayer for Peace" and Joe MacDonald's "Fixing-to-Die Rag." Even combatants in Vietnam wrote cynical songs to pre-existing tunes. Set to the tunes of "The Battle Hymn of the Republic," "The Wabash Cannon Ball," "The Night Before Christmas," "Froggy Went A-Wooing," "Silent Night," "On Top of Old Smokey," or many other folk tunes, the soldiers, sometimes with considerable profanity and black humor, sang of their fears, their hopes, their despairs, and even their good-natured fun while in Vietnam.

Not only did composers make fun of their own troops, they wrote laments for the enemy or considered the enemy's suffering equal with that of their own country. Ned Rorem dedicated his *War Scenes* (no. 1181) "to those who died in Vietnam, both sides, during the composition: 20-30 June 1969." Mayer showed the suffering of the Vietnamese in his *Letters Home* (no. 1176) through "letters from N. Vietnamese soldiers along with those of our own servicemen."[31] The most famous lament during the war, however, was Pete Seeger's popular song "Where Have All the

Flowers Gone," which Neil Sheehan claims was "perhaps the best known song of Vietnam."[32]

Other U. S. composers concerned themselves entirely with the tragedy of the Vietnamese victims. Arnold Rosner created a large-scale orchestral composition entitled *A Mylai Elegy* (no. 1182) because he "was particularly enraged, or you might say ashamed, about the fact that the American machine was perpetrating such things . . . [as the] ruthless brutality on the part of Lieutenant Calley and Captain Medina."[33] Morgan Wood composed a requiem "for the victims of Mylai," the Pulitzer Prize-winning composer Wernick provided a *Kaddish-Requiem* (no. 1189) for the victims of Indochina, and Francis Schwartz dedicated his *Caligula* (no. 817) to "victims of massacres," including Mylai. Dai-Keong Lee based his "symphonic prayer for world peace," *Canticle of the Pacific* (no. 1171), "on a Vietnamese children's song, a theme from the "Star Spangled Banner" to indicate our commitment in Vietnam, and a Buddhist chant from the Sanscrit."[34] In the program notes Lee wrote, "Although it is not programmatic, one can sense the calm, rolling countryside with children peacefully singing and dancing, imagine the devastation as the result of the conflict in Vietnam, and hear the chanting of Buddhists, who believe in non-violence and abhor the degradation of the people."[35] In no war before this had composers, as a whole, been so humanitarian in their concern for the enemy their own country was fighting, rightly or wrongly.

As in earlier wars of this century, composers actively wrote genuine war laments for their own soldiers wounded and killed. John Beall's *Lament for Those Lost in War* (no. 1150), Hill's *A Requiem for Vietnam* (no. 1167), Bruce Rogers Jackson's *Quartet in Memoriam for the Dead and Dying in Vietnam* (no. 1200), Donald Lybbert's *Lines for the Fallen* (no. 1174), and Robert Lombardo's *Largo for String Quartet* (no. 1173), commemorated America's war dead. Lybbert's composition is particularly poignant in its use of indeterminacy, clusters, and microtones to create a foreboding and tragic lamentation.

Victory compositions like those that applauded the end of World War II are almost nonexistent in the United States and other Western countries after 1973; a phenomenal number of peace compositions have taken their place. During World War II, composers wrote perhaps eight peace pieces world-wide, accounting for approximately five percent of the total number of war-related compositions. From 1965 to 1973, composers produced over thirty peace works, constituting approximately twenty percent of the total number of war-related works composed during these years. In the past two decades, composers from more than fifteen countries have written over sixty peace compositions.

Since 1965, most American composers have written war works as expressions of outrage and frustration with America's involvement in Vietnam. In less than three decades, American composers had moved from almost exclusive support for their government to outspoken individualistic protestations against what they felt were the evils of their country and their era. In no time before the Vietnam conflict had such a large number of composers produced such an extensive body of war-related art music contrary to the desires and policies of the government. In this short period, composers of war-related music turned a volte-face and radically changed their role in society, and, of necessity, their art itself.

In almost all cases, however, the art music failed to reach a wide audience. Despite Siegmeister's optimism that his composition may have helped speed up the end of the war, the art music failed to make a significant impact upon the war or the musical world itself (although George Rochberg and Krzysztof Penderecki, who wrote no works dealing with the Vietnam conflict, changed their styles radically near the end of the war). Only a small percentage of these works appears on recordings, usually in one recorded version on minor labels (with the exception of Crumb's *Black Angels* [no. 1158]); major publishers have exhibited little enthusiasm for publishing many of these works. While a large educated public reads novels about the Vietnam conflict, few (if any) of the art compositions dealing with Vietnam are known even in the music/academic world that produced so many of them.

During the last decade, films and novels about the Vietnam conflict have proliferated; however, no significant resurgence has appeared in either popular or art music. Since 1975, Americans have composed fewer than a dozen art-music compositions about the war. Composers, at least the major ones today, appear to have little interest in writing music related to the disastrous Vietnam conflict.

Nonetheless, the genre of war-related music continues. Over thirty popular war songs in the United States were recorded within a year of the Gulf War, and almost all uniformly supported the conflict. The few art compositions about the war that have appeared thus far, however, have been unanimous in their protest of U.S. involvement in the war. John Adams, Aaron Jay Kernis, and Jerome Kitzke have continued the tradition that grew out of the Vietnam conflict (nos. 1209, 1221, 1223). Although war music has changed significantly in the past seven centuries, there is no indication that this well-established tradition will die out anytime soon. As long as war exists, so too will the music that has accompanied, applauded, and cursed it. These hundreds of compositions, if nothing else, are a testimony to that fact.

ANNOTATED LISTING OF MUSIC DEALING WITH THE
VIETNAM CONFLICT: 1965-1990

America (United States)

Beall, John (b. 1942)

1150. *Lament for Those Lost in War.* Orchestra [November 1971-
       January 1972]. #Rochester, 1972.
          M1045.B42X L3
          In the preface to the score, Beall claimed this work was not
       a political statement, and was not necessarily related directly to
       any war. This Adagio, however, was written during the dark days
       of Vietnam and includes glissandos, indeterminate rhythms,
       clusters, and playing inside the piano to lament those killed
       because of war.

Bernstein, Leonard (1918-1990)

1151. *Mass.* A theater piece for singers, players, and dancers [1971].
       1st: Washington, D.C., 8 September 1971. #New York: G.
       Schirmer, 1971. *CBS M2K-44593. Text from the Liturgy of
       the Roman Mass and additional texts by Stephen Schwartz and
       the composer.
          M1503.B53M4 1971b
          While there are apocalyptic tinges in the Credo, the Agnus Dei
       turns into a nightmarish plea for peace of chaotic proportions,
       with the chorus and soloists singing and screaming "Dona nobis
       pacem," telling God they are tired of the violence and God's
       seeming inability to help us out here on earth. In this passage
       marked *ffff*, the chorus sings notated music, while members of
       the orchestra and blues singers freely shout and improvise at
       will. While not specifically about the Vietnam conflict, its anger
       grew out of the era in which it was composed.

Blumenfeld, Harold (b. 1923)

1152. *Songs of War.* Chorus with guitar obbligato [1970]. #New
       York: Seesaw Music, 1971. Text by Siegfried Sassoon.
          M1586.B655

A thirteen-minute work consisting of four songs: "Autumn," "Before the Battle," "Suicide in the Trenches," and "The Death Bed." The music is intense, forceful, and quite dissonant. Some falsetto is called for in the first song and Sprechstimme in the last.

1153.   *War Lament.* Chorus and obbligato guitar [1970]. 1st: St. Louis, 22 October 1972. *Gregg Smith Singers Recording Company. Text by Siegfried Sassoon.
         [No LC number available]
         Written because of the unwarranted war in Vietnam (letter to author, January 1985).

Byrd, Joseph (20th c.)

1154.   *The Defense of the American Continent from Viet Cong Invasion.* Octet [1968]. 1st: 3 December 1968. #John Cage, *Notation* (New York: Something Else, 1969), [n.p.].
         ML 96.4 C33 no. 1
         Called a "patriotic octet for eight or more instruments." Contains no decipherable music notation, only a map of Vietnam and California and the air attacks on various places in California.

Clarke, Henry Leland (b. 1907)

1155.   *The Young Dead Soldiers.* Chorus, solo, and piano [1970]. 1st: Boston, 18 October 1977. #New York: American Composers Alliance, 1970. Text by Archibald MacLeish.
         AMC M1552 C598 Y7
         Performed on the tenth anniversary of the date when drafted soldiers first turned in their draft cards. A straightforward work with options that the soloist may recite instead of sing and the chorus may sing in unison instead of in the three parts written. The music is somewhat dissonant and in traditional meters and rhythms.

Corner, Phil (b. 1933)

1156.   *One antipersonnel-type CBU bomb will be thrown into the audience.* No instruments [1969]. Never performed. #*Source* 6 (1969).
         [No LC number available]

Represents a philosophical statement instead of sound. Cope refers to this music as "an example of danger music used to express anti-war political views" (*New Directions in Music*, p. 103). Words instead of notes on score.

1157.   *Oracle* [c. 1969]. Tape.
[No LC number available]
Dedicated "to the opposition against the bombing of Hanoi."

Crumb, George (b. 1929)

1158.   *Black Angels.* Electric string quartet. [1970]. 1st: Ann Arbor, Michigan, 23 October 1970. #New York: C.F. Peters, 1971. *Elektra Nonesuch 9 79242-2.
M452
A protest against war, this is the most important war-related composition to come out of the Vietnam conflict. It consists of thirteen symbolic sections with numbers 7 and 13 representing good and evil. The middle section "7. Threnody II: Black Angels!" contains the most violent music and innovative string techniques and requires the performers to shout at various points the word "thirteen" in Japanese, Russian, Swahilli, and German. Other important recordings: CRI SC 283, Philips 6500 881, and Vox SVBX 5306.

Dello Joio, Norman (b. 1913)

1159.   *Evocations.* Mixed chorus and orchestra [1970]. 1st: 2 October 1970, Tampa, Florida. #New York: Edward B. Marks, 1970.
M1533.D358 E92
Contains two parts: "Visitants at Night" (text from Robert Hillyer's "Visitants in a Country House at Night") and "Promise of Spring" (text from Richard Hovey's "Spring"). The composer requests that the second part be sung by a "Young People's Chorus" if possible. The work is traditionally notated and ends with the "promise of spring" and a C-major chord.

Downey, John W. (b. 1927)

1160.   *Almost 12.* Chamber orchestra [1971, revised 1974]. #Bryn Mawr: Theodore Presser. *Non-commercial recording at AMC.
AMC M985.D751A4

A seventeen-minute, anti-war protest using spatial (unmetered) notation. The music is improvisatory, even though pitches and rhythms are notated for the most part. In between two furioso improvisatory sections sound distorted fragments of "The Star Spangled Banner" and "America." Includes numerous uses of glissandos, flutter-tonguing, pizzicatti, dissonant aleatoric processes, and bomb sounds from plucked bass strings.

Fink, Robert (b. 1933)

1161.   *Lysistrata and the War.* Opera with piano and trumpet in C (or any solo or piano alone) [1967-1970]. #Greenwich-Meridian, 1977.
M1503.F5025 L9 1978
A two-act, five-scene opera with a simplistic, diatonic score based on Aristophanes's *Lysistrata.* According to the detailed preface printed in the score, the composer described the music as "essentially Mozartian with a mixture of styles reminiscent of Handel, *My Fair Lady* and silent movie music." Its 28 May 1967 scheduled performance was cancelled because it was "too political" (and also because the leading male singer was drafted). The composer then "withdrew his opera permanently." Characters in the opera include Richard Stillouse Noxious, Spiral Upyou, General Wantsmorewar, and Democratea Diarrhea.

Hannay, Roger Durham (b. 1930)

1162.   *America Sing!* Tape and visuals [1967]. *Cassette at University of North Carolina at Chapel Hill.
[No LC number available]
Contains sounds of machine gun fire and sirens in a parody of America in Vietnam.

1163.   *Sayings for Our Time.* Chorus and orchestra [1968]. 1st: Winston-Salem, N.C., 2 August 1968. #Photocopy of Holograph and *cassette at University of North Carolina at Chapel Hill.
M1530.H36S3
Consists of three movements, "Getting With It," "Contextual Dynamics," and "Winning Hearts and Minds." Music is all notated, except for directed aleatoric passages near the end where everything is destroyed. Texts taken from newspaper items include such gems as "Groovy!! What's

Happening?! It's Wiggy! It's Twiggy," and catch-words and phrases of the time: "War of attrition, interrogation, de-escalation, pacification, and troop concentration."

Harrison, Lou (b. 1917)

1164.   *Peace-Piece I: from the Metta sutta.* Chorus and instrumental ensemble [1968]. 1st: 17 August 1968. #*Soundings* no. 3/4 (1972), pp. 112-28.
         JMM 78-18 no. 3/4 (NYPL call number)
         A warm, intensely lyrical work dedicated "to the memory of Martin Luther King." Displays Eastern influence in "slides" and other ornaments found in Buddhist chant and Korean court songs; strings and harp prevail, but ornamented by tasteful use of percussion.

1165.   *Peace-Piece II.* Narrator/singer and percussion [1960s]. #*Soundings* no. 3/4 (1972), pp. 129-37. Text by Robert Duncan.
         JMM 78-18 no. 3/4 (NYPL call number)
         An anti-war work (unlike *Peace-Piece I*) with an incessant narrator over ostinato percussion. Text compares President Johnson with Hitler and Stalin and intensifies from there.

1166.   *Peace-Piece III.* Voice, violin, harp, and drone strings [1953-1968]. #*Soundings* no. 3/4 (1972), pp. 138-39.
         JMM 78-18 no. 3/4 (NYPL call number)
         Subtitled a "Little Song on the Atom Bomb," a short song with a chant-like melody under sparse, sustained accompaniment.

Hills, Arthur (20th c.)

1167.   *A Requiem for Vietnam.* Chorus, narrator, soloists, and organ [1974]. 1st: 3 March 1974. #Holograph at LC.
         M2021.H672R4
         An elaborate service of twenty-five sections including pop music, church hymns, peace songs, newly composed protest works, dialogues, meditation, and calls for activism and understanding.

Kubik, Gail (1914-1984)

1168.   *A Record of Our Time.* Chorus, narrator, and orchestra [1970].
         1st: Manhattan, Kansas, 11 November 1970. #Melville, N.Y.:
         MCA Music, 1975. Texts by Mark Twain, Yeats, Vanzetti,
         John Jay Chapman, and from the Bible and a Negro spiritual.
         M1533.3.K8 R4
             An eight-part, forty-minute, oratorio-like protest piece.
         Most of the music is conventionally notated except for part IV:
         the most explosive section of the work consisting purely of war
         and political slogans, leading to a howling confusion of disorder.

Lang, David A. (b. 1957)

1169.   *Frag.* Flute, oboe, and cello [1985]. 1st: 1 October 1985. #New
         York: G. Schirmer, 1985.
         AMC M362.L269F8
             A seven-minute, minimalistic work taken from the idea of
         "fragging"—the intentional killing of officers by their own
         soldiers during the Vietnam Conflict. Not highly descriptive.

1170.   *Illumination Rounds.* Viola and piano [1982]. 1st: New York 22
         April 1982. #New York: G. Schirmer, 1983. *CRI CD 625.
         AMC +M22.L269I2
             A ten-minute work dealing with the mechanism of the guns
         themselves from a technical point of view instead of expressing
         their murderous intent.

Lee, Dai Keong (b. 1915)

1171.   *Canticle of the Pacific.* Chorus and orchestra [1968]. 1st: 10
         November 1969. #New York: Belwin Mills, 1970.
         M2020.L325C3
             In two parts, with the second based upon text from
         Saddharma Pundarika Sutra chanted and set to Buddhist music. A
         lyrical fifteen-minute work which, in addition to the chant,
         contains a Vietnamese children's song and "The Star Spangled
         Banner."

Lentz, Daniel (b. 1942)

1172.   *Anti Bass Music.* Graphic score: drawing of various guns and
         tanks, and cannons for speaker and "stringer." [c. 1969].

#Example of score printed in David Cope, *New Directions in Music*, 3rd. ed. (Dubuque, Iowa: William C. Brown, 1981), p. 103.

[No LC number available]

Uses graphic notation to bring the sounds of the battlefield to the audience. See Cope (p. 103) for additional information.

Lombardo, Robert (b. 1932)

1173.　*Largo for String Quartet.* String quartet [1969]. *Crystal Records S 861.

[No LC number available]

A very slow, seven-minute work with no programmatic effects other than its dreadfully lethargic tempo and sustained chords. An effective work with string harmonics and a striking sense of dissonance and resolution.

Lybbert, Donald (1923-1981)

1174.　*Lines for the Fallen.* Soprano and two pianos tuned a quarter-tone apart [1967]. #New York: C.F. Peters, 1969. *Odyssey 3216 0162. Text by William Blake and from the Mass for the Dead.

M1621.L

A poignantly dissonant, eight-minute work serially organized except for clusters and sporadic aleatoric sections. Rhythms are not notated specifically; instead, certain shaped-notes indicate longer note values creating a proportional score. The music is largely pointillistic and contains a new system of dynamic markings using a "+," "x," "z," and "-" for directions.

Martirano, Salvatore (b. 1927)

1175.　*L's.G.A.* A gas-masked performer, helium bomb, two-track tape, and three 16mm movie projectors [1967-1968]. *Polydor 24.5001. Text by Abraham Lincoln.

[No LC number available]

Perhaps the most outrageous anti-war work of the period. See page 322 for additional information.

Mayer, William (b. 1925)

1176.   *Letters Home*. Mixed chorus, soloists, speakers, and orchestra [1968]. 1st: 24 May 1968. #New York: MCA Music, 1968. Texts are taken from letters of soldiers fighting in Vietnam.
         M1533.3.M
         This eight-minute work includes various speaking parts (e.g., officials and generals) and soloists (soldiers, a pop singer, and a Buddhist monk). Although not recorded and not well-known, its power lies in its convergence of graphic text with its austere, dissonant music.

Morrow, Charlie (b. 1942)

1177.   *The Birth of the War God*. Vocal sextet. #Other Media, 1981. *Laurel Record LR-840CD. Text from Angel Marta Garibay's *Epica Hahuat 1*.
         M1529.5.M
         Experiments with several fascinating vocal techniques, primarily a type of chanting (trance singing) which makes it unique among the war-related works; also includes various types of styles including moments of blues and gospel. Its focus is on the ancient mythology that connects the Aztecs with the Asians who were conquered by the invading Europeans.

Noon, David (b. 1946)

1178.   *Psalm*, Op. 17. Chorus, tenor, flute, cello, and piano [1968]. #Claremont: D. Noon, 1968. Text from Psalm 120.
         [OCLC 18757352]
         A subtle, intense, work in a dissonant style; the tenor represents "the voice of the prophet raging against injustice. The instrumental trio is often called upon to reflect the anguish of war. The wordless chorus symbolizes the great mass of suffering people, people caught in the midst of war" (cited in Arnold, *War, Peace and the Apocalypse in Art Music*, p. 540).

Powell, Morgan (b. 1938)

1179.   *Darkness No. 2*. Brass quintet and percussion [1970-1971]. 1st: Festival of Contemporary Arts at the University of Illinois, 1971. #La Jolla, California: Lingua, 1978. *Ubres EN-203.
         M785.P

An experimental, proportionally notated work with improvisatory passages, including laughter, conversation, cuckoos, whistles, whispers, and hand sirens.

Riley, Terry (b. 1935)

1180. *A Rainbow in Curved Air*. Instrumental ensemble [1970]. *Columbia MS 7315.
[No LC number available]
A minimalistic work with an idealistic preface about the end of war and a world with no need for the Pentagon. The music has no direct relation to war other than the preface itself.

Rorem, Ned (b. 1923)

1181. *War Scenes*. Baritone and piano [1969]. 1st: 5 November 1969. #New York: Boosey & Hawkes, 1971. *Desto DC 7107. Texts by Walt Whitman.
M1621.R
Consists of five songs dedicated "to those who died in Vietnam, both sides, during the compositions: 20-30 June 1969." Harsher and angrier than usual for Rorem's music.

Rosner, Arnold (b. 1945)

1182. *A Mylai Elegy*, Op. 51. Orchestra [1971]. 1st: Evergreen Colorado, 1974. #NYPL.
AMC M1045.R822Mp
Dedicated to the victims of Mylai, Kent State, and Jackson State. A large-scale, impressive, twenty-six-minute symphonic poem in a musical language reminiscent of Shostakovich. Rosner stated: "I had very strong feelings about the Vietnam War and about Mylai and was motivated by the idea of working on such a composition. . . . When I read the news of the Kent State massacre, I was so angry about that that . . . I was full speed ahead working on *Mylai Elegy*" (cited in Arnold, *War, Peace, and the Apocalypse in Art Music*, p. 548).

Schifrin, Lalo (Boris) (b. 1932) [Argentine born]

1183. *Rock Requiem*. Chorus, electronic instruments, and orchestra [c. 1968]. *Verve V6 8801.
[No LC number available]

A large-scale fusion of rock elements with the requiem format written for those killed in the Southeast Asia War.

Schwartz, Francis (b. 1940)

* *Caligula.* Voices, prepared piano, concrete sounds, and tape [1975]. See item 817 above.

Sens, Charles (20th c.)

1184.   *War Songs.* Voice and piano [1973]. #Unpublished manuscript. Texts by Olivier de Magny, Ts'Ao Sung, Ralph Chaplin, Marcel Martinet, Jacques Prevert, Eva Marriam, Basho, Stephen Crane, Archibald MacLeish, Toyohiko Kagawa, a G.I. who scribbled lines on a latrine wall during World War II, and a little girl in a Nazi death camp.
         [No LC number available]
         Dedicated to those who do not believe in war. Consists of ten songs written on diverse texts and well ordered to make an effective cycle in a dissonant, yet often tonal, musical language.

Siegmeister, Elie (1909-1991)

1185.   *The Face of War.* Songs for voice and orchestra or piano [1968]. 1st: New York, 24 May 1968. #New York: Carl Fischer, 1978. *CRI 416. Text by Langston Hughes.
         M1613.S57F3
         Consists of five short songs highlighted by a touching, simple setting of "Peace" and a dramatic "War."

Smith, Gregg (b. 1931)

1186.   *Beware of the Soldier.* Chorus and orchestra [1975]. 1st: Fort Worth, May 1969. #New York. G. Schirmer, 1975. *CRI SD 341. Texts by Thomas Hardy, William Blake, John Keats, Stephen Crane, and Mark Twain.
         M1609.S
         A traditional forty-minute oratorio based upon selected war texts and quoting "L'Homme Armé"; it uses some twelve-tone structures for the elegies, but largely is tonal and simple. Smith thought of the work as a "religious composition," although he admits it could be thought of as anti-war.

Talma, Louise (b. 1906)

1187.   *Voices of Peace.* Chorus and strings [1973]. 1st: Philadelphia, 10 February 1974. Text based on the Bible, the missal, St. Francis of Assisi, and Gerard Manley Hopkins.
         [No LC number available]
         "It owed its inspiration to the news on January 28, 1973, that peace was coming to Vietnam" (Ewen, p. 651).

Tenney, James (b. 1934)

1188.   *Viet Flakes.* Electronic tape [1970s]. For a Carolee Schneemann film on the Vietnam war.
         [No LC number available]
         "Consists of snatches of popular rock'n'roll songs from the mid-sixties . . . Asian musics (probably Vietnamese) and western classical music, all more or less randomly spliced together." Cited in "Music of James Tenney," (*Sounding*, 1984), p. 173.

Wernick, Richard F. (b. 1934)

1189.   *Kaddish-Requiem for the Victims of Indo-China.* Mezzo-soprano, cantor, flute, alto flute, clarinet, bass clarinet, violin, sitar, piano, and percussion [1971]. 1st: Philadelphia, 1971. #Bryn Mawr: Theodore Presser, 1971. *Nonesuch 71303.
         [No LC number available]
         A nineteen-minute, deftly orchestrated work that grew out of the turbulent sixties. The first movement uses fragments of Brahms's *German Requiem* in a highly dissonant and rhapsodic manner; the second is a collage of the *Kaddish* and the last a setting of the *Requiem aeternam* with quotes from Palestrina's *Veni Sancti Spiritus.*

Canada

Pentland, Barbara (b. 1912)

1190.   *News.* Virtuoso voice and orchestra [1968-1970]. 1st: Ottawa, 15 July 1971.
         [No LC number available]

Sets various texts from the news media in styles including plain-chant, nursery rhymes and carols, and contrapuntal quotations, and uses musical quotations from the "Dies irae" and "We Shall Overcome." In twenty-six minutes, she includes Sprechstimme, quarter-tones, and text-distortion. See Sheila Eastman and Timothy J. McGee, *Barbara Pentland* (Toronto: University of Toronto Press, 1983), p. 111.

Czechoslovakia

Košut, Michal (b. 1954)

1191.   *America Dies in Asia With Me.* Chorus and piano [1979, revised 1986].
          [No LC number available]
          A six-minute composition based on text taken from a fragment of the Peace Agreement of King George of Podebrady and letters of American soldiers killed during the Vietnam conflict. Cited in "Michal Košut," CZECH.

Kubík, Ladislav (b. 1946)

1192.   *Lament of Fighter's Wife.* Soprano, Vietnamese female narrator, viola, bass clarinet, piano, and percussion [1974]. Based on a Vietnamese poem by Dang-tram-Tson and Doan-thi-Diem.
          [No LC number available]
          An eleven-minute chamber cantata protesting those who planned and executed the war in Vietnam during the sixties and seventies. Won first place in the UNESCO Composers' Tribune for Young Composers in 1974. Cited in "Ladislav Kubík," CZECH.

France

Tomasi, Henri (1901-1971)

1193.   *Chant pour le Vietnam.* Symphonic poem for wind ensemble and percussion [c. 1969]. 1st: Paris, 7 December 1969. #Bryn Mawr: Theodore Presser, 1970.
          M1002.T655.C5
          Inspired by a text from Sartre quoted in the preface to the score about the difficulties of acting human in an inhuman world. An angry, fifteen-minute work characterized by loud

dynamics (and markings of marcato, pesante, etc.), changing meters, numerous repeated-pitched melodies, and ostinatos bordering on primivitism.

Germany

Dessau, Paul (1894-1979)

1194. *Geschäftsbericht*. Cantata for solo voices, percussion, two pianos, and double basses [1967]. 1st: 29 April 1967. #Berlin: Neue Musik, 1969. *Reel tape at Indiana University. Text by Volker Braun.
      M1531.D44 G3
      An enormous polemic work based upon six photographs dealing with American politics and U.S. involvement in the Vietnam conflict. The first shows Lyndon Johnson and Hubert Humphrey at a barbecue. The remaining five show scenes from the conflict, concluding with one of dead U.S. soldiers in Da-Dran Valley. The chorus relies upon Sprechstimme, shouting, and glissandos, while the piano uses clusters (which end the work) and the percussion plays short *fortissimo* blasts. Soprano solo concludes *ff* on a high "D."

Italy

Nono, Luigi (1924-1990)

1195. *Al gran sole carico d'amore*. Opera [1975]. 1st: 11 February 1978. #Milan: Ricordi, 1978. Libretto by Bertolt Brecht, Tania Bunke, Fidel Castro, Che Guevera, Dimitrov, Gorki, Gramsci, Lenin, Marx, Louise Michel, Pavese, Rimbaud, Celia Sanchez, and Haydée Santamaria.
      ML410.N667A8 1978
      Deals with various wars including Vietnam, particularly in the sixth part of the second act: Prigionieri politici in carcere: a) guerrigliere del Sud Vietnam.
      Nono also wrote several other works that in some way dealt with the Vietnam conflict: *A floresta é jovem e cheja de vida.* Oratorio [1966]. Texts taken from declarations by the Vietnam guerilla fighters. Dedicated to the Vietnam Nationalen Befreiungsfront; *Contrappunto dialettico alla mente* [1968]. *DG 2561 044. A protest of Vietnam and the death of Malcolm X; and *Siamo in gioventù del Vietnam* [1973].

The Netherlands

Schat, Peter (b. 1935)

1196.   *On Escalation*, Op. 18. Six solo percussionists and orchestra
         [1968]. 1st: Amsterdam, 31 May 1968 at a "politico-
         demonstrative experimental concert." #Amsterdam: Donemus,
         1968. *Attacca Babel 8531-6.
         M1038.S28O5
         Dedicated to the memory of Che Guevara, this experimental
         composition, written primarily in graphic notation, includes
         considerable improvisation, clusters, and double harmonics in
         the winds, for which a table is given at the beginning of the
         score to show how to create these sounds.

SUPPLEMENT OF MUSIC DEALING WITH THE
VIETNAM CONFLICT: 1965-1990

1197.   Anderson, T.J. [Thomas Jefferson] (b. 1928). America. *Soldier
         Boy Soldier*. Opera [1982]. 1st: Bloomington, Indiana, 23
         October 1982. #New York: American Composer's Alliance,
         1982. *(at Indiana University). M1500.A74 S6 1982.
1198.   Ardévol, José (1911-1981). Cuba [Spanish born]. *Por Viet-Nam*
         [1966]. Text by Fidel Castro. [Cited in BAKER, p. 51].
1199.   Blanco, Juan (b. 1920). Cuba. *Poema espacial No. 3 ("Viet-
         Nam")*. Tape [1968]. [Cited in BAKER, p. 192].
1200.   Jackson, Bruce Rogers (20th c.). America. *Quartet in Memoriam
         for the Dead and Dying of Vietnam* [1978]. [Cited in *Give Peace
         a Chance: Music and the Struggle for Peace*, ed. Marianne
         Philbin (Chicago: Chicago Review, 1983), p. 121].
1201.   Ohki, Masao (1901-1971). Japan. Symphony No. 6
         ("Vietnam"). Orchestra [1970]. [Cited in BAKER, p. 1332].
1202.   Pentland, Barbara (b. 1912). Canada. *Songs of Peace and Protest*.
         Piano [1968]. [Cited in Eastman and McGee, p. 111].
1203.   Ruzicka, Peter (b. 1948). Germany. *Esta noche*. Alto flute,
         English horn, viola, and cello [1967]. [Cited in NEW GROVE,
         vol. 16, p. 353]. Funeral music for Vietnamese victims.

1204.   Rzewski, Frederic (b. 1938). America. *Lost and Found.* Solo
        percussion [1985].
1205.   Salzman, Eric (b. 1933). America. *The Peloponnesian War.*
        Full-evening dance/theater work [1967-1968]. 1st: Brockport,
        N.Y., 1968. Choreographed and performed by Daniel Nagrin.
1206.   Tuominen, Harris (20th c.). Finland. *My Lai.* Percussion and
        strings [1971]. #Finnish Music Center.
1207.   Wesley-Smith, Martin (b. 1945). Australia. *Vietnam Image.*
        Tape [1969-1970]. [Cited in *International Who's Who in Music
        and Musicians Directory* (Cambridge: Melrose, 1990), p. 890].
1208.   Wood, Morgan (20th c.). America. *Dona eis requiem (for the
        Victims of My Lai)* [1970s]. [Cited in *Give Peace a Chance:
        Music and the Struggle for Peace,* p. 122].

ANNOTATED LISTING OF WAR COMPOSITIONS:
1965 to 1990

America

Adams, John (b. 1947)

1209. *El Dorado.* [1991]. 1st: New York, January 1992.
        [No LC number available]
        The first movement was Adams's response to the Gulf War.
        See Andrew Porter, *New Yorker* (3 February 1992), p. 74.

Albright, William (b. 1944)

1210. *Jericho Battle Music.* Organ and trumpet [1976]. #New York:
        Henmar, 1981.
        M184.A
        In three movements, this fifteen-minute work is dramatic in
        its irregular rhythms and dissonances. The last movement is a
        ground bass (usually in the organ pedals) symbolizing the seven-
        day siege.

Anderson, Eugene (b. 1944)

1211. *The Perception of War.* Symphonic poem. *Commercially
        released by composer.
        [No LC number available]
        Depicts a man seeing first-hand the terrors of the battle he is
        in the midst of and incorporates the sounds of cymbals, drums,
        and low brass to create this horrifying experience.

Ballard, Louis (b. 1931)

1212. *Incident at Wounded Knee.* Chamber orchestra [1974]. St. Paul
        Minnesota, 1st: 4 May 1974. #New York: Belwin Mills, 1975.
        M1003.B182 I5
        A four-movement work written as a commemoration of the
        massacre of the Oglala Sioux in 1890. The work is not
        programmatic, but the third movement ("Blood and War") evokes

war with its changing meters, sporadic trills, glissandos, and repeated sixteenth-note patterns.

Bazelon, Irwin Allen (b. 1922)

1213.   Symphony No. 6 ("Day War"). Orchestra [1970]. 1st: Kansas City, Missouri, 17 November 1970. #Unpublished.
[No LC number available]
Incorporates music the composer wrote for the film *Survival '67* dealing with the Israeli Six-day War. The opening movement does not use sound effects to depict the war, but rather attempts to capture the dramatic intent of the war experience. Cited in BAKER, p. 127.

Binkerd, Gordon (b. 1916)

1214.   *The Battle.* Two trumpets, two cornets, three horns, four trombones, and five percussionists [1973]. #New York: Boosey & Hawkes, 1973.
M985.F
A six-minute arrangement and elaborate glorification of Frescobaldi's keyboard work *Capriccio sopra la battaglia.* See item number 118.

Dana, Walter (b. 1902)

1215.   *Israelis' Victory Dance: Dancing in the Streets After the Six Days War.* Orchestra [1971]. #Miami Beach: Dana, 1971.
AMC M1045.D171I8
A brief, five-page score full of ostinatos and repeated pitches but with no real programmatic effects.

Eaton, John (b. 1935)

1216.   *Danton and Robespierre.* Opera [1978]. 1st: Bloomington, 21 April 1978. #Delaware Water Gap, Pa.: Shawnee, 1978. *CRI IUS 421. Libretto by Patrick Creagh.
ML50.E17D3 1978 (Libretto)
Based on the events of the French Revolution, this massive opera has extended scenes of mass demonstrations and reeks with conspiracies and infightings of the protagonists.

Fulkerson, James (b. 1945)

1217.   *Bombs*. Bass trombone and prepared piano [1976]. #New York:
        Seesaw Music, 1982.
            JNH 86-10 (NYPL call number)
            A four-page, experimental work with numerous special
        effects. It begins *fff* with a sustained E-flat in the trombone over
        which the piano plays tremolo-like alternating chords as fast as
        possible, intensifying to *ffff* and louder. After numerous clusters,
        multiphonics, glissandos, and repeated notes, the work ends with
        the last measure repeated over and over again "until exhaustion."

Horner, Wesley (20th c.)

1218.   *War Prayer*. Chorus, flute, oboe, bassoon, French horn, guitar,
        and two clarinets. [1971]. #Manuscript in Library of Congress.
        Text by Mark Twain.
            M2020.H778W4
            Uses whispering and spoken text in addition to singing. In
        four brief movements and includes some dramatic flutter-
        tonguing in the flutes.

Husa, Karel (b. 1921) [Czech born]

1219.   *Music for Prague 1968*. Band (later orchestra) [1968]. 1st:
        Washington, D. C., January 1969. #New York: Associated
        Music, 1969. *Louisville S-722.
            M1060.H95M9
            Without doubt, the most performed war-related work
        composed after World War II, having received over 7,000
        performances since 1969. The four-movement work contains
        some aleatoric passages, one movement of only percussion
        instruments, the theme of the Hussite war song "Ye Warriors of
        God and His Law," and a fierce, concluding Toccata. Written as a
        protest against the Soviet invasion of Czechoslovakia in 1968.

1220.   *The Trojan Women*. Ballet for orchestra [1981]. 1st: Louisville,
        28 March 1981. #New York: G. Schirmer, 1981. *Louisville
        775.
            M1003.H955 T7 1988
            A polemic to awaken us all to the extended history humans
        have of killing one another in the name of war. See Ellen Hall,

"Karel Husa's ballet: a plea for peace," *Potential* 6 (12 March 1981), p. 1.

Kernis, Aaron Jay (b. 1960)

1221. Symphony No. 2. Orchestra [1991]. 1st: 15 January 1992.
[No LC number available]
In three movements "Alarm," "Air/Ground," and "Barricade," it directly confronts issues raised by the Gulf War. The ending is noteworthy for its *ffffff* ending with the explosive sounds of tam-tams. See Andrew Porter, *New Yorker* (3 February 1992), p. 74.

Kitzke, Jerome (b. 1955)

1222. *Box Death Hollow: Wounded Knee Creek (1890-1990)*. Male and female voices, male chorus, and orchestra including unusual instruments such as twelve harmonicas [1990]. #Jerome Kitzke, 1990. Text by the composer.
AMC M1531.K62B7
"Written on the centennial of the massacre of Big Foot's Miniconjous Sioux," this work has eighteen sections, with the only texts being the names of Indians and places related to the massacre. The climactic part occurs when the chief is murdered, depicted by glissando clusters in harmonicas and a screaming chorus shouting "with unbearable agony." Each of the names of the massacred Indians is called out one after another with strong, punctuated *sfz* blasts from the orchestra. At the end of naming fifty-eight people, a four-second silence ensues before breaking out "like a machine gun—insane," the full orchestra and chorus gradually emerges into a *fff* climax.

1223. *Mad Coyote Madly Sings*. Four actors (preferably two women and two men), tenor saxophone, bass, and drum set [1991]. 1st: New York, 5 April 1992. #Jerome Kitzke, 1991. Texts by Tewa, Allen Ginsberg, and the Lakota.
AMC M1625.K62M2
An eight-minute work written in response to the Persian Gulf War and war in general. An intense, angry work with constantly changing meters, syncopation, and vocal directions including "a bit insane." The instrumental parts are clearly notated, and the vocal parts are chiefly Sprechstimme. The middle section is a calmer, blues lament but also contains

screams of glissandos on "Ahs." After a long silence, a scream erupts from the instruments with *ff* sixteenth notes and sounds of bombs.

Kraft, William (b. 1923)

1224. *Encounters III*. Duel for trumpet and percussion [1971]. #Los Angeles: Avant Music, 1973. *Avant AV-1003.
        M298.K915 E5
        A sixteen-minute encounter with trumpet and percussion battling one another.
        Kraft has two other works that have some war-relationships as well: 1) *Encounter IV*. Trombone, percussion, and optional tape [1972]. #Van Nuys: New Music West, 1975. *Crystal S-641. JNF 89-61 (NYPL call number). In three parts, "Strategy," "Truce of God," and "Tactics"; and 2) *Encounter VII: Blessed are the peacemakers*. Two percussionists [1977-1978]. #Van Nuys: New Music West, 1977. M298.K733 E5.

La Montaine, John (b. 1920)

1225. *Be Glad Then America*, Op. 43. Opera [1974]. 1st: University Park, Pennsylvania, 6 February 1976. #Hollywood: P.J. Sifler, 1975.
        M1503.L245B4 1975
        Depicts the Battle of Lexington during the American Revolutionary War (p. 110) and is followed by a lament for the dead. The libretto was constructed from actual texts of the revolutionary period, and the music, which is written in a tonal and highly diatonic language, quotes Billings' revolutionary hymn "Chester."

Lang, David A. (b. 1957)

1226. *By Fire*. Small mixed chorus and percussion [1984]. #Lang, 1984. Texts from Sun Tzu's *The Act of War* and an unidentified CIA analyst as quoted by Robert Scheer.
        AMC M1582.L269B9
        The text of the CIA analyst deals with a bird incinerated by atomic bomb testing. The music is disjunct, atonal, and severe.

Lindenfeld, Harris (b. 1945)

1227.   *The War Prayer*. Oratorio for narrator, soloists, chorus, and orchestra [1975]. Text by Mark Twain.
AMC M1530.3.L744W2 (NYPL call number)
A bravura, sectionalized work with crowds talking and yelling to celebrate the Fourth of July, while violins, flutes, and piccolos spit out fast sixteenth-note repeated passages. A particularly effective moment appears when the text "terrible" is repeated over and over again in clusters.

Newman, Anthony (b. 1941)

1228.   Sinfonia No. 1 ("On Fallen Heroes"). Organ and Orchestra [1989]. *Newport Classic NCD 60140.
[No LC number available]
A fifteen-minute lament written to "memorialize the heroes of Tienneman Square." The music opens darkly with solo trumpet over tremolo strings and an occasional timpani thud. The music is tonal, melodic, and not overtly programmatic.

Penn, William A. (b. 1943)

1229.   *Guernica*. Violin or viola [1975]. 1st: Michigan State University, 26 April 1970. #New York: Seesaw Music, 1975.
M44.P45G8
An eight-minute unaccompanied work filled with trills, trill-glissandos, snaps, and double stops, and employs double-stop harmonics at the end. In his preface, Penn writes that Picasso's *Guernica* inspired his work, but the virtuosic composition is not in any way explicitly programmatic. The work concludes with a coda the composer labeled "Requiem."

Rollin, Robert (b. 1947)

1230.   *The Song of Deborah*. Chamber orchestra with soprano [1985]. 1st: New York, 14 July 1988. #New York: Seesaw Music, 1987. Story from Judges 4-6.
JMG 89-61 (NYPL call number)
An eleven-minute, three-movement work including "Sinfonia (Battaglia)," "Song of Thanksgiving," and "Song of Victory." The story deals with Deborah and Barak leading the Jewish army over the Sisra army. The Battaglia (scored for

percussion and brass only) is in 3/4 and 4/4, chromatic, but is more melodic than many of the battle-like works. The victory celebration is elaborate, more chromatic, and ends softly with spoken text.

Rothrock, Carson (20th c.)

1231. *For Johnny Would A Soldier Be.* Viola and percussion [1985]. #Rothrock, 1985.
       AMC M298.R8465F6
       In three movements: 1) Johnny leaves his lover to join the army; 2) Her life at the home front; and 3) The battle, Johnny's wound, and the letter reaching his lover announcing his death. The battle scene incorporates extended trill-like, sixteenth-note passages, syncopations, and repeated notes, crescendoing to *ff* with glissandos in the viola.

Rouse, Steve (b. 1953)

1232. *Dense Pack.* Chorus and tam-tam [1983-1984]. 1st: Ann Arbor, 29 April 1985. *at NYPL.
       [No LC number available]
       A protest work that uses clusters to dismember "The Star Spangled Banner." Cited in Glenn Watkins, *Soundings: Music in the Twentieth Century* (New York: G. Schirmer, 1988), p. 499.

Rzewski, Frederic (b. 1938)

1233. *The People United.* Piano [1975]. #Tokyo: Zen-On Music, 1979. *Vanguard VSD 71248.
       M24.R98P4
       Based on Sergio Ortega's and Quilapayun's revolutionary song, these thirty-six variations (nearly fifty minutes long) have formed one of the most important piano works since World War II. Though not a pictorial account of war and revolution, it creates at times an atmosphere of struggle and tragedy, and symbolically represents strong support for the Chilean resistance movement in the seventies.

Smit, Leo (b. 1921)

1234.   *Copernicus: Narrative and Credo.* Chorus, narrator, and
        instrumental ensemble [c. 1982]. #New York: C. Fischer, 1982.
        Text by Sir Fred Hoyle.
             M1533.3.S64C6 1982
             A twenty-five minute work in eight sections, one of which
        deals with the Teutonic War. This section is only three pages
        long and consists chiefly of bass tremolos over which the
        narrator tells how the Teutonic Knights invaded Poland and how
        Copernicus defended the city.

Argentina

Kagel, Mauricio (b. 1931)

1235.   *... den 24.xii.1931. Verstümmelte Nachrichten (Garbled
        News).* Baritone, two pianos, percussion, violin, viola, cello,
        and bass [1988-1991]. *Disques Montaigne 1 CD 782009.
             [No LC number available]
             A seven-movement, thirty-minute work based, in part, upon
        news reports the day Kagel was born. Movement three deals with
        General Honjó and the Japanese occupation of Manchuria. Uses
        considerable percussion, ostinatos, and pentatonic motives with
        the baritone loudly declaiming the words of General Honjó.

Austria

Rubin, Marcel (b. 1905)

1236.   *Variationen über ein französisches Revolutionslied.* Eleven
        players and instruments [1976]. #Vienna-Munich: Ludwig
        Doblinger, 1978. *Preiser SPR 148.
             M985.R
             An eleven-minute set of variations on a theme from the
        French Revolution.

Bulgaria

Dimov, Bojidar (b. 1935)

1237.   *Continuum II: Trauerminuten für Dana Kosanová.* Chamber
        orchestra [1968-1969]. 1st: Graz, 25 October 1969. #Köln: Hans
        Gerig, 1969.
            M1002.D56C76 No.2
            Commemorates a fifteen-year-old-girl student (Dana
        Kosanová) killed in the Soviet invasion of Czechoslovakia on
        21 August 1968 and was written during this occupation of
        Czechoslovakia. The music is notated in a space-time
        relationship and incorporates numerous aleatoric devices. A
        single, unchanging chord provides the structure for the entire
        composition.

Canada

Lanza, Alcides (b. 1929) [Argentine born]

1238.   *Ekphonesis IV.* Electronic music and slides [1971]. 1st: Berlin,
        12 May 1973.
            [No LC number available]
            The composer composed several works called *Ekphonesis*
        which include political messages and center on human
        holocausts that the composer feels should never have happened.
        This work in particular is based upon Picasso's *Guernica* and
        includes street sounds from New York City, non-comprehensible
        conversation about Guernica, and quotations from the
        composer's other music.

China

Chen, Pei-xun (b. 1921)

1239.   Symphony No. 2 ("Ching Ming"). Orchestra [after 1976].
        *Hong Kong 6.340101.
            [No LC number available]
            In three movements about the Chinese Cultural Revolution
        in 1967 and later: "Before the Tombstone of the Martyrs,"
        "Dance of Righteousness," and "Hope of the Dead Transformed."
        Awarded a Gold Medal in a National Symphonic Competition.

Feng, Tian (b. 1933)

1240.   *Last Night.* Symphonic poem [1980]. *Hong Kong 6.340101.
[No LC number available]
Attempts to depict the Chinese Revolution through its uprising and its ultimate victory. Awarded a prize in the First National Symphonic Competition.

Czechoslovakia

Fišer, Luboš (b. 1935)

1241.   *Caprichos.* Chamber chorus [1966].
[No LC number available]
A ten-minute composition inspired by the anti-war drawings of Goya. Cited in BAKER, p. 546.

1242.   *Nárek nad zkázou mesta Ur (Lament over the Destruction of Ur).* Soprano, baritone, three narrators, children's chorus, chorus, kettledrums, and bells [1969]. A second version for ballet appeared in 1978.
[No LC number available]
A ten-minute composition based on Sumerian texts about the destruction of the ancient city Ur. Cited in BAKER, p. 546.

1243.   *Report.* Wind instruments, piano, and percussion [1971]. #New York: C.F. Peters, 1971. *American Wind Symphony Orchestra AWS-102.
M1245.F53 R4
In four sections ("Report" and three marches) performed in eight minutes and written in memory of the Russian invasion of Czechoslovakia in 1968. The work includes both proportional and metric notation with enormous amounts of repetition.

Tausinger, Jan (1921-1980) [Russian born]

1244.   *Ave Maria.* Soprano, narrator, and orchestra [1972]. #Prague: Panton, 1974.
M2103.T34
A twelve-minute anti-war composition which won first prize in the UNESCO International Composers' Tribune in Paris.

Válek, Jiří (b. 1923)

1245.   Symphony No. 5 ("Guernica"). Orchestra [1968].
          [No LC number available]
          A nineteen-minute symphony inspired by Picasso's sketches
          and painting of the massacre in Guernica. Cited in "Valek, Jiří,"
          CZECH.

Denmark

Ruders, Poul (b. 1949)

1246.   *Tre breve fra den ukendte Soldat (Three Letters from the
          Unknown Soldier)*. Piano [1967]. #Copenhagen: Engstrom &
          Sodring, 1973.
          M25.R8xT7
          A brief, three-movement work with violent uses of clusters
          and dissonance incorporating experimental, non-metric notation:
          "March," "Bells," and "Prayer." Ruders intended his work to
          express "compassion for a human being" and uses markings such
          as "Cold, heartless and with heavy aversion and disgust" to
          instruct performers how to play the work.

France

Zanettovich, Daniele (20th c.)

1247.   *Appunti in un cimitero di guerra*. Flute and percussion [c. 1976].
          #Paris: A. Leduc, 1976.
          JMH 77-13 (NYPL call number)
          A ten-minute composition in six sections: "Dedicaa,"
          "Brindisi," "Segnali," "Marcia," "Litania," and "Ripresa della
          marcia." The music is often unmetered and includes some
          graphic notation in its highly fragmented style.

Germany

Henze, Hans Werner (b. 1926)

1248.   *We Come to the River*. Opera, actions for music [1974-1975].
          1st: 12 July 1976. #Mainz: B. Schott Söhne, 1976. *(at Indiana
          University). Libretto by Edward Bond.
          M1500.H48W4 Case

In two parts and eleven scenes, this work is a vicious,
black-humored, anti-war work set in an imaginary empire where
the soldiers violently put down a people's uprising. Using three
stage orchestras and a military band, the work creates chaos as
rarely created. The text is graphic throughout and deals with the
agony of wounded soldiers as well as women digging up buried
soldiers looking for buried valuables. The last scene is entitled
"Madhouse."

Hölderle, W.-Joseph (20th c.)

1249. *Wartime (The Blake-Light-Tragedy)*. Soloist, chorus, and
orchestra [1984]. 1st: 18 May 1984. #Darmstadt: Wilhelm Lutz,
1986. Text from Allen Ginsburg's "Howl," but uncredited in
score.
JMF 89-261 (NYPL call number)
A wild, experimental thirty-minute work not just about the
war, but often describing the "war-time blues" referred to in
Ginsburg's poem. Full of special effects which the composer
explains in a two-page table in front of the score.

Hufschmidt, Wolfgang (20th c.)

1250. *We Shall Overcome*. Speaker, singers, chorus, and nine
instruments including guitar and accordion [1983-1984].
#Dortmund: Verlag pläne, 1985?. Text by Bertolt Brecht.
M1531.H9 W4 1985
A twenty-five minute, eclectic work in ten movements
proclaiming peace.

Steffens, Walter (b. 1934)

1251. *Guernica: Elegie*, Op. 32. Viola and orchestra [1976-1978].
#Frankfurt and New York: Wilhelm Hansen, 1979.
M1014.S84G8 1979
An eighteen-minute composition using proportional
notation at times, opening with over thirty graphic
representations of B-52 bombers. The music is then metered,
predominantly in 5/4. Numerous aleatoric devices, rapid repeated
patterns, and long held notes are employed. Near the end, the
graphics of the B-52s return before diminishing to nothingness
(*ppp*). Steffens writes in the score: "Ich versuche, das bewegende
Geschehen um Guernica in der für Bratsche und Orchester

nachzuempfinden, Furcht, Schrecken und Trauer auszulösen und musikalisch zu gestalten."

Wolschina, Reinhard (b. 1952)

1252. *Fünf Caprichos.* Wind quartet and percussion [1973]. 1st: Weimar, 17 April 1974. #Leipzig: Deutscher Verlag für Musik, 1979.
        M585.W
        An eighteen-minute composition consisting of five pieces, each based upon a particular painting from Goya's *Los caprichos.* Although there is no particular tone-painting, the style is bold and adventurous with progressive musical notation. The third piece in particular is rhythmically very free.

Great Britain

Biggin, Tony (20th c.)

•   *The Gates of Greenham: A Peace Passion for Today.* See item number 928.

Holloway, Robin (b. 1943)

1253. *From Hills and Valleys: War Memorials No. 2,* Op. 50 No. 2. Brass band and percussion [1984]. #London: Boosey & Hawkes, 1984.
        M1245.H
        Prefaced with a poem by Charles Hamilton Sorley who died in 1915. It is a large-scale, lyric reflection of war. The music is chromatic, rhythmically simple, traditionally notated, and highly sectionalized.

Singer, Malcolm (b. 1953)

1254. *York—A Cantata.* Soprano, narrator, wind octet, and strings [1990]. 1st: York, May 1990. Text by Michelin Wandor.
        [No LC number available]
        Based upon three medieval chants: "Ja nuns hons pris," "Sainte Marie," and "Olenu."

Lloyd-Webber, Andrew (b. 1948)

1255. *Requiem.* Soloists, chorus, children's chorus, organ, and orchestra [1985]. #New York: Hal Leonard, 1985. *Angel DFO 38218.
M2013.L79R4 1985
A fifty-minute, well-publicized work dedicated in part to those murdered by the Khmer Rouge in Cambodia during the 1970s.

Osborne, Nigel (b. 1948)

1256. *I am Goya.* Baritone and chamber orchestra [1977]. #London: Universal, 1982. *Unicorn-Kanchana DKP 9031. Text by Andrey Voznesensky.
M1613.3.O75I2 1982
An extraordinary poem set in a lyrical and rather beautiful way that almost seems incongruous with the text itself. Particularly striking is the opening baritone falsetto.

Walton, William (1902-1983)

1257. *Battle of Britain: Battle in the Air.* Film music for orchestra [1969]. *HMV ASD 3797 and HMV ED 29 0190 1.
[No LC number available]
Contains snarling brass and considerable syncopation with trilling strings amidst driving rhythmic patterns.

Italy

Nono, Luigi (1924-1990)

1258. *Y entonces comprendio (And Then He Understood).* Six female voices and tape [1969-1970]. #Milan: Ricordi & Editori, 1970. *DG 2530436.
M1531.N65Y2 folio
In three short movements composed on graph paper and divided into seconds with emphasis on blocks of sound.

Lebanon

El-Khoury, Becham (b. 1957)

1259. *Requiem for Orchestra*, Op. 18. Orchestra [1980]. *Erato ERA
       9260.
       [No LC number available]
       In memory of Lebanese martyrs during the 1975 war
       between Moslems and Christians, this twenty-minute orchestral
       lament highlights the soaring strings of film music.

1260. Symphonic Poem No. 1 ("The Lebanon in Flames"), Op. 14.
       Orchestra [1980]. *Erato ERA 9260.
       [No LC number available]
       A twenty-minute, somber work in the nineteenth-century
       harmonic tradition with strings dominant and some occasional
       martial overtones through the timpani and brass. It attempts to
       illustrate the struggle and death of war.

The Netherlands

Straesser, Joep (b. 1934)

1261. *Intervals II: Music on War and Peace*. Mezzo-soprano, chorus,
       and instruments [1979]. #Amsterdam: Donemus, 1979. Texts by
       Marlowe, Milton, Frank B. Kellogg, and from Goethe's
       "Wanderers Nachtlied" and the Bible.
       JMH 80-42 (NYPL call number)
       Begins "Accursed by he that first invented war" and
       continues as a vehement anti-war work with speaking and
       whispering in four explosive movements. Straesser creates the
       anxiousness of war through his frequently changing meters and
       numerous irregular divisions in its fourteen minutes.

Poland

Przybilski, Bronislaw (b. 1941)

1262. *Guernica: Pablo Picasso in memoriam*. Orchestra [c. 1977].
       #Crakow: Polskie wydawnictwo muzyczne, 1977.
       M1045.P978G8

A fifteen-minute chance composition written in the memory of Picasso and in remembrance chiefly of his painting of the horrors at Guernica.

Slovenia

Božič, Darijan (b. 1933)

1263. *Requiem (to the Memory of a Murdered Soldier, My Father).* Sound collage for narrator, chorus, instruments, and concrete sounds [1969]. *Helidon FLP 10-003. Text by Robert Rozdestvenski.

[No LC number available]

Based on the classical requiem movements, the work illustrates how we have glorified violence and war in this century in its movements: "Gloria mortis," "Decus irae," "Agon hominis," "Sancitatas mortuorum," "Benedice," and "Credar." Cited in BAKER, p. 228.

South Africa

Joubert, John (b. 1927)

1264. *South of the Line,* Op. 109. Cantata for soloists, chorus, two pianos, and percussion [1985]. #London: Novello, 1989. Text by Thomas Hardy.

M1531.J86 S72 1989

Deals with the Boer War and contains five movements lasting twenty-eight minutes: "Embarcation," "A wife in London," "Drummer Hodge," "The Man He Killed," and "A Christmas Ghost Story."

Soviet Union

Chaikovsky, Boris (b. 1925). Russia

1265. Symphony No. 3 in B-flat major ("Sevastopol"). Orchestra [1980]. 1st: 25 January 1981. #Moscow: Soviet Kompozitor, 1985. *Melodiya C10 20245 002.

JMF 87-479 (NYPL call number).

Deals with the sieges and battles at Sevastopol in both the nineteenth and twentieth centuries. The work in over forty-five minutes is more adventuresome than some Soviet works in its use of dissonance and its dramatic, abrasive outbursts in the second half.

Eshpay, Andrey (b. 1925). Russia

1266.   *Cantata: "Lenin is Amongst Us."* Chorus and orchestra [1968]. #Moscow: Soviet Composer, 1975. *Olympia OCD 201. Text by Mayakovsky.
         JMF 77-77 (NYPL call number)
         The first section is a brief examination of war subtitled "The Last Page of the Civil War." Its march-like rhythms and brass fanfares create a stirring remembrance of the excitement and furor of revolution.

Mustafayev, Ramiz (b. 1926)

1267.   *October*. Oratorio for baritone, chorus, and orchestra. #Moscow: Soviet Composer, 1973.
         M2003.M95O3
         In five movements, it is in an adventurous Soviet style with a bitonal opening, narration, and a heroic ending on an E-flat seven chord.

Petrov, Andrey (b. 1930). Russia

1268.   *Petr Pervyi (Peter I)*. Vocal-symphonic frescoes for soloists, chorus, and orchestra [1972]. #Leningrad: Edition Music, 1975. *Melodiya C10-15525. Texts by Natalii Kasatkina and Vladimir Vasilyov.
         M1530.P45P5
         A story of Peter the Great set to music. The third section is entitled "The Battle Against the Swedes," and the concluding section is "The Hymn to Russia and Russian troops." The excerpts are taken from an opera of the same name published in 1984.

Shostakovich, Dmitry (1906-1975). Russia

1269.   *October*, Op. 132. Symphonic poem [1967]. 1st: 26 September 1967. #Moscow: Muzyka, 1969. *Olympia OCD 201.
         *MTA (NYPL call number)
         A fourteen-minute reminiscence of the glory days of the Russian Revolution in which Shostakovich uses many

characteristics from his earlier war symphonies, particularly the Eighth.

Spain

Balada, Leonardo (b. 1933)

1270. *Guernica.* Orchestra [1966]. 1st: New Orleans, 25 April 1967. #New York: General Music, 1969. *Louisville Orchestra LS686.
        M1045.B2426G8
        A highly dissonant, non-melodic work full of clusters, repetition, and intense aleatoric devices aimed for what the composer calls "anti-beauty" and which evokes the horrors that took place at Guernica during the Spanish Civil War.

SUPPLEMENT OF WAR COMPOSITIONS:
1965 to 1990

1271. Bargielski, Zbigniew (b. 1937). Poland. *Danton or Some Pictures from the History of the Great French Revolution.* "A surrealistic historical opera." [1968-1969]. [Cited in BAKER, p. 108].
1272. Beadell, Robert M. (b. 1925). America. *Napoleon.* Opera [1972]. *Interview with composer about opera at LC.
1273. Bilash, Aleksandr (b. 1931). Ukraine. *Ballad about War.* Opera [1971]. *Melodiya C10-18197 006. [Cited in HO, p. 57].
1274. Björklund, Staffan (b. 1944). Sweden. *War-Game.* Soprano, flutes, horns, organ, and strings [1973-1974].
1275. Boiko, Rostislav (b. 1931). Russia. *The Year 1917.* Chorus and orchestra [1957]. [Cited in HO, p. 65].
1276. Bonsel, Adriaan (b. 1918). The Netherlands. *Peace-War-Peace? Moto-Perpetito?* Orchestra [1975]. [Cited in BAKER, p. 213].
1277. Bucht, Gunnar (b. 1927). Sweden. *Jerikos murar (The Walls of Jericho).* Opera/oratorio (electronic version, 1970) [1966-1967]. [Cited in BAKER, p. 263].
1278. Butsko, Yury (b. 1938). Ukraine. *The Tale of Pugachyov's Uprising.* Oratorio [1968]. [Cited in HO, p. 77].

1279. Chyrgal-Ohol, Aleksey (b. 1924). Tuva. *Military Glory*. Oratorio [1978]. [Cited in HO, p. 99].

1280. Cikker, Ján (1911-1989). Czechoslovakia. *Epitaph (Over an Old Trench)*. Symphonic image [1973]. *Opus 9112 0124. [Cited in BAKER, p. 334].

1281. Delden, Lex van (b. 1919). The Netherlands. *Canto Della Guerra*. Chorus and orchestra [1967]. #New York: Henmar. [Cited in BAKER, p. 411].

1282. Dmitriyev, Georgy (b. 1942). Russia. Symphony ("On the Kulikovo Field"). Orchestra [1979]. [Cited in HO, p. 116]. Commemorates the 600th anniversary of the Battle on the Kulikovo Field.

1283. Farberman, Harold (b. 1929). America. *War Cry on a Prayer Feather*. Soprano, baritone, and orchestra [1976]. 1st: Colorado Springs, 11 November 1976. [Cited in BAKER, p. 516].

1284. Fotek, Jan (b. 1928). Poland. *The Last War*. Rhapsody for narrator, chorus, and orchestra [1971]. [Cited in BAKER, p. 564].

1285. Fried, Alexej (b. 1922). Czechoslovakia. *Guernica*. Quintet for soprano saxophone and string quartet [1978]. [Cited in "Alexej Fried," CZECH].

1286. Gaburo, Kenneth (b. 1926). America. *Antiphony VIII: Revolution*. Percussion and tape [1983]. [Cited in BAKER, p. 590].

1287. Gavrilin, Valery (b. 1939). Russia. *War Letters*. Oratorio [1970]. *Melodiya C10-19871 002. [Cited in HO, p. 165].

1288. Gefors, Hans (b. 1952). Sweden. *Krigets eko/Sonido de la guerre*. Percussion solo [1982-1983].

1289. Grantham, Donald (b. 1947). America. *Musica para "Los desastres de la guerra."* Orchestra [1974]. [Cited in BAKER, p. 661].

1290. _____. *The War Prayer*. Baritone and orchestra (or piano) [1974]. Text by Mark Twain. [Cited in BAKER, p. 662].

1291. Guerra-Peixe, César (b. 1914). Brazil. *A Retirada da Laguna*. Symphonic suite [1971]. *Pro-Memus MMB 79.001. Deals with the 1865 War between Brazil and Paraguay.

1292. Hahn, Gunnar (b. 1908). Sweden. *Krig och fred i svensk folklore*. Brass sextet [1976]. 1st: 8 January 1977.

1293. Hoddinott, Alun (b. 1929). Great Britain. *The Charge of the Light Brigade*. Ballad for male chorus and piano. #Cardiff: University College Cardiff Press, 1982. Text by Alfred, Lord Tennyson. M1560.M.

1294. Kalistratov, Valery (b. 1942). Russia. *Kulikovskaya Bitva* [1981]. [Cited in HO, p. 233].
1295. Kalmanoff, Martin (b. 1920). America. *Kaddish for a Warring World*. Tenor, baritone, chorus, and orchestra [1970]. 1st: Toronto, 1978. [Cited in *Who's Who in American Music*, p. 300].
1296. Karminsky, Mark (b. 1930). Ukraine. *Ten Days That Shook The World*. Opera [1970]. [Cited in HO, p. 242]. Deals with the turbulent days of the Russian Revolution.
1297. Khachaturyan, Aram (1903-1978). Georgia. *A Moment of History*. Oratorio [1971]. Deals with the Russian Revolution.
1298. Kochan, Günter (b. 1930). Germany. *Aurora*. Women's voices, chorus, and orchestra [1966]. Deals with the Russian Revolution. [Cited in BAKER, p. 934].
1299. Koetsier, Jan (b. 1911). The Netherlands. *Piet-Hein Variaties*, Op. 99 [1984]. #Amsterdam: Donemus, 1985. Music (Sheet) 88-168 (NYPL call number).
1300. Kravchenko, Boris (1929-1979). Russia. *Thoughts on Peace and War*. Oratorio [1969]. [Cited in HO, p. 285].
1301. Lilburn, Douglas (b. 1915). New Zealand. *Poems in Time of War*. Tape [1967]. *KIWI SLD 44-46.
1302. Lindroth, Peter (b. 1950). Sweden. *A Piece of War*. Mezzo-soprano, clarinet, and cellos [1981].
1303. Luciuk, Juliusz (b. 1927). Poland. *Battleship Potemkin*. Ballet [1967].
1304. Matthus, Siegfried (b. 1934). German. *Judith*. Opera [1985]. 1st: Berlin, 28 September 1985. #Leipzig: Deutscher Verlag für Musik, 1985. Based on Friedrich Hebbel's play and texts from the Bible. M1503.M4467J8 1985.
1305. Molchanov, Kirill (1922-1982). Russia. *Neizvestnyi soldat (The Unknown Soldier)*. Opera [c. 1972]. #Moscow: Soviet Composer, 1972. Libretto by the composer. M1503.M717N4 1972.
1306. Nikolayev, Aleksey (b. 1931). Russia. *Song about the Death of the Cossack Army*. Voice and orchestra [1973]. *Melodiya C10-06695-96. [Cited in HO, p. 378].
1307. Ovchinnikov, Vyacheslav (b. 1936). Russia. *War and Peace*. Film score [1961-1967]. #Moscow: Soviet Kompozitor, 1985. *Melodiya/Capitol SWAO 2918. M1527.09V6 1985.
1308. Peck, Russel (b. 1945). America. *Le tombeau de l'inconnu (The Tomb of the Unknown)*. String orchestra [1974].

1309.	Peiko, Nikolay (b. 1916). Russia. *In the Throes of War*. Five symphonic tableaux [1975]. #Moscow: Sov. Kompozitor, 1989. JMF 91-539 (NYPL call number).
1310.	Pirumov, Aleksandr (b. 1930). Georgia. *Days of October*. Oratorio [1967]. [Cited in HO, p. 407].
1311.	_____. *Requiem in Memory of a Brother Soldier* [1975]. [Cited in HO, p. 407].
1312.	Pol'sky, Il'ya (b. 1924). Soviet. *Heroes of Brest*. Opera [1965]. [Cited in HO, p. 411].
1313.	Prigozhin, Lyutsian (b. 1926). Russia. *In Memory of the Great Battle*. Bass, chorus, and orchestra [1975]. [Cited in HO, p. 415].
1314.	Przybilski, Bronislaw (b. 1941). Poland. *Requiem—In Memory of the Children-Martyrs of the war*. Voice and orchestra [1976]. [Cited in BAKER, p. 1453].
1315.	Pylkkänen, Tauno (1918-1980). Finland. *Tuntematon sotilas (The Unknown Soldier)*. Opera [1967]. #Finnish Music Center. [Cited in BAKER, p. 1458].
1316.	Rudziński, Witold (b. 1913). Poland. *The Nike of the Vistula*. War ballads and scenes for narrator, four soloists, chorus, and orchestra [1973]. [Cited in BAKER, p. 1559].
1317.	Salva, Tadeáš (b. 1937). Slovenia. *War and the World*. Baritone, women's chorus, double bass, organ, and chamber orchestra [1972]. [Cited in BAKER, p. 1580].
1318.	Sanches, Blas (20th c.). Spain. *Guernica 2, etude*. #Editions Max Eschig, 1972. M127.S.
1319.	Tylik, Vladimir (b. 1938). Soviet. *Sevastopol*. Voice and orchestra [1976].
1320.	Vacek, Miloš (b. 1928). Czechoslovakia. *Poema o padlých hrdinech (Poem of the Fallen Heroes)*. Soprano and orchestra [1974]. *Panton 11 0528. [Cited in BAKER, p. 1928].
1321.	Yossifov, Alexander (b. 1940). Bulgaria. Symphony No. 4 ("April Insurgents"). Orchestra [1974]. *Balkaton BCA 1969. [Cited in BAKER, p. 2087].
1322.	Zeidman, Boris (1908-1981). Russia. *Songs of Struggle*. Orchestra [1966]. [Cited in HO, p. 617].
1323.	Zupko, Ramon (b. 1932). America. *La guerre*. Soprano, piano, vibraphone, clarinet, and two percussion groups [1965]. Texts by Ezra Pound, Randall Jarrell, and e.e. cummings. M1613.3.Z86G8.

NOTES

1. Stanley Karnow, *Vietnam: A History* (New York: Viking, 1983), p. 15.

2. Marshall McLuhan and Quentin Fiore, *War and Peace in the Global Village* (New York: Bantam, 1968), p. 134.

3. Cited in Cecil B. Arnold Jr., *War, Peace, and the Apocalypse in Art Music Since World War II* (Ph.D. dissertation: University of Kentucky, 1986), p. 538.

4. Cited in David Ewen, *American Composers: A Biographical Dictionary* (New York: G.P. Putnam's Sons, 1982), pp. 396-97.

5. Cited in Arnold, p. 531.

6. Robert Fink, *Lysistrata and the War* (Saskatoon: Greenwich-Meridian, 1977).

7. Cited in Arnold, p. 555.

8. Charlie Morrow, notes to phonodisc *The Birth of the War God* (Laurel Records LR-840CD, 1988), p. 3.

9. Cited in Arnold, p. 552.

10. Barbara Pentland, program notes to CBC Ottawa - Radio Canada of *News*.

11. David Halberstam, "Once-Banned French Folk Song Becomes Vietnam War Protest," *New York Times* (14 August 1966), p. 16.

12. Gene Lees, "War Songs II: Music goes AWOL," *Hi-Fidelity/Musical America* 29 (January 1979), p. 21.

13. Bernard Weinraub, "A Vietnamese Guitarist Sings of Sadness of War," *New York Times* (1 January 1968), p. 3.

14. Weinraub, p. 3.

15. Weinraub, p. 3.

16. Joseph B. Treaster, "Saigon Bans the Anti-war Songs of Vietnamese Singer-Composer," *New York Times* (12 February 1969), p. 18.

17. Raymond Ericson, "Bernstein to Conduct Inaugural Day Peace Concert," *New York Times* (12 January 1973), p. 20.

18. Linda Charlton, "Concerts Reflect Moods of Divided Washington," *New York Times* (20 January 1973), p. 3.

19. Allan Hughes, "Inaugural-Concert Work Deleted as 'Not in Spirit,'" *New York Times* (14 January 1973), p. 1.

20. Cited in Karnow, p. 9.

21. Philip P. Beidler, *American Literature and the Experience of Vietnam* (Athens, Ga.: University of Georgia Press, 1982), p. 12.

22. Gilbert Adair, *Vietnam on Film* (New York: Proteus, 1981), p. 10.

23. William Mayer, *Letters Home* (Melville, N.Y.: MCA Music, 1968), p. 14.

24. Gail Kubik, *A Record of Our Time* (Melville, N.Y.: MCA Music, 1975), pp. 47-49.

25. Kubik, p. 46.

26. Mark Behm, "American Society of University Composers Region V. Conference University of Illinois, Urbana-Champaign, November 5-8, 1981," *Perspectives of New Music* 20 (1981-1982), pp. 606-07.

27. David Cope, *New Directions in Music,* 3rd ed. (Dubuque, Iowa: William C. Brown, 1981), p. 103.

28. Edwin London, "Salvatore Martirano," *Dictionary of Contemporary Music,* ed. John Vinton (New York: E.F. Dutton, 1974), p. 456.

29. London, p. 456.

30. Joseph Byrd, letter to author, February 1985.

31. Cited in Arnold, p. 538.

32. Neil Sheehan, *A Bright Shining Lie: John Paul Vance and America in Vietnam* (New York: Random House, 1988), p. 23.

33. Cited in Arnold, p. 547.

34. Dai-Keong Lee, *Canticle of the Pacific* (New York: Belwin Mills, 1970), p. i.

35. Lee, p. i.

1. Illustrated excerpt from Peter Welden's *The Battle of Baylen* (c. 1810).

2. Excerpt from the "Sturmmarsch" of Beethoven's *Wellington's Victory* (1813).

3. Title page of Tobias Haslinger's *Deutschlands Triumpf* (c. 1826)

4. Excerpt from B. R. Lignoski's *Battle of Palo Alto* (1851).

5. Excerpt from Donald Erb's *God Love You Now* (1973). © 1973 Merion Music, Inc. Used by permission of the publisher.

SELECTED WAR-RELATED BIBLIOGRAPHY

Abraham, Gerald, ed. *The Music of Tchaikovsky*. New York: W.W. Norton, 1946.

_____. *Eight Soviet Composers*. London: Oxford University Press, 1946.

Adams, Stephen. *R. Murray Schafer*. Toronto: University of Toronto Press, 1983.

Adler, Kurt, ed. *Songs of Many Wars: From the Sixteenth to the Twentieth Century*. New York: Howell & Soskin, 1943.

Adorno, Theodore W. *Introduction to the Sociology of Music*. Trans. E.B. Ashton. New York: Seabury, 1976.

_____. *Philosophy of Modern Music*. Trans. Anne G. Mitchell. New York: Seabury, 1973.

Anderson, E. Ruth, ed. *Contemporary American Composers: A Biographical Dictionary*. Boston: G.K. Hall, 1976.

Antheil, George. *Bad Boy of Music*. New York: Doubleday & Doran, 1945.

Apel, Willi. *The Harvard Dictionary of Music*. Cambridge: Belknap Press of Harvard University Press, 1969.

Arnold, Ben. "Art Music and the Holocaust." *Holocaust and Genocide Studies* 6 no. 4 (1991), pp. 335-49.

_____. "Music, Meaning, and War: The Titles of War Compositions." *International Review of the Aesthetics and Sociology of Music* 22 (June 1991), pp. 19-28.

_____. "War Music and the American Composer During the Era of the Vietnam War." *Musical Quarterly* 75 (Fall 1991), pp. 316-35.

_____. [Arnold, Cecil B. Jr.]. *War, Peace, and the Apocalypse in Art Music Since World War II*. Ph.D. dissertation: University of Kentucky, 1986.

Arnold, Denis. "Monteverdi and the Art of War." *Musical Times* 108 (May 1967). 412-14.

Arnold, Denis, ed. *The New Oxford Companion to Music*. Oxford: Oxford University Press, 1983.

Austin, William. *Music in the Twentieth Century: From Debussy through Stravinsky*. New York: W.W. Norton, 1966.

Bailey, Walter B. *Programmatic Elements in the Works of Schoenberg.* Studies in Musicology no. 74. Ann Arbor: UMI Research Press, 1984.

Baker's Biographical Dictionary of Musicians. 7th ed. Ed. & rev., Nicolas Slonimsky. New York: Schirmer, 1984.

Bakst, James. *A History of Russian-Soviet Music.* New York: Dodd & Mead, 1966.

Ballantine, Christopher. "Charles Ives and the Meaning of Quotation in Music." *Musical Quarterly* 65 (April 1979), pp. 167-84.

_____. *Music and Its Social Meanings.* New York: Gordon & Breach, 1984.

Barzun, Jacques. *Berlioz and the Romantic Century.* 3rd ed. New York: Columbia University Press, 1969.

Bauer, Marion. *Twentieth Century Music.* Rev. ed. New York: G.P. Putnam's Sons, 1947.

Becherini, Bianca. "La canzone 'Alla battaglia' di Henricus Isaac." *Revue belge de musicologie* 7 (1953), pp. 5-25.

Becker, Heinz, ed. *Die "Couleur locale" in der Oper des 19. Jahrhunderts.* Studien zur Musikgeschichte des 19. Jahrhunderts, vol. 42. Regensburg: Gustav Boose, 1976.

Beckwith, John, and Udo Kasemets. *The Modern Composer and His World.* Toronto: University of Toronto Press, 1961.

Beidler, Philip P. *American Literature and the Experience of Vietnam.* Athens, Ga.: University of Georgia Press, 1982.

Bell, Carla Huston. *Oliver Messiaen.* Boston: Twayne, 1984.

Bennett, John R., compiler. *Melodiya: A Soviet Russian L.P. Discography.* Westport, Conn.: Greenwood, 1981.

Bernard, Kenneth A. *Lincoln and the Music of the Civil War.* Caldwell, Id.: Caxton, 1966.

Betz, Albrecht. *Hanns Eisler Political Musician.* Trans. Bill Hopkins. Cambridge: Cambridge University Press, 1982.

Bienefeld, Elsa. "Essai sur la Bataille en musique." *Le Guide Musicale.* Brussels, 1888.

Billeter, Bernhard. *Frank Martin: Ein Aussenseiter der neuen Musik.* Frauenfeld, 1970.

Bliss, Arthur. *As I Remember.* London: Faber & Faber, 1970.

Blok, Vladimir, compiler. *Sergei Prokofiev: Materials, Articles, Interviews.* U.S.S.R.: Progress, 1978.

Blokker, Roy, and Robert Dearling. *The Music of Dmitri Shostakovich: The Symphonies.* Cranbury, N.J.: Associated University Presses, 1979.

Boardman, John. *Greek Art.* Rev. ed. New York & Toronto: Oxford University Press, 1973.

Boretz, Benjamin, and Edward T. Cone, eds. *Perspectives on American Composers*. New York: W.W. Norton, 1971.

Bors, Josef. *The Terezín Requiem*. New York: Knopf, 1963.

Bowen, Meirion. *Michael Tippett*. London: Robson, 1982.

Bowman, Kent A. *Voices of Combat: A Century of Liberty and War Songs, 1765-1865*. New York: Greenwood, 1987.

Branson, L., and G.W. Goethals, eds. *War: Studies from Psychology, Sociology, Anthropology*. New York: Basic, 1964.

Broder, Nathan. *Samuel Barber*. New York: G. Schirmer, 1954.

Broeckx, Jan L. *Contemporary Views on Musical Style and Aesthetics*. Antwerp: Metropolis, 1979.

Brown, Alan. "Battaglia," NEW GROVE, vol. 2, p. 290.

Brown, Calvin S. *Music and Literature: A Comparison of the Arts*. Athens, Ga: University of Georgia Press, 1948.

Brown, Howard M. *Music in the Renaissance*. Englewood Cliffs, N.J.: Prentice Hall, 1976.

Brown, Malcolm H. "The Soviet Russian Concepts of 'Intonazia' and 'Musical Imagery.'" *Musical Quarterly* 60 (October 1974), pp. 557-67.

_____. *The Symphonies of Sergei Prokofiev*. Ph.D. dissertation: Florida State University, 1967.

Bruckner, D.J.R., Seymour Chwast, and Steven Heller. *Art Against War*. New York: Abbeville, 1984.

Budden, Julian. *The Operas of Verdi: From Oberto to Rigoletto*. New York: Praeger, 1973.

Cage, John. *Notations*. New York: Something Else, 1969.

Callaway, Frank, and David Tunley, eds. *Australian Compositions in the Twentieth Century*. Melbourne: Oxford University Press, 1978.

Caputo, Philip. *The Rumor of War*. New York: Holt, Rinehart, & Winston, 1977.

Cardew, Cornelius. *Stockhausen Serves Imperialism*. London: Latimer New Dimensions, 1974.

Casella, Alfredo. *Music in My Time: The Memories of Alfredo Casella*. Trans. Spencer Norton. Norman, Ok.: University of Oklahoma Press, 1955.

Castiglione, Baldesar. *The Book of the Courtier*. Trans. Charles S. Singleton. New York: Doubleday, 1959.

Charlton, David. "Revolutionary Hymn." *NEW GROVE* vol. 15, p. 777.

Charlton, Linda. "Concerts Reflect Moods of Divided Washington." *New York Times* (20 January 1973), p. 30.

Chase, Gilbert. *The American Composer Speaks*. Baton Rouge, La.: Louisiana State University Press, 1966.

Chinn, Jennie A. "There's a Star-Spangled Banner Waving Somewhere: Country-Western Songs of World War II." *JEMF Quarterly* 16 (Summer 1980), pp. 74-80.

Claphan, John. *Smetana*. The Master Musicians Series. New York: Octagon, 1972.

Clark, J. Bunker, ed. *Anthology of Early American Keyboard Music 1787-1830, Part I*. Recent Researches in American Music, vol. 1. Madison: A-R Editions, 1977.

_____. "Battle Piece List Updated." *Sonneck Society* 11 (Fall 1985), p. 85.

_____. *The Dawning of American Keyboard Music*. Contribution to the Study of Music and Dance no. 12. New York: Greenwood, 1988.

_____. "Worklists prepared for, but there was no room for, *The New Grove Dictionary of American Music*." *Sonneck Society* 11 (Summer 1985), p. 53.

Cohen, Aaron, ed. *International Encyclopedia of Women Composers*. New York: Bowker, 1981.

Collaer, Paul. *Darius Milhaud*. Geneva-Paris: Slatkine, 1982.

Collier, Jeremy. "An Instrument for War and Peace." *Pleasures of Music,* ed. Jacques Barzun. Chicago: University of Chicago Press, 1977, pp. 236-37.

Cooper, Martin, ed. *The Modern Age 1890-1960. New Oxford History of Music*, vol. 10. London: Oxford University Press, 1974.

Cope, David, *New Directions in Music*. 6th ed. Dubuque, Iowa: William C. Brown, 1993.

Copland, Aaron, and Vivian Perlis. *Copland: 1900 through 1942*. New York: St. Martin's, 1984.

_____. *Copland: Since 1942*. New York: St. Martins, 1989.

_____. *The New Music*. New York: W.W. Norton, 1968.

Cowell, Henry, ed. *American Composers on American Music: A Symposium*. New York: Frederick Ungar, 1933.

_____. "In Time of Bitter War." *Modern Music* 19 (January-February 1942), pp. 83-87.

_____. "Shaping Music for Total War." *Modern Music* 22 (May-June 1945), pp. 223-26.

Dahl, Ingolf. "Symphony in Three Movements." *Concert Bulletins of the Boston Symphony Orchestra 1945-1946*, p. 1046.

Dahlhaus, Carl. "Programmusik heute." *Neue Zeitschrift für Musik* 133 (December 1972), p. 682.

Dane, Barbara, and Irwin Silber, eds. *The Vietnam Songbook*. New York: Guardian, 1969.

Daniel, Keith W. *Francis Poulenc: His Artistic Development and Musical Style*. Studies in Musicology no. 52. Ann Arbor, Michigan: UMI Research Press, 1982.

Dawidowicz, Lucy S. *The War Against the Jews: 1933-1945*. New York: Holt, Rinehart, & Winston, 1975.

Dean, Winton. *Handel's Dramatic Oratorios and Masques*. London: Oxford University Press, 1959.

Del Mar, Norman. *Richard Strauss: A Critical Commentary on His Life and Works*. 3 vols. London: Barrie & Rockliff, 1962-69.

Denisoff, R. Serge. *Great Day Coming: Folk Music and the American Left*. Chicago: University of Illinois Press, 1971.

_____. *Songs of Protest, War and Peace: Bibliography and Discography*. Rev. ed. Santa Barbara, CA: ABC Clio, 1973.

Dickinson, A.E.F. *Vaughan Williams*. London: Faber & Faber, 1963.

Donakowski, Conrad L. *A Muse for the Masses*. Chicago: University of Chicago Press, 1972.

Drechsler, Nanny. *Die Funktion der Musik im deutschen Rundfunk 1933-1945*. Ph.D. dissertation: University of Freiburg, 1985.

Dumezil, Georges. *The Destiny of the Warrior*. Trans. Alf Hiltebeitel. Chicago & London: University of Chicago Press, 1970.

Dyer, Gwynne. *War*. New York: Crown,1985.

Dyson, Freeman. *Weapons and Hope*. New York: Harper & Row, 1984.

Einemann, Marita. "Luigi Nono: Die unendliche Bereitschaft zum Suchen." *Neue Zeitschrift für Musik* 145 (May 1984), pp. 16-19.

Engel, Hans. "Battalia," *Die Musik in Geschichte und Gegenwart*. Kassel & Basel: Bärenreiter, 1949-51, vol. 1, pp. 1406-11.

Engel, Lehman. "Songs of the American Wars." *Modern Music* (1943), pp. 147-52.

Enschedé, J.W. "Zur Battaglia del Re di Prussia." *Internationale Musik-Gesellschaft* 4 (1903), pp. 677-685.

Eösze, László. *Zoltán Kodály: His life and Work*. Trans. Istvan Farkas & Gyula Gulyás. Boston: Crescendo, 1962.

Erding, Susanne. *Apocalyptica. Eine multimediale Ballettoper von Fernando Arrabal, Milko Kelemen und Edmund Kieselbach*. Rohrdorf: Rohrdorfer, 1979.

Erhardt, Ludwik. *Contemporary Music in Poland*. Trans. Eugenia Tarska. Warsaw: Polonia, 1966.

Ericson, Raymond. "Bernstein to Conduct Inaugural Day Peace Concert." *New York Times* (12 January 1973), p. 20.

Etzkorn, K. Peter. *Music and Society: The Late Writings of Paul Honigsheim*. New York: John Wiley & Sons, 1973.

Evans, Peter. *The Music of Benjamin Britten*. Minneapolis: University of Minnesota Press, 1979.

Evenson, Pattee E. *A History of Brass Instruments, Their Usage, Music, and Performance Practices in Ensembles During the Baroque Era.* Ph.D. dissertation: University of Southern California, 1960.

Ewen, David. *American Composers: A Biographical Dictionary.* New York: G.P. Putnam's Sons, 1982.

_____. *Complete Book of 20th Century Music.* Englewood Cliffs, N.J.: Prentice-Hall, 1959.

_____. *Composers Since 1900: A Biographical and Critical Guide - First Supplement.* New York: H.W. Wilson, 1981.

Fabian, Imre. "Two Opera Composers." *Tempo* 88 (Spring 1969), pp. 10-19.

Farmer, Henry G. *Military Music.* New York: Chanticleer, 1950.

Fellerer, Karl Gustav. "Die Battaglia des 16. Jahrhunderts." *Musik* (April 1940), pp. 231-33.

Fénelon, Fania. *Playing for Time.* New York: Atheneum, 1977.

Ferguson, Donald. *Music as Metaphor.* Minneapolis: University of Minnesota Press, 1960.

Finkelstein, Sidney. *How Music Expresses Ideas.* Rev. & enlarged ed. New York: International, 1970.

Fish, Lydia M. "General Edward G. Lansdale and the Folksongs of Americans in the Vietnam War." *Journal of American Folklore* (October-December 1989), pp. 390-411.

Fitzgerald, Frances. *Fire in the Lake: The Vietnamese and the Americans in Vietnam.* Boston: Little & Brown, 1972.

Flam, Gila. *Singing for Survival: Songs of the Lodz Ghetto, 1940-45.* Urbana: University of Illinois, 1991.

French, Peter. "The Music of Andrzej Panufnik." *Tempo* 84 (Spring 1968), pp. 6-14.

Friedwald, Russell E. *A Formal and Stylistic Analysis of the Published Music of Samuel Barber.* Ph.D. dissertation: State University of Iowa, 1957.

Fussel, Paul. *The Great War and Modern Memory.* Oxford: Oxford University Press, 1975.

Gagne, Cole and Tracy Caras. *Interviews with American Composers.* Metuchen, N.J.: The Scarecrow Press, 1982.

Gardavsky, Cenek, ed. *Contemporary Czechoslovak Composers.* Prague: Panton, 1965.

Gilmore, P. S. *History of the National Peace Jubilee and Great Musical Festival, Held in the City of Boston, June, 1869.* New York: Lee, Shepard, & Dillingham, 1871.

Gläsel, Rudolf. *Zur Geschichte der Battaglia.* Ph.D. dissertation: Leipzig, 1931.

Goetze, Ursula. *Johann Friedrich Klöffler*. Ph.D. dissertation: Westfalischen Wilhelms-Universität zu Munster, 1965.

Goss, Madeline. *Modern Music Makers: Contemporary American Composers*. New York: E.P. Dutton, 1952.

Gottschalk, Louis Moreau. *Notes of a Pianist*, ed. Jeanne Behrend. New York: Knopf, 1964.

Grabs, Manfred, ed. *Hanns Eisler: A Rebel in Music*. Trans. Marjorie Meyer. New York: International, 1978.

Gradenwitz, Peter. *The Music of Israel: Its Rise and Growth Through 5000 Years*. New York: W.W. Norton, 1949.

Gramann, Heinz. *Die Ästhetisierung des Schreckens in der europäischen Musik des 20. Jahrhunderts*. Bonn: Verlag für systematische Musikwissenschaft GmbH, 1984.

Greene, David M. *Greene's Biographical Encyclopedia of Composers*. Garden City: Doubleday, 1985.

Greenway, John. *American Folksongs of Protest*. New York: Octagon, 1970 .

Gretchaninoff, Alexandre. *My Life*. Introduction & trans. Nicholas Slonimsky. New York: Coleman-Ross, 1952.

Grey, J. Glenn. *The Warriors: Reflections on Men in Battle*. New York: Harper & Row, 1970.

Griffiths, Paul. *A Concise History of Avant-Garde Music From Debussy to Boulez*. New York: Oxford University Press, 1978.

_____. *György Ligeti*. London: Robson, 1983.

_____. *Modern Music: The Avant Garde Since 1945*. New York: George Braziller, 1981.

_____. *New Sounds, New Personalities: British Composers of the 1980s*. London: Faber Music, 1985.

_____. *Olivier Messiaen and the Music of Time*. Ithaca, New York: Cornell University Press, 1985.

Grinde, Nils. *Contemporary Norwegian Music 1920-1980*. Trans. Sandra Hamilton. Oslo: Universitets-forlaget, 1981.

Gruen, John. *Menotti: A Biography*. New York: Macmillan, 1978.

Gutman, Robert W. *Richard Wagner: The Man, His Mind, and His Music*. New York: Harcourt, Brace & World, 1968.

Hadley, Arthur. *The Straw Giant: Triumph and Failure in America's Armed Forces*. New York: Random House, 1986.

Haithcock, Michael L. "Karel Husa: Talks About Composing." *The Instrumentalist* (April 1982), pp. 23-25.

Halberstam, David. *The Best and the Brightest*. New York: Random House, 1972.

_____. "Once-Banned French Folk Song Becomes Vietnam War Protest." *New York Times* (14 August 1966), p. 16.

Hall, Barrie. "Andrzej Panufnik's *Sinfonia Sacre.*" *Tempo* 71 (1965), pp. 14-22.

Harrison, Michael M. "Verdi, Wagner, and the Legacy of Politics in the Nineteenth Century." *Opera Quarterly* 2 (Spring 1984), pp. 95-103.

Hartman, Dominik. *Gottfried Von Einem: Eine Biographie.* Vienna: O. Sterreichischer, 1967.

Hartog, Howard, ed. *European Music in the Twentieth Century.* London: Routledge & Kegan Paul, 1957.

Hartzell, Lawrence W. "Karel Husa: The Man and the Music." *Musical Quarterly* 62 (June 1976), pp. 87-104.

Harvard Dictionary of Music, s.v. "Battaglia."

Heifetz, Vladimir. *Songs of the Holocaust.* Brooklyn: Isabel Belarsky, 1985.

Helbig, Otto M. *A History of Music in the Armed Forces during World War II.* Philadelphia: M.W. Lads, 1966.

Henahan, Donald. "'Song of Terezín' is Given Premiere by Little Orchestra." *New York Times* (20 March 1968), p. 37.

_____. "Why Music in a Time of War?" *New York Times* (3 March 1991), p. 23, 30.

Hennig, Julia A. *Battle Pieces for the Pianoforte Composed and Published in the United States Between 1795 and 1820.* D.M.A.: Boston University, 1968.

Henze, Hans Werner. *Music and Politics.* Trans. Peter Labanyi. Ithaca: Cornell University Press, 1982.

Herring, George C. *America's Longest War: The United States and Vietnam 1950-1975.* New York: John Wiley & Sons, 1979.

Hesbacher, Peter, and Les Waffen. "War Recordings: Incidence and Change (1940-1980)." *Popular Music and Society* 8 (1982), pp. 77-100.

Hess, Howard. "Fanfares by Americans." *Modern Music* (1943), pp. 189-91.

Hiller, Lejaren, and Leonard Isaacson. *Experimental Music.* New York: McGraw-Hill, 1959.

Hines, Robert S. *The Composer's Point of View.* Norman, Ok.: University of Oklahoma Press, 1963.

_____. *The Orchestral Composer's Point of View.* Norman, Ok.: Oklahoma University Press, 1970.

Hitchcock, H. Wiley. *Music in the United States: A Historical Introduction.* 2nd ed. Englewood Cliffs, N.J.: Prentice-Hall, 1974.

Hollander, Hans. *Leoš Janáček: His Life and Work.* Trans. Paul Hamburger. New York: St. Martin's, 1963.

Holmes, Richard. *Acts of War: The Behavior of Men in Battle.* New York: Free, 1985.

Holst, Gail. *Theodorakis: Myth and Politics in Modern Greek Music.* Amsterdam: Adolf M. Hokkert, 1983.

Honegger, Arthur. *I Am a Composer.* Trans. Wilson O. Clough in collaboration with Allan Arthur Willmar. New York: St. Martin's, 1966.

Howard, John T. *Our Contemporary Composers.* New York: Thomas Y. Crowell, 1941.

Howes, Frank. *The English Musical Renaissance.* London: Secker & Warburg, 1966.

_____. *The Music of Ralph Vaughan Williams.* London: Oxford University Press, 1954.

Hughes, Allan. "Ancerl Conducts the Torontians in 'Anne Frank.'" *New York Times* (16 April 1972), p. 49.

_____. "Inaugural-Concert Work Deleted as 'Not in Spirit.'" New York Times (14 January 1973), p. 1.

Hughes, Edwin. "Music in Wartime and Post-War America." *MTNA Proceedings* (1942), pp. 17-30.

_____. "War Reactions on Music." *MTNA Proceedings* (1944), pp. 58-65.

Hughes, Robert. *The Shock of the New.* New York: Knopf, 1981.

Ikonnikov, A. *Miaskovsky: His Life and Work.* New York: Philosophical Library, 1946.

Kaczerginski, Szmerke. *Lider fun di getos un lagern.* New York: Tsiko, 1948.

Kakutani, Michiko. "Novelists and Vietnam: The War Goes On." *New York Times Book Review* (15 April 15 1984), pp. 1; 39-41.

Kalisch, Shoshana. *Yes, We Sang: Songs of the Ghettos and Concentration Camps.* New York: Harper & Row, 1985.

Kappel, Vagn. *Contemporary Danish Composers.* Denmark: Det Danske Selskab, 1967.

Karas, Joža. *Music in Terezín: 1941-1945.* New York: Beaufort Books Publishers in association with Pendragon, 1985.

Karnow, Stanley. *Vietnam: A History.* New York: Viking, 1983.

Katz, Ruth. *Diving the Powers of Music: Aesthetic Theory and the Origins of Opera.* Aesthetics in Music, vol. 3. New York: Pendragon, 1986.

Keegan, John. *The Face of Battle.* New York: Viking, 1976.

Kennedy, Michael. *A Catalogue of the Works of Ralph Vaughan Williams.* London: Oxford University Press, 1982.

_____. *Portrait of Elgar.* London: Oxford University Press, 1968.

_____. *The Works of Ralph Vaughan Williams.* New Edition. London: Oxford University Press, 1980.

Kivy, Peter. *The Corded Shell*. Princeton, N.J.: Princeton University Press, 1980.

_____. *Music Alone: Philosophical Reflections on the Purely Musical Experience*. Ithaca, N.Y.: Cornell University Press, 1990.

_____. *Osmin's Rage: Philosophical Reflections on Opera, Drama, and Text*. Princeton: Princeton University Press, 1988.

_____. *Sound and Semblance: Reflections on Musical Representation*. Princeton: Princeton University Press, 1984.

Kome, Penny, and Patrick Crean, eds. *Peace: A Dream Unfolding*. San Francisco: Sierra Club, 1986.

Krauss, Ernst. *Richard Strauss: The Man and His Work*. Trans. John Coombs. London: Collet's, 1964.

Krebs, Stanley Dale. *Soviet Composers and the Development of Soviet Music*. New York: W.W. Norton, 1970.

Laks, Szymon. *Music of Another World*. Evanston, Il.: Northwestern University Press, 1989.

Landon, H. C. Robbins. *Haydn: The Years of 'The Creation' 1796-1800*. Bloomington: Indiana University Press, 1977.

Lang, Paul Henry. *George Frideric Handel*. New York: W.W. Norton, 1966.

_____. *Music in Western Civilization*. New York: W.W. Norton, 1941.

Lang, Paul Henry, ed. *Problems of Modern Music*. New York: W.W. Norton, 1960.

Langer, Lawrence L. *The Holocaust and the Literary Imagination*. New Haven, Conn.: Yale University Press, 1976.

Langer, Suzanne K. *Philosophy in a New Key*. New York: Mentor, 1951.

Large, Brian. *Martinů*. New York: Holmes & Meier, 1976.

Lederer, Sidonie K. *Soviet Wartime Music: A Russian War Relief Report*. New York: Russian War Relief, 1948.

Lees, Gene. "War Songs II: Music goes AWOL." *High Fidelity-Musical America* 29 (January 1979), p. 20+.

_____. "War Songs: Bathos and Acquiescence." *High Fidelity-Musical America* 28 (December 1978), pp. 41+.

Lerner, Gerald. "Music and War." *The Listener* (17 March 1966), pp. 386-87.

Lipman, Samuel. *Music After Modernism*. New York: Basic, 1979.

List, Kurt. "Ode to Napoleon." *Modern Music* 21 (March-April 1944), pp. 139-45.

Loesser, Arthur. *Men, Women & Pianos: A Social History*. New York: Simon & Schuster, 1954.

Longyear, Rey M. "Ferdinand Kauer's Percussion Enterprises." *The Galpin Society Journal* 27 (May 1974), pp. 2-8.

_____. "The 'Banda Sul Palco': Wind Bands in Nineteenth-Century Opera." *Journal of Band Research* 13 (Spring 1978), pp. 25-40.

_____. *Nineteenth-Century Romanticism in Music*. 3rd. ed. Englewood Cliffs, N.J.: Prentice-Hall, 1988.

Lust, Patricia D., ed. *American Vocal Chamber Music, 1945-1980: An Annotated Bibliography*. Music Reference Collection no. 4. Westport, Conn.: Greenwood, 1985.

Malan, Clement T. *Music and Morale in Wartime*. State of Indiana: Department of Public Instructions, (Bulletin no. 139), 1943.

Marek, Tadeusz and David Drew. "Górecki in Interview (1968)—And 20 Years After." *Tempo* 168 (March 1988), pp. 25-29.

Matonti, Rev. Charles J. "A Prayer for Peace Now: Britten's War Requiem Revisited." *The Choral Journal* (October 1983), pp. 21-30.

Matthew-Walker, Robert. "Copland as Symphonist—II." *Music and Musicians* (December 1985), pp. 12-13.

Mayer-Reinach, Albert. Carl Heinrich Graun. "La battaglia del Re di Prussia." *Internationale Musik-Gesellschaft* 4 (1903), pp. 478-84.

McGee, Timothy J. "'Alla Battaglia': Music and Ceremony in Fifteenth-Century Florence." *Journal of the American Musicological Society* 46 (Summer 1983), pp. 287-302.

McLaurin, Donald M. *The Life and Works of Karel Husa with Emphasis on the Significance of his Contribution to the Wind Band*. Ph.D. dissertation: Florida State University, 1985.

McLuhan, Marshall, and Quentin Fiore. *War and Peace in the Global Village*. New York: Bantam, 1968.

Mechell, Harry. *Dmitry Shostakovich (1906-75): A Critical Study of the Babi Yar Symphony with a Survey of his Works Involving Chorus*. D.M.A. dissertation: University of Illinois at Urbana-Champaigne, 1985.

Mellers, Wilfred. *Music in a New Found Land*. London: Barrie & Rockliff, 1964.

Merrick, Paul. *Revolution and Religion in the Music of Liszt*. Cambridge: Cambridge University Press, 1987.

Messiaen, Oliver. *The Technique of My Musical Language*. Paris: Alphonse Leduc, 1950.

Meyer, Herman H.B. *A Check List of the Literature and Other Material in the Library of Congress on the European War*. Washington: Government Printing Office, 1918. See pp. 211-93.

Meyer, Leonard B. *Emotion and Meaning in Music*. Chicago: University of Chicago Press, 1956.

_____. *Explaining Music: Essays and Explorations*. Chicago: University of Chicago, 1973.

_____. *Music, The Arts, and Ideas.* Chicago: University of Chicago Press, 1967.

Meylan, Pierre. *Arthur Honegger.* Frauenfed & Stuttgart: Huber, 1970.

Miller, Malcolm. "Clifford's Tower: A Commemoration at York." *Musical Times* 31 (May 1990), p. 278.

Mlotek, Eleanor, and Malke Gottlieb, compilors. *We Are Here: Songs of the Holocaust.* New York: Educational Department of the Workmen's Circle and Hippocrene Books, 1983.

Morgan, Robert P. "On the Analysis of Recent Music." *Critical Inquiry* 4 (Autumn 1977), pp. 38-53.

_____. *Twentieth-Century Music: A History of Musical Style in Modern Europe and America.* New York: W.W. Norton, 1991.

Moseley, Caroline. "'When Will Dis Cruel War Be Ober?' Attitudes Toward Blacks in Popular Song of the Civil War." *American Music* (Fall 1984), pp. 1-26.

Mueller, Kate Hevner. *Twenty-Seven Major American Symphony Orchestras.* Bloomington: Indiana University Press, 1973.

Nef, Karl. *Schlachtendarstellungen in der Musik.* Grenzbote, 1904.

Nestyev, Israel V. *Prokofiev.* Trans. Florence Jonas with a foreword by Nicolas Slonimsky. Stanford, Ca.: Stanford University Press, 1960.

Newhouse, John. *War and Peace in the Nuclear Age.* New York: Knopf, 1988.

Newman, Ernest. "Elgar's 'Fourth of August.'" *Musical Times* (1 July 1917), pp. 295-97.

_____. "Programme Music." *Musical Studies.* (London: Johne Lane The Bodley Head), pp. 103-88.

_____. "The Spirit of England." *Musical Times* (1 November 1917), p. 506.

_____. "'The Spirit of England': Edward Elgar's New Choral Work." *Musical Times* (1 May 1916), p. 235.

Nieckes, Frederick. *Programme Music in the Last Four Centuries.* 1907. Reprint: New York: Haskell House, 1969.

Norris, Christopher, ed. *Shostakovich: The Man and His Music.* Boston: Marion Boyars, 1982.

Nyman, Michael. *Experimental Music: Cage and Beyond.* New York: Schirmer, 1980.

Oja, Carol J., ed. *American Music Recordings: Discography of Twentieth-Century U. S. Composers.* Brooklyn: Institute for Studies in American Music, 1982.

Olson, Kenneth E. *Music and Musket: Bands and Bandsmen of the American Civil War.* Contributions to the Study of Music and Dance no. 1. Westport, Conn.: Greenwood, 1981.

Orga, Antes. "Krzysztof Penderecki." *Music and Musicians* 22 (October 1973), pp. 38-41.

Orrey, Leslie. *Programme Music: A Brief Survey from the Sixteenth Century to the Present Day*. London: Davis-Poynter, 1975.

Palisca, Claude V. "French Revolutionary Models for Beethoven's Eroica Funeral March." *Music and Context: Essays for John M. Ward*. Ed. Anne Dhu Shapiro (Cambridge, Mass.: Department of Music, Harvard University, 1985), pp. 198-209.

Panufnik, Andrzej. *Impulse and Design in My Music*. London: Boosey & Hawkes, 1974.

Parmenter, Ross. "Britten's Interweaving of Two Strands of Pity." *New York Times* (24 October 1963), p. 36.

Peatman, John. "Non-Militant, Sentimental . . ." *Modern Music* 20 (November-December 1942), pp. 152-56.

Percy, Gosta, ed. *Swedish Music—Past and Present*. Trans. Dick Litell. Stockholm: Musikrevy, 1967.

Perris, Arnold. *Music as Propaganda*. Westport, Conn.: Greenwood, 1985.

Philbin, Marianne, ed. *Give Peace a Chance: Music and the Struggle for Peace*. Chicago: Chicago Review, 1983.

Philips, Tom. "Vietnam Blues." *New York Times* (8 October 1967), pp. 12-28.

Pirie, Peter J. "Music Reviews: Music Against War." *Musical Times* (August 1984), p. 448.

Pleasants, Henry. *The Agony of Modern Music*. New York: Simon & Schuster, 1955.

Pollack, Howard. *Walter Piston*. Studies in Musicology no. 50. Ann Arbor: UMI Research Press, 1982.

Potter, Pamela M. "Strauss's *Friedenstag:* A Pacifist Attempt at Political Resistance." *Musical Quarterly* 69 (Summer 1983), pp. 408-24.

Price, Kingsley, ed. *On Criticizing Music: Five Philosophical Perspectives*. Baltimore: Johns Hopkins University Press, 1981.

Prod'homme, J.G. "Music and Musicians in Paris During the First Two Seasons of the War." *Musical Quarterly* (1918), pp. 135-60.

Rajterova, Alzbeta. "Symphonie 1945." Trans. Ján Albrecht. Foreword to score *Symfonia 1945* by Ján Cikker. Bratislava: Opus, 1976.

Reich, Willi. *Schoenberg: A Critical Biography*. Trans. Leo Black. Vienna: Fritz Molden, 1968.

Reis, Claire R. *Composers, Conductors, and Critics*. New York: Oxford University Press, 1955.

Rhodes, Willard. "On the Warpath, 1942." *Modern Music* 20 (November-December 1942), p. 157.

Ringbom, Nils-Eric. *Über die Deutbarkeit der Tonkunst.* Helsinki: Fazer, 1955.

Ringer, A.L. "Musical Composition in Modern Israel." *Musical Quarterly* 2 (1965), p. 295.

Robertson, Alec. *Requiem: Music of Mourning and Consolation.* New York: Praeger, 1968.

Robinson, Harold. *Sergei Prokofiev.* New York: Viking, 1987.

Robinson, Ray. "Krzysztof Penderecki: An Interview and an Analysis of Stabat Mater." *The Choral Journal* 24 (November 1983), pp. 7-16.

_____. "The Polish Requiem by Krzysztof Penderecki." *Choral Journal* 26 (November 1985), pp. 5-11.

_____. *Krzysztof Penderecki: A Guide to His Works.* Princeton, N.J.: Prestige, 1983.

Rochberg, George. *The Aesthetics of Survival: A Composer's View of Twentieth-Century Music.* Ann Arbor: University of Michigan Press, 1984.

Rockwell, John. *All-American Music: Composition in the Late Twentieth Century.* New York: Knopf, 1985.

_____. "Music under Hitler." *Opera News* 36 (15 January 1972), pp. 8-13.

Rogers, Cornwell B. *The Spirit of Revolution in 1789.* Princeton, N.J.: Princeton University Press, 1949.

Rosen, Charles. *The Classical Style: Haydn, Mozart, Beethoven.* New York: W.W. Norton, 1972.

Rossi, Nick, and Robert A. Choate. *Music of Our Time.* Boston: Crescendo, 1969.

Routh, Francis. *Contemporary British Music.* London: MacDonald, 1972.

Rubin, Ruth. *Jewish Folksongs in Yiddish and English.* New York: Oak Publications, 1965.

Runciman, Steven. *A History of the Crusades,* vol. 3. Cambridge: Cambridge University Press, 1954.

Rushton, Julian. *The Musical Language of Berlioz.* Cambridge Studies in Music. Cambridge: Cambridge University Press, 1983.

Russcol, Herbert. "Music Since Hiroshima: The Electronic Age Begins." *Breaking the Sound Barrier.* ed. Gregory Battock. New York: E.P. Dutton, 1981.

Rzewski, Frederick. "Prose Music." *Dictionary of Contemporary Music.* ed. John Vinton. New York: E.P. Dutton, 1974.

Sachs, Harvey. *Music in Fascist Italy.* New York: W.W. Norton, 1987.

Safranek, Milos. *Bohuslav Martinů: His Life and Works.* Trans. Roberta Finlayson-Samsourova. London: Allan Wingate, 1962.

Salisbury, Harrison. *The 900 Days: The Siege of Leningrad.* New York: Harper & Row, 1969.

Salzman, Eric. *Twentieth Century Music: An Introduction.* Englewood Cliffs, N.J.: Prentice-Hall, 1974.

Schell, Jonathan. *The Fate of the Earth.* New York: Knopf, 1982.

Schafer, R. Murray. "Threnody: A Religious Piece For Our Time." *American Organist* 4 (May 1970), pp. 33-37.

_____. *British Composers in Interview.* London: Faber & Faber, 1967.

Schenk, Erich. "Zur Battaglia des 17. Jahrhunderts." *Musik* (Oktober 1940), pp. 26-28.

Schmidt, Christian Martin. "Schoenberg *Kantate Ein Überlebender aus Warschau*, Op. 46." *Archiv für Musikwissenschaft* 33 no. 4 (1976), pp. 174-88.

Schoenberg, Arnold. *Style and Idea.* Trans. Dika Newlin. New York: Philosophical Library, 1950.

Schrade, Leo. *Monteverdi: Creator of Modern Music.* London: Gollancz, 1951.

Schreiber, Flora R. and Vincent Persichetti. *William Schuman.* New York: G. Schirmer, 1954.

Schuffett, Robert Vernon. *The Music, 1971-1975, of George Crumb: A Style Analysis.* D.M.A. dissertation: Peabody Conservatory of Music, 1979.

Schwartz, Elliott S. and Barney Childs. *Contemporary Composers on Contemporary Music.* New York: Holt, Rinehart & Winston, 1967.

Schwartz, Elliott S. and Daniel Godfrey. *Music Since 1945: Issues, Materials, and Literature.* New York: Schirmer, 1993.

Schwartz, Joe, ed. *Pete Seeger: The Incompleat Folksinger.* New York: Simon & Schuster, 1972.

Schwartz, Nancy E. *The Nazi and the Musician.* Ann Arbor, Mich.: University Microfilms International, 1990.

Schwarz, Boris. *Music and Musical Life in Soviet Russia.* Bloomington: Indiana University Press, 1983.

Schwarz, K. Robert. "For Steve Reich, War and Rediscovery." *New York Times* (28 May 1989), II, p. 21.

Schwinger, Wolfram. *Krzysztof Penderecki: His Life and Work: Encounters, Biography, and Musical Commentary.* London: Schott, 1989.

Searle, Humphrey. *The Music of Liszt.* 2nd. rev. ed. New York: Dover Publications, 1966.

Sears, Richard S. *V-Discs: A History and Discography.* Westport, Conn.: Greenwood, 1980.

Seroff, Victor. *Sergei Prokofiev: A Soviet Tragedy.* New York: Funk & Wagnalls, 1968.

Sessions, Roger. "No More Business as Usual." *Modern Music* 19 (March-April 1942), pp. 159-62.

Sheehan, Neil. *A Bright Shining Lie: John Paul Vann and America in Vietnam*. New York: Random House, 1988.

Shirer, William L. *The Rise and Fall of the Third Reich*. New York: Simon & Schuster, 1959.

Shostakovich, Dmitri. *Testimony: The Memoirs of Dmitri Shostakovich*. Ed. Solomon Volkov. New York: Harper & Row, 1979.

Simms, Bryan. *Music of the Twentieth Century: Style and Structure*. New York: Schirmer, 1988.

Simpson, Robert, ed. *The Symphony*. 2 vols. New York: Drake, 1972.

Slonimsky, Nicholas. "Roy Harris." *Musical Quarterly* 33 (1947), p. 17.

_____. *Music Since 1900*. 4th ed. New York: Charles Scribner's Sons, 1971.

Small, Christopher. *Music—Society—Education*. New York: Schirmer, 1977.

Smith Brindle, Reginald. *The New Music: The Avant-garde Since 1945*. London: Oxford University Press, 1975.

Smith, Julian. *Aaron Copland*. New York: E.P. Dutton, 1955.

Sollertinsky, Dmitri and Ludmilla. *Pages from the Life of Dmitri Shostakovich*. Trans. Graham Hobbs & Charles Midgley. New York: Harcourt Brace Jovanovich, 1979.

Solomon, Maynard. *Beethoven*. New York: G. Schirmer, 1977.

_____. "Beethoven and Bonaparte." *Music Review* 29 (1968), pp. 96-105.

Spangemacher, Friedrich. "Hiroshima in der Musik: Bemerkungen zu einigen Kompositionen mit dem Thema der nuklearen Bedrohung." *Schweiz Musik* 120 no. 2 (1980), pp. 78-88.

Speer, Albert. *Inside the Third Reich*. Trans. Richard & Clara Winston. New York: Macmillan, 1970.

Starr, Chester G. *A History of the Ancient World*. 3rd. ed. Oxford: Oxford University Press, 1983.

Steblin, Rita. *A History of Key Characteristics in the Eighteenth and Early Nineteenth Centuries*. Studies in Musicology no. 67. Ann Arbor: UMI Research Press, 1983.

Stehman, Dan. *Roy Harris: An American Musical Pioneer*. Boston: Twayne, 1984.

_____. *The Symphonies of Roy Harris: An Analysis of the Linear Materials and of Related Works*. Ph.D. dissertation: University of Southern California, 1973.

Steiner, George. *In Bluebeard's Castle: Some Notes Towards the Redefinition of Culture*. London: Faber & Faber, 1971.

Stevens, Halsey. *The Life and Works of Béla Bartók*. New York: Oxford University Press, 1953.

Stone, James. "War Music and War Psychology in the Civil War." *Journal of Abnormal and Social Psychology* 36 (October 1941), pp. 543-60.

Strickland, William. "Musicians in the Army." *MTNA Proceedings* (1945), pp. 17-21.

_____. "The Army Way Today." *Modern Music* 21 (January-February 1944), pp. 82-85.

Strunk, Oliver. *Source Readings in Music History.* New York: W.W. Norton, 1950.

Stuckenschmidt, H.H. *Schoenberg: His Life, World and Work.* Trans. Humphrey Searle. New York: Schirmer, 1978.

_____. *Twentieth Century Music.* Trans. Richard Deveson. New York: McGraw-Hill, 1969.

Swan, Alfred J. *Music 1900-1930.* New York: W.W. Norton, 1929.

Swanzy, David P. *The Wind Ensemble and Its Music During the French Revolution (1789-1795).* Ph.D. dissertation: Michigan State University, 1966.

Tashjian, Beatrice. *Stravinsky's Symphony in Three Movements: An Analysis.* D.M. dissertation: Northwestern University, 1985.

Thomas, Lewis. *Late Night Thoughts on Listening to Mahler's Ninth Symphony.* New York: Viking, 1983.

Thomson, Virgil. *American Music Since 1910.* New York: Holt, Rinehart, & Winston, 1971.

Thucydides. *A History of the Peloponnesian War.* London: Penguin, 1954.

Tischler, Barbara L. *An American Music.* New York & Oxford: Oxford University Press, 1986.

Treaster, Joseph R. "G-Eye View of Vietnam." *New York Times* (30 October 1966), VI, pp. 100-09.

_____. "Saigon Bans the Anti-War Songs of Vietnamese Singer-Composer." *New York Times* (12 February 1969), p. 18.

Tuso, Joseph F. *Singing the Vietnam Blues: Songs of the Air Force in Southeast Asia.* College Station: Texas A & M University Press, 1990.

Vale, Malcolm. *War and Chivalry.* Athens, Ga.: The University of Georgia Press, 1981.

Vinton, John, ed. *Dictionary of Contemporary Music.* New York: E.F. Dutton, 1974.

Vogel, Jaroslav. *Leoš Janáček: A Biography.* Rev. & ed. Karel Janovicky. 1st ed. trans. Geraldine Thomsen-Muchova. New York: W.W. Norton, 1981.

Vogt, Hans. *Neue Musik seit 1945.* Stuttgart: Philipp Reclam, 1982.

Vogt, Matthias Theodor. "Auflösung der verhaltnisse: Luigi Nonos 'Intolleranza 1960' in Hamburg." *Neue Zeitschrift für Musik* 146 (April 1985), pp. 42-43.

Walker, Alan. *Franz Liszt: The Virtuoso Years 1811-1847.* New York: Knopf, 1983.

Wallenstein, Barry. *Visions and Revisions: An Approach to Poetry.* New York: Thomas Y. Crowell, 1971.

Warrack, John, ed. *Carl Maria von Weber Writings on Music.* Trans. Martin Cooper. Cambridge: Cambridge University Press, 1981.

Watkins, Glenn. *Soundings: Music in the Twentieth Century.* New York: Schirmer, 1988.

Weiner, Lazar, arr. *Songs of the Concentration Camps: From the Repertoire of Emma Shaver.* New York: Schulsinger Bros., 1948.

Weinraub, Bernard. "A Vietnamese Guitarist Sings of Sadness of War." *New York Times* (1 January 1968), p. 3.

Weissmann, Adolf. *The Problems of Modern Music.* Trans. M.M. Bozman. London: J.M. Dent, 1925.

Welsh, R.D. "Music in America." *Music Review* 4 (1943), pp. 32-34.

Wheeler, Mortimer. *Roman Art and Architecture.* New York: Oxford University Press, 1964.

White, Eric Walter. *Stravinsky: The Composer and His Works.* Berkeley: University of California Press, 1979.

Whittall, Arnold. *The Music of Britten and Tippett.* Cambridge: Cambridge University Press, 1982.

_____. *Music Since the First World War.* London: J.M. Dent, 1977.

Whitwell, David. *Band Music of the French Revolution.* Tutzing: Hans Schneider, 1979.

Wiant, Bliss. *The Music of China.* Hong Kong: Chinese University of Hong Kong, 1965.

Winstock, Lewis. *Songs and Music of the Redcoats: A History of the War Music of the British Army 1642-1902.* London: Leo Cooper, 1970.

Wulf, Joseph. *Musik im Dritten Reich: Eine Dokumentation.* Gütersloh: Sigbert Mohn, 1963.

Yarustovsky, Boris. *Sinfonie o voine i mire.* Moscow, 1966.

Yates, Peter. *Twentieth Century Music.* New York: Pantheon Books, 1967.

Zakariasen, William. "The Musician as Activist." *High Fidelity* (July 1971), pp. 50-55.

Zuck, Barbara A. *A History of Musical Americanism.* Studies in Musicology no. 19. Ann Arbor: UMI Research Press, 1980.

Zwerin, Mike. *La Tristesse de Saint Louis: Jazz Under the Nazis.* New York: Beech Tree Books, 1985.

TITLE INDEX

Numbers in plain type refer to item numbers. Numbers in parentheses refer to secondary works listed within item numbers. Numbers in italic type refer to page numbers.

INDEX OF COMPOSERS

Numbers in plain type refer to item numbers. Numbers in italic type refer to page numbers.

SUBJECT INDEX

Numbers in plain type refer to item numbers. Numbers in parentheses refer to secondary works listed within item numbers. Numbers in italic type refer to page numbers. Names of authors, artists, historical figures, songs, and events are included.